ACROSS THE ATLANTIC AND BEYOND:
The migration
Swiss Immigra

Charles R. Haller

HERITAGE BOOKS
2008

HERITAGE BOOKS

AN IMPRINT OF HERITAGE BOOKS, INC.

Books, CDs, and more—Worldwide

For our listing of thousands of titles see our website
at
www.HeritageBooks.com

Published 2008 by
HERITAGE BOOKS, INC.
Publishing Division
100 Railroad Ave. #104
Westminster, Maryland 21157

Other books by the author:
Distinguished German-Americans,

International Standard Book Numbers
Paperbound: 978-1-55613-697-9
Clothbound: 978-0-7884-7104-9

The book begins in Part 1 with a tale of three centuries of migration history of Gerrit Hendricks (ca. 1649-1691), and his descendants, and ends in Part 7 with another detailed family history of a later American arrival, Jacob Marzolf (1780-1870), and his descendants.

The two families are representative of the numerous German speaking peoples who comprised a significant portion of European emigrants departing from the key Dutch port of Rotterdam for America. The laborious migration of such adventurous individuals to America, typically to either Philadelphia or New York, often resulted eventually in subsequent movement to the Midwest.

In the five parts separating the two family histories, we go through a step-by-step analysis of how these family histories were derived and what motivated the families to make so many changes in locale. Much of the motivation is shown to be related to war, famine, and disease.

The first step involves the introduction of printing in Mainz about 1450 by the unique individual Johannes Gutenberg, whose technology was promoted by his former apprentice, Peter Schöffer.

Step two considers the Reformation which was initiated in Wittenberg in 1517 by Martin Luther, and later supported by his multiple assistants. The Wittenberg group quickly adapted printing as a means of mass communication in order to expound Protestant ideas.

The third step involves the complex relationship between printing and the Reformation and the spread of the ideas of the Reformation. Documentation is given as to the rapid advances made by the Protestant movement, through the effects of mass marketing which occurred at the Frankfurt and Leipzig book fairs, particularly in the late 16th century.

From the beginning, the Protestants felt the heavy pressure of the Catholics represented for the most part by the Hapsburg regime in Vienna and the governing bishoprics in Mainz, Köln, and Trier.

Outstanding presses in Europe were the Froschauer presses of Zürich, Switzerland, during the 16th century and the Merian presses in Frankfurt of the 17th century. Both presses are shown to have contributed much to the preservation of the book fairs which provided a vital link between the ruling classes and the common citizen.

In the early 17th century, the Dutch financial capitol of Amsterdam provided much of the necessary capital for step four which was the evolution of map making from block prints to the advanced technology of copper plate printing.

In the late 17th century, the seemingly bottomless coffers of Versailles in France provided capital that elevated map making to a fine art. By the 18th century, these superior maps were in full use by migrants and as well as by the warlords of Europe with their dreams of territorial expansion.

Thanks to the busy Englishman William Penn and the other European evangelists, the 17th and 18th century English and German migrants to America were nearly all Protestant. Through the means of advertising and personal representation, Penn "pulled" many Europeans to America.

The fifth step details two aspects of the multi-faceted ramifications of the industrial revolution. The first was that steam started replacing sails as a primary mode of power, beginning in America about 1806. The second was the dominant use of steam in American railroad transportation by the 1840's.

Along the way, many names are cited. As a necessary diversion, the change in spelling of representative Germanic names is documented through various family histories from its origin in a European country to its modern occurrence, often Anglicized, in America. The text reviews important books on linguistic histories and overviews the use of this knowledge as an aide to deciphering family history.

Considerable space is devoted to the Rhine River as a transportation route whose ease of transport, from the earliest times up to the age of steam technology, for both migrants and goods, can not be underestimated. The river was, at various times, an important barrier separating antagonistic groups living on either bank. Control of the Rhine was a major military objective all through recorded history and residents along its banks suffered accordingly. After 1683, the numerous conflicts compelled many Rhinelanders to seek their fortunes in America.

Extensive lists of references are cited and partly annotated for all of the seven parts of the book.

C. R. Haller
Kronberg/Taunus
August, 1992

This book is dedicated to a few of the world's better libraries, whose resources are freely open to the public:

Clayton Genealogical Library, Houston
Bayerischer Staatsbibliothek, München
Deutsche Bibliothek, Frankfurt am Main
Fondren Library, Rice University, Houston
Genealogical Society of Pennsylvania Library, Philadelphia
Goethe-Institut Library, Houston
Houston Public Libraries, both the Central Library and the
Jungman Branch, and their interlibrary loan services
Koninklijke Bibliotheek, Den Haag
LDS Family History Library, Salt Lake City
Library of Congress, Washington, D.C.
Library of Congress, Geography & Map Division, ibid
Mennonite Archives & Libraries, Lancaster, Pennsylvania
Mid-Continent Public Library, Independence, Missouri
Münchener Städtische Bibliotheken, München
Stadt- u. Universitätsbibliothek, Frankfurt am Main
Universität-Bibliothek Heidelberg
Universiteits Bibliotheek van Amsterdam

Major contributions by individuals are acknowledged throughout the book.

ART 1, BEING TITLED **GERRIT HENDRICKS of Krisheim, Germany,** describes in detail some 300 years of an evolving family history, that of the Hendricks family. Fleeing from the clouds of war hovering over the Rhine in the 1680's, the Hendricks began their long and cumbersome journey westward. The migration path of this family is traced from the middle Rhine, across the Atlantic, and into the gateway of Philadelphia and Germantown, in Pennsylvania.

After settling initially at Germantown, near Philadelphia, the second generation began the expansion westward. The initial movement was a relatively short distance into the western part of what later became Montgomery County. By 1713, the Hendricks were to reside in a small geographic area of eastern Pennsylvania until the depletion of the fertility of the farm land, and the subdivision of land through inheritance, made the settlement economically unlivable.

By 1848, the younger members of the various family groups were again on the move westward. Some went to Lancaster, Pennsylvania. Remaining there only until 1851, because of the already relatively dense population and limited finances, the group responded to the greater opportunity offered by new settlement programs in western Illinois.

In 1878, having been firmly established in Illinois for some 20 years, the appeal of joining in the settlement of yet another new frontier, the plains of north central Kansas, proved overwhelming. Mitchell County, Kansas, was the final stop on a trek that had covered much of Europe, the Atlantic, and a good portion of a constantly growing America. It is a typical trail of the millions who eventually occupied the Midwest.

The Hendricks were to carry with them an ingrained, passive support of warfare, as evidenced by their limited participation in the American Revolutionary War and the Civil War.

Anyone who has ever attempted to deal with historical records was almost immediately confronted with the perplexing questions regarding name changes. One goal of this text is to bridge the formidable linguistic barriers between Dutch, German, and English for the benefit of the English reading public. We use four case studies of name changes involving Rhineland immigrants in America.

The first essay of **Part 2,** namely **Hendriks and Hendricks,** examines modern-day records for the many variations in spelling of the relatively common name Hendricks in its major English and Dutch varieties. With a curious logic, the most likely origin of the name is pinpointed, about 1655, to an area along the Lower Rhine near the German-Dutch border. Modern-day telephone books from Belgium, The Netherlands, and the western part of Germany are shown as useful source materials and as a means of searching backwards for historical records.

The second essay, **Surnames and Personal Names**, delves into virtually all the current etymological dictionaries, and in particular, those of the three "B's" (Bach, Bahlow, and Brechenmacher), commonly used for researching German personal names. For linguistic purposes, Germany is subdivided into four broad linguistic areas. These four linguistic areas within Germany are cited in an overview and related to adjacent language areas. A list of some common surnames and given names is tabulated and the German versions are tied to the Dutch and English spellings.

The third essay of **Part 2, Mechanics of Name Changes**, deals with the common name Shoemaker, transferred to America in 1685 in its English variant. The forty-seven varieties in spelling include German and Dutch versions.

The fourth essay, **Heinrich Buchholtz alias Henry Pookeholes**, begins with the tale of common citizen and native German Heinrich Buchholtz who probably set some sort of a record for having his name grossly misspelled, as "Henry Pookeholes," in 1682-1687 Pennsylvania ship's arrival records. This example is English folk etymology at its finest, or perhaps worst, as the case may be. Likely, researchers familiar with both the German and English languages would immediately recognize this faux pas while others may note from this example, and from the following paragraphs, the rather obvious difficulties encountered in transliteration.

In addition, the essay illustrates, with the comparison of names of thirteen other villagers and co-religionists, the intricacies of dealing with centuries' old European records. Handwritten records invariably are transcribed anew by each reader with a concurrent variation in spelling.

For comparative purposes, the fourth essay also includes a synopsis of name changes of prominent American citizens, such as Eisenhower, Hoover, Pershing, Rockefeller, Roosevelt, Van Buren, Vanderbilt, Astor, and Guggenheim. Here, we examine the apparent original spelling, the changes that take place in Europe, and the changes, usually Angelization, that take place upon arrival in America.

Part 3 follows up on Part 2 with a history of variations in the spelling of European city and village names, specifically in communities along the ancient travel conduit of the Rhine River. These changes are set in the context of major events, such as wars, and their concurrent territorial reversals.

Changes in the spelling of major cities are illustrated by reference to antique maps and to books containing old maps, the maps dating from the 15th to the 18th centuries. One clear advantage of using old maps is that they contain printing which is unmistakably distinct as contrasted to the often obscure handwriting in manuscripts.

The collecting of maps, and arranging them in order according to printing date, gives a pattern of logical changes, especially when integrated with historic background data. For instance, over the centuries, the famous cathedral city of Köln (Cologne) has undergone an unimaginable 450 variations in spelling, in part because of profound Latin, German, French, Dutch, and English influences upon the name.

The first essay of Part 3, City and Village Names, lists thirty-four common variants of the famous city of Mainz as used on old maps and manuscripts dating from the period of 1300-1800. In another table of this essay, ten major Rhenish cities are listed and their spelling variants for the period 1491 to 1803 are compared.

The second essay, **Griesheim/Krisheim/Kriegsheim**, refers to documents, over a time frame of more than two centuries, as a case history of the classic variation in spelling of the small German villages of Kriegsheim and Monsheim, as given both on old maps and also in old books and manuscripts. The more radical changes in spelling of these particular villages, as well as nearby villages, are tied to linguistic differences of migrating populations and also to conquering overlords, to political events such as wars, and to legalities imposed by reigning powers, in particular to the French generals of Napoleon's armies.

Two other Rhineland towns, each famous in their own right, are given as an example showing numerous historic variations in their spelling. The towns are Nierstein, which has long produced a remarkable wine of high quality, and Krefeld, which was the origin of some of the first German immigrants to America.

While the techniques of printing evolved in 15th century Europe, the more complex techniques of map making were dependent not only on proper types of paper, printing presses, and copper and steel plate engraving, but also upon the development of more sophisticated techniques provided by advanced surveying tools.

One technological advance fed upon the other. Maps were vital to establish trade routes as exemplified by the utilitarian maps drafted by the Dutch merchants of the 15th century. Maps were necessary to fight wars in Europe as exemplified by the superior maps of Louis XIV's armies. Maps for the latter purpose were brought to a high level by the French, culminating in the work of the famous cartographer Guillaume Del'Isle (1652-1726), who also provided important maps of inland America. Maps of the New World were much sought after by migrants as travel guides in attempts to visualize the land of the unknown.

The last two essays of Part 3 delve into the broad history of early maps and their importance in the study of the migration of peoples, of changes in political boundaries, and in interpreting the vast realm of graphic description of European history. The cliché that a picture is better than a thousand words holds for maps, even a graphic map, which by its simplistic nature illuminates the darkness in a way that no printed description can.

Thus the third essay, **Old European Maps**, deals with antique maps and cites examples of their usefulness in researching historical records.

The essay provides the possibility of tracing migration routes across Europe and separates the probable from the unlikely. The text concentrates on Dutch, French, and German cartographers. A useful bibliography is given.

The fourth essay of **Part 3, Early American Maps**, concerns maps from early America whose quality and quantity, until the present century, never really approached that of maps printed in Europe. This important fact illustrates that technology transfer was very late in materially assisting the lives of the immigrants. Nonetheless, atlases and sectional maps of various portions of America are highly useful in studying the development and the populating of America, regardless of whether the maps are in manuscript form or in printed form.

The transformation of the waves of 17th century European migrants, who settled initially in isolated communities along the Atlantic coast, then moved across the Allegheny and the Appalachian barriers in the 18th century, and eventually swept across the Mississippi River and the Rocky Mountain barriers in the 19th century, is superbly documented through the various stages of map development.

Both the third and the fourth essays of **Part 3** give the reader lists of references useful for isolating the specific geographic areas of his or her map interest.

The sixteenth and seventeenth century saw great numbers of evangelists traveling to every corner of Europe. **Part 4** delves into the lives and influence of two evangelistic personalities of the time, namely Menno Simons and William Penn.

The first essay **The Wandering Menno Simons** concerns this noteworthy, but relatively obscure, mid-16th century religious leader who, in a curious way, gave his name to one of the many religious factions, some conservative, some radical, of that time. Simons' migratory life is described very briefly.

The second essay, **The Beginnings of English Quakerism**, discusses the start of this religious group and their evangelical work in Europe.

Which leads us to the third essay titled **William Penn's Travels in Europe**. This essay surveys the more or less complete travel records of William Penn (1644-1718), the dynamic evangelist who spent much of his life traveling, not only around England and Ireland, but also on three occasions in northwestern Europe. The records of Penn's travels on the continent are so good that little is left to the imagination in considering the difficulties of travel in the days before steam, electricity, petroleum, and atomic power. The evangelical travels of William Penn and his role in "pulling" immigrants to American are discussed in some detail also in the first essay of Part 6.

On his European trips, Penn was in contact with a considerable number of personalities who gave their sympathy and religious and political support to his cause. Penn gained near diplomatic immunity from an extensive and wide ranging circle of nobility, one of whom was Elisabeth (1618-1680) Pfalzgräffin bei Rhein. Penn also gained important financial support from a prominent group of Protestants in Frankfurt, the Frankfort Companie, who thereby assisted in the first important German settlement in America.

The fourth essay of **Part 4, Early German Quakers: A Small Minority**, delves into the lives of late 17th century Quakers in Krisheim and Krefeld. This group would probably have gone down in history virtually unnoticed, but for their association with William Penn and his enormous influence in the development of Pennsylvania. As it was, the Quakers played a unique role in the settlement of early America.

The fifth essay **The Frankfort Companie** briefly traces the history of that small but important group of investors.

The last essay of **Part 4, Germantown and the Susquehanna Subscribers**, uses the family names of an entire community from Germantown, Pennsylvania, in order to emphasize the challenge of deciphering early American records. Penn's attempt around 1696 to start a similar community in the Susquehanna valley never succeeded. The list of subscribers to the Susquehanna project survives; it includes many from the Germantown community whose names are repeated here in their quaint, originally recorded form. The most likely correct spelling of these names is also given.

Part 5 focuses upon the advancement of printing in central Europe during the period of, say, 1400 through 1700. Until the progress made in printing in the late 16th and early 17th centuries, the common citizen in Europe had little recourse to the world beyond the distance that could be covered by horseback in one or two days.

Concurrent with the great technological advances in printing and in map making, the vast hordes of everyday citizens in Europe received another stimulus in the form of mental provocation by the great Reformers. Religious reformers sprang up everywhere in Europe and issued printed works by the hundreds of thousands. The ecclesiastical and ruling authorities, whose loyalty lay in Rome, reacted with an endless series of bans. For instance, The German Diet attempted to restrict the rights of the Reformers (later called Protestants) during the trial years of 1520, 1521, 1524, 1529, and periodically thereafter throughout the 16th century. Each ban on the publication or distribution of Protestant thoughts, however, was mainly counterproductive, creating a new crisis and inflaming the interest of every citizen. No doubt the authorities were dumbfounded when their official ultimatums were virtually ignored as the world of Protestantism swept by them.

The Protestant ideas of freedom of religion generated mass migrations, not only through Europe, but on to America. Indeed, data show that the populating of 16th and 17th century America was basically a result of the Protestant movement.

The printing of books, which flourished in the era after 1500, and the 16th century development of copper and steel plate engraving for illustrations, and eventually for maps, marked significant technological advances. These advances broadened the knowledge of men everywhere, opened the doors for mass communication, and unleashed the first of the modern tools adapted for migration purposes.

It was in Frankfurt that the book industry flourished following the achievements, about 1448, of Johann Gutenberg in nearby Mainz, as the first essay of **Part 5, Mainz and Gutenberg**, relates. The curious life of the unique individual Johann Gutenberg is briefly examined and the many changes in the spelling of his name, as cited in numerous legal records, are repeated. The spread of printing from Mainz to other major European cities is briefly examined.

After the short era of Gutenberg, which lasted only until about 1468, one of the many ramifications of relatively large press runs and their mass marketing, exemplified by the Luthern Bible of 1522-34, was to raise the literacy level of the man on the street.

In historic context, by 1500, most major cities in northern Europe were involved in the rapidly developing book industry.

The second essay of **Part 5, Frankfurt and the Book Fair**, celebrates the famous Frankfurt Book Fair, one of the most important bi-annual marketing events in Europe. An overview is given of the Book Fair, which began about 1462-1466. The initiation of the Book Fair is credited to Peter Schöffer, who was an apprentice to Johannes Gutenberg.

By 1525, the Book Fair was a critical aid to the famous personality of Martin Luther, his co-workers, and many other writers. Frankfurt, which for centuries has attracted refugees like a magnet, became known as the crossroads of Germany in the 16th and 17th centuries, and as a key outlet for the Protestant book trade. No event in recent history has had a more profound effect upon the migration of the peoples of western Europe than the period of the early 16th century, formally known as the Reformation. And without a doubt its nominal leader, Martin Luther, accomplished in his relatively brief lifespan more for the advancement of European literacy than any other single person.

The life of Martin Luther (1483-1546) is briefly described in the third essay titled **Martin Luther and the Book Wars**. Luther recognized that Latin, the dominant printed language of the time, was phonetically antagonistic to German speech patterns. His writings in the vernacular and in simplified German sold like hotcakes; they were in effect the newspapers of their day.

With his access to the facilities of mass printing in Wittenberg and other publishing centers, and to the marketing centers of Frankfurt and Leipzig, Luther acted as a focal point for the Reformation. There were tens of other minority religious leaders who are much less well-known because they did not possess the writing genius of Luther and his editors, nor did they have the means to distribute their ideas to the public.

The fourth essay of **Part 5, The Froschauer Presses of Zürich**, cites one example of the publication of Bibles and other religious items, items which formed an important element in many European households during the religious turmoil of the 16th and 17th centuries. The example used happened to involve the Froschauer publishing firm, established about 1521 in Zürich, but may well have chosen any one of a half dozen other publishers operating in other cities in Europe. The role of these historic documents in transmitting literacy to America, with the migration of immigrants of the 18th century, is an unique aspect of Part 3; nearly 120 Froschauer Bibles, dating from 1524-1581, have been located in various repositories in the United States.

The fifth essay **Matthäus Merian and the House of Merian**, surveys the enormous output of the famous Merian Printing House of Frankfurt, beginning about 1624, and refers to their pictorial documentation of the early history of German cities, a documentation which is universally cited in modern day studies on the history of central Europe. The use by the Merian firm of copper and steel plate engraving in large quantities exemplifies the advanced technology applied in the 17th century. This technology is related to the introduction of the vastly superior maps which evolved in the last part of the 17th century. Early 17th century Dutch map makers, followed by French map makers, and to some extent by German map makers, played a vital role in bridging the Atlantic with their cartography. Once firmly established in America, English firms of the 18th century also assisted in mapping migration routes, as discussed earlier in Part 3.

Printed travel guides span a considerable range of time, having evolved as they did not long after the introduction in Mainz of modern day printing. Travel along the great migration route of the Rhine waterway spawned a host of legends, some here mentioned.

The sixth essay, **The Rhine Travel Guides**, lists a number of little known early travel guides for areas along the Rhine, as well as early travel guides for other parts of Europe. Beginning about 1641, there were a whole series of road maps, followed by 18th century postal route maps, to guide the weary traveler along his way. Doubtless, many 19th and 20th century migrants used the famous guides of the Baedeker and the Michelin publishing houses.

From A.D. 843 until 1806, the Holy Roman Empire, vested in the Emperor resident in Vienna and in the bishoprics of Mainz, Köln, and Trier, was a dynamic force in the development of central Europe. These Catholic forces controlled the life of the ordinary citizen in the German States until the mid-16th century. One of the long-term results of the Protestant revolts against these forces was the search for new homelands. Just as Protestantism was initially a phenomena originating in the German States, so was the great movement of migrants across the Atlantic before 1800 basically a Protestant phenomena.

Current literature provides astonishing claims as to the number of Protestants who gave up their homeland and became permanent settlers in America. Migration was both a matter of push and pull, as the text implies. Numerous short-term causes resulting in actual migration are cited: war, famine, and disease being the primary ones.

In the case of German-speaking peoples, the first essay of **Part 6, The German Americans,** brings together much of this literature in a few short pages. The estimated total numbers of German-speaking migrants quoted, perhaps seven to eight million as from 1683, are believable. Descendants occupied every niche in American society from Presidents down to common laborer. In a comparative sense, by far the majority made a definite contribution to the welfare of American society.

Even though the accomplishments and marks of this important group upon American history are somewhat glazed over by a host of other nationalities, their numbers form the backbone of the "German Belt" and the "Swiss Belt," a farm belt which stretches from Pennsylvania westward to Kansas and beyond, with significant outliers in Texas and other states.

The second essay, **The Land of Wars,** considers an isolated portion of the Empire, the Palatinate, along the left bank of the central Rhine, an area with a pivotal and long history of nearly constant involvement in numerous the political and religious wars of central Europe. The causes of war, and the effects of war, especially upon the migration of peoples to America, are shown once again, to be a primary contributor to the initiation of migration.

From a migration-causing standpoint, the most notable of the many wars in central Europe were the Thirty Years' War, 1618-1648; the Wars of Louis XIV, 1676-1697; the successive Wars of the French Revolution, 1792-1800; and the Napoleonic Wars of 1800-1815.

Control of the Rhine was a major military objective all through recorded history. Along the Rhine migration route, the triple threat of war, famine, and disease resulted in large population turnovers. After each depopulation, notably in 1650 and 1720, the rulers of the afflicted lands sent appeals to more stable areas, Switzerland and the Lowlands especially, for adventurous family groups to repopulate their fiefdoms.

The third essay, **Of Kings and Queens and Lesser Nobility,** is geared in particular toward understanding something of the ancestry and complexity of the many noble German houses. The essay cites indexes to the numerous records in various archives and in major publications. A list of the Holy Roman Emperors, whose residences typically were in Vienna, Austria, is tabulated for easy reference and for use in other parts of the book.

Among the long list of Emperors, the reign of Karl V (1519-1556) of the influential House of Hapsburg, stands out, not only for its longevity, but more importantly for its occurrence during the critical embryonic stages of the Reformation. The indexes to the lists of nobility are shown to be useful in pinpointing many Germanic names of ordinary citizens to their general area of origin. The literature describing early travel is scattered. An unique attempt is made in the next two essays to bring together the many diverse records, not only regarding modes of primitive travel, but also in an effort to consolidate descriptions and accounts of travel, as well as references to maps.

The fourth essay of **Part 6, The Rhine as a Migration Route**, deals with real and imagined experiences of travel on the Rhine waterway, from the days of the 11th century robber barons, and the subsequent multitude of toll stations, until the age of steamships, which began about 1816. From the times of early Roman occupation until recent times, the Rhine has been a major, if not the dominant, artery for movement of goods and people living in central and northern Europe.

The fifth essay, **Across the Atlantic and Beyond**, brings together numerous records which relate the trials and tribulations of early travel. Even in Europe, technological advances contributed little to progress in modes of travel until late in the 19th century, the period known as the Industrial Revolution; the transfer of technology to the Americas was slow to follow.

This essay also follows up on the land travel discussed previously and deals with oceanic travel from the 17th through the 19th centuries, including Penn's three physically taxing trips to America between 1682 and 1701. Due to the ceaseless efforts of Penn, the period 1681-1685 was the embryonic period of the formation of Philadelphia, a city destined to become America's largest city by the time of the Revolutionary War.

The essay further explores the settlement of Pennsylvania and the prominence of Philadelphia as a seaport and primary population center in the 18th century, as well as its role as a gateway for millions of migrants to America.

If the mass of migrating peoples found land travel through Europe to be burdensome, they were in for a shock when they boarded a small, bouncy and smelly ship headed for a little known destination, thousands of miles away, and came face-to-face with the grim and grimy realities of a two month or so sea voyage. The relative comfort of steamships was not to be available to most migrants until about 1848.

And even after crossing the Atlantic, most travelers of the 18th and 19th centuries had yet another formidable experience awaiting them: the agonizingly slow and uncomfortable land journey across the frontiers of primitive America.

Once in America, the immigrants also had to contend with numerous armed conflicts, the major ones being the French and Indian War (1754-63), the first conflict for independence during the American Revolutionary War (1775-83), and the second conflict for independence during the War of 1812 (1812-15). The latter two wars were the result of more than a century of pent-up hostility which had developed between the haughty English overlords and the Americanized English, Dutch, Germans, Swedes, and all the other minority groups.

In terms of migration patterns inland, the American Revolution is a convenient milestone to separate the settlement of the Atlantic coastal strip of America from that of the settlement of the wilderness beyond the Alleghenies. The subsequent settlement of the Louisiana Purchase in 1803, between the French and the Americans, provided a much needed boost for territorial expansion westward.

The history of construction of ordinary roads in America is surveyed as is river transportation before and after the introduction of steamboats to inland waterways, the latter beginning only after 1807.

The last essay of **Part 6, Bridging the Prairies of Kansas,** details the relative comfort of the early trains in the Midwest and what impact the laying of new railroad lines had upon isolated frontier settlements. In the second half of the 19th century, the rapid expansion of railroads across the Midwest went hand-in-hand with the migration of millions. The one supported the other.

After the American Civil War (1861-1865), the great grain-bearing states, north of the Ohio River and west of the Mississippi River, contributed their enormous natural resources. Railroads provided the necessary means for the exchange of goods and a vital American economy.

Part 7, finally, summarizes the family history of one small branch of the Marzolf family, another typical, relatively large, immigrant family led by an early 19th century Alsatian emigrant. The part documents, and in some cases, speculates upon the means of transportation down the greater length of the Rhine, across the Atlantic, and overland, first to New York, and later to Kansas. The initial immigrants left Alsace after the bad experience of the Napoleonic wars and subsequent economic recession; ironically, the third generation in America became deeply involved in the Civil War.

The Marzolf name is one of relatively simple spelling; however, the census takers and Civil War record keepers of the 19th century, being barely literate in English, much less German, managed to misspell the name in at least twenty-one different versions. It is another classic example of English folk etymology.

errit Hendricks of Krisheim, Germany

N 1970, THE AUTHOR BECAME CURIOUS AS to the origin of the Hendricks name. My mother Edna Haller, née Hendricks, was one of ten children of Charles R. Hendricks (1859-1934), who had their homes mainly in Mitchell County, Kansas, and Whiteside County, Illinois. At that time, we, the grandchildren of Charles R. Hendricks numbered forty-two, all then still living. During family get-togethers, there was much speculation and some few facts regarding our common origin. Family records showed that Ephraim D. Hendricks was the father of Charles R. and that Ephraim came to Kansas from Montgomery County, Pennsylvania about 1878 via the Sterling, Illinois and Lancaster County, Pennsylvanian Mennonite route.

At that point, tracing the records came to a standstill until, through persistent query, Aunt Mabel Nusbaum, née Hendricks, then in her eighties, remembered that the "D" in Ephraim D. stood for Delph, later found to be Delp. This clue provided the key, after further inquiry at the Mennonite Archives in Lancaster, Pennsylvania, to eventually trace our particular Hendricks to one Gerrit Hendricks who came to Philadelphia on October 16, 1685, and settled in Germantown. Even though the lineage involved mainly farmers of Mennonite religion, whose historical records are above average, it was a challenging experience to search back ten generations, and 300 years, to the immigrant ancestor.

Until about 1975, we were still lacking records of an ancestral immigrant. Through some good fortune, Hull's 1935 provocative book on the *Dutch Quakers* had been reprinted and a copy was ordered for general background notes. By coincidence, Hull's book contains considerable discussion and documentation of ancestral Hendricks' in Europe and in southeast Pennsylvania who happened to be the ones initiating our line.

Thus, the records showed a beginning and an end to our Hendricks line. It remained to gather the scattered literature and unpublished records to fill in the gap. Especially important for this purpose were publications by Boorse (1953), and by Delp (1962), as well as the monumental work on the Rosenberger clan by Fretz (1906).

During the course of research, it rapidly became apparent that early arrivals in Pennsylvania, and later generations, with some exceptions, tended to have large families. Families with eight to twelve children, including some from second marriages, were common.

By 1982, enough data was available to do this short story on Gerrit Hendricks of Germantown, Pennsylvania, and a few of his numerous descendants who first settled in eastern Pennsylvania and who eventually moved westward. For most of the 18th century, as we now know, our Hendricks congregated around an area in southeast Pennsylvania, which in 1728 officially became Towamencin Township. Figure 1 shows the area of Towamencin in the center of the illustration. This small area of about 4 1/2 miles by 3 miles (some 6, 000 acres) contained four related Hendricks families in 1734 (Bean, 1884, p. 1085), and at least seven related Hendricks families as late as 1776 (Bean, 1884, p. 1090). Many of these Hendricks are buried in the Towamencin Mennonite Church graveyard, located in the southwest corner of the township.

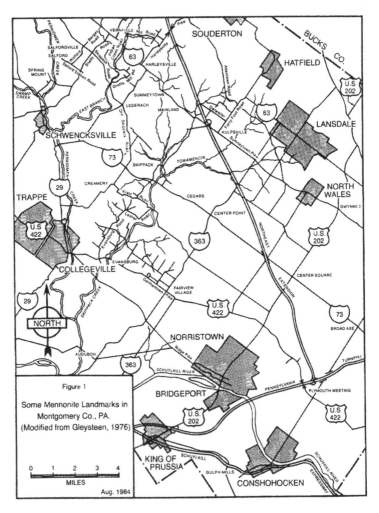

Figure 1

Some Mennonite Landmarks in Montgomery Co., PA. (Modified from Gleysteen, 1976)

Aug. 1984

The core of the Gerrit Hendricks clan remained in Montgomery County, Pennsylvania (county officially named only in 1784) well into the 19th century as shown by the 1972 publication of R. T. and M. C. Williams who cite Will records from 1759-1850 of some twenty-eight persons, mainly males, under the name of Hendricks. Moreover, the

1790 U.S. Census shows fifteen households with ninety-eight individuals under the name Hendricks in Montgomery County. Even as late as 1849, Morris' *Map of Montgomery County* shows a concentration of twelve households under the name Hendricks as follows:

Hatfield Township	1
Towamencin	3
Worchester	2
Franconia	2
Lower Salford	3
Upper Salford	1

Even today, a tiny village in Upper Salford Township with the name Hendricks remains. Probably, it refers to part of the clan which lived there during 1868 when the Reading Railroad, formerly the Perkiomen Railroad, was built. The railroad follows Perkiomen Creek; the village Hendricks is on the northeast side of the Creek, between Salford and Perkiomenville.

KRISHEIM TO GERMANTOWN. The records show that on May 8, 1685, Gerhardt Hendricks, Hans Peter Umstadt, and Peter Schumacher filed, at Horcheim, Germany, a petition for a passport. The request was repeated on June 11, 1685. The petition was granted shortly thereafter. On August 15, 1685, while still in Krefeld, Germany, Hendricks and Schumacher bought 200 acres each from Dirck Sipman (Philadelphia Deed Book E4, vol. 7, p. 180).

Following a trip down the Rhine to Rotterdam (see Figure 3 on page 240), and across the North Sea to London, we find further records that Gerrit Hendricks and his group departed London in late August 1685 for the promised land. The trip across the Atlantic lasted about eight weeks.

So it was that on October 16, 1685, the good ship *Francis and Dorothy,* under commander Richard Bridgeman, arrived in Philadelphia with the family of Gerrit Hendricks, consisting of his wife Maria, a daughter Sarah (born Oct. 2, 1678), and apparently also two sons, Lambert and Willem (Hull, 1935, p. 398). A certain Heinrich Frey accompanied the family as a "servant."

Due to the paucity of records, historians are uncertain as to whether or not the two boys, Willem and Lambert, who would have been respectively about fifteen and thirteen in 1685, or possibly even twins, accompanied their parents on this trip, or whether they came at a later date.

The two boys' names do not appear on the sketchy passenger list of the *Francis and Dorothy,* arriving in Philadelphia on 16 October 1685, as published in 1884 in the *Pennsylvania Magazine History & Biography.* But in 1694 a Lambert Hendricks is named as Gerrit Hendricks' son in Germantown records. And in 1698 a Willem Hendricks is recorded as a property owner there.

An alternative theory is that the two boys were nephews of Gerrit Hendricks and were actually from the Krefeld Mennonite Hendricks. Possible evidence for this alternative theory is as follows:

1. The Gerrit Hendricks property in Germantown, Pa., was occupied by Sarah Hendricks after 1694. This suggests that Willem and Lambert were either not part of the immediate family or that they sold their interests to Sarah and her husband Isaac Shumacher (Shoemaker).
2. There were a number of "Henderichs" families living in the Krefeld Mennonite community during the years 1678-91 (Niepoth, 1939).

GENERATION I: GERMANTOWN. Gerrit Hendricks, along with three other Quakers, namely Derick op den Graeff, Francis Daniel Pastorius, and Abraham op den Graeff, are renowned for their signing of the "Protest Against Slavery" in Germantown on April 18, 1688, in the house of Thunnes Kunders. In keeping with the English text of the "Protest," Hendricks' name was signed "garret hendricks."

The Gerrit Hendricks house, built in 1687, of local stone (*Germantown stone*, also called by the German name *Glimmerstein*, or, technically, *mica schist*) was in Lot 8, Germantown Division, east side of Germantown Road, along the east side of Wingohocking Creek, between Lukens Mill Road/Church Lane and Weavers Mill Road/Shoemakers Lane/Penn St. Nearby was the house of Hendricks' daughter Sarah (1678-1742) and his son-in-law Isaac Shumacker (1669-1732). Today, the location is Belfield Aveneu at Penn Street.

Maria Hendricks ("Mary Henrix"), evidently a widow by 1693, was shown on the tax list for Germantown in that year. Lambert Hendricks, son of Gerrit Hendricks, appears in the Germantown court records in 1694 for grievances against Peter Schumacker, Jr.

In summary, it is supposed that Gerrit Hendricks was born in Germany about 1649 and died in Germantown in early 1691.

In the literature, there is much confusion regarding "Gerhard Hendrick Dewees" (especially in Pennypacker, 1899, p. 119). A number of records indicate that Dewees dropped the last name on occasion and became simply Gerhard Hendricks, or Gerrit Hendricks. The house of "Gerret Hendricks Dewees" (as in Tinkcom, et al, 1955), built about 1692, was at 6200 Germantown Avenue, about 3/4 miles northwest of and on the opposite side of Germantown Road from our Gerrit Hendricks' house. Dewees was married to "Zijtijen" (probably Sijtie Boekenoogen) and had the following children: Cornelis, Willem, Lodewijk (Lewis), and Wilhelmina. Dewees died about 1700 (La Munyan, 1905).

GENERATION II: GERMANTOWN TO TOWAMENCIN. Willem Hendricks, probably one of Gerrit Hendricks' two sons, was born about 1670, apparently in Krisheim, Germany. He is also recorded under the names Wilhelm and William.

Willem is recorded as having owned seventy-five acres in Germantown in 1698 and as having lived there at least during the period 1698-1709 as a property owner. He apparently was initially a Quaker, but later followed the Mennonite religion, perhaps because of the influence of George Keith, a controversial leader of the Mennonites. Willem was naturalized in 1709 together with his sons Hendrick and Laurens (Lawrence) according to the Colonial Records of Pennsylvania, vol. 2, p. 493-494. Willem eventually had five sons (Boorse, 1953, p. 25), known as Hendrick, Laurens, Paulus, Leonhard, and Petrus. In Table 1.1 below, the "ca.", as in circa, is an inferred date extrapolated from other known dates of ancestors, descendants, brothers, and historical events. These Hendricks sons are recorded as follows:

TABLE 1.1
THE CHILDREN OF WILLEM HENDRICKS

Name (other names)	born	died	married	no. children
Hendrik (Hendrick) (Henry)	ca. 1692	1749	Rachel Linderman	8
Laurens (Lorentz) (Lawrence)	ca. 1693	1753	Yanicken Tyson	9
Leonhard (Lenart) ((Leonard)	ca. 1698	1776	Elizabeth Turner (Tuenes)	5
Paulus (Paul)	ca. 1700	1775	Margaret Johnson (Jansen)	11
Petrus (Pieter) (Peter)	ca. 1705	1750	?not married	0

Willem is reported to have died in 1749 in Towamencin Township, probably at the home of his oldest son Hendrick, who died in the same year. It is likely that both were buried in the graveyard of the Towamencin Mennonite Meeting House which was established at least as early as 1728.

Two of Willem's sons, Leonard and Paul, are recorded as having been married at the First Presbyterian Church in Philadelphia, the former on December 19, 1718, and the latter on September 19, 1719.

GENERATION III: TOWAMENCIN TOWNSHIP. Hendrick Hendricks was born about 1692 in Germantown, as the oldest of five sons of Willem Hendricks (Boorse, 1953, p. 24-25, 31-32; Hull, 1935, p. 407). He appears as one of the "German's naturalized by Act of Council at Philadelphia, September 29, 1709." Of the some sixty families on this naturalization list, by far the majority of family names were of Dutch spelling. Following the start of the Keithian controversy about 1692, the Quakers in the colonies became polarized. George Keith (1638-1716) was a controversial leader of the Mennonites in New Jersey in 1684 and in Philadelphia in 1689. His radical ideas led many of the Germantown Quakers eventually to become Mennonites. Many of them later migrated to the western part of what later became Montgomery County. This migration started with the purchase in early 1702 of a 6,000 acre tract by Matthias van Bebber in the Skippack Creek area, later known as Perkiomen Township, and, for a time, as "van Bebber land." The first Mennonite settlement along Skippack Creek began in 1703. The settlements spread northward to Towamencin Township.

Hendrick Hendricks was among the later arrivals in Towamencin Township. He acquired a tract of 123 acres in 1713 and still later added more acreage. Thus, he and his brother Lorentz, along with Jacob and Henry Frey, were among the pioneer Mennonites settling in Towamencin. A leader of the Mennonites, Jacob Godshalk, and his brother Godshalk Godshalk, also settled in Towamencin Township about 1713. By 1728, the first Mennonite Meeting House was built.

Hendrick Hendricks was a signer in March, 1727 of a petition for a road which extended from the North Branch of the Perkiomen Creek to the Great Road (Sumneytown Pike). This road was built in 1735. Like most roads, the Great Road, or North Wales Road, built in 1704, was originally an old Indian Trail. Hendrick was also one of the petitioners, in March 1728, for the erection of Towamencin Township. At this time, the population of Towamencin Township was about 125 persons, of whom twenty-eight were landowners.

Four of the five Hendricks brothers are among the thirty-two "landholders and tenants" on the 1734 tax list for Towamencin Township (see Table 1.2).

Hendrick Hendricks died in February, 1749, survived by a widow and eight children; his widow was Rachel Linderman (d. 1765), daughter of John Linderman of Roxborough in Philadelphia County, who came from Mülheim-an-der-Ruhr, Germany, sometime prior to 1698.

The primary Will records of the five brothers survive in the Philadelphia City Hall Annex as follows:

1. Hendrick Hendricks, Phila. Admin. Book F/312, no. 58, dated March 13, 1749, and Phila. Deed Book I, vol. 12, p. 248.
2. Lowrentz Hendricks, Will Book K, p. 101, no. 66, 1753 (written in English and also, separately, in German by third parties; signed "L H").
3. Leonard Hendricks, Will Book Q, p. 264, no. 220, 1776 (written in English by a third party).

4. Paul Hendricks, Will Book Q, p. 114, no. 96, 1775 (written in English by a third party; signed "P")
5. Peter Hendricks, Admin. Book F, p. 347, no., 35, 1750 (written in English by a third party; signed "P")

TABLE 1.2
HENDRICKS GENERATIONS III AND IV
Towamencin Township Land Records

Name/Period	Date Acquired	Initial Acreage	1734 Tax List Acres	1769 Tax List Acres	1776 Tax List Acres
Lawrence Hendricks	1713	123	150	x	x
(ca. 1693-1753)					
(brother of Hendrick)					
Leonard Hendricks	1720	158	n/a	x	x
(ca. 1698-1776)	1729	150	150	125	125
(brother of Hendrick)					
Hendrick Hendricks	1729	150	123	x	x
(1692-1749)					
(oldest of 4 brothers)					
Paul Hendricks	1729	200	100	x	x
(ca. 1700-1775)					
(brother of Hendrick)					
William Hendricks	x	x	x	60	60
(ca. 1720-1800)					
(son of Leonard					
Paul Hendricks	x	x	x	99	99
(ca. 1724-1815)					
(son of Paul)					
Samuel Hendricks	1764	x	x	100	100
(1735-1807)					
(son of Hendrick)					
Leonard Hendricks	x	x	x	89	89
(1744-1825)					
(son of Hendrick)					
Peter Hendricks	1753	x	x	88	88
(ca. 1730-1785)					
(son of Lawrence					
Benjamin Hendricks	1753	x	x	88	88
(ca. 1732-1792)					
(son of Lawrence)					
William Hendricks	x	x	x	lot	lot
(ca. 1733-1794)					
(son of Hendrick)					

GENERATION IV: TOWAMENCIN TO LOWER SALFORD, PENNSYL-
VANIA. Leonard Hendricks was born in 1744 in Towamencin, apparently as the sixth child of eight children of Hendrick Hendricks (Boorse,
1953, p. 30-32; Roach, undated manuscript) and Rachel Linderman. The
eight children were:

1. William, ca. 1733-ca. 1794
2. Samuel, ca. 1735-1807
3. John, ca. 1739-1775
4. Christina, 1741-1801
5. Catharina, ca. 1742-ca. 1790
6. Leonard, 1744-1825
7. Susanna, ca. 1745-?
8. Jacob, ca. 1746-?

Leonard married Catharina Boorse, daughter of Gesbert Boorse and
Margareth Boorse, née Kuster, about 1771. They had four children.
Leonard was a farmer and resident of Towamencin Township until
about 1776 when he sold the eighty-nine acres that he had inherited
from his father and acquired 154 acres of land in Lower Salford Township. Being a Mennonite, he refused to bear arms during the Revolutionary War, but paid the absentee fines levied upon the non-associator,
which in 1777 amounted to 20 pounds, 17 shillings, 6 pence.

On March 10, 1783, Leonard acquired eighty acres and 135 perches
(a perch is the same as a rod, namely 16 1/2 linear feet, or 272 square
feet) of land from Bernard Getz. This land was near the West Branch of
Skippack Creek along the Sumneytown Pike, just inside the Lower
Salford Township boundary.

Leonard died in December, 1825, and was buried in the graveyard
of the Mennonite Meeting House at Towamencin, Pa. The Meeting
House is located near present day Kulpsville (see Figure 1 on page 14).

GENERATION V: LOWER SALFORD TOWNSHIP. Jacob Hendricks
was born on October 5, 1775 in Towamencin Township as the second of
four children of Leonard Hendricks (Boorse, 1953, p. 60) and Catharina
Boorse (ca. 1753-1790), the other children being as follows:

1. Margaret, ca. 1771-1830
2. Jacob, 1775-1828
3. Elizabeth,
4. Rachel, 1781-1856

Jacob carried on the farmer tradition, purchasing on May 3, 1812 the
homestead from his father in Lower Salford Township, which he retained until his death in 1828. Probably in the year 1796, Jacob married a
cousin, Sybilla Boorse (b. Feb. 25, 1777; d. June 12, 1859), who was

known also as "Isabella" and as "Bilke." They had four children.

Jacob died on September 28, 1827, and was buried in the yard of the Mennonite Meeting House at Towamencin, at the side of his father (Boorse, 1953, p. 61).

GENERATION VI: TOWAMENCIN, PENNSYLVANIA, TO STERLING, ILLINOIS. John Boorse Hendricks was born on September 14, 1797, oldest son of four children of Jacob Hendricks and Sybilla Hendricks, née Boorse, the children being as follows (Boorse, 1953, p. 61):

1. John B., 1797-1883
2. Susanna, 1799-1833
3. Jacob B., 1809-1875?
4. Samuel B., 1818-1897

John B. married on November 14, 1819, at the Zwingli Reformed Church at Tohickon (Bucks Co., Pa.) a first cousin, Elizabeth Delp, daughter of George Delp (1776-1841), and Rachel Delp, née Hendricks (1781-1856) (see Delp, 1962, p. 23). The marriage was recorded under the names "John Henry and Elizabeth Delp" (see Hinke, 1925). Elizabeth was born on May 22, 1799. John and Elizabeth had seven children.

Morris' 1849 *Map of Montgomery Co., Pa.* indicates that the "J. Hendricks" residence was located on the Sumneytown Pike, just northwest of the boundary between Lower Salford and Towamencin Townships. John inherited the farm from his father Jacob on November 17, 1829. Thus, this same small plot of farmland supported three generations:

1. Leonard Hendricks 1783-1812
2. Jacob Hendricks 1812-1829
3. John B. Hendricks 1829-1853

John B. appears as a resident of Lower Salford Township, Montgomery Co., Pa. in the U.S. census tabulation of 1850. His wife Elizabeth died on August 28, 1851, and was buried in the Salford Mennonite Cemetery (unpublished records of Salford Mennonite Cemetery - fide Wilmer Reinford, 1978).

After his farm was sold by Court order in 1853, John B., along with his brothers Jacob B. and Samuel B., is supposed to have emigrated to Whiteside County, Illinois (Heckler, 1888, p. 364). However, he apparently returned to Pennsylvania a few years later as the Salford Mennonite Cemetery records indicate he is buried there, having died on June 11, 1883.

GENERATION VII: LOWER SALFORD, PENNSYLVANIA, TO CAWKER CITY, KANSAS. Ephraim D. Hendricks was born on August 16, 1825, probably in Lower Salford Township, Montgomery Co., Pa. He was the third child of seven of John B. Hendricks and Elizabeth Hendricks, née Delp (Boorse, 1953, p. 91), the children being:

1. Leonard D., ca. 1821- ?
2. Rachel, ca. 1823-1841
3. Ephraim D., 1825-1903
4. Margaret, ca. 1827- ?
5. Sabilla, 1829- ?
6. John D., 1832-1875?
7. Samuel D., 1834-1902

On November 18, 1848, Ephraim married Mary Rosenberger (or Rosenberry) at the Zwingli Reformed Church at Tohickon (Hinke, 1925), which was located about 3 miles north of Perkasie, Bucks Co., Pa. Mary's father had died in 1831 and her mother in early 1848. Mary was born on December 6, 1825, daughter of Jacob Rosenberger (1797-1831) and Mary Rosenberger, née Detweiler (1799-1848). Both Mary's father and paternal grandfather were buried in the cemetery near the Methacton Mennonite Meeting House in Worcester Township (Fretz, 1906).

In 1848, Ephraim and Mary dissolved their ties with Montgomery County and migrated to East Lampeter Township (near Strasburg), Lancaster County, Pa., where they joined the Church of the Reformed Mennonites (Herrite Denomination, schism of the Mennonite Church led by John Herr).

John Herr (1782-1850) had founded the Reformed Mennonite Church in 1812 at Strasburg, Lancaster Co., Pa. In the same sense that various European Quaker groups separated from the Mennonites, so did the American Reformed Mennonites form a splinter group from the main body of the Mennonites. The Reformed Mennonites apparently never had more than a few thousand members; in 1948, for instance, they numbered about 950 members in Canada and about 733 members in the United States.

The first two sons of Ephraim and Mary, namely, Allen R. and Benjamin Franklin, were born in Lancaster County. The 1850 U.S. Census shows Ephraim Hendricks as living in Lampeter Township, Lancaster Co., Pa. under the phonetic spelling of "Epharum Hendrix." His occupation was listed as a "talor" (tailor).

In 1851, the family migrated to Sterling, Whiteside Co., Ill. Here, the two younger sons, John Rosenberry and Charles Rosenberry, were born. By some good fortune, the family survived the 1854 cholera epidemic in Sterling.

The 1860 U.S. Census shows Ephraim D. Hendricks living in Jordan Township (New Jordan Post Office), Whiteside Co., Ill.; he was classified as a farmer with real estate valued at $2500.00, and personal property valued at $600.00. Ephraim's uncles Jacob and Samuel (Generation VI), as well as his brothers Leonard D., John D., and Samuel D. Hendricks were also recorded as living in Whiteside Co., Ill., during the Federal and State census years of 1860 and 1865.

In 1877, Ephraim was listed as a Deacon in the Reformed Mennonite Church at Sterling, Ill. (Bent, 1877, p. 439). This Church had been founded about 1820 and reorganized in 1868 with a membership of sixty-five with the building of a frame structure in Sterling. By 1868, Ephraim Hendricks occupied land in Tampico Township, sections 25-26, Whiteside Co., Ill.

In 1878, Ephraim D., his wife, and their two youngest sons moved to Cawker City, Kansas. In 1899, Ephraim D. and his wife, as well as son Charles R., and his wife Emma, née Marzolf, were listed as members of the Naomi Mennonite Church, Walnut Creek Township, Mitchell Co., Kansas.

Ephraim D. died on September 6, 1903, in Cawker City, Kansas, and was buried in the Naomi Mennonite Cemetery which is located about eight miles south-southwest of Glen Elder, Kansas, amongst the rolling prairie wheat farms of north central Kansas. Mary D. died on March 24, 1904, and was buried next to her husband.

The westward migration of Ephraim D. Hendricks, which was typical of numerous families in that era, is nicely shown in Table 1.3.

TABLE 1.3
FEDERAL & STATE CENSUS RECORDS
Ephraim D. Hendricks (1825-1903)

Year	State	County	Township/City	Spelling
1830	Pennsylvania	Montgomery	Lower Salford	Hendricks
1840	Pennsylvania	Montgomery	Lower Salford	Hendricks
1850	Pennsylvania	Lancaster	East Lampeter	Hendrix
1860	Illinois	Whiteside	Jordan	Hendricks
1865	Illinois	Whiteside	x	x
1870	Illinois	Whiteside	Tampico	Hendricks
1880	Kansas	Mitchell	Pittsburgh	Hendrick
1890	x	x	x	x
1900	Kansas	Mitchell	Cawker	Hendricks

GENERATION VIII: STERLING, ILLINOIS, TO GLEN ELDER, KANSAS. Charles Rosenberry Hendricks was the youngest of the four boys of Ephraim Delp Hendricks and Mary (Rosenberry or Rosenberger) Hendricks:

1. Allen R., 1849-1939
2. Benjamin Franklin, 1851-1927
3. John R., 1855-1927
4. Charles R., 1859-1934

Charles R. Hendricks was born on August 29, 1859, near Sterling, Ill. (probably in Jordan Township, Whiteside County). About 1878, he moved, with his parents and brother John, to Mitchell County, Kansas., where he bought a homestead relinquishment in Pittsburgh Township. In 1879, the railroad line was laid to Glen Elder.

On March 27, 1883, Charles R. married Emma Marzolf (1861-1931), daughter of Jacob (1831-1919) and Anna Elizabeth Marzolf, née Shafer (1836-1925). (See Part 7 for more information on the Marzolf family). The marriage was performed by Jacob Baay, Pastor of the Presbyterian Church in Cawker City. Soon thereafter, they occupied a farm in Sections 13/14 of Pittsburgh Township. The bitter cold blizzard of January, 1886, when the temperature dropped to twenty-eight degrees below zero, was a challenge.

In the fall of 1888, the family moved to a farm in Section 36 of Carr Creek Township. Charles R. lived here and farmed this land for a period of forty years during which time he became fairly prosperous and accumulated a half section (360 acres) of land. About this time, the couple apparently joined the Naomi Mennonite Church group. The family eventually comprised ten children: three boys and seven girls.

The turn of the century saw major advances in farm mechanization in the form of mechanized threshers, automobiles, trucks, and the like. Primitive steam engines were used in Mitchell Co. as early as 1890 to run stationary threshers. Automobiles first appeared in the Glen Elder community about 1909, that being the year following Henry Ford's mass production of the famous Model T.

Although electricity arrived in the towns and villages along the Solomon valley as early as 1905, farm households did not benefit until 1920 or later from the invention of vacuum cleaners, dial telephones, light bulbs and the like.

Life in the Kansas wheat belt consisted of cold winters and hot summers. Periodic temperatures above 100 degrees were common during the months of June, July, and August. Typical harvest weather was 104 to 105 degrees. The hot summers were mitigated by nearly constant breezes blowing out of the northwest. In the winter months of January and February, it was not uncommon to have temperatures below zero degrees Fahrenheit.

Charles R. became a member of the Reformed Mennonite Church, Naomi Meeting House in 1892. He was chosen a deacon in 1929. In 1928, Charles R. retired to a home in Glen Elder, Kansas; Emma Marzolf died on December 24, 1931. A second marriage to Sadie E. Watson of Lancaster, Pa., took place on August 6, 1933.

Charles R. died on December 5, 1934. Both Charles R. and Emma are buried in the Naomi Cemetery as are three of their ten children. These cemetery records are documented in the 1981 book by D. and M. Reling; they record forty-seven family names, mostly non-Mennonite although nearly all somehow related.

ACKNOWLEDGEMENTS
Many individuals kindly took a direct interest in this brief research on the Gerrit Hendricks family of southeastern Pennsylvania. Among those who contributed are the following:

Elinor Claire, née Boorse, of Souderton, Pa.
Theo I. Delp, of Monticello, Fla.
Priscilla L. Delp, of Souderton, Pa.
Edna Haller, née Hendricks, of Independence, Mo.
Carroll D. Hendricks, of Harleysville, Pa.
David Leah Hendricks, née Moss, of Glen Elder, Kansas.
Ed R. Hendricks, of Sterling, Ill.
Lelia M. Hendricks of Auburndale, Fla.
Leroy R. Hendricks, of Sterling, Illinois.
Pearl F. Hendricks, of Glen Elder, Kansas.
Mary Medearis, of Boulder, Colorado.
Charles K. Nusbaum, of Dixon, Ill.
Mabel Nusbaum, née Hendricks, of Sterling, Ill.
Benjamin H. Shoemaker, 3rd, of Germantown, Phila., Pa.
Helen Smith Shoemaker, of Stevenson, Maryland.
Jacob B. Stouffer, of Sterling, Ill.
Ruth Stuart, née Hendricks, of Beloit, Kansas.

Many organizations generously contributed their expertise, of which a few were:

Genealogical Society of Pennsylvania, Philadelphia, Pa.
    Margaret Fox
Germantown Historical Society, Philadelphia, Pa.
    Patricia A. Henning
Germantown Mennonite Church, Philadelphia, Pa.
    Robert F. Ulle
Mennonite Archives & Libraries, Lancaster, Pa.
    Ira D. Landis
Mennonite Historians of Eastern Pa., Creamery, Pa.
    Wilmer Reinford

REFERENCES.

Bean, T. W., 1884, *History of Montgomery County, Pennsylvania*. Everts & Peck, Philadelphia, Pa., 2 vols., 1197 p., appendices. Reprinted in 1975 by Unigraphic, Evansville, Indiana.

Bent, Charles (ed.), 1877, *History of Whiteside County, Illinois*. Privately printed, Morrison, Ill., 532 p., map. Reprinted by The Bookmark, Knightstown, Indiana., 1978.

Boorse, H. E., 1953, *The Boorse Family*. Privately printed, Boorse Family Assoc., Asheville, N.C., 298 p., illus., map.

Burkhalter, Sheldon, et al, 1975, *A Mennonite Response 1776-1976*. Franconia Mennonite Conf., Souderton, Pa., 16 p.

Cassel, D. K., 1896, *A Genealogical History of the Cassel family in America*. M. R. Wills Publ., Norristown, Pa., 463 p.

Delp, Leonard, A., 1971, *Delps Galore*. Privately printed, Monticello, Fla., 137 p.

Delp, Priscilla L., 1962, *A Genealogical History of the Delp and Delp-Cassel Families*. Privately printed, Souderton, Pa., 58 p., illus.

Fretz, A. J., 1906, *A Genealogical Record of the Descendants of Henry Rosenberger of Franconia, Montgomery Co., Pa*. Privately printed, Milton, N.J., 336 p.

Haller, C. R. 1985, "The Gerrit Hendricks Line of Montgomery County, Pennsylvania." *Mennonite Family History*, vol. IV, no. 2, p. 58-63, illus. (including front cover).

Heckler, J. Y., 1888, *History of Lower Salford Township*. Weekly News Office, Harleysville, Pa., 456 p.
_____, 1960, *History of Franconia Township*. Compiled by Roy C. Kulp, published by Carroll D. Hendricks. Schlecters Printing, Allentown, Pa., 112 p.

Hinke, W. J., 1925, *A History of Tohickon Union Church*. Tribune Publ. Co., Meadville, Pa., 483 p.

Hocker, E. W., 1938, *Abstracts of Tombstone Inscriptions, Mennonite Churches in Central Montgomery County, Pa*. Privately printed, Germantown, Pa.

Hull, Wm. I., 1935 (reprinted 1970), *William Penn and the Dutch Quaker Migration to Pennsylvania*. Genealogical Publ. Co., Baltimore, Maryland., 445 p., illus.

La Munyan, P. E., 1905, *The DeWees Family: Genealogical Data, Biographical Facts and Historical Information*. W. H. Roberts Publ., Norristown,

Mathews, Edward, 1892, *The Rosenberger Family of Montgomery County: Historical and Genealogical Sketches*. J. R. Haldeman Co., Harleysville, Pa., 60 p.
_____, 1897, *History of Towamencin Township*. A. E. Dambly's Estate, Skippack, Pa.

Medearis, Mary, 1985, "The J. V. Hendricks Family in Smithville, 1879-1902." Lawrence County (Ark.) *Historical Quart.*, Vol. 8, no. 1, p. 17-31, illus.

Miller, J. S., & Marcus Miller, 1983, *The Mennonites of Southeastern Pennsylvania 1693-1983*. Germantown Mennonite Church Corp., Philadelphia, Pa., 32 p., figs. map.

Munro, J. C., 1976, *Franconia Mennonites, The Eighteenth Century Settlement*. Privately printed, Harleysville, Pa., 26 p.

Rathmell, J. K., Jr., & Robert Ziegler (eds.), 1978, *Towamencin Township 250th Anniversary Book*. Montco Business Forms, Center Square, Pa., 66 p., figs.

Reling, Dorothy, & Mildred Reling, 1981, "Naomi Cemetery." In *Mitchell County Cemeteries*. North Central Kansas Genealogical Society, Cawker City, Kansas. Vol. II, p. 6-11.

Roach, H. B., undated, probably 1967-76, *Godshalk, Hendricks and Hudders Families*. Unpubl. manuscript, about 250 p. (Chestnut Hill, Phila., Pa.)
An unique copy exists in The Genealogical Soc. of Penna., Phila.

Rosenberger, J. L., 1923, *The Pennsylvania Germans*. Univ. Chicago Press, Chicago, Ill., 173 p.
_____, 1929, *In Pennsylvania German Land*. Ibid, 91 p.

Rosenberger Family Association, 1973, *Rosenberger and Swartley Family History*. Rosenberger Family Assoc., Hatfield, Pa.
Reprint of 8 books including Fretz, 1906a, 1906b; M. Rosenberger, 1973; Kramer, 1953; A. C. Rosenberger, 1944; F. C. Rosenberger, 1950a, 1950b, Baker, 1956, totals 625 p.

Smith, C. H., 1929, *The Mennonite Immigration to Pennsylvania in the Eighteenth Century*. Norristown Press, Norristown, Pa., 412 p., illus.

Wenger, J. C., 1937, *History of the Mennonites of the Franconia Conference*. Franconia Mennonite Historical Soc., Telford, Pa., 523 p.

Williams, R. T., & M. C. Williams, 1971-72, *Index of Wills & Administration Records, Philadelphia, Pa., 1682-1782*. Privately printed, Danboro, Pa., 213 p.

_____, & _____, 1972, *Index of Wills & Estate Settlements, Montgomery County, Pennsylvania, 1784-1850*. Ibid, 146 p.

Yoder, Dan, 1980, *Pennsylvania German Immigrants, 1709-1786*. Genealogical Publ. Co., Inc., Baltimore, Maryland., 394 p.

_____, et al, 1971, *Christopher Dock Bicentennial Commemoration Program*. Mennonite Publ. House., Scottsdale, Pa., 32 p.

Part 2

Changes in German Surnames and Personal Names

EVERAL GENEALOGIES ON THE HENDRICKS name have been printed, among which are those of Charles T. Hendricks (1923), Marguerite H. Allen, ed., (1963), and Florence Hendricks Moore (1985). The lineages in those publications, except for their incomplete footnotes, involve mainly persons outside the scope of this research. Most historians, including the three publications mentioned above, imply that the name Hendricks is of Dutch origin. In fact, current records suggest that the various Hendricks families mostly originated in the Lowlands of Belgium, The Netherlands, and the Lower Rhine of Germany.

During the turmoil of the 17th and 18th centuries, there was considerable migration to other lands from the Lowlands, and in many cases, eventually to America. Families bearing the Hendricks name independently settled in colonies which later became Massachusetts, New York, Pennsylvania, and Delaware.

THE FIRST PENNSYLVANIA GERMANS, 1683-1709. Pennsylvania Germans (known also as Pennsylvania Dutch, an Anglization of Deutsch or Duitsch, meaning German) came to America en masse, but the first large numbers of Germans did not come until about 1709. After 1708, the "Dutch Quakers" from Krefeld (near Köln, see Figure 3 on page 240) and from Krisheim (near Worms) of 1683, 1684, 1685, and 1686 were rapidly outnumbered, especially in southeastern Pennsylvania, by the Rhenish Germans, many of whom were Mennonites. The Dutch names Hendricks and Boorse, among others, became a minority, albeit persistent, among the German names Rosenberger, Delp, Schwardle, Schuhmacher, and many others.

As Hull (1935, p. 399) aptly states: "as small bodies (of migrants) tend to be drawn towards and absorbed in larger ones, the tendency was to Germanize the Dutch names" and the "Germans were in turn largely Angelicized." This was a very important process for the understanding of genealogy, a process which in this case occurred not only in Krefeld and in Krisheim, but was carried over to Philadelphia and Germantown.

The records show numerous variations in spelling in given and familial names. Depending upon the background of the census taker or the surrogate, the immigration or naturalization officer, or other record keeper, the Dutch names Hendriks and Hendricks become Heinrich or Heinrichs in Germany, Hendrickx in Belgium (Flemish), and Henry (or Henri) in England and France. All these names may have been derived from the Old High German name Hangarih, meaning "chief of the house." Misspellings include Henrix, Hendericks, Hendricsz, etc. (See also Table 2.3 on page 36.)

GERRIT HENDRICKS, SON OF HENDRICK GERRITS. We know that by about 1657, there was an active Mennonite community in the small German village of Krisheim, led by Yelles Kassel (1618-1681). In 1657, however, the English Quaker William Ames and others arrived in Krisheim in 1657. Seven or eight families soon converted to Quakerism.

Among the converts were Hendrick Gerrits and his son Gerrit Hendricks. We know little of Hendrick Gerrits, except that two of his cows ("worth twenty-seven Guilders") were confiscated in 1663 because he persisted in attending Quaker meetings. One might suppose that he was part of a group of Mennonites who migrated from the Lower Rhine to Krisheim in the aftermath of the Thirty Years' War, say about 1655.

Hendrick disappears from the records after this, but his son Gerrit took up his father's leadership in Krisheim's Quaker circle, and came with his family to Pennsylvania in 1685 (Hull, 1970, p. 294).

The small German village of Griesheim or Krisheim (after 1794, called Kriegsheim and today Monsheim/Kriegsheim postal district) is located about seven miles west of the City of Worms, on the west flank of the Rhine River, in the heart of the German Lower (Rhenish) Palatinate (see Figure 4 on page 241). After his first visit in 1657 William Ames returned to Krisheim in 1661 and spent some time there helping with the grape harvest and converting more Mennonites to Quakerism. William Penn came to Krisheim in 1677 during one of his trips in western Europe to convert people to Quakerism.

The spelling of both the name Gerrit and the name Hendricks, as well as his father's name Hendrick Gerrits, leaves little doubt that the family was originally of Dutch origin, if that is the proper term for people from the Low Countries. It was a Low Country custom for the son to take as his last name, the first name of the father with the addition of the suffix -sen or -son, or the genitive 's'. This is called a patronymic.

The Dutch name Gerrit becomes Gerhard or Gerhardt in German, and Garret in English.

FROM THE PAST TO THE PRESENT: SEARCHING BACKWARDS. Twenty-three cities from the Low Countries (Netherlands, Belgium, Lower Rhine of Germany) were analyzed for present-day occurrences of the Hendricks name and for related spellings. The thirteen cities in the Lowlands show twenty-two variations of the Hendricks surname and twelve variations of the use of Gerrits as a surname. The ten cities in Germany show twenty-eight variations of the surname Hendricks. The data sources were telephone directories dating from 1985/86. In the following Tables 2.1 and 2.2, several conclusions stand out.

TABLE 2.1
LISTING OF GERRITS/GERRITSEN AND RELATED NAMES
from current telephone directories

City	The Netherlands											Belgium	
	Groningen	Leeuwarden	Amsterdam	Haarlem	Utrecht	Arnhem	Nijmegen	The Hague	Rotterdam	Eindhoven	Maastricht	Antwerp	Brussels
Population	149,500	85,400	866,800	171,000	261,000	128,000	136,100	604,100	731,000	174,000	93,400	253,296	170,489
Province	Groningen	Friesland	N. Holland	N.Holland	Utrecht	Gelderld	Gelderld	S. Holland	S.Holland	N. Brabant	Limburg	Antwerp	Brabant
Gerets	0	0	0	0	0	0	1	0	0	0	12	1	1
Gerits	0	0	3	1	1	0	0	2	0	3	7	3	4
Gefitz	0	0	0	0	0	0	0	6	0	0	1	0	0
Geritzen	0	0	10	0	0	0	0	0	0	0	0	0	12
Gerrets	0	0	2	0	0	0	0	2	1	0	0	0	0
Gerretse	2	5	15	0	3	1	5	0	0	0	0	0	0
Gerretsen	29	1	44	12	31	39	150	21	6	3	2	0	2
Gerrits	0	6	30	2	0	3	10	28	7	40	3	9	6
Gerritse	29	5	181	33	63	209	61	22	41	5	2	0	0
Gerritsen	5	6	21	3	4	4	3	90	70	17	9	6	1
Gerritsma	0	0	10	1	2	3	12	10	6	2	0	0	0
Gerritzen	0	0	0	0	0	0	0	12	3	1	0	0	0
Totals	65	23	316	52	104	259	242	193	134	71	36	19	26
Per 100,00	43	27	36	30	40	202	177	32	18	41	39	8	15

Data Sources:
Names from 1986 Telephone Directories
Population from 1961-1963 Census

TABLE 2.2
LISTING OF HENDRIKS/HENDRIKSEN AND RELATED NAMES
from current telephone directories

City	The Netherlands											Belgium	
	Groningen	Leeuwarden	Amsterdam	Haarlem	Utrecht	Arnhem	Nijmegen	The Hague	Rotterdam	Eindhoven	Maastricht	Antwerp	Brussels
Population	149,500	85,400	866,800	171,000	261,000	128,000	136,000	604,100	731,000	174,000	93,400	253,296	170,489
Province	Groningen	Friesland	N.Holland	N.Holland	Utrecht	Gelderld	Gelderld	S.Holland	S.Holland	N.Brabant	Limburg	Antwerp	Brabant
Henderick	0	0	0	0	0	0	0	0	0	0	0	0	0
Henderickx	0	0	0	0	1	0	0	0	0	0	0	51	18
Henderik	0	0	0	0	7	0	0	0	1	0	0	0	0
Henderiks	1	0	9	0	1	0	1	3	1	0	1	1	2
Henderikx	0	0	1	0	0	1	0	0	0	0	0	7	0
Henderix	0	0	0	0	0	0	0	0	0	0	4	1	0
Hendrich	0	0	0	0	0	0	0	0	0	1	0	0	0
Hendrichs	0	0	0	0	0	0	0	0	0	0	0	0	2
Hendrick	0	0	2	1	0	0	3	3	1	3	1	1	26
Hendricks	2	0	3	0	0	0	5	1	0	2	3	1	5
Hendrickx	0	0	10	0	1	0	6	2	0	6	8	322	194
Hendrik	0	0	6	0	1	0	0	4	1	0	0	0	0
Hendrikman	0	0	1	0	0	0	0	5	0	0	0	0	0
Hendriks	64	17	343	95	145	191	436	197	159	188	52	23	8
Hendrikse	4	1	23	10	8	2	4	13	13	4	0	2	0
Hendriksen	4	3	40	3	20	22	13	40	16	11	0	0	0
Hendriksma	1	0	9	0	1	0	0	0	4	0	0	0	0
Hendrikson	0	0	1	0	0	0	0	0	2	0	0	0	0
Hendriksz	0	0	2	0	1	0	0	1	0	0	3	0	0
Hendriksze	0	0	3	0	0	0	0	0	0	0	0	0	0
Hendrikx	1	0	1	0	4	0	6	1	5	0	34	23	6
Hendrix	1	1	22	3	0	3	10	6	3	19	19	26	20
Totals	79	26	476	112	190	220	484	287	206	234	125	458	285
Per 100,00	53	30	55	65	73	172	356	48	28	134	134	181	167

Data Sources:
Names from 1986 Telephone Directories
Population from 1961-1963 Census

The Hendricks spelling is concentrated in the small area between Nijmegen in the Netherlands and Kleve in Germany - these two cities are only about twenty kilometers (twelve miles) apart. The Hendricks name is spelled in various forms in local environments. Four dominant spellings are as follows:

Country	City	Dominant Spelling	Composite Spelling per 100,000
Netherlands	Arnhem	Hendriks	172
Netherlands	Nijmegen	Hendriks	356
Netherlands	Eindhoven	Hendriks	134
Belgium	Antwerp	Hendrickx	181
Belgium	Brussels	Hendrickx	167
Germany	Kleve	Hendricks	493
Germany	Düsseldorf	Heinrich(s)	only 49
Germany	Köln	Heinrich(s)	only 57

The Dutch town of Maastricht, lying on the crossroads of the three countries, Netherlands, Belgium, and Lower Rhine of Germany, contains a composite of the dominant spellings of Hendriks and Hendrikx, both of which show the Dutch and the Belgium influence. In Germany, the Hendricks name, or its variants, becomes less common outside the Lower Rhine area as shown by comparable data from Frankfurt, Mainz, Worms, and Mannheim. The addition of 'sen' (meaning son of) to the Hendricks name appears as a local phenomena, most commonly used in the Dutch cities of Arnhem and Nijmegen.

EARLY HENDRICKS' RECORDS IN THE LOWER RHINE. The records show that there were Anabaptists (an early Reform group), at Nijmegen in 1539, 1557, 1569, 1639, 1652, 1654-57, and in later years. A prominent Mennonite preacher at Nijmegen in the period from about 1690 to 1714 was Laurens Hendriks. His son, named Hendrik Laurens, was a minister at Nijmegen from 1714 to 1759.

Another well-known couple was Pieter and Elizabeth Hendricksz, both leading Quakers in Amsterdam during the period of about 1660-1690. She was active as a Quaker preacher, missionary, and author of pamphlets. He was a button-maker and apparently a merchant of some means who traveled with William Penn, later founder of Pennsylvania, from Amsterdam to Harlingen in September, 1677. Pieter Hendricksz (1634/36-1704) was a son of Hendrick Pietersz from Holstein in northern Germany; the family was exiled from the area of Hamburg for religious reasons. Some reports show Pieter Hendricks as Pieter Hendricksz Deen, the last appendage apparently having been adopted in later years, possibly reflecting his original area of origin (Deen is Dutch for a Dane).

There is also a mention of a Herman Hendricks (or Harmon Hendricks) from Rotterdam who in 4/82 (April, 1682) was a "first purchaser" of 2000 acres of Pennsylvania. Niepoth (1950, p. 154) lists the following citizens of Krefeld, Germany, whose relationships to the other Hendricks of the Lower Rhine are not clear: Henderichs, Aret, 1687; Henderichs, Henderich, 1679; Henderichs, Jacob and sons, David and Johannes, 1694; Henderichs, Mattheis, 1695; and Henderichs, Veit, 1679.

TABLE 2.3
LISTING OF HEINRICH AND RELATED NAMES

City	The Netherlands			Germany									
	Arnhem	Nijmegen	Maastricht	Aachen	Krefeld	Kleve	Duesseldorf	Koeln	Muenster	Frankfurt	Mainz	Worms	Mannheim
Population	128,000	136,100	93,400	177,700	223,500	22,500	696,000	859,000	200,300	678,500	146,200	63,500	329,000
Province	Gelderld	Gelderld	Limburg	Nordrhein	Nordrhein	Nordrhein	Nordrhein	Nordrhein	Westfalen	Hessen	h.-Pfal	h.-Pfal	Baden
Heinrich	0	0	0	18	83	4	105	166	29	130	55	22	70
Heinrichs	0	1	0	84	152	1	111	165	18	25	17	1	6
Henderick	0	0	0	0	n/a	0	0	0	0	0	0	0	0
Henderickx	0	0	0	0	n/a	0	0	0	0	0	0	0	0
Henderik	0	1	1	0	n/a	0	0	0	0	0	0	0	0
Henderiks	1	0	0	0	n/a	0	0	0	0	0	0	0	1
Henderikx	0	0	4	0	n/a	0	0	0	0	0	5	0	0
Henderix	0	0	0	0	2	0	5	8	0	11	1	33	2
Hendrich	0	0	0	4	17	0	8	18	0	1	1	1	0
Hendrichs	0	3	1	0	n/a	0	2	0	0	2	0	0	2
Hendrick	0	5	3	20	111	101	31	26	10	0	1	0	0
Hendricks	0	0	0	0	8	1	0	0	0	0	2	0	0
Hendricksen	0	0	0	0	n/a	0	0	0	0	0	0	0	0
Hendrickson	0	6	8	2	n/a	0	0	2	0	0	2	0	0
Hendrickx	0	0	0	0	n/a	0	1	1	1	0	1	0	0
Hendrik	0	0	0	0	n/a	0	0	0	0	7	0	0	1
Hendrikman	0	436	52	8	43	2	10	5	0	0	1	0	0
Hendriks	191	4	0	0	n/a	0	0	0	0	0	0	0	0
Hendrikse	2	13	0	0	n/a	0	1	0	0	0	0	0	0
Hendriksen	22	0	0	0	n/a	2	0	0	0	2	0	0	0
Hendriksma	0	0	3	0	n/a	0	0	0	0	0	0	0	0
Hendrikson	0	0	0	0	n/a	0	0	0	0	0	0	0	0
Hendriksz	0	0	0	1	n/a	0	2	2	1	2	0	2	0
Hendriksze	6	0	34	3	n/a	0	9	0	0	1	20	1	1
Hendrix	3	10	19	4	46	0	30	45	0	0		0	27
Hendrix	0	0	0	1	n/a	0	25	52	1	0	1	2	1
Henrich													
Henrichs													
Totals	220	485	125	145	462*	111	339	490	59	183	103	59	110
Per 100,000	172	356	134	82	207*	493	49	57	29	27	70	93	33

Data Sources: *Krefeld only - 1986 Adressenbuch; note most spellings not tabulated (includes individuals 19 and older)
All other German cities: telephone directory for 1986/87
German cities population estimate: 1966;
Dutch cities: 1985/86 telephone directory; population estimate: 1961/63

REFERENCES

Allen, M. H., 1963, *Henry Hendricks Genealogy.* Hendricks Family Organization/Woodruff Printing & Litho, Salt Lake City, Utah, 578 + 80 p.

Haller, C. R., 1985, "The Gerrit Hendricks Line of Montgomery County, Pennsylvania." *Mennonite Family History,* vol IV, no. 2, p. 58-63, figs. This was an early version, now much expanded.

Hendricks, C. T., 1923, *The Hendricks Genealogy.* The Tuttle Co., Rutland, Vermont, 699 p.

Hendrix, R. L., 1980, *The Hendrix Family of Mobile County, Alabama.* Privately printed, Cazenovia, N.Y., 93 p., (1986, Additions & Corrections, 9 p.)

Kannegieter, J. Z., 1971, *Geschiedenis van de Vroegere Quakergemeenschap Te Amsterdam.* Schelteman & Holkema N.V., Amsterdam, 350 p.

Moore, F. H., 1985, *Albert(us) Hendricks(on).* Beidel Printing House, Inc., Skippensburg, Pa., 321 p. Includes the probable lineage of former Vice President Charles A. Hendricks (1819-1885), no evident relation to Gerrit Hendricks of Part 1.

Niepoth, Wilhelm, 1939, *Die Mennonitengemeinde in Krefeld und ihre Beziehungen zu ihren Nachbargemeinden.* Mennonitischen Geschichtsverein Weierhof (Pfalz), Schriftenreihe Nr. 2, p. 131-143
_____, 1950, "Das Bürgerbuch der Stadt Krefeld." *Die Heimat,* Bd. 21, p. 148-155.

HE THREE "B'S" OF GERMAN ETYMOLOGY. With regard to names of Germanic origin, there exist today numerous dictionaries which you may use to get an idea in which area you should be looking for the place of origin of your ancestors. Large areas of the German speaking countries have names which tend to be concentrated in that particular area. In some cases, names are typical to the countries of Switzerland, Germany, or the Netherlands. In other cases, minor variations in spelling give a clue as to origin in more localized areas.

These statements assume, of course, that the spelling of the name has not been radically altered. The most extreme alteration is the Latinization of a name. Fortunately, Latinization was not overly common for the average family, and in fact occurred in relatively few well-known instances, mainly those of highly educated individuals.

The bibliography lists nearly all of the better-known name dictionaries. Prominent among this list are the three "B's," that is, Bach, Bahlow, and Brechenmacher. Books by these three experts on German name etymology may be found in nearly all large libraries in the United States, especially in genealogical libraries.

TYPICAL GERMAN NAMES. Many, many German names end in "-er". In most cases, but not all, the "-er" is part of an occupational name, such as in Müller (miller). Also typical, but not confined to German names, is the use of the umlaut form, as in ä, ö, and ü; in America, the umlaut form invariably becomes a, o, or u, with the vowel sometimes being followed by an e. The combination of the vowels au and e, as in Bauer and Mauer, is easily recognizable, as is the combination of 'eu', and e in the prefixes Neue or Neu, as in Neumann. A similar German vowel combination is ie, as in Nieder, or ei, as in Breitweiser, which originally was probably Breitwieser (a locality name, meaning wide meadow).

The flood of 19th century Germans, of course, brought to Midwest America the art of beer making as represented by the characteristic and universally known brewery names of Anheiser, Budweiser, Busch, Miller (probably Müller), Pabst, Schlitz, Stroh, and many others. And where would we be without that marvelous thing called "blue jeans" which were developed and promoted by former Bavarian Levi Strauss.

Bavarian names often show a characteristic spelling whereby a vowel apparently is omitted from the name, especially when preceding an "l". Some of the numerous examples include: Brandl, Diebl, Glasl, Haslberger, Kriegl, Reichl, Steibl, Waltl, and the like.

TYPICAL SWISS NAMES. Names of Swiss origin often have a characteristic identity. Such names as Amstutz, Binggeli, Gerber, Habegger, Hirschi, Huber, Lehmann, Liechti, Mast, Nussbaum (Nusbaum), and

Stouffer, are common to the northwestern part of the country. The names ending in "i" probably indicate an Italian or Latin influence; following the migration in the late 17th century of Swiss families such as Binggeli and Hirschi down the Rhine into Germany, where the former became Binkele. In America Binkele and Hirschi changed to Binkeley (or some close variation) and Hershey. These families contributed their names to the baby food, chocolate, and hotel industries.

Numerous other typical Swiss family names are given in the publications by Faust & Brumbaugh, 1920-25, by Schelbert & Luebking, 1981, by Zürcher, 1988, and in an unpublished document prepared by the well-known Swiss Mormon genealogist Julius Billeter (see References).

LANGUAGE AREAS IN GERMANY. Writers on the etymology of German names have long recognized that certain names are characteristic of particular regions within Germany. This applies to both surnames (family names) and to given names (first names).

The first broad division is between High and Low German (Figure 2). Pure linguists have long recognized the geographic distinction between High German (residents of southern Germany and Switzerland) and Low German (those families from northern, coastal Germany). The invisible line dividing the north and the south, according to Donaldson (1983), may be called either the Benrather Line (named after a small town near Düsseldorf in Germany), which extends east of the Rhine, or the Uerdinger Line (named after the town of Uerdingen, near Krefeld) which extends west of the Rhine into the Netherlands.

A further division of Germany for etymological purposes is the one into four quarters, as shown by an anonymous 1988 publication in the quarterly *German Genealogical Digest*. In that article, Germany (that is, pre-World War II Germany, including Prussia) is divided into four quadrants, as shown in Figure 2, with corresponding broad dialects.

The four quadrants in Figure 2 have been relabeled in accordance with the language tree inside the back cover of *The American Heritage Dictionary of the English Language* under 1969 copyright by the American Heritage Publishing Co., N.Y. One should note that the divisions between the quadrants are marked by dashed lines indicating, of course, nebulous boundaries between the various language areas. Family names are characterized by pronounced variations in spelling within each quadrant; moreover, family names may also have characteristic prefixes (beginnings) or suffixes (endings), diagnostic of a broad general area.

In the northwest quadrant, especially in the area under Frisian linguistic influence, family names are often characterized by the endings of "-inga", "-stra", and "-ma". Moreover, prefixes of the prepositions and adjectives "van", "van den", and "op den" invariably indicate a western or Dutch origin, meaning "from" or "of."

To the east, Germans less commonly use the similar prefixes "Von" (for ordinary citizens) and "von" (for nobility). Common German suffix-

Figure 2

MAJOR DIALECTIC DIVISIONS
IN GERMANY

Legend

———— THE RHINE RIVER

es include the nouns "-bach", "-bauer", "-breit", "-haus", "-mann", "-müller", and many others.

In Germany, some nouns, such as "stein" may occur either as a prefix or as a suffix, as in the family names Steinmetz and Gradstein, or just plain Stein (meaning Stone in English). The German penchant for combining two words, either adjectives or nouns, led to many combinations, as in Wagner (shortened from Wagenbauer, meaning wagon maker); in America, many variations exist for this name.

In eastern Germanic areas, an obvious Slavic influence is shown by the suffixes "-ski", "-ow", "-ek", "-ak", and "-vic".

In the old days, spelling of both surnames and given names usually changed when an individual moved from one country to another, or from one quadrant in Germany to another. A good example is the common name Meyer which may have many variations, depending upon locality. The name apparently occurs mainly in the western part of Germany with Meyer and Meier being typical of the northwest and Maier, Mayer, and Mayr in the southwest. Other variants include Mair, of possible Slavic influence, of eastern Germany. The probable Dutch variants Majer and Meijer are indicated by the "j" in place of an "i" or a "y"; the combination "ij" is another indication of Dutch origin.

Thode (1983, p. 16-17) published an interesting sketch map showing the distribution of some common masculine and feminine given names over the area of modern day West Germany. Certain first names are characteristic of certain areas, although of course, not exclusively so. For instance, the feminine names Annetje, Anneke, and Geertje, with their characteristic diminutive endings, show a basic Dutch influence and are typical of the northwest quadrant in Germany. Similarly, the feminine names Brunhilde, Gudrun, and Ingeborg occur most commonly in the northeast quadrant. The feminine names Erika, Irene, and Wilhelmine are fairly representative of the southeast quadrant, and the feminine names Barbara, Monika, and Veronica are generally diagnostic of the southwest quadrant. Less commonly, Germans as a group use feminine diminitive endings of "-chen" and "-lein", as in Gretchen and Evelein.

EXAMPLES OF ENGLISH, DUTCH, AND GERMAN INFLUENCE. In the course of research on family history, one commonly finds individuals with given names that show spelling reflecting either German, Dutch, or English influence without regard to the individual's residence. Table 2.4 on the next page recognizes thirty-six common masculine given names and gives the equivalents in English, German, and Dutch, as well as the apparent origin of the given name. Interestingly, the very common German name of Johannes was nearly always recorded as John at American ports of disembarkation; in a few cases the Germanic label survived, but virtually never beyond the immigrant generation.

Table 2.5 is a checklist of some common feminine names and their equivalents. The list is much simplified. For instance, in the case of the very common name Elisabeth, Dutch etymological dictionaries show at least seventy-five variants such as: Betje, Elisa, Elise, Elly, Elsbet, Elsje, Lies, Lizette, and so on. The appendages "tje" and "je" are common to many Dutch variants.

Of course, only a few variants of any given name are shown in Tables 2.4 and 2.5. A good reference to the spelling of northern European given names, both masculine and feminine, is Van der Schaar (1984). Spelling often depended upon the interpretation of the record keeper, and not necessarily upon birth records. German historians and record keepers are prone to use German spelling, just as English scribes invariably use English spelling. In American records, it is obvious that many 19th century census takers were barely literate and usually of English background.

TABLE 2.4
CHECKLIST OF SOME COMMON MASCULINE NAMES
Much Simplified

ENGLISH	GERMAN	DUTCH	PROBABLE ORIGIN
Abraham	n/a	Abraham	Abraham (Hebrew)
Adrian	Adriaen	Adriantje	Adriaan (Latin)
Andrew	Andreas	Andries	Andreas (Greek)
Antony	Anton	Antonius, Teunis	Antonius (Latin)
Albert	Albrecht	Albertus	Adelbert (German)
Arnold	Arnolf	Arent, Arend	Arnout (Germanic)
Arthur	n/a	Artur	Arthus (English)
Benjamin	n/a	Benjamin	Benjamin (Hebrew)
Bernard	Bernhard	Barent	Bernhard (Germanic)
Bartholomew	Barthold	Bart	Bartholomeus (Hebrew)
Christopher	Christoph	Cristoffel	Christoforus (Greek)
Conrad	Conrad, Kurt	Coenraad	Koenraad (Germanic)
Cornelius	Cornelius	Cornelis	Cornelis (Latin)
David	n/a	(Vijt)	David (Hebrew)
Derek	Dietrich	Diederik, Dirk	Diederik (Germanic)
Ephraim	n/a	Efraim	Efraim (Hebrew)
Garret, Gerard	Gerhard	Gerard, Gerrit	Gerhard (Germanic)
George	Georg	Joris	Georg(e) (Greek)
Henry, Harry	Heinrich	Hendrik, Hendrick	Hendrik (Germanic)
Herman	Hermann	Harmen	Herman (Germanic)
Jacob, James	Jakob	Jacob	Jacob(us) (Hebrew)
John	Johan(nes), Hans	Jan, (etc.)	Johan(nes) (Hebrew)
Joseph	n/a	Jozef	Jozef (Hebrew)
Lambert	Lambert	Lambert	Lambert (Germanic)
Lawrence, Larry	Laurenz, Lorenz	Laurent, Laurens	Laurentius (Latin)
Lewis, Louis	Ludwig	Lodewijk	Lodewijk (Germanic)
Leonard	Leonhard	Lennart, Lenard	Leonhard (Germanic)
Matthew	Matthaeus	Mattheus	Mattheus (Greek)
Matthias	Matthias	Matthias	Matthais (Hebrew)
Nicholas	Klaus, Niels, Nikolaus	Nicolaas, Klaas, Claas	Nicolaas (Greek)
Paul	Paul(us)	Paul(us)	Paulus (Latin)
Peter	Peter	Petrus, Pieter	Petrus (Greek)
Rayner	Rainer, Reiner	Reinier	Reginher (Germanic)
Richard, Dick	Reichert	Richard	Richard (Germanic)
Walter	Walther, Walter	Wouter, Wolter	Walt(h)er (Germanic)
William, Bill	Wilhelm	Willem, Wim	Wilhelm (Germanic)

TABLE 2.5
CHECKLIST OF SOME COMMON FEMININE NAMES
Much Simplified

ENGLISH	GERMAN	DUTCH	PROBABLE ORIGIN
Ann, Nancy	Anna, Anne	Anna	Anna (Greek)
Amy	(rare)	Aimee	Aimee (French)
Alice	Heidi	Aaltien, Heide	Adelheid (Germanic)
Barbara	(Barbe(l))	Barbertje	Barbara (Greek)
Beatrice, Tricia	Beatrix	Beatrix	Beatrix (Latin)
Catherine, Kathleen	Katharina	Catharina, Karen	Catharina (Greek)
Diana	(rare)	Diana	Diana (Latin)
Dorothy, Dot	Dorothea	Doortje	Dorothea (Greek)
Edith	Edith	Editha	Edith (Germanic)
Ellen	Eleonore	Eleonora	Eleonora (Arabic)
Emma	Emma	Emmeken	Emma (Germanic)
Evelyn	Eveline	Evelijn, Eve(lien)	Eva (Hebrew)
Frances	Franziska	Fransje	Franciscus, m (Latin)
(rare)	Gerda	Geertje	Gerard, m (German)
Gertie	Gertrud(is)	Gertrude, Gertie	Geertruida (Germanic)
Margaret, Peggy	Grete, Gretchen	Griet(ke), Maggie	Margaretha (Greek)
Harriet Henrietta	Henrike	Hendrika, Henriette	Hendrik, m (Germanic)
Helen	Helena	Helen(e)	Helena (Greek)
Irene	Irene	(rare)	Ireneus, m (Latin)
Jane, Janet	Hanna	Janice, Janet	Johannes, m (Hebrew)
Jeanne	(rare)	Jeanne(tte)	Johannes, m (Hebrew)
Joan	(rare)	Joan	Johannes, m (Hebrew)
Judy	Judith, Jutta	Judith	Judith (Hebrew)
Jill, Juliana	Julia	Juliana	Julius, m (Latin)
Laura	Laura	Laura, Laurie	Laurentius, m (Latin)
Luisa	Luise	Louise	Lodewijk, m (Germanic)
Madeline	Alena	Le(e)na	Magdalena (Hebrew)
Mary	Maria	Maria, Marie	Maria (Hebrew)
Martha	Martha	Martha, Martje	Martha (Hebrew)
Patty	(rare)	Patricia	Patricius, m (Latin)
Pauline	Paula	Paula	Paulus, m (Latin)
Rebecca	(rare)	Rebecca	Rebekka (Hebrew)
Ruth	(rare)	Ruth	Ruth (Hebrew)
Sue, Susan	Sanna	Suzanne	Susan(na) (Hebrew)
Wilma	(rare)	Wilhelmina	Wilhelm, m (Germanic)

REFERENCES

Anonymous, 1988, "Factors Influencing the Establishment of Surnames and Given Names." *German Genealogical Digest*, Vol. IV, no. 3, p. 106-109.

Bach, Adolf, 1952, *Deutsche Namenkunde: Die deutschen Personennamen.* Carl Winter Universitätsverlag, Heidelberg, Vol. 1, 331 p., Vol. 2, 295 p.

_____, 1956, *Deutsche Namenkunde: Registerband.* Ibid, 457 p.

_____, 1965, *Geschichte der Deutschen Sprache.* Quelle & Meyer, Heidelberg, 495 p.

Bahlow, Hans, 1967, *Deutsches Namenlexikon.* Keyersche Verlagsbuchhandlung, München, 588 p.
This very popular book was reprinted in 1976, 1985, etc. It lists more than 15,000 family names.

_____, 1972, *Niederdeutsches Namenbuch.* Dr. Martin Sändig OHG., Walluf bei Weisbaden, 572 p.

_____, 1975, *Mittelhochdeutsches Namenbuch nach schlesischen Quellen.* Verlag Degener, Neustadt/Aisch, 184 p.

_____, 1976, *Deutsches Namenlexikon.* Ibid, 558 p.

_____, 1982, *Pommersche Familiennamen.* Ibid, 99 p.

Bailey, R. F., 1954, *Dutch Systems in Family Naming, New York-New Jersey.* National Genealogical Soc. Gen. Publ. No. 12, 21 p.
This an interesting and rather detailed short article outlining some of the complexities applicable to Dutch names with emphasis on the numerous Dutch names characteristic of New York and New Jersey.

Billeter, Julius, (1973), *Verzeichnis der genealogischen Arbeiten von Julius Billeter.* LDS microfilm, Salt Lake City, 51 pages
Includes more than 1200 Swiss family names and their location by village in northwest Switzerland. The microfilm is available in the numerous LDS branch libraries in the United States. The author has a print-out copy.

Brechenmacher, J. K., 1957-1963, *Etymologisches Wörterbuch der Deutschen Familiennamen.* C. A. Starke Verlag, Limburg/Lahn, Vol. 1, 1957-60, 788 p., Vol. 2, 1960-63, 879 p.

de Vries, Jan, 1971, *Het Nederlands etymologisch woordenboek.* E. J. Brill, Leiden, 977 p.
A standard work on the etymology of Dutch words.

Donaldson, B. C., 1983, Dutch, *A Linguistic History of Holland and Belgium*. Martinus Nijhoff, Leiden, 200 p., 11 maps, illus.
Although the text discusses a rather sophisticated subject matter, it is written for the general public with a short chapter format and a moderate bibliography. Emphasis is on the period from the 12th century through the 19th century.

Drosdowski, Günther (ed.), 1974, *DUDEN, Lexikon der Vornamen*. Dudenverlag, Mannheim, 237 p., 75 illus., 2nd ed.
_____, 1976, *DUDEN. Das grosse Wörterbuch der deutschen Sprache*. Bibliographisches Institut AG und Zechnersche Buchdruckerei Speyer, 6 Vols. (Vol. 1, A-C, 464 p., etc.)
The Duden series is nearly always present in major libraries.

Faust, A. B., & G. M. Brumbaugh, 1920-25, *List of Swiss Emigrants in the Eighteenth Century to the American Colonies*. National Genealogical Soc., Washington, D.C., vol. I, (Zürich, 1734-1744; 1925), 122 p., vol. II (Bern, 1706-1795 & Basel, 1734-1794; 1929), 243 p.

Ferguson, Laraine, 1988, "German Surnames and Surname Etymology." In *German Genealogical Digest*, Vol. IV, No. 1, p. 7-9.

Fleischer, Wolfgang, 1968, *Die deutschen Personennamen*. Akademie Verlag, Berlin, 137 p.

Förstemann, Ernst, 1900, *Altdeutsches Namenbuch, Erster Bd: Personennamen*. P. Hanstein's Verlag, Bonn, 1700 p.

Gottschald, Max, 1982, *Deutsche Namenkunde. Unsere Familiennamen*. Walter de Gruyter, Berlin, 567 p.

Grimm, Jacob, & Wilhelm Grimm, 1854, *Deutsches Wörterbuch*. Verlag von S. Hirzel, Leipzig, 16 volumes, numerous pages.
The multi volumes of this 19th century classic on the German language were recently reprinted and are available in most major libraries.

Heintze, Albert, 1882, *Die deutschen familien-namen, geschichtlich, geographisch, sprachlich*. Buchhandlung des Waisenhauses, Halk a.S., 227 p.
This classic was followed by numerous later editions.

_____, & Paul Cascrebi, 1967, *Die Deutschen Familiennamen*. Georg Olms Verlagsbuchhandlung, Hildesheim , 536 p., 7th reprint ed.
The works by Heintze and co-workers were pioneering efforts and are universally cited by later students of German etymology. The first edition dates from 1933.

Hilbig, F. W., 1958, *Americanization of German Surnames and the Related Process of Changes in Europe*. M.A. Thesis, Univ. Utah, 83 p.

Jensen, L. O., 1988, "The World of Germanic Names." *German Genealogical Digest*, Vol. IV, No. 1, p. 2-6, No. 2, p. 62-66.

Johnson, A. F., 1981, *A Guide to the Spelling and Pronounciation of German Names*. The Copy Shop, Columbus, Ohio, 57 p.
_____, 1984, *The Origins, Development, and Meanings of German Names*. Ibid, 44 p., illus.

Jones, G. F., 1990, *German-American Names*. Genealogical Publ. Co. Inc., Baltimore, 268 p.
Includes scholarly text of 59 pages (in English) and a list of 12, 700 family names on pages 61-268 in abbreviated dictionary form; text unfortunately does not include a bibliography.

Knaur, Drömer, 1985, *Knaurs Vornamen Buch*. Drömersche Verlaganstalt, Th. Knaus Nachf., München, 588 p.

Lockwood, W. B., 1972, *A Panorama of Indo-European Languages*. Hutchinson Univ. Lib., London, 281 p.
_____, 1976, *An Informal History of the German Language*. Andre Deutsch, London, 265 p., maps.

Naumann, Horst, 1987, *Familiennamenbuch*. VEB Bibliographisches Institut, Leipzig, 328 p.

Peters, Victor, & Jack Thiessen, 1987, *Mennonitische Namen - Mennonite Names*. N. G. Elwert Verlag, Marburg, 247 p., 7 maps, illus.
Concentrates on German names from East Prussian and from Russian Mennonite colonies of 19th century.

Reuter, Monika, 1991, *Das neue Vornamen-lexikon*. Gondrom Verlag GmbH & Co., KG, Bindlach, 341 p.

Sahl, Hans, 1983, "Die Pennsylvania-Deutschen: Geschichte eines Dialektes (Hoerspiel)." In *Die Heimat*, Krefelder Jahr., Jahrg. 53, p. 12-14.

Schelbert, Leo, & Sandra Luebking, 1981, "Swiss Mennonite Family Names." In *Rhineland Emigrants*. Genealogical Publ. Co., Baltimore, p. 122-144.
This is a reprint from *Pennsylvania Folklife*, 1977, vol. 26.

Smith, H. C., 1973, *New Dictionary of American Names*. Harper & Row, N.Y., 570 p.

Storrer, N. J., & L. O. Jensen, 1977, *A Genealogical and Demographic Handbook of German Handwriting, 17th-19th Centuries*. Vol. *1, Births & Baptisms*. Privately printed, Pleasant Grove, Utah, 157 p.
One of the better texts illustrating the vagaries of German handwriting. Modern German handwriting tends to be among the poorest in the world; this may have come about as a result in changes in style of certain letters.

Suess, J. H., 1978, *Central European Genealogical Terminology*. The Everton Publishers, Inc., Logan, Utah, 168 p.

Thode, Ernest, 1983, *Atlas for Germanic Genealogy*. Heritage House, Indianapolis, I, Ind., 2nd ed., 74 p.
The work contains a series of interesting sketch maps showing the language areas, in general, of Germany.

Van der Schaar, J., 1984, *Voornamen*. Prisma Woordenboek. Uitgeverij Het Spectrum, Utrecht, 375 p.
This book contains a nearly comprehensive list of Dutch first names with their numerous variants related to geographic parts of the Netherlands. Also included are the variants in other major European languages. Contains good bibliography.

Waterman, J. T., 1976, *A History of the German Language*. Univ. Washington Press, Seattle, 284 p., illus., revised ed.
This highly scholastic summary is one of the few published in English. Originally published in 1966, the revised edition contains an extensive bibliography. The emphasis is on High German language complexity for the period from the 11th through the 19th centuries.

Wimmer, Otto, & Hartmann Melzer, 1982, *Lexicon der Namen und Heiligen*. Tyrolia Verlag, Innsbruck, 980 p.

Zürcher, Isaac, 1988, "Anabaptist-Mennonite Names in Switzerland." *Mennonite Quarterly Review*, Vol. LXII, no. 4, p. 461-495.
First published in 1985 in *Informations-Blätter*, vol. VII, p. 28-61.

**WENTIETH CENTURY PENNSYLVANIA RECORDS.** For several generations, Pennsylvania descendants of the German family name Schuhmacher or Schumacher have made an intensive effort to compile lists of families by that name. These published lists are cited in the accompanying bibliography. It is readily apparent that the name Schuhmacher was largely angelicized during the transition across the Atlantic. As the publications show, Shoemaker became by the far the dominant spelling in America.

The recent publication by Benjamin H. Shoemaker III shows forty-seven variants of the Shoemaker name in America, of which the most common variants are Shoemake, Schumacher, and Schoonmaker, in that order. Benjamin H. Shoemaker III, is a descendant of the Germantown, Pennsylvania, Shoemakers who came to America in 1685. This group traces its origin to the Schuhmachers or Schumachers in the small German village near Worms which in 1685 was called Griesheim or Krisheim. Before the family settled in Krisheim, it is likely that they migrated up the Rhine from the area called Siebengebirge, as various publications in the bibliography relate.

In the Philadelphia area, the Shoemaker name became fairly common. In fact, during the early generations, three members of the clan were mayors of Philadelphia.

EUROPEAN AND AMERICAN CODING SYSTEMS. In checking numerous census and immigration records, one must recognize the logic behind the considerable variation in spelling even while conceding that not all these variants were related.

First, the Germanic Coding System recognizes that a number of consonants may substitute for one another. The learned Hanns Jäger-Sunstenau in his *General-Index zu den Siebmacher'schen Wappenbüchern, 1605-1961* (General Index to Siebmacher's Coats of Arms Books) indexes the first letter of surnames in only one of nineteen categories, as follows:

1. A	11. N
2. B, P	12. O
3. D, Dh, T, Th	13. Q
4. E	14. R, Rh
5. F, V	15. S
6. H	16. U, Ue
7. I, J, Y	17. W, V
8. K, Kh, C, Ch, G, Gh	18. X
9. L	19. Z, Zh, Zs, Zsch, C, Ch, Cs, Cz
10. M	

The principle behind this classification is illustrated by the grouping of "B" and "P" together, which suggests that they are almost indistinguishable in oral communication. On the same principel, "D" and "T" form another composite group, as do "K", "C", and "G", etc. Thus, the Europeans recognize the considerable variation in spelling of the same Germanic surname even before its migration to America. Migration to America provides considerable additional complexity because of the crossing of linguistic boundaries at which time the spelling was changed.

Secondly, the U.S. National Archives uses the well-known Soundex Coding System. This indexing system covers the censuses of 1880, 1900, and part of 1910. Soundex recognizes that vowels may freely substitute for one another in immigration, naturalization, and census records. The Soundex Coding System was devised to facilitate the indexing and filing of millions of family names, many of which were misspelled in the records.

In the Soundex Coding System, all vowels (a, e, i, o, u) and the consonants w, y, and h are dropped unless these vowels or consonants begin a family name. The first letter is kept as is, but the remaining letters in a surname are replaced by a numerical code. No more than three numbers are used. Short surnames add zeros to the end of the code. The basic six number system is as follows:

1. B, P, F, V
2. C, S, K, G, J, Q, X, Z
3. D, T
4. L
5. M, N
6. R

For example, in the four most common spellings of the Shoemaker name, the Soundex Coding System works as follows:

Shoemaker is coded as	S 526
Schoemake is coded as	S 250
Schumacker is coded as	S 252
Schoonmaker is coded as	S 255

Schuhmacher without question is a German occupational name which means shoemaker. A related name, Schoonmaker, is apparently derived from the Dutch word Schoenmaker, which also means shoemaker. A Swiss equivalent apparently is the name Sutter. These examples indicate that families with names of similar occupational origin are not necessarily related.

In summary, it is readily apparent that a considerable amount of research is needed to encompass all forty-eight variants of the Shoemaker name as they are listed in the U.S. Federal Census records. Fortunately, much of the work has been done by the Shoemaker family of Philadelphia and printed in a series of six publications listed in the references at the end of this essay.

TABLE 2.6
VARIOUS SPELLINGS OF SHOEMAKER

Variant	Number of Occurrences	Variant	Number of Occurrences
Schermacher	2	Shoemacher	3
Schoemaker	4	Shoemake	2
Schoenmacker	1	Shoemake	1
Schoenmager	1	Shoemacker	168
Schoenmaker	6	Shoemark	3
Schomacher	1	Shomacher	1
Schomacker	1	Shomack	1
Schomaker	1	Shomacker	1
Schoomaker	1	Shomake	1
Schoonmaker	30	Shomaker	1
Schowmacker	1	Shoomach	1
Schuemaker	1	Shoomack	1
Schuhmacher	7	Shoomak	1
Schumach	4	Shoomaker	4
Schumache	1	Showmaker	1
Schumacher	92	Schumach	1
Schumacherin	3	Shumack	1
Schumacker	3	Shumake	18
Schumager	1	Shumaker	10
Schumaker	10	Shumarke	6
Shamaker	2	Soomake	1
Shewmak	1	Suemaker	1
Shewmake	24	Simack	1
Shewmaker	5		

*U.S. data according to Shoemaker, 1986, p. 505-507

MECHANICS OF NAME CHANGES. Surname variations are summarized by Ferguson (1988, p.7-9). These variations may fall under one or more of the following categories:

1. dialectic changes: very common
   a. vowel changes
   b. consonant substitutions
      labials (f and v; b and p; v and w, etc.)
      dentals (t and z; d and t; etc)
      velars (c and k; k and g; ch and k, etc)
      spirants (c and z; etc.)
2. translation: common only for certain names
3. Latinization: relatively uncommon
4. Anglicization: relatively common

To the above classification, one may add the following:

5. phonetization of name spelling across nationality boundaries
6. changes involved in going from a Germanic language to a Romance language
7. deletion of unnecessary letters (simplification)

The forty-seven variations of the Shoemaker name of Table 2.6 (on page 51) incorporate many of the above name-spelling changes, especially vowel changes and consonant substitution of velars. The Schuhmacher name commonly becomes Shoemaker by virtue of translation. Anglicization is a very common occurrence for this particular surname. The common omission of the second 'h' and the final 'r' in the original German fall under categories 6 and 7 above.

Latinization probably does not occur with the name Schuhmacher. In fact, Latinization was relatively uncommon, occurring in some cases of well-educated families before the widespread use of the vernacular came strongly into effect, i.e., the 16th and 17th centuries. Well-known examples of the Latinization are the following: the Swedish naturalist Carolus Linnaeus (1707-1778), whose original family name was von Linne; the Flemish cartographer Gerhardus Mercator (1512-1594), whose family name was Kaufmann; the German lawyer Francis Daniel Pastorius (1651-1719), whose family name possibly was either Schaefer or Hirt, and the German theologian Philipp Melanchthon (1497-1560), originally named Schwarzerd.

REFERENCES

Ferguson, Laraine, 1988, "German Surnames and Etymology Books." *German Genealogical Digest*, Vol. III, no. 1, p. 7-9.

Jäger-Sunstenau, Hanns, 1964, *General-Index zu den Siebermacher'schen Wappenbüchern, 1605-1961.* Akademische Druck- u. Verlagsanstatt, Graz, Austria, 586 p.
This important index was reprinted in 1984.

Niepoth, Wilhelm, 1956, "Die Wanderungen und die Wandlung der Mennonitenfamilie Schuhmacher." *Der Mennonit*, Frankfurt am Main (Feb., 1956), p. 27-28.
_____, 1957, "From Kriegsheim to Pennsylvania: origin and career of the brothers Peter and George Shoemaker, of Kriegsheim, in the Palatinate." *Germantown Crier*, vol. IX, no. 1, March, p. 7-9, 26.
Translation of above article from the original German was by Edward W. Hocker.

Risler, Walther, 1955, "Taüfer im bergischen Amt Löwenburg, Siebengebirge." *Mennonitische Geschichtsblatter*, 12. Jahr., p. 6-21
Contains mainly historical information of the area.

_____, 1956, "Taüfer im bergischen Amt Löwenburg (Schluss)." *Ibid*, 13. Jahr., p. 31-45
Lists numerous heads of families including various "Schomecher."

Shoemaker, B. H., 1903, *Genealogy of the Shoemaker Family of Cheltenham, Penna..* J. B. Lippincott Co., Phila., 524 p.

Shoemaker, B. H., 3rd, 1951, *Annals of the Shoemaker family of Germantown.* reprint of articles from the Germantown Crier, 7 p.
_____, 1955, *Guide to Shoemaker Pioneers in Colonial America.* privately printed, Germantonwn, Pa., 155 p., mimeographed
_____1975, *Shoemaker Pioneers.* Deford & Co., Baltimore, Md., 566 p., figs. (Supplement, 1982, 24 p.).
_____1986, *Shoemaker Pioneers.* Maran Graphic Specialities, Inc., Baltimore, 530 p., + Supplements 1982, 24 p., and 1986, 6 p.
_____, & R., K. Shoemaker, 1955, *Shoemaker Pioneers.* Privately printed, no address, 155 p.
An unique copy exists in the Genealogical Soc. of Pa., Phila.

I N AN ARTICLE DATED 1884, HENRY POOKE-holes and his wife Mary were cited among the "Partial List of the Families who arrived at Philadelphia between 1682 and 1687." The average reader would not recognize the name of "Henry Pookeholes" as being actually one Heinrich Buchholtz, resident prior to 1685 of Krisheim (or Griesheim, alternate spelling) in the Palatinate. The Buchholtz descendants may be amused about this orthographic curiosity!

NAME CHANGES, THE CHALLENGE OF GENEALOGY. Poor old Heinrich Buchholtz would have been amazed to know that he had been called Henry Pookeholes by means of phonetic English spelling. He might also be astounded to know that the American historian William I. Hull (1935, p.412) calls him "Hendrick Boekwolt" (Dutch version). Another well-known American historian, M. D. Learned (1908, p. 161) quotes a similar Dutch version from court records of Germantown, Pa., dating 1691 as being "Hindrick Bookwolt."

We may assume that Heinrich Buchholtz was probably the son of Mennonite Peter Buchholtz of Krisheim in the Palatinate. An undocumented source suggests that Heinrich Buchholtz and his wife (unnamed) were from "Mulheim" (actually the German town of Mülheim-an-der-Ruhr, near Essen). In any event, he was a property owner in Germantown, near Philadelphia, in 1689, and he was on the well-known Germantown Naturalization List of 1691. He additionally appears on the Naturalization List of 1709 as Henry Bucholtz (Colonial Records of Pennsylvania, vol. 2, p. 493).

In America, the dominant English group applied phonetic spellings at ports of enmbarkation and in most official city and county records. The English, of course, were not overly found of their German cousins, or other Europeans for that matter, the latter including Dutch, French, and Spanish settlers, all of whom were relegated to a lower status.

Almost as curious and as troublesome as name changes of individuals are orthographic changes of European cities and villages. The name changes of a small German village under the succession Griesheim / Krisheim / Kriegsheim is documented in a companion essay in Part 3.

CHANGES IN FAMOUS AMERICAN NAMES OF EUROPEAN ORIGIN. Only slightly more plausible are the name changes of some of America's more prominent citizens. Many of the following immigrants were part of the early wave arriving in America long before the Revolutionary War.

There is, for instance, Johann Nicol Eisenhauer (c. 1695-c. 1760) who came to Philadelphia in 1741. Some reports indicate that he may have been of Bavarian Mennonite descent and that his birth place may have been near Darmstadt in Germany, not far east of the Rhine. The U.S. name, of course, is exemplified by Dwight D. Eisenhower (1890-1969), the former President and direct descendant of the immigrant. Other records of the President's ancestors indicate an origin in one Johannes Eisenhauer who lived in Odenwald in 1446. Odenwald is the wooded, hilly area between Darmstadt and Heidelberg.

Former President Herbert C. Hoover (1874-1964) was born in Iowa of Quaker parents. An immigrant ancestor, Andreas Huber (1723-1783), from Ellerstadt (near Ludwigshafen, just west of the Rhine) came to America about 1750. The name originally was from Oberkulm in Switzerland. American relatives spelled the name Hover, Hoober, Hoeber, and Hoofer, although these spellings were in the minority.

Former President Martin Van Buren (1782-1862) was a descendant of Pieter Martense (1670-1743) (whose descendants added Van Buren) and who came to America in 1693. The old Dutch system of patronymics is well reflected in the names of Pieter Martense's father who was Martin Cornelisz whose father in turn was Cornelis Maessen (the suffices "-sz" and "-sen" or "-se" mean "son of"). The assumed appendage of "van Buren" (the "van" meaning "from") indicates that perhaps the family came from the small village of Buren in Gelderland or from the tiny village of the same name on the island Ameland in Friesland.

Presidents Theodore Roosevelt, Jr. (1858-1919) and Franklin Delano Roosevelt (1882-1945) had a common ancestor in Claes Martenszen van Rosenvelt who came to America from Holland before 1650. Rosenvelt means "rose field." The immigrant settled in New Amsterdam, which was renamed New York by the English when they conquered New Netherland in 1664.

The well-known American capitalist Cornelius Vanderbilt (1794-1877) was a descendant of Jan Aersten van der Bilt, who came from Holland about 1650. The name likely comes from the town of de Bilt, near Utrecht. In the United States, the name is reported to have changed from van der Bilt to Van Derbilt to Vanderbilt.

The famous soldier John J. Pershing (1860-1948), otherwise informally known as "Black Jack" Pershing, was a descendant of Frederick Pfoerschin who came to America before 1750. Anglization of the difficult German or French name in America evidently was a quick process. In America, the name has been listed also as Pfersching, Pfirsching, Pfoershing, Parshing, Pershin, Pairshen, Persian, and likely many other variations. Various accounts attribute the family origin to parts of Alsace, Swabia, Württemberg, and to the city of Darmstadt, in Germany.

A relatively minor change occurred in the name of Johann Peter Rockenfeller (1682-1766) who arrived with his second wife in New Jersey in 1723. Rockenfeller came from the area of Wied, along the north side of the Rhine, about seven miles downstream from Koblenz. The well known businessman, John D. Rockefeller (1839-1937), was just one of many of the family who used this minor variation in name spelling;

other family members used different variants, including Rockfellow, Rockafellar, Rockafellow, and Rockfeller.

It is suspected that the Rockefeller name originated from a small village formerly called Rochenfeld (also spelled Rockenfeld and Rokkenfeld). On current German maps, the spelling is Rockenfeld and the community, which in 1910 had 54 residents, is now part of the city of Neuwied ("Neu" meaning "new"), being about five kms (3 miles) to the northwest of the city center. The 19th century spelling of Rochenfeld is a peculiar, although not unique, French-German combination meaning 'rocky field'. Neuwied was founded in 1652 and partly populated by Mennonites at that time. The Rockefeller name was present in Lutheran or Reformed Church records in the area of Wied at least as early as 1590. Curious attempts have been made to relate the Rockefeller family to the German word Roggenfelder, meaning "rye field," and also to an ancient castle in France which was spelled either Roquefeuil, or Roquefeuille.

In 1910, the Rockefeller Family Association had one of their finest days in recalling the participation of at least eighteen New York Rockefellers in the struggle for independence during the Revolutionary War. In these records, the name is misspelled as Rockenfeller, Rockafelow, Rockafellow, Rockafeller, Rockifellow, Roackaffalter, Rockalow, and Rockfellow, among others. At least six Rockefellers from New Jersey also served on the American side in the first war for independence. During the War of 1812, there were at least six New York Rockefellers on the rolls of the American Army. And during the Civil War of 1861-65, there were more than sixty-four Rockefellers supporting the Union cause. An interesting aspect of this latter tabulation shows twenty-six joining New York regiments, eighteen enlisting in Pennsylvania regiments, nine from New Jersey, and the remainder scattered westward across Michigan, Illinois, Wisconsin, and Kansas.

A relative late-comer to the American scene was Johannes Jacob Astor (1763-1848) who came to the United States in 1783. Astor was born in the town of Walldorf, south of Heidelberg, some twelve kilometers (seven miles) east of the Rhine.

The Astor family fortune was founded in the fur trade and real estate investments. The Astor name lent itself to one of New York's premier hotels, the Walldorf-Astoria, and to the city of Astoria, Oregon. Astor is not a typical German name and likely stems from the Italian-Piemonte region where the name was Astore, meaning hawk.

Also prominent in the American financial world was Meyer Guggenheim (1828-1905) who was born to a Jewish family in Lengnau, canton of Aargau, Switzerland. Fleeing repression against his religion, Guggenheim came to the U.S. in 1847 and settled in Philadelphia. Achieving success as mining and smelting capitalists, the Guggenheim family was active in many large mining ventures, most notably as partners in the enormous Kennecott Copper mining operations in Utah. The elder Guggenheim sired eight sons and three daughters, who in turn vastly expanded the mining operations. It was a rare case where the family name apparently resisted changes in spelling.

The noted American linguist H. L. Mencken (1880-1956) would have been amused at the above mentioned linguistic problems, large and small. No doubt, he could have expanded this short essay into a third large supplement to the 1936 edition of his well-known series titled *The American Language*. The Mencken name itself shows a trace of a Slavic element, coming as it did to America in the 1800's from the area of Leipzig in Germany.

The migration of millions of Swiss, Alsatians, and Germans down the Rhine and across the Atlantic will be expanded on in a series of essays which follow.

ACKNOWLEDGMENTS
The writer gratefully acknowledges use of library facilities at the Mennonitische Forschungsstelle, Weierhof (Rheinland-Pfalz), and in particular, the assistance of Dr. Gary J. Waltner, Dr. Horst Gerlach, and Librarian Christa Kägy.

The author thanks also Mr. Joseph W. Ernst, Director Emeritus of the Rockefeller Archive Center, Pocantico Hills, North Tarrytown, New York, for correspondence and for the transmittance of news clippings and printed information. The family name Ernst is fairly common both in Germany and in America; those from New York apparently had their origin in an unknown locality along the Rhine.

REFERENCES

Anonymous, 1884, "A Partial List of the Families who arrived at Philadelphia between 1682 and 1687." *Pennsylvania Mag. Hist. Biogr.*, vol.
8, p. 328-340
The editorial comments of this publication were by F. D. Stone.

Cassel, R. N., & M. H. Cassel, 1978, *Cassel Family*. Project Innovation,
Chula Vista, CA, 76 p., illus.
Cites dates of 1590-1681 for Yelles Cassel without obvious docu-
mentation.

Cobb, W. T., 1946, *The Strenuous Life: The "Oyster Bay" Roosevelts in
Business and Finance*. William E. Rudge's Sons, N.Y., 99 p.

Dohan, Mary Helen, 1990, *Making of the American Language*. Dorset Press,
N.Y., 315 + xliii p.
A valuable guide to Anglified and Americanized names, common
nouns, and verbs; originally published in 1974 under another title.

Friederichs, H. E., 1961, "The Eisenhower Genealogy." *The Pennsylvania
Genealogical Mag.*, vol. XXII, no. 2, p. 144-146.
Friederichs was a well known German genealogist; his short paper
on the Eisenhower genealogy summarizes an intensive effort to
locate Eisenhower's ancestors.

Guth, Hermann, Guth, Gertrud, Mast, J. L., & L. A. Mast, 1987, *Palatine
Mennonite Census Lists, 1664-1793*. Mennonite Family History. Spec.
Pub., Elverson, Pa., 115 p., maps.

Hoyt, E. P., 1964, *The Vanderbilts and Their Fortunes*. Doubleday & Co.,
Inc., Garden City, N.Y., 434 p., chart.

Hull, W. I., 1935 (reprinted 1970), *William Penn and the Dutch Quaker
Migration to Pennsylvania*. Genealogical Publishing Co., Baltimore,
Md., 445 p., illus.

Johnson, A. P., 1933, *Franklin D. Roosevelt's Colonial Ancestors*. Lothrop,
Lee & Shepard Co., Boston, 222 p., illus.

Learned, M. D., 1908, *The Life of Francis Daniel Pastorius*. William J.
Campbell Co., Phila., 324 p., illus.

McLean, H. H., 1967, *Genealogy of the Herbert Hoover Family*. Hoover Inst.
War, Revolution, & Peace, Stanford, CA, 486 p.

Mencken, H. L., 1936, "Proper Names in America." In *The American Language*. Alfred A. Knopf, N.Y., 4th ed., p. 474-554.
_____, 1948, "Proper Names in America." In *The American Language*. Alfred A. Knopf, N.Y., Supplement II, p. 396-642.

O'Connor, Harvey, 1941, *The Astors*. Alfred A. Knopf, N.Y., 488 p., index.

Pershing, E. J., 1924, *The Pershing Family in America*. George S. Ferguson Co., Phila., 434 p., illus.

Roberts, G. B., 1989, *Ancestors of American Presidents*. Carl Boyer, 3rd, Publisher, Santa Clarita, Calif., 236 p.

Rockefeller, H. O. (ed.), 1910, *The Transactions of the Rockefeller Family Association (for the years 1905-1909)*. Knickerbocker Press, N.Y., Vol. I, 383 p.
_____, 1915, *ibid, (for the years 1910-1914)*. J. J. Little & Ives Co., N.Y., Vol. II, 338 p.
_____, 1926, *ibid, (for the years 1915-1925)*. J. J. Little & Ives Co., N.Y., Vol. III, 294 p., illus.
_____, 1958, *ibid*. J. J. Little & Ives Co., N.Y., Vol. IV, 325 p.

Scheiffarth, Engelbert, 1969, "Der New Yorker Gouverneur Nelson A. Rockefeller und die Rockefeller im Neuwieder Raum." *Genealogisches Jahrbuch*. Neustadt/Aisch, Bd. 9, p. 17-42

Schriftgiesser, Karl, 1942, *The Amazing Roosevelt Family, 1613-1942*. Wilfred Funk, Inc., Boston, 367 p.

Part 3

Changes in City and Village Names

AMOUS CITIES THROUGH TIME. VIRTUALLY all German cities, towns, and villages have gone through a series of changes in the spelling of their names, just as German family names have changed. In some cases, it is difficult to relate one version to the other without extensive searches in the literature. Especially valuable in such a search is a series of old maps which show the geographic position of the community in question and the different spellings of its name through time.

Prof. Klaus Stopp of the University of Mainz has called my attention to his publication documenting the Latin, Italian, French, and German variations in spelling of the large German city of Mainz for the period 1300-1800. The conclusions of Stopp's little known work published in 1964 are abstracted here as Table 3.1.

TABLE 3.1
VARIATION IN SPELLING OF THE GERMAN CITY OF MAINZ

Date	Spelling	Date	Spelling	Date	Spelling	Date	Spelling
a. 1300	Mogoncia	1536	Magonce	1610	Mainz	ca. 1700	Moguntium
1493	Maguncia	1552	Magontia	ca. 1626	Mayence	1717	Magontiacum
1493	Mentz	1558	Macontia	1641	Mayen	1745	Maynz
1497	Maguntia	1561	Magonza	1646	Maintz	1793	Meinz
a. 1500	Mayntz	1570	Ments	1674	Mogonza	ca. 1800	Moyance
1501	Meincz	1578	Moguntiacum	ca. 1689	Maience	ca. 1800	Mayance
1502	Moguncia	1578	Moguntia	ca. 1690	Mayense	ca. 1800	Maince
1520	Mauntz	1592	Meintz	1690	Meyntz		
1524	Maentz	1604	Mogontia	ca. 1700	Maguntiacum		

Note: Data abstracted from K. Stopp, 1964

Current European maps vary between the currently recognized German spelling of Mainz and the French spelling of Mayence. Historically, there are at least some thirty-four variations.

During the long reign of Louis XIV (1654-1715), the French made a determined effort to change the name of Zweibrücken to the translated name of Deux Ponts (two bridges). Similarly, the City of Aachen varied between the German Aken and the French Aix la Chapelle. The Germans, of course, never accepted the French usage as permanent.

In addition to Mainz, Table 3.2 on the next page shows the historic and wide variation in the spelling of some thirteen other German cities. The cities are all located along the Rhine except for Aachen, Frankfurt, Alzey, and Zweibrücken which, however, are in the vicinity of the Rhine. Many of the European famous map-makers of the 15th to 18th centuries are also cited in Table 3.2.

Through some good fortune, I was able to locate at The Royal Library in The Hague an original copy of the massive work titled *Atlas Noveau*, dated 1692, by Sanson and Jaillot. For those unacquainted with this work, it consists of two large volumes, approximately 22 x 26 x 2 inches, each volume weighing possibly twenty-five lbs. The volumes

TABLE 3.2
MAP VARIATION IN SPELLING OF MAJOR GERMAN CITIES

Modern Spelling

Date	Map Author	Aachen	Koeln	Mainz	Frankfurt	Oppenheim	Worms	Alzey	Mannheim	Kaiserlauter	Zweibruecken
1491	(after N. Cusanus)	Aqvisgranv	Colonia ve Agrippina	Magvntia	Franckfordi	n/a	Wormatia	n/a	n/a	n/a	n/a
1493	H. Muenzer	Aquisgranu	Colonia	Mentz	Franckfurt	n/a	n/a	n/a	n/a	n/a	n/a
ca. 1500	E. Etzlaub	Ach	Ccoln	Maynss	Frankfuzt	n/a	Wormatia	n/a	n/a	Kayserlater	n/a
1507	B. Wapowski	Aqvisgrana	Colonia	Magonza	Fracfordia	n/a	n/a	n/a	n/a	n/a	n/a
1513	M. Waldseemueller	Aquismanum	Colonia	Mayunna	Franitfordi	Oppenheun	Wormana	Altzheim	Manheim	n/a	n/a
n/a	H. Zell (1518-64)	Ach	Coltne	Mientz	Franctfurt	n/a	Wurms	n/a	Manheim	n/a	Zweibruck
1540	S. Muenster	Ach	Coeln	Mentz	Franckfurt	Oppnheim	Worms	n/a	Manheim	Keisers	Zweybrug
1550	(after Zell)	n/a	Coeln	Meintz	Franckfurd	Oppheim	Worms	n/a	n/a	KeisersLate	Zweybrug
1552	J. Gastaldi	Aquisgrena	Colonia	Magontia	Francfor	n/a	n/a	n/a	n/a	n/a	n/a
1553	M. Tramezini	n/a	Colonia	Mogvntia	Francfor	Openhvn	Vormatia	n/a	Meinheim	Lvtern	n/a
1555	C. Vopel	n/a	n/a	Mentz	Franckfort	Openhvn	Worms	Altzheim	n/a	Keysersluter	Zweibrucken
1560	T. Stella	Ach	Coln	Mencz	Francfurt	Oppehei	Worms	n/a	n/a	Keiserslute	Zweibruck
1569	G. de Jode	n/a	Colln	Mentz	Francfort	Oppenheim	Worms	Altzheim	Manheim	Keisersluter	Zweibrucken
1570	A. Ortelius	Aken	Coelen	Ments	Francfort	Oppenheim	Wormbs	n/a	n/a	Keiserlauter	Zweibrucken
1585	G. Mercator	Aken	Coln	Meitz	Francfurt	Oppenheim	Worms	Altzei	Manheim	Keisersluter	Zweibrucken
1587	G. de Jode	Aken	Collen	Mentz	Francfurt	Oppenheim	Vrms	Alvzheim	Manheim	Keyserleutre	Sweybrug
1595	M. Quad	Aquen	Colonia	Mentz	Franckfurt	Oppenheim	Wurmbs	Altzen	Manheim	Keiserslate	Zweibruck
1607	J. Hondius	Aeken	Coln	Mentz	Francfurt	Oppenheim	Worms	Altzei	n/a	n/a	Zweibrucken
1617	J. Hondius II	Aken	Coln	Mentz	Francfurt	Oppenheim	Worms	n/a	n/a	Keisersloere	Zweibrucken
ca. 1624	J. Janssonius	Aken	Coln	Mentz	Francfurt	Oppehaim	Worms	Altsei	n/a	Keisrslaute	Zweibrucken
1626	H. Hondius	Aken	Coln	Mentz	Francfurt	Oppehaim	Worms	n/a	n/a	Keiserlautr	Zweibruckn
1631	W. Blaeu	?	Colln	Mentz	Francfurt	n/a	n/a	n/a	n/a	n/a	n/a
1633	C. Tassin	n/a	n/a	Mayence	Franckfort	n/a	Uorms	Altzey	Manheim	KeisersLutte	Les deux pont
1662	(after Blaue)	Aken	Coln	Mentz	Franckfort	Oppenheim	Worms	n/a	n/a	n/a	Zweibrucken
1679	N. Sanson	Aix la Chap	Cologne	Mayence	Franckfort	Oppenheim	Worms	Alstzhei	Manheim	Keyerslauter	Zweybruck
n/a	Sanson (1600-67)	Aix la Chayeslle	Cologne	Mayence	Franckfort	n/a	n/a	n/a	n/a	n/a	n/a
1692	Sanson & Jaillot	Aix la Chapelle	Cologne	Mayence	Francfort	Oppenheim	Worms	Altzheim	Manheim	Keyserlauter	Zweybrucken
1701	G. Deslisle	Aix la Chapelle	Cologne	Mayence	Francfort	Oppenheim	Worms	Altzey	Manheim	Kayserslaute	Deux Ponts
ca. 1705	J. Homann	Aachen	Coeln	Maintz	Francfur	Oppenheim	Worms	Altzheim	Manheim	n/a	Zweybruk
1714	J. Nell	Achen	Coeln	Maintz	Frankfur	Oppenheim	Worms	n/a	Manheim	n/a	Zweybrueck
ca. 1720	J. Homann	Achen	Coeln	Maintz	Francfur	Oppenheim	Worms	Altzheim	Manheim	n/a	Zweybrueck
1730	M. Seutter	Aix	Coeln	Mavutz	Franckfort	Oppenheim	Worms	Altzey	Manheim	KaysLautern	Zweybrucken
1759	G. LeRouge	n/a	n/a	Mayence	Franckfort	Oppenheim	Wormbs	Altzheim	Manheim	Kayserslaute	Deux Ponts
1803	F. Guessefeld	Acken	Coeln	Maynz	Frankfurth	n/a	Worms	Alzey	Manheim	Lautern	Zweybruecken

contain 200 maps as well as a city-town index for each map and sixteen pages of text. Most maps are double page size, i.e., they cover two facing pages; some are larger. A large part of the *Atlas Noveau* deals with the various areas along the Rhine. In fact, this atlas shows a series of "war maps" with the Rhine area in some detail. The Rhine was, of course, then at the center of attention as far as Louis XIV and France were concerned.

By comparing maps of the same area with those from other atlases, it is noteworthy that many cities show variation in spelling within any given atlas, and also within their indices. Köln, for instance is shown as Cöln, Colln, and Cologne, with the latter term preferred on many old map titles. According to the book by Keyser (1956, p. 251) there are some 450 ways to spell Köln; this compendium lists only a few. Many of these no doubt concern the old Roman designations.

The preferred spelling of modern French and English maps is Cologne. Modern Dutch maps invariably use the Dutch version Keulen. All are derived from the original Latin designation "Colonia vel Agrippina" (the Colony of Agrippina) which in everyday use was shortened to Colonia, which later became simply Coln or Cöln. Then, about 1899, a Prussian edict ordered that all German cities formerly written with "C" would henceforth be spelled with "K" thus changing Cöln into Köln. The same happened with Krefeld which is located some miles north of Köln.

Occasionally, some cities are shown on old maps in abbreviated form for economy of space, such as "Zweybruck" and "Keyserlauter." Kaiserslautern, for instance, was shown as "Keisers" or even simply as "Lautern." Other shortened names include "Ach" for Aachen.

SMALLER VILLAGES OF THE PAST. Early maps show the variation in spelling of the well-known Lower Rhine early Mennonite community of Krefeld (modern spelling), tabulated in Table 3.3.

TABLE 3.3
VARIATION IN SPELLING OF KREFELD

Publications:
    Österley, 1883
        ?1050, **Krinvelde**
    Keyser, 1956
        1105, **Krinvelde, Krienfelde**
        1166, **Crinvelt**
        12th cent., **Creinvelt, Crinelt, Crevelt**
        13th cent., **Creynelt, Creivelt, Crevelt**
        14th cent., **Creinvelt, Creinelt**
        15th cent., **Creveldia, Creyveldia, Crefeldia** (Latin forms)
        1542, **Creynelt** (Pfarrsiegel); **Crefelt** (Stadtsiegel)

Sturmfels, 1961
1013, **Creginfeld**
1166, **Creinvelt**
1598, **Creyfeldt**

Early Maps (map makers, dates, and names used on maps)
1600, Matthias Quad, **Crevelt**
?1630, Claes Janszoon Visscher, **Crevelt**
1646, Matthäus Merian, **Creuelt**
1647, Hendrik Hondius, **Crevelt**
1662, Johannes Blaeu, **Crevelt**
1673, Sanson & Jaillot, **Crevel**
1692, Sanson & Jaillot, **Crevelt** on map; **Creuelt** in index
1723-1736, Engelbronner, **Crefeld** (city plan)
1803, Franz Ludwig Güssefeld, **Crevelt**
1803, Tranchot & Müffling, **Creveld**
1886, Hofacker, **Crefeld** (city plan)

Addressbuchen (Krefeld City Address Books)
1827-1898, **Crevelt**
1899-1986, **Krefeld**

Some irregularities in spelling on maps, especially of the smaller villages, may be due to apprentice copiers and their errors in copying. The maps themselves indicate a different origin stemming from different copper plate engravers whose training, nationality, and native speech influence whatever spelling they engraved on the map. Fortunately, the legibility of engraving on copper plate is superb, with little doubt as to the configuration of individual letters.

South of Mainz, on the left bank of the Rhine is the famous German village of Nierstein. Over the years, Nierstein has been known for producing high quality wines. Table 3.4 shows the diverse spelling of this village name. According to Fabricus (1914, p. 15) the village name is known on old manuscripts as early as 993, and again in 994, as Nerstein; and in 1000, as Nerestein.

VILLAGE LOCATORS TODAY. Readers of the periodicals *Mennonite Family History* and *German Genealogical Digest* periodically ask for help in locating obscure German villages. If the requested name dates from 1900 or if there has been little change in spelling of the village name, then it is a relatively simple matter to locate these small communities.

Two well-known indexes to German cities, towns, and villages available at all major European libraries and some American libraries are the following:

TABLE 3.4
VARIATION IN SPELLING OF NIERSTEIN

Date	Map Maker	Spelling	Date	Map Maker	Spelling
1540	Muenster	Nirstein	1689	de Wit	Nerstein
1585	Mercator	Naersheim	1689	Pfann	Nerstein
1593	de Jode	Naersheim	1690	Coronelli	Nerstein
1621	Visscher	Viderstein	1692	Sanson &	
1625	Bellus	Niersheim		Jaillot	Nersheim
1626	Kaerius	Nidervlm	1695	Jaillot	Nerstein
1630	Janssonius	Niderstein	1695	de Fer	Nerstein
1630	Danckerts	Niderstein	1695	Funk	Nerstein
1633	Tassin	Niderstein	1700	Jaillot	Nerstein
1634	"	"	1704	Delisle	Nerstein
1644	Janssonius	Niderstein	1707+	Schenk	Nerstein
1645	Merian	Nierstein (map)	1708	Baillieul	Nerstein
		Nerstein (view)	1712+	Homann	Nerstein
1647	Hondius	Niderstein	1720	de Fer	Nerstein
1660	Merian	Nierstein	1724	Liebaux	Nerstein
1660	Blaeu	Niderstein	1728+	Seutter	Nerstein
1662	"	Nerstein	1729	Homann	Nerstein
1664	"	Niderstein	1737+	Ottens	Nerrestein
1674+	Waltheu	Niderstein	1744	Reinhardt	Nierstein
1681	Sanson	Nerrestein	1759	LeRouge	Nerstein
1686	Hoffman	Nierstein	1766	Lamey &	
1688	Danckerts	Nerstein		Denis	Neristein
1688	Visscher II	Nerstein	1766	Pfister	Nirstein
1688	Cantelli	Nerestein	1770+	Crepy	Nerbeim
1688	Desgranges	Niderstein	1791+	von Reilly	Nierstein
1689	Person	Nerstein	1794	Dewarat	Nierstein
1689	Visscher II	Nerstein	1803	von Reilly	Nierstein

Müller, Joachim, 1991/92, *Müllers Grosses Deutsches Ortsbuch.* Post- und Ortsbuchverlag, Postmeister A.D. Friedrich Müller, Wüppertal, 24th ed., 966 p.

Weber, Willy, 1986, *Ortsbuch der Bundesrepublik Deutschland.* Verlag für Standesamtswesen, Frankfurt am Main, Vol. I, 507 p., (A) Systematische Verzeichnisse; Vol. II, 725 p., (B) Alphabetische Verzeichnisse.

The Weber compilation is similar to the Müller compilation, but is somewhat more complete and easier to read. Both books are updated periodically.

The German automobile club, ADAC (Allgemeiner Deutscher Automobil-Club e.v.), publishes annually for members a series of thirty-seven maps covering Germany in great detail at a scale of 1:200,000. There is an ADAC office in most major towns and cities. The address of the main office is as follows:

Allgemeiner Deutscher Automobil-Club e.v.
Am Westpark 8
8000 München 70

Virtually all villages and farm communities are shown on the ADAC maps. Unfortunately, there is no index. It is therefore necessary to resort to the two above mentioned indices to locate the general area of interest. In many cases, the same name applies to several villages and the indices list all villages with the same name and indicate their corresponding state.

Another useful series of maps is the annual series published by the oil and gas marketing firm under the name ARAL Aktiengesellschaft, Bochum, popularly known simply as ARAL. This series contains seven maps at a scale of 1:400,000 for Western Germany plus six other general maps of Europe at varying scales. There is also an index to the cities and larger towns. The ARAL maps may be ordered through the publisher at:

Kartographischer Verlag Busche GmbH
Kaiserstrasse 129
46 Dortmund

In eastern Germany, the following are useful:

Balkow, Karla, & Werner Christ, 1986, *Orts-Lexikon der Deutschen Demokratischen Republik*. R. v. Decker's Verlag, G. Schenck GmbH, Heidelberg, 352 p.

Kraus, Th., et al, 1959, *Atlas Östliches Mitteleuropa*. Velthagen & Klasing, Bielefeld, 68 folio maps, with 4 key maps at a scale of 1:300,000.

Staatsarchivs Potsdam, dates vary 1962 to 1983, *Historisches Ortslexikon für Brandenburg*. In seven parts, maps as of 1900.

In the Netherlands, a useful guide is the following:

Beekman, A. A., et al, 1936, *Lijst der Aardrijkskundige Namen van Nederland*. E. J. Brill, Leiden.

For individuals wishing still more detailed recent maps of western Germany, an article I wrote for the *Quarterly Mennonite Family History* (1987, vol. VI, p. 48) lists the addresses of government offices in the various German States which provide maps at scales of 1:50,000 and 1:100,000. Each of the German States has a catalog listing of their comprehensive sets of maps. These addresses are:

Landesvermessungsamt Baden-Württemberg
Büchsenstrasse 54, Postfach 1115
7000 Stuttgart 1

Bayerisches Landesvermessungsamt
Alexanderstrasse 4
8000 München 22

Landesvermessungsamt Brandenburg
Grosse Scharrnstrasse
O1200 Frankfurt/Oder

Hessisches Landesvermessungsamt
Postfach 3249, Schaperstrasse 16
6200 Wiesbaden 1

Landesvermessungsamt Mecklenburg Vorpommern
Lübecker Strasse 289
O2761 Schwerin

Niedersächsisches Landesvervaltungsamt
Postfach 107, Warmbüchenkamp 2
3000 Hannover 1

Landesvermessungsamt Nordrhein-Westfalen
Postfach 205007, Muffendorder Strasse 19-21
5300 Bad Godesberg 1

Landesvermessungsamt Rheinland-Pfalz
Postfach 1428, Ferdinand-Saürbruch-Strasse 15
5400 Koblenz 1

Landesvermessungsamt des Saarlandes
Neugrabenweg 2
6600 Saarbrücken 3

Landesvermessungsamt Sachsen
Olbrichtplatz 3 - PF 306
O8060 Dresden

Landesamt für Landesvermessung und Datenverarbeitung
Land Sachsen Anhalt
Barbarastr. 2 - PF 616
0-4020 Halle/S.

Landesvermessungsamt Schleswig-Holstein
Postfach 5070, Mercatorstrasse 1
2300 Kiel 1

Thuringer Landesverwaltungsamt -
Landesvermessungsamt Schmidtstedter
Ufer 7
O5010 Erfurt

In addition, the major metropolitan areas of Berlin, Bremen, and
Hamburg retain a semi-independent political status. Two of these cities
have map distribution offices as follows:

Senatsverwaltung Bau und Wohnungswesen
Abteilung V (Vermessungswesen)
Mansfelder Strasse 16
W1000 Berlin 31

Vermessungsamt Hamburg
Wexstrasse 7
2000 Hamburg 36

Some years ago, various European historians made a coordinated
effort to put in bibliographic form the names of various papers describing locality names in their area of interest. Consequently, individuals
with names derived from European localities may be able to locate that
locality also by reference to one of the following publications which are
contained in major European libraries: Dollinger, Wolff, & Guenee, 1967,
(France), Guyer, 1960 (Switzerland), Keyser, 1969, (German), Rausch,
1984 (Austria), and Van Herwijnen, 1978 (The Netherlands). These
publications are cited in the Reference section.

REFERENCES

Bach, Adolf, 1954, *Deutsche Namenkunde: Die deutschen Ortsnamen.* Carl Winter Universitätsverlag, Heidelberg, Bd. 1, 615 p.; Bd. 2, 451 p.
A more recent listing of German city, town, and village names with a brief history.

Bahlow, Hans, 1962, *Deutschlands Älteste Fluss und Ortsnamen.* Grindeldruck GmbH, Hamburg, 190 p.
_____, 1965, *Deutschlands Geographische Namenwelt.* Vitorio Klostermann, Frankfurt am Main, 554 p.
Bahlow's listings include rivers and other German geographic terms. Both of these publications have been reprinted several times by different publishers under varying titles.

Dollinger, Philippe, Philippe Wolff, & Simonee Guenee, 1967, *Bibliographie d'historie des villes de France.* Librarie C. Klincksieck, Paris.

Fabricus, Wilhelm, 1914, *Erlauterungen zum Geschichtlichen Atlas der Rheinprovinz. Bd. 6, Die Herrschaften des Unteren Nahegebietes.* Hermann Behrendt, Bonn, 668 p., 2 maps.
Deals mainly with the history of the Nahe valley.

Fischer, Rudolf, E. Eichler, H. Naumann, & H. Walther, 1963, *Namen deutscher Städte.* Akademie Verlag, Berlin, 137 p.

Förstemann, Ernst, 1913-1916, *Altdeutsches Namenbuch.* Peter Hanstein Verlagsbuchhandlung, Bonn. Zweiter Bd., Erste hälfte, A-K, 1766 p. (1913); Zweiter Bd., Zweite hälfte, L-Z, 1942 p. (1916).
A massive pioneering compilation of most German cities, towns, and villages with a brief history.

Gleysteen, Jan, 1984, *Mennonite Tourguide to Western Europe.* Herald Press, Scottdale, Pa., 340 p., maps.
Contains index maps and short discussion of many key European Mennonite communities.

Guyer, Paul, 1960, *Bibliographie der Städtgeschichte der Schweiz.* Verlag Leemann, Zürich.

Keyser, Erich, 1956, *Deutsches Städtebuch. Rheinisches Städtebuch.* W. Kohlhammer Verlag, Stuttgart, vol. III, pt. 3, 441 p., map.
_____(ed.), 1964, *Deutsches Städtebuch. Städtebuch Rheinland-Pfalz und Saarland.* W. Kohlhammer Verlag, Stuttgart, vol. IV, pt. 3, 550 p., map (a series of short histories of key cities).
_____, 1969, *Bibliographie zur Städtgeschichte Deutschlands.* Böhlau Verlag, Köln, 404 p., map.

The first two volumes are part of a series which list German cities and larger towns and provide an historical sketch of each. The sketches, ranging up to 20 pages, were written by local authorities.

Österley, Hermann, 1883, *Historisch-geographisches Wörterbuch des deutschen Mittelalters*. Verlag Justus Perthes, Gotha, 806 p.
An early pioneering effort concerning German geographic names.

Polenz, Peter von, 1969, "Namenkunde." In *Dahlmann-Waitz, Quellenkunde der Deutschen Geschichte*. Anton Hiersemann Verlag, Stuttgart, Bd. I, Abschnitt 33, Nr. 1-838 (33 pages).
_____, 1980, ibid, Bd. 5, Abschnitt 216, Nr. 1-38 (3 pages).
Basically a bibliographic citation of references dealing with German geographic names.

Rausch, Wilhelm, 1984, *Bibliographie zur Geschichte der Städte Österreichs*. Druckerei J. Wimmer GmbH, Linz, 329 p., map.

Uetrecht, E., (ed), 1912/1913, *Meyers Orts- und Verkehrs-Lexikon des Deutschen Reichs*. Bibliographisches Institut, Leipzig und Wien, 5th ed., Vol I (A-K), 1092 p., Vol. II (L-Z), 1246 p., plus Anhang, 76 p.
Gives 210,000 community names, including the smallest farm communities, with their 1910 populations. Especially important for locating communities in Alsace-Lorraine and in Poland, the names of which often changed before and after the Second Reich period of 1871-1918.

Verdenhalven, Fritz, 1970, *Kleiner historischer Städtenamen-Schlüssel für Deutschland und die ehemaligen deutschen Gebiete*. Verlag Degener & Co., Neustadt/Aisch, 80 p.
Lists some 5, 000 locality names and a few variant spellings mainly relating to Slavic alternatives. Contains a useful bibliography for greater detail of some areas.

Van Herwijnen, G., 1978, *Bibliographie van de Stedengeschiedenis van Nederland*. E.J. Brill, Leiden, 355 p., map.
Virtually all references are in Dutch; the title refers to city histories in the Netherlands.

MISPLACED VILLAGE. WHILE SEARCHING for the location of early Mennonite and Quaker communities in the German Palatinate, I had difficulty in relating village names used in recent publications to names shown on old European maps. Motivation for this study was provided in part by the uncertainty of Wm. I. Hull in his extensive and often cited 1935 documentary on the "Dutch Quakers". Thanks to the recent able assistance of Prof. Klaus Stopp of the University of Mainz, I was able to verify and document variations in spelling of two small villages, Kriegsheim and Monsheim, over the period of about 1650-1985. Both villages are located some twelve kilometers (seven miles) west of Worms.

Following the 1984 publication of the book titled *Landkarten der Pfalz am Rhein, 1513-1803* by F. Helwig, W. Reiniger, and K. Stopp, it became a relatively easy matter to clarify the name changes for Kriegsheim, the etymology of which is exemplified by the succession Griesheim/Krisheim/Kriegsheim. Table 3.5 on the next page shows the variations in spelling as used by French, Dutch, and German map-makers.

GRIESHEIM, 1688-1704. The name Griesheim appears as early as 1688 on old maps and apparently much earlier in printed texts. We can verify that this is the predominant spelling used in the 16th century. The word "Gries" or "Griess" appears to have originated from the German word referring to gravel or grit, and thus to a quarrying operation (Sand U. Tonwerk), still located in the west end of the village. As in the old days, the current quarrying operation produces both quartz sand for glass-making and kaolin clay products for pottery and porcelain.

The suffix "-heim" is a very common appendage for several thousand village names along the left bank of the Rhine, between Basel and Mainz. The use of this appendage is in fact shown on a map published by Winkler (1935, illus. 5). The origin of the ancient word heim is obscure; in modern Germanic languages, it refers to a home. Examples are:

German: -heim (Mannheim, Oppenheim)
Dutch: -hem (Arnhem, Lochem)
Flemish: -gem (Balegem)
English: -ham (Birmingham, Chatham)
Old English: -hâm

KRISHEIM, 1704-1794. The name Krisheim appears as early as 1704 on old maps. This term apparently reflects the regular alternation in Germanic languages of the letters 'G', 'C', and 'K'.

English influence upon the name may date from the year 1657 when the English Quaker evangelist William Ames first went to Griesheim.

TABLE 3.5

SPELLING OF GERMAN TOWNS KRIEGSHEIM AND MONSHEIM

DATE	AUTHOR	VILLAGE	VILLAGE	MAP TEXT
ca. 1688	J. Danckerts	n/a	Mantheim	Latin
ca. 1688	N. Visscher	Griesheim	Mantzheim	Latin
1689	N. Person	Griesheim	Mansheim	Latin
1690	W. Pfann	Greisheim	Mansheim	German
1692	N. Sanson & C. Jaillot	Griesheim	Muntzheim	French
1695	N. de Fer	Griesheim	Muntzheim	French
ca. 1695	D. Funk	Griesheim	Mantzheim	Latin
1695	C. Jaillot	Griesheim	Muntzheim	French
ca. 1696	P. Mortier	Griesheim	Mantzheim	French
1704	G. Delisle	Krisheim	Muntzeim	French
1705	C. Jaillot	Griesheim	Mantzheim	French
ca. 1705	T. Bowles	Krisheim	Muntzheim	English
1707 +	R. Schenk	Griesheim	Mantzheim	Latin
1708	G. Baillieul	Greisheim	Muntzheim	French
ca. 1712	J. B. Homann	Griesheim	Mantzheim	Latin
1720	N. de Fer	Griesheim	Mantzheim	French
1728 +	M. Seutter	Griesheim	Mantzheim	Latin
1729 +	J. B. Homann	Griesheim	Mantzheim	Latin
1734	A. Felseckers	Krisheim	Muntesheim	German
1744	A. Reinhardt	Griesheim	n/a	German
1745	G. Le Rouge	Griesheim	Muntzheim	French
1766	A. Lamey & F. Denis	Kreikesheim	Munulfesheim	Latin
ca. 1770	L. Crepy	Krisheim	Muntzheim	French
1794	P. Dewarat	Kriegsheim	Monsheim	German
1795	J. B. de Bouge	n/a	Monsheim	French

Later, during the grape harvest season of 1661, he and other Englishmen spent several months there helping with the harvest and in converting some seven or eight families of the local Mennonite community to Quakerism. From his publications of 1660 and 1661, Ames appears to have been conversant in Dutch, and probably had a good working knowledge of German as well.

With the migration of the smaller Quaker group from the village to America in 1685, the name was transferred to America in the English version either as Cresheim or as Crisheim. Various 17th and 18th century misspellings of the term Griesheim / Krisheim / Kriegsheim, mainly by English authors unfamiliar with Germanic languages, include Griesham, Crisheim, Kriesheim, Christein, Kircheim, Cressinge, and Kreysheim.

In America Cresheim was, prior to 1700, a subdivision of Germantown. Today, Cresheim, as a part of Philadelphia, is represented only by Cresheim Creek, Cresheim Road, and Cresheim Valley. The name

Krisheim was made well known to American readers with D. K. Cassel's 1896 publication of his massive work on the Cassel clan in America.

KRIEGSHEIM, 1794-1985. In 1985, the author visited Kriegsheim. The modern name Kriegsheim first appears on old maps in 1794. The name figuratively means 'home of wars', or in more lucid English, a 'battleground'. Following the devastation of the area during the war and occupation periods of 1618-48, 1677, 1688-89, 1740-48, 1756-63, and 1792-1813, the name seems oddly appropriate. The 'battleground' tradition was carried on in more recent years. Just in front of the train station at neighboring Monsheim is a Prussian-style memorial honoring soldiers from the area lost during the war years 1848, 1870-71, 1900, and 1914-18. In the main churchyard of Kriegsheim, a granite plaque lists the names of nineteen soldiers lost in World War I (1914-18), and twenty-five lost in World War II (1941-45).

In 1905, the village had eighty-seven dwellings and 449 residents of which 307 residents were Protestants ("Evangelical"), 107 were Catholic, and thirty-five belonged to other religions (probably mainly Mennonite).

The name Kriegsheim has resisted further change except that today it is part of the Monsheim/Kriegsheim postal district; the 1986 combined population was 2,338. The two villages are separated by the Pfrimm tributary, with Kriegsheim located on the north bank. This is an ideal location for grape vines which are grown in profusion on the sunny, south slope of the valley. The main industry is wine-making. The southern slope of the Pfrimm valley supports a varied crop of annuals, notably barley, sugar beets, and of course, potatoes.

Kriegsheim is in the southeast corner of the wine district called "Rhinehessen". The hillside vineyards produce, among others, a palatable Spaetlese labeled *Kriegsheimer Rosengarten*.

At the time of the author's visit in 1985, the old Rathaus (city hall) had just been demolished. For historical comparison, a picture of the old Rathaus is shown in Shoemaker (1903, opposite his page 2). In 1820, the Mennonite Church body was relocated from Kriegsheim across the Pfrimm to Monsheim, a distance of about one kilometer (six-tenth of a mile). Mennonite Church membership records in Monsheim apparently did not survive the Napoleonic Wars and the 1820 move. In any event, according to Rev. G. Becker, pastor of the small Mennonite Church in Monsheim in 1985, a fire during the German Revolution of 1848 appears to have destroyed what few church records were left.

MONSHEIM PARTIAL FRENCH ORIGIN. Coincidentally, the name Monsheim was apparently also first used on maps in 1794. As indicated in Table 3.5 on page 76, there were a variety of spellings for this village, the most common being Mantzheim. The prefix Mon(s) appears to be of French origin. The official usage of the name Monsheim dates from the time of the French occupation of 1792-1813.

ACKNOWLEDGEMENTS
In addition to the assistance of Prof. Stopp, as mentioned earlier, an early version of this section was read by Dr. B. C. Donaldson, of the University of Melbourne. Dr. Donaldson is recognized as an authority on Germanic languages through his several books, in particular a 1983 book titled *Dutch, A Linguistic History of Holland and Belgium* (Martinus Nijhoff/Leiden).

REFERENCES

Besse, Joseph, 1753, *Sufferings*. Luke Hinde, London, Vol. 1, 767 p., Vol. 2, 638 p.
Vol. 2, p. 450-454 lists heads of families of the Cresheim Quakers.

Bender, H. S., et al, 1957, *The Mennonite Encyclopedia*. Mennonite Publishing House, Scottsdale, Pa., vol. 3, p. 241-242.
Uses the term Kriegsheim, but refers to Griesheim. This is a standard four (originally four, now five) volume work detailing numerous subject matter relating to European Mennonite history. It was preceded some two decades by a similar compendium in German.

Brilmayer, K. J., 1985 (reprint of 1905 edition), *Rheinhessen in Vergangenheit und Gegenwart*. Weidlich Reprints, Wuerzburg, 513 p.
Lists villages in Rheinhessen including, on page 255, Kriegsheim; cites names on old documents: Kreikesheim, 766; Crigesheim, 1137; Crigisheim, 1276; Crisheim, 1306; Criegekeim, 1335; Krysheim, 1344; Griesheim, 1450, and Criesheim, 1496.

Cassel, D. K., 1896, *A Genealogical History of the Cassel Family in America (Being the Descendants of Julius Kassel or Yelles Cassel of Kriesheim, Baden, Germany)*. M. R. Wills Publ. Co., Norristown, PA, 463 p.
A well worn and rebound copy in the LDS Library in Salt Lake City, missing the original cover and the title page, is labeled simply "The Cassel Family" - its text gives the date of writing as 1895 and refers to the town as being in the Palatinate rather than in Baden; this book recently has been reprinted by Selby Publishing Company.

Dunn, M. M., & R. S. Dunn (eds.), 1981, *The Papers of William Penn: vol. I (1644-1679)*. Univ. Pennsylvania Press, Phila.
Quotes Penn as using the term Crisheim and, in a footnote, refers to this village with the modern name Kriegsheim.

Fabricus, Wilhelm, 1914, *Erklauterungen zum Geschichtlichen Atlas der Rheinprovinz. Bd. 6, Die Herrschaften des Unteren Nahebegietes.* Hermann Behrendt, Bonn, 668 p., 2 maps
On page 211, cites Crigisheim, 1137; Criechesheim, 1194; and Crisheim, 1361.

Fellmann, W., 1938, *Kriegsheimer Mennoniten und Quäker in ihrer religiösen Verschiedenheit: in Beiträge zur Geschichte der Mennoniten*. Schriftenreihe des Mennonitischen Geschichtsvereins, Nr. 1, Weierhoff

Gerlach, Horst, 1983, *Mennoniten in Rheinhessen*. Alzeyer Geschichtsblätter. Verlag der Rheinhessischen Druckwerkstätte, Alzey, p. 20-47, illus.

Guth, Hermann, with Gertrud Guth, J. Lemar Mast & Lois Ann Mast, 1987, "Palatine Mennonite Census Lists, 1664/1793." *Mennonite Family History*, Spec. Publ., Elverson, Pa., 115 p., illus. Uses term Kriegsheim.

Hellwig, Fritz, Wolfgang Reiniger, & Klaus Stopp, 1984, *Landkarten der Pfalz am Rhein, 1513-1803*. Druckerei Foerner GmbH, Bad Kreuznach, 275 p., illus. See Table 3.5 on page 76 in this paper.

Hubben, Wilhelm, 1929, *Die Quaeker in der deutschen Vergangenheit*. Quaeker-Verlag, Leipzig, 202 p. Includes chapter on Kriegsheim, p. 61-73.

Hull, Wm. I., 1970, *William Penn and the Dutch Quaker Migration to Pennsylvania*. Genealogical Publishing Co., Baltimore, Md., 445 p., figs. Uses terms Griesheim, Kriegsheim, and Krisheim, but prefers the latter; reprint of Swarthmore Coll. Monograph No. 2, dated 1935.

Lloyd, S. M., & M. B. Tinkcom (eds.)., 1983, *Germantown and its founders*. publisher not cited (William Penn Foundation, Germantown, Pa.,), 20p., figs. Uses term Krisheim.

Lutz, R. H., 1911, "A Recent Visit to Kriegsheim." *The Pennsylvania German*, vol. XII, p. 85-86 Mentions the two Churches, the Evangelical Church on the hillside to the northeast, and the more modern Catholic Church to the west and higher up, the latter being erected over the ancient Mennonite graveyard; also mentions some variations in spelling of village.

Michel, Paul, 1965/66, *Täufer, Mennoniten und Quäker in Kriegsheim bei Worms*. Der Wormsgau, Bd. 7, Worms am Rhein, p. 41-52
_____, 1981, *Chronik von Monsheim*. Druckerei Kunke GmbH, Monsheim, 195 p., figs. Cites use of names Munnesheim, Munisheim, Muniusheim, Monnisheim, Munsheim, Munesheim, during period of 1196 to 1329; also refers to use of term Monsheim from period of 1343 to 1575; I have been unable to verify this early apparent spelling of Monsheim.

Österley, Hermann, 1883, *Historischer geographischer Wörterbuch des Deutschen Mittelalters*. Verlag Justus Perthes, Gotha, 806 p. Cites Kriegsheim spelling of Crichesheim, 1251; and Chriesheim, 1449; Monsheim in an early ca. 1196 manuscript is noted as Munnesheim and later in 1260, as Mumesheim.

Seidensticker, Oswald, 1883, *Die erste Deutsche Einwanderung in Amerika.* Globe Printing House, Phila., Pa., 94 p.
Uses term Krisheim.

Sewel, Willem, 1717, *Histori van de Opkomste, aanwas en voortgang der Christenen, bekend by den naam van Quakers.* R. & G. Wetstein, Boekverkoopers, Amsterdam, text 784 p., appendix 56 p., index 12 p.
Uses term Kriesheim, p. 614.

Sewel, William, 1722, *The History of the Rise, Increase and Progress of the Christian People called Quakers.* J. Sowle Publ., London text 723 p., index 16 p. ("written originally in Low-Dutch by William Sewel and by himself translated into English")
Uses term Chrisheim, p. 559.

_____, 1811, *The history of the Rise, Increase and Progress of the Christian People called Quakers.* B. & T. Kite & S. Pike Publ., Phila., Pa., vol. I, 578 p., vol. II, 603 p.
Uses term Criesheim; this very popular book was issued in at least 14 printings dating from 1722 to 1876 after the initial Dutch edition of 1717.

Sewel, Wilhelm, 1742, *Die Geschichte von dem Ursprung, Zunehemen und Fortgang des christlichen Volckes, so Quaeker gennent werden.* Leipzig, 647 p.

Shoemaker, B. H., 1903, *Genealogy of the Shoemaker Family of Cheltenham, Penna..* J. B. Lippibncott Co., Phila., 524 p., illus.
Uses modern term Kriegsheim.

Tinkcom, H. M., Margaret B. Tinkcom, and Grant M. Simon, 1955, *Historic Germantown.* Mem. American Philosophical Soc., Phila., Pa., vol. 30, 154 p.
Uses term Cresheim.

Waltner, Gary J. (ed.), 1982, *300 Jahre Mennoniten Gemeinde Weierhof, 1682-1982.* Ph. Pfeiffer's Buchdruckereien und Verlage, Kaiserslautern, 83 p., illus.

Winkler, Wilhelm, 1935, *Pfälzischer Geschichtsatlas.* Verlag der Pfälzischen Gesell. z. Förderung d. Wissenschaften, Neustadt an der Haardt, text 18 p., 40 illus.
Note Winkler's illustration 5 with distribution of heim, etc., also his illustration 16, German migration in SE Pa.

EARCHING FOR OLD MAPS. SOME YEARS ago, while doing research on family history, I conceived the imaginative, if unoriginal, idea of attempting to buy an old map which showed the European village of origin of my ancestors. Fortunately, I happened to be stationed in The Hague (better known on the continent as Den Haag) on a foreign assignment at that time. This major Dutch city, which embraces a population of some 600,000 not surprisingly contained several shops specializing in rare books as well as old maps. Unfortunately, a mere glance in the windows of several of the more prominent rare book shops indicated phenomenal prices for hand-colored, copper-plate maps printed by well-known map-makers. The search continued for an affordable conversation piece. A few months later, I happened to spot a small sign in a window of a tiny shop along a cobbled, pedestrian alley in the very center of The Hague's business district. The sign mentioned rare books and maps. The shop window contained a clutter of old toys, bric-a-brac, and mineral oddities, as well as a few old books.

I had taken a few Dutch language lessons, at least enough to bargain in the book stalls of the open air market held every Thursday in a city square. But to communicate my exact desires in a small, cluttered shop was another matter. Consequently, in my hesitation, I passed by the shop several months before finally entering and inquiring about old maps. The shop keeper, a tall, lanky man by the unlikely Dutch name of Loose, as I recall, spoke fluent English as the learned Dutch are wont to do, for an insignificant percent of the world's population speaks Dutch.

At any rate, Meneer Loose indicated a map rack in one corner containing a number of loosely held maps. There were perhaps 50 maps in the unbound assemblage, nearly all being folio size as originally printed for insertion in some giant atlases.

Within fifteen minutes, I had located my prize. A deal was quickly struck for the asking price was relatively nominal. It was a 1704 original print by the superb map-maker Guillaume Del'Isle, born 1652, died 1726. The map was a fine quality, highly legible print of 49 x 63.5 cm (19.3 x 25.0 inches) and was titled with the imposing name of *Le Cours du Rhin depuis Worms jusqua Bonne et les Pays adjaces*. In simple English, the title translates as "The Rhine from Worms to Bonn."

Del'Isle was in fact French and occupied the position of royal map-maker to the over-bearing, flamboyant, and neurotic French King Louis XIV, who reigned 1654-1715. The King may have depleted the coffers of France by sponsoring large armies, map makers, and artistic talents, but the marauding armies of the King needed good maps if they were to conquer in 1688-89, first the Rhine area, and then, much of Europe.

At the very bottom of the Del'Isle map lies the tiny German village I was seeking. The map gives it the old name of Krisheim. The location is slightly more than two leagues (roughly seven miles) west of the city of Worms amidst the vineyards of the Pfrimm valley.

Krisheim was the home of my Hendricks and Schuhmacher ancestors, who were, in those days, of Quaker and Mennonite persuasion. It is well documented that William Penn, founder of Pennsylvania, preached to the Quakers in Krisheim in 1677. And thanks to the encouragement of Penn, the Hendricks and the Schuhmachers were able to escape to America in 1685, just a scant four years ahead of the rampaging armies of Louis XIV who ordered all cities in the area burnt to the ground.

The next question was: how did William Penn reach this remote village during his evangelistic circuit of some 700 miles through Holland and northern Germany. Again, the obvious answer was to be found in an old European map.

Some months later, I spotted another classic map in Meneer Loose's tiny shop. This second map was by the famous German map-maker Johann Baptist Homann, born 1663, died 1724.

"Would Meneer Loose make a better price for the Homann map and also another Del'Isle map?"

"No," came the distinctly frosty, tight-fisted reply. "The price for the Homann was low enough," he said as he turned away to wait on another customer. And so, the Homann was purchased alone.

The title of the Homann map, whose size is 45 x 57 cm (17.7 x 22.4 inches), is an equally imposing *Neu vermehrte Post Charte durch gantz Teutschland*. The map can be dated at about 1714. The title means simply "Postal Route Map of Entire Germany," which as the map indicates, theoretically included all lands from the North Sea southeastward to Hungary. As the Homann map shows, a network of pony-express type postal routes ran between all cities and towns of any consequence. Not only did the mail wagons carry letters and documents, but the coaches were filled with passengers such as William Penn.

On his 1677 trip through Holland and Germany, Penn averaged about twenty-three miles a day, a record which might challenge some modern day postal services.

THE DUTCH SCHOOL, 1581-1689. In the Lowlands, the story of map-making starts in 1566 with the Dutch revolt against the rule of Phillip II of Spain. After the Dutch finally freed themselves from Spanish domination in 1581, Dutch banking and commercial enterprise, especially in Amsterdam, began to dominate Europe. At the same time, a vast amount of capital was being generated by the Dutch merchant marine trade in Asia.

The Dutch East Indies Company was founded in 1602; their ships brought spices, tea, china, and cotton from Asia. The Dutch West Indies Company was founded in 1621; their ships brought sugar, tobacco, and furs from America. Other ships plied the North Sea and the Baltic Sea carrying lumber, grain, cattle, copper and wool. Parts of the Dutch fleet went southward along the Atlantic coast and into the Mediterranean Sea; they carried back wine, silk, and silver to the main central marketplace of Amsterdam.

In the century after the Dutch gained independence, Amsterdam's population grew from an estimated 30,000 to more than 200,000 people. The Amsterdam Borse (stock market) was started in 1602 with the issue of paper of the Dutch East Indies Company and during the 17th century became the "Wall Street" of the time, that is, a financial powerhouse. It remains the world's oldest active stock market.

The period from about 1581 to 1689 came to be called the Golden Age of the Dutch influence in world affairs. Artistically, it was the age of famous painters including Frans Hals (c.1580-1666), Pieter de Hooch (1629-c.1683), Jan Vermeer (1632-1675), and Rembrandt Harmensz van Rijn (1607-1669). Although basically a Calvinist state, the Netherlands, and Amsterdam in particular, tolerated Catholics, Anabaptists, Jews, and other minority religions.

During the turmoil created by the Thirty Years' War (1618-1648) in central Europe, Amsterdam, which was considerably west of the zone of warfare, increasingly became a center of the arts as cartographers, engravers, and printers flocked there. For the Netherlands, it was a time of political power and glory, economic prosperity, and a remarkable development in the fields of culture and science, in spite of, or perhaps because of, the series of wars directly involving the Dutch during 1652-53, 1665-67, 1672-78, and 1690-97.

During this era, European map-making was dominated by the following four Dutch families and by a number of less well-known individuals of Dutch nationality:

1. Willem Janszoon Blaeu, 1571-1638
   son, Joan Blaeu, 1596-1673

2. Claes Jansz. Visscher, 1587-1652
   son Nicolaes Visscher I, 1618-79
   grandson Nicolaes Visscher II, 1649-1702

3. Jan Jansson, 1588-1664

4. Jodocus Hondius, 1563-1612
   son Jodocus Hondius 1594-1629
   grandson Henricus Hondius, 1587-1638

The Dutch promoted the engraving of maps on copper-plate, many of the actual plates being passed on to other Dutch families, and in some cases being sold to other European families.

THE FRENCH SCHOOL, 1648-1718. The French map makers during the latter part of the 17th century and the early 18th century are well-known for providing nice, clean maps, showing great geographical detail, at scales which were highly legible. The French school was dominated by the Sanson and Jaillot families:

1. Nicolas Sanson, 1600-67
   son Nicolas Sanson, 1626-48
   son Guillaume Sanson, d. 1703
   son Adrien Sanson, d. 1708
   grandson Pierre Moulard-Sanson, d. 1730
   son-in-law Pierre Duval, c. 1619-83

2. Alexis Hubert Jaillot, c. 1632-1712
   son Bernard Jean Jaillot, 1673-1739
   grandson Bernard Antonio Jaillot, d. 1749

There were, of course, other well-known French map makers; among them was Guillaume Del'Isle (1652-1726). Del'Isle brought the systematic and detailed mapping of the Rhine area to a fine art by producing a whole series of adjoining maps at large scale.

On Del'Isle's 1704 map of the central Rhine the small village Krisheim, for instance, is plainly marked by the symbol of a church, no doubt Protestant. At least one small village, namely Ubersheim (today Ibersheim) is distinguished as "Cense de Anabapuits", that is, regarded as Anabaptist, being decidedly contrary to the dominant French Catholic philosophy of the time. Nearby villages include "N. Flersheun, Pfedersheim, Hocheim, Dalsheim, and Wackenheim", all of which exist today, most of them with some variation in spelling.

Another interesting map in the author's collection is a photocopy of a 1673 map by Sanson and Jaillot titled *Provinces-Unies des Pays-Bas* (in simple English: Provinces of the Low Countries). This map shows villages in the area of Cologne including the early Mennonite communities of "Creuelt, Kaldekirche, and Brugge" (that is, Krefeld, Kaldenkirchen, and Brugge; near the border with Holland). Three companion maps dating 1675, 1681, and 1689 show essentially the same features with map coverage extended further east and south. These reduced scale photocopies range from 30 x 47.5 cm to 32.5 x 46.5 cm.

THE GERMAN SCHOOL, 1702-1744. Even though the use of movable type for printing originated in Mainz in the mid-16th century, perhaps only some fifty-six volumes of the 40,000 editions of incunabula (that is, books printed before 1500) contained maps. At this early stage, the Germans almost invariably used woodcuts for maps and town scenes.

The most notable of the earliest German map makers was Cardinal Nicholas of Cusa (ca. 1401-1464) who evidently devised a manuscript about 1439-54, with a pioneering map of northern and central Europe. This so-called "Eichstätt map" was engraved on copper plate in 1491. Documentation is not available to know whether the engraving was done in Italy, Germany, or elsewhere. Incidentally, Cusa went by a host of names including Canzer de Coesze, Chrypffs, Cryftz, Cues, Cusanus, Khryfts, Khrypffs, Krebs, Kues, and other variants. The Cardinal was born as Nicholas Khrypffs at Kues on the Moselle.

Martin Waldseemüller's maps, most notably the one in 1513, and those of Sebastian Münster, especially 1540, tended to follow the Eichstätt map, all of which were printed long before modern cartographic methods were introduced.

The German School arrived comparatively late on the map publishing scene. German printers relied mainly on public support and had little access to funds provided by either the government, noble families or royalty, as was the case for the French school. An abbreviated list of the more prominent German map-making families is:

1. Johann Baptist Homann, 1663-1724
   son Johann Christoph Homann, c. 1703-30

2. Georg Matthaeus Seutter, 1678-1756
   son Georg Matthaeus Seutter, 1729-60
   son Albrecht Carl Seutter,
   son-in-law Tobias Conrad Lotter, engraver

The Seutter family, working in Augsburg, produced more than 500 different maps, of which many copies exist today.

CURRENT REPOSITORIES. There are a number of dealers scattered across Europe who sell old maps. However, originals of these maps may range up to several hundred dollars for a simple map with little original hand coloring. Complete atlases of older maps, such as the citation here for the *Atlas Noveau* of 1692 by Sanson & Jaillot are rare and range to more than $50,000. Fairly inexpensive photocopies of individual maps may be purchased at most major libraries.

Well-known repositories for the vast collections of old European maps include the following:

Bayerischer Staatsbibliothek, München, Germany
Bibliothèque Nationale, Paris, France
The British Museum, London, England
Herzog-August-Bibliothek, Wolfenbüttel, Germany
Library of Congress, Washington, D.C.
Staatsbibliothek Preussischer Kulturbesitz, Berlin, Germany

A more thorough listing of repositories is given in Wolter & Grimm, 1986, cited in the selected list of references attached. A similar compilation of repositories of Germany was made earlier by Zögner, 1983, as cited in the bibliography.

RECENT EUROPEAN MAPS AND REPRODUCTIONS. In October of each year, one of Europe's largest book fairs is held in Frankfurt, Germany. In 1992, there was a very nice display of German State maps by the sixteen States of the Federal Republic of Germany. Each of the German States publishes a catalog of current maps.

The catalogs are approximately 6 x 8 inches and 1/8 to 1/4 inch thick and concentrate on topographic maps in scales of 1:200,000, 1:100,000, and 1:50,000. Nearly all tiny farm communities are shown on the 1:200,000 scale. However, for enlargement of a specific area, one should order the 1:100,000 scale, or better yet, the 1:50,000 scale. The catalogs include also a good selection of geologic maps, county (Kreis) maps, and the so-called *Wanderkarte* or natural park maps, as well as aerophoto maps. The addresses for ordering these maps was given earlier at the end of the *City and Village Names* essay.

An introduction to European map-makers and many of the key recent publications concerning European maps is given in the attached bibliography. The listing is hardly exhaustive, but rather concentrates on German-speaking lands, in particular areas along the Rhine.

REFERENCES

Aubin, Hermann & Josef Niessen, 1926, *Geschichtlicher Handatlas der Rheinprovinz*. Verlag J. P. Bachem GmbH, Köln, text 18 p., 56 illus.
Especially interesting is their illustration 30 titled "Zollstaetten am Rhein um 1200-1400," (toll stations on the Rhine from 1200 to 1400).

Bonacker, Wilhelm, 1966, *Kartenmacher Aller Länder und Zeiten*. Anton Hiersemann, Stuttgart, 244 p., illus.

Campbell, Tony, 1981, *Early Maps*. Abbeville Press, N.Y., 148 p., 67 pls.

Degn, Christian & Uwe Muuss (eds.), 1977, *Topographischer Atlas Bundesrepublik Deutschland*. Paul List Verlag, München, 196 p., 82 maps.
Spotty coverage of Germany, but good basic reference.

Deutschenweininstitut, 1980, *German Wine Atlas and Vineyard Register*. Mitchel Beazley London Ltd., London, 104 p., maps, illus. 4th ed.;
Places heavy emphasis, of course, with detailed maps on the wine growing areas of the Middle Rhine. The Atlas was originally printed in German.

Hellwig, Fritz, Wolfgang Reiniger, & Klaus Stopp, 1984, *Landkarten der Pfalz am Rhein, 1513-1803*. Druckerei Förner GmbH, Bad Kreuznach, 275 p.,
Numerous illustrations of high quality; of special interest are the 'War Maps' of the Middle Rhine dated 1689, 1744, and 1794-1799.

Hilgemann, Werner, 1984, *Atlas zur deutschen Zeitgeschichte 1918-1968*. R. Piper GmbH & Co. KG, München, 208 p., maps
Numerous good recent maps - example: "Frankfurt 40-50% destroyed in World War II."

Koeyman, G., 1970, *Joan Blaeu and his Grand Atlas*. Theatrum Orbis Terrarum Ltd., Amsterdam, 114 p., 27 figs.
Joan Blaue was a premier Dutch map-maker; his 17th century Atlas included virtually all that was known of the World.

Lindgren, Uta, 1986, *Alpenübergänge (von Bavaria nach Italie, 1500-1830)*. Hirmer Verlag/Deutsches Museum, München, 208 p., illus.
Subtitle translates as: maps, roads, travel. Area included is southern Germany to Italy.

Loeb-Larocque, Louis, 1985, *Karten deutscher Gebiete aus der Produktion französischer Verleger des 17. Jahrhunderts*. Speculum Orbis, 1. Jahrg., Nummer 1, p. 3-23, maps.
Includes maps of Germany by French map-makers.

Meurer, Peter N., 1984, *Mappae Germaniae*. Verlag Dietrich Pfaehler, Bad Neustadt a.d. Saale, 22 map reproductions loose, Folio size, bound text 72 p., 28 figs.
Includes 22 map reproductions for the years 1482-1803. Map quality is suitable for framing; covers western Europe.

Moreland, Carl, & David Bannister, 1986, *Antique Maps*. Phaidon - Christie's Collectors Guides, 332 p., 168 p., illus.
One of the best concise references available; covers all of Europe.

Niessen, Josef, 1946, *Geschichtlicher Handatlas Deutschen Länder am Rhein (Mittel und Niederrhein)*. J. P. Bachem, Köln/Res. Gentium Verlag, Lörrach, 64 p., numerous illus.
Note especially map p. 20, "Rheingebiet um das Jahr 1610"; that is, the Rhine area about 1610.

Romer, Gerhard (ed.), 1981, *Die Oberrheinlande in alten Landkarten (1618-1828)*. Badischen Landesbibliothek, Karlsruhe, 131 p., 71 illus.

Sandler, Christian, 1905, *Die Reformation der Kartographie um 1700*. R. Oldenbourg, München, 25 p., tables.

Sanson, Nicolas (d'Abbeville), & Jaillot, Charles Hubert Alexis, 1692, *Atlas Nouveau, Continenant Tout Les Parties du Monde*. Pierre Mortier, Libraire, Amsterdam, vol. 1, maps 1-99; vol. 2, maps 100-200.
A classic work showing maps for all countries of Europe; maps have alphabetical city and town indices.

Stopp, Klaus, 1967, *Maps of Germany with Marginal Town Views*. The Map Collector's Circle, London, 21 p., 22 pls.
Maps illustrated date 1607 to 1680. Stopp also has a massive series of at least eight other publications containing reproductions of town views from Germany, Switzerland, and Czechoslovakia, these books date from 1979 to 1985.

Tooley, R. V., 1978, *Maps and Map-makers*. Crown Publishers, Inc., N.Y., 6th ed., 140 p., figs.
Note especially his illustration five showing villages with appendages of heim along the west bank of the middle Rhine.

Wolter, John A., E. Grimm, & D. K. Carrington (eds.), 1986, *World Directory of Map Collections*. K. G. Saur Co., München, 405 p., 2nd ed..

Zögner, Lothar, 1983, *Verzeichnis der Kartensammlungen in der Bundesrepublik Deutschland einschliesslich Berlin (West)*. Otto Harrassowitz, Wiesbaden., 417 p., map.

THE ENGLISH, BEING THE LANDLORDS OF America until 1776, jealously guarded their mapping technology. Under these circumstances, the immigrants in America improvised as best they could with manuscript maps and a few copies, mostly of a short life. Early American maps were of a comparatively primitive nature up until the time of the mid-19th century. In America, there was in fact no organized effort to make good maps for the better part of the North American continent. Locally, maps of fair quality were devised at an early date for certain key, populated areas in the eastern part of America. Financing by federal agencies was not available for map making purposes, and in general, also not through state and local agencies. Until mid 19th century, nearly all printed maps were privately funded, mainly by their publishers who, at best, received moderate degrees of compensation.

Many of the earliest American maps were hand drawn and laboriously engraved on soft copper plate whose rapid wear during the printing process limited the number of copies to one thousand or so. The better quality maps of America, and parts thereof, continued to be printed in Europe until recent times; these were done on copper and steel plate with high quality engraving.

In 1822, the process of lithography was first used in the United States; it was cheaper, faster, and more adaptable for color printing of maps. In 1824, the introduction of cerography (wax engraving) speeded up the printing process, especially for commercially published atlases. Still, the use of copper and steel plates was stubbornly maintained by the larger American printers until the 1840s.

EARLY PRINTED MAPS OF AMERICA. One good example of a high quality map of a detailed nature was that produced by Thomas Holme in 1687 and printed in London. This map was produced at the request of William Penn, then proprietor of a little known and sparsely settled area around Philadelphia in Pennsylvania. The Holme map is titled *A Map of the Improved Part of the Province of Pennsilvania*. The counties of Chester, Philadelphia, and Bucks were covered. The map shows the names of about 670 early Pennsylvanians. However, the many names of individuals in Radnor, Haverford, Plymouth, Germantown and Dutch Townships are omitted. For instance, Germantown Township is shown only with the name of Van de Walle, who was of course a leader of the participants in the German investment company known as *The Frankfort Companie*, but who never actually lived in America.

A fine publication by Tinkcom, et al, 1955, gives a list of maps covering Germantown. The cited maps date from 1683 to 1943. Particular note is made of Germantown maps dated 1683, 1687, ca. 1700, 1740, 1746, 1750, etc. The book by Tinkcom, et al, shows inside the front and back covers a diagrammatic sketch of Germantown Township with the names of property owners of about 1690.

Twenty other notable early maps, mainly of high quality, include the following, listed in chronological order:

1. Thomas Holme, 1683, *A Portraiture of the City of Philadelphia*, London.
   The first printed plan of an American city.
2. Cyprian Southack, 1717, *A New Chart of North America*, Boston.
   First known general map published in America, eastern part only.
3. Guillaume Del'Isle, 1718, *Carte de la Louisiane et du Cours du Misisipi*, Paris.
   The main printed source for all later maps of the Mississippi River drainage shed.
4. John Bonner, 1722, *Map of the Town of Boston*, Boston.
   Earliest extant town plan published in the United States.
5. Jacques Nicolas Bellin, 1744, *Carte des Lacs du Canada*, Paris.
   An early and important, detailed map of the Great Lakes region by another well-known French cartographer.
6. Nicholas Scull and George Heap, 1750, *A Map of Philadelphia, and Parts Adjacent*, Philadelphia.
   The first map of Philadelphia printed in America.
7. John Mitchell, 1755, *A Map of the British Colonies in North America*, London.
   This map and its editions up to 1781 has been described as "the most important map in American colonial history," having been used as a primary basis for territorial boundaries
8. Harry Gordon, 1766, *River of Ohio*, manuscript map in the Library of Congress, Washington DC.
   The first accurate map and the first hydrographic survey of the Ohio.
9. J. B. Eliot, 1778, *Carte du Theatre de la Guerre Actual Entre les Anglais et les Treize Colonies Unies de l'Amerique Septrentrionale*, Paris.
   The first map to use the name United States, in French.
10. Christopher Colles, 1789, *A Survey of the Roads of the United States of America*, New York.
    A "strip map," being among the first road maps printed in America. Deals mainly with roads around New York City.
11. Abraham Bradley, Jr., 1796, *Map of the United States, Exhibiting the Post Roads, etc.*, Philadelphia.
    One of the first maps for commercial purposes.
12. William Maclure, 1809, *Observations on the Geology of the United States*, Philadelphia.
    One of the first geologic maps in the United States.
13. Tanner, Henry S., 1827, *Virginia, Maryland, and Delaware*, Phila.
    In 1819-23, Tanner initiated modern map-making in the United States with his New American Atlas. The above listed map is representative of his well-known high quality workmanship.

14. William Norris, 1834, *Map of the Railroads and Canals Finished, Unfinished and In Contemplation in the United States*, New York.
    Shows the eastern seaboard States and as far west as Illinois.
15. S. A. Mitchell, 1835, *Mitchell's Travellers Guide Through the United States*, Philadelphia.
    Covers the eastern States as far west as Missouri; J. H. Young was the engraver.
16. David H. Burr, 1839, *Map of the United States of North America, published as part of The American Atlas*, London.
    An atlas of postal maps - a series of 12 maps designed to show every post office in America; it was the most complete map of the United States to that date.
17. John C. Fremont, 1845, *Map of Oregon and Upper California*, Washington, D.C.
    One of the early, important printed maps used as a basis for the settlement of the American West. The maps accompanying Fremont's report were done also in 1846 by the firm of August Hoen in Baltimore. These included an important topographical map of the wagon trail from Missouri to Oregon and were issued in seven sheets.
18. Samuel A. Mitchell, 1849, *A General Map of the United States with the contiguous British & Mexican Possessions*, Philadelphia.
    A good example of the high quality work Mitchell inherited from Tanner, and which he improved upon.
19. Lt. C. K. Warren, 1858, *Map of the Territory of the United States from the Mississippi to the Pacific Ocean*, Washington, D.C.
    Probably the best map resulting from the extensive 1853-55 government surveys of the West.
20. Edward Freyhold, 1868, *Cordilleras*
    A revision of G. K. Warren's general map of the West; the first recognizable modern map of the West.

THE HOLLAND LAND COMPANY IN WESTERN NEW YORK. Early on, the Dutch investment companies, later collectively named The Holland Land Company, realized the necessity of having maps of the almost three million acres which they had purchased in western New York and in Pennsylvania. Representative examples of these manuscript maps are shown in the 1976 publication by W. C. Pieterse. Most of these examples are undated. However, the systematic and detailed mapping of the area probably occurred between 1795 and 1819.

In 1824, Amos Eaton made a geological survey of the route covered by the Erie Canal, which traversed much of the acreage held by the Holland Land Co. The resulting map was one of the early geologic maps of a significant part of the United States.

THE EMIGRANT GUIDES. Among the many emigrant guides published in the United States after the Revolutionary War, some notable examples which partly satisfied the needs of ever increasing waves of migrants and travelers west of the Allegheny Mountains, are the following:

1. John Filson, 1784, *Map of Kentucky* and accompanying book titled *The Discovery, Settlement, and Present State of Kentucky.*
2. Mathew Carey, 1796, *Pocket Atlas for Travelers*, Philadelphia
3. Zadok Cramer, 1801, *Ohio Navigator*, Pittsburgh (later editions were titled *The Ohio and Mississippi Navigator* and *The Navigator*, ibid).
   These works by Zadok Cramer were primarily concerned with boat travel along the Ohio, Allegheny, Monongahela, and Mississippi Rivers. This very popular series of publications was carried on even after Cramer's death (he was b. 1773, d. 1813) with the 9th improved and enlarged edition being published in 1817.
   The series is basically an expansion of the 1766 maps and published data of Capt. Harry Gordon and Ensign Thomas Hutchins for the Ohio River portion, and of Lieutenant Philip Pittman's 1770 publication of data from Mississippi River surveys. Gordon, Hutchins, and Pittman were all English Army officers.
4. James Melish, 1812, *Travels in the United States of America etc.* Philadelphia, 2 vols., 8 maps.
   This guide was based on his personal 1806-11 trip covering some 2,400 miles in Ohio, upper New York, and Massachusetts.
5. William Darby, 1818, *Emigrant's Guide to the Western and Southwestern States and Territories*, Kirk & Mercein, N.Y.
6. D. Hewett, 1825, *The American Traveller, etc.*
   Apparently the first guide of national scope and the first comprehensive list printed list of United States roads.
7. H. S. Tanner, 1828, *New Pocket Atlas of the United States with the Roads and Distances Designed for Travellers*, Philadelphia.
8. S. A. Mitchell, 1832, *Traveller's Guide Through the United States, etc.*, Philadelphia.
9. H. S. Tanner, 1834, *Traveller's Guide of Map of the Roads, Canals, and Rail Roads of the United States etc.*, Philadelphia.
   The first of a large series of traveler's guides published by Tanner. The 10th edition is dated 1846.
10. S. A. Mitchell, 1834, *Tourist Pocket Maps*, Philadelphia.
    Concentrates individually on various states in the Midwest.
11. J. H. Colton, 1839, *Western Tourist and Emigrant's Guide*, N.Y.
    The map includes Ohio, Michigan, Illinois, Missouri & Iowa.
12. Henry I. Simpson, 1848, *The Emigrant's Guide to the Gold Mines* (of California), Joyce & Co., N.Y.
13. T. H. Jefferson, 1849, *Map of the Emigrant Road from Independence, Missouri, to St. Francisco, California* (four sheets), Berford & Co., N.Y.
14. Joseph E. Ware, 1849, *Emigrant's Guide to California*, J. Halsall Co., St. Louis.

THE IMPACT OF RAILROAD CONSTRUCTION. With the beginning of the construction of the American railroads in the early 18th century, decent maps became a necessity. These maps covered parts of the eastern seaboard at first, and eventually preceded the railroad expansion westward to the Mississippi River. In the 1840's, the expansion, or at least the dream of expansion, of the railroads to the Pacific gave impetus to government surveys west of the Mississippi. These dreams were stimulated in part by the discovery in 1848 of gold at Sutter's Mill in California.

The dreams of a railroad to the Pacific apparently were first published anonymously in 1832 in a small journal titled *The Emigrant*, which was printed in Ann Arbor, Michigan. During the years 1844-1852, Asa Whitney (1797-1872) took up the cause and expended much of his mercantile fortune in publicizing various proposals for the creation of a railroad to the Pacific. His 1845 proposal, for instance, requested from Congress a tract of land sixty miles wide extending from Lake Michigan to the Pacific. The proposal was to sell sections along the right of way to settlers in order to finance construction of the railroad. The culmination of Whitney's widespread newspaper campaign was a 1849 pamphlet titled *A Project for a Railroad to the Pacific*.

In 1849, four railroad conventions were organized: in Chicago, Boston, St. Louis and in Memphis. Each city was attempting to gain support as the all important eastern terminus of the railroad to the Pacific. By this time, there was general agreement that San Francisco was the most logical city for the western terminus of the railroad.

By 1849, Julius Hutawa of St. Louis had published a *Map and Profile Sections showing Railroads of the United States*. This important map accompanied a report of the Project for a Pacific Railway which was exhibited at the convention in St. Louis in October, 1949.

The Corps of Topographical Engineers had been established in July, 1838, primarily to map the West. In the years 1853-1855, the U.S. army surveyed four potential railroad routes across the western part of the United States. These four routes were:

1. Isaac I. Stephens/Capt. George B. McClellan - west from St. Paul, (Minnesota).
2. Lt. John W. Gunnison - west from Fort Leavenworth (Kansas).
3. Lt. Amiel Weeks Whipple - west from Fort Smith, Arkansas.
4. Lts. John G. Parke & John B. Pope - west from north Texas.

In addition, Lt. Henry L. Abbott explored a route from Fort Vancouver in Washington south to San Diego in California, with the view of connecting all then important coastal cities to the western terminus of the transcontinental railroad when it was build. Route maps were prepared in 1857 by Lt. Governor Kemble Warren of the U.S. Topographical Engineers.

Ironically, the final route of the transcontinental railroad (built in the 1860's) did not follow any of these surveys, but was a compromise, with the eastern terminus at Omaha, Nebraska, and the western terminus at Sacramento, California. A key deciding factor in the selection of this route was the desire to use the Donner Pass in California.

Thirteen massive volumes of reports on these railroad surveys were issued between 1854 and 1859. Warren's 1857 map compilation was one of the most important maps of the West ever drawn, being the first adequate topographic treatment of the West. A diagrammatic sketch of the survey routes is nicely illustrated in the current literature, as for instance, that shown by Goetzmann, 1982, p. 76-77. The map series was completed in large part due to the efforts of transplanted Germans, namely Edward Freyhold, compiler; Baron F. W. Egloffstein, former Prussian artist and cartographer; and Julius Bien (1826-1909), German born lithographer and printer. Bien, who was of Jewish extraction, was involved in the civil disturbances in 1848 in Germany and came to America at that time in order to escape prosecution.

In the United States, Bien soon was actively involved in printing maps in America of the western surveys; the various projects lasted for most of the last half of the 19th century. Bien in fact produced literally thousands of maps for use by state and federal governments. One of his more notable efforts was the atlas series to accompany the 1870-80 *Report of the Geological Exploration of the Fortieth Parallel* under the direction of Clarence King.

GOVERNMENT SURVEYING AND WESTWARD MIGRATION. In 1785, Thomas Hutchins was authorized by the Congressional Ordinance of 1785 to begin systematic mapping of lands west of the Ohio River. Townships six miles square were surveyed and established; these were subdivided into thirty-six sections. Each section contained about 640 acres. Government land sales provided the opportunity to purchase plots of 160, 320, or 640 acres or multiples thereof. Most of the early migrants could only afford 160 acre plots.

A further ordinance of 1796 changed the order of numbering of the thirty-six sections in a township. The systematic government surveys continued across the west, at first close to the Mississippi River, later across the grain belt west of the Mississippi, and eventually on to the Pacific Ocean. The various waves of migrants generally followed the surveys and in relatively short order occupied virtually all of the more fertile parts of the surveyed land, starting with the lands along the rivers. These surveys lasted for more than a century.

The establishment of the General Land Office (part of the Treasury Department) in 1812 reorganized the pioneering efforts of Thomas Hutchins and standardized the format and content of the government mapping. Revisions to this format were made in 1831. About the same time, the U.S. Topographical Bureau (part of the War Department) was organized; the bureau lasted until 1863 when it was abolished because of the priorities of the Civil War. In 1813, Major Stephen H. Long was charged with filling the military's mapping needs, notably the mapping of strategic water ways and coasts in the Great Lakes area. His surveys eventually extended westward to the Rocky Mountains.

Other notable army officers attached to the bureau included John C. Fremont, John W. Gunnison, Howard Stansbury, and Governor K. Warren. All these contributed a fair share to early mapping of the West.

On an individual basis, by 1840, some thirty or more state maps of eastern states had been published. Nearly all were private efforts organized by local publishers, although many publishers received some delayed support from state government by purchases of multiple copies for state use. Virtually every town had an official full- or part-time surveyor whose data eventually was incorporated into a state map.

Some of the eastern States had established geological survey divisions in the 1820's and 1830's. By the 1840's, about twenty eastern States had established a geological survey division; most of the early state surveys disappeared by the late 1800's, however. As previously mentioned, one of the more notable mapping efforts of the State surveys was the 1824 survey along the route of the Erie Canal in western New York.

However, there was no unified or systematic effort for government support of mapping. Even during the Civil War, good topographic maps of certain key areas either did not exist or were not readily available. The Armies of the North and the South often depended upon local knowledge for information regarding the topography of key battlefield areas in states such as Kentucky, Tennessee, Georgia, and North and South Carolina. In fact, overall Civil War maps were created only in 1891-95. These are shown by the massive publications of Somers (1978), and Yoseloff (1958), cited here.

The most notable of the 19th century territorial expansions involved the large acreage acquired from the French by the Louisiana Purchase, which became in effective in March, 1804. Settlement of Spanish claims over part of the territory was done at the same time.

Subsequently, the well-known exploration of the Missouri and Columbia Rivers westward to the Pacific in 1804-06 by Meriwether Lewis (1774-1809) and William Clark (1770-1838) was a pioneering effort which provided basic data for numerous later government-sponsored exploration parties in the West. The sketch maps and other documentation drawn by Lewis and Clark did not reach the general public until 1814, when they were consolidated and published by Nicholas Biddle and Paul Allen. The Lewis and Clark maps provided settlers with basic knowledge of territories along the Missouri River extending from St. Louis toward Kansas City.

Zebulon Montgomery Pike (1779-1813) led another early exploration. In 1805, Pike's party traversed the headwaters of the Mississippi River and later concentrated their efforts on exploring much of what is now the State of Kansas by following and mapping the Missouri, Osage, and Arkansas Rivers.

After the Civil War, systematic mapping of the far West by the Federal government was developed under four great survey teams nominated as follows:

1. Hayden Surveys, 1867-78
2. King Surveys, 1867-72
3. Powell Surveys, 1869-79
4. Wheeler Surveys, 1869-79

The four survey teams covered the enormous, but less fertile portion of the United States' western regions. Their mapping efforts provided a foundation for understanding the complex geologic history of the Rocky Mountain area as well aiding in the search for numerous deposits of economically important minerals such as silver and copper. Innumerable mining towns developed all along the north-south extent of the Rockies. In some local valleys, where water was available for irrigation, important farming communities developed.

The Hayden, King, and Powell survey teams were government sponsored, but run by civilians, who, for the most part, had been educated in eastern Universities. The three civilian team leaders were Ferdinand Vandever Hayden (1829-1886), Clarence King (1842-1901), and John Wesley Powell (1834-1902). The Wheeler survey team was led by Lieutenant George M. Wheeler (1842-1905) of the Army Topographic Engineers.

A summary of the areas mapped by the four survey teams is diagramed in the recent publication of Goetzmann, 1982, p. 84-85. The trials and tribulations of all four surveys are covered in some detail by the lively and interesting summary written by Bartlett in 1962.

The U.S. Geological Survey was finally established in March, 1879, basically to consolidate the work of the four above mentioned western surveys. In 1879, Clarence King became the first Director of the Survey, but resigned the following year in order to seek his fortune elsewhere. King was succeeded by Powell who remained the chief until 1894.

A primary function of the U.S. Geological Survey is the development of topographic maps; the map series was first systematically organized in 1882. Today, vast sections of the more populous parts of the United States are covered by topographic maps at a scale of 1:50,000. The maps show farming areas in great detail along with geographic names which can be related directly to historic family records as done in the first and last chapters of this book.

One should write to the Survey for a free index to a particular area of interest, as for instance, as used in this book, indices to topographic maps of Illinois, Kansas, Pennsylvania, etc. The address is:

U.S. Geological Survey, Map Distribution
Federal Center, Building 41
Box 25286
Denver, CO 80225

NOTABLE 19TH CENTURY MAP PRINTERS IN THE EAST. For the most part, early printing in America tended to concentrate in the three major cities of Philadelphia, Boston, and New York. Eventually, Philadelphia and New York developed the primary printing infrastructure needed to become important printing and publishing centers.

The 19th century in America was marked by the publication of atlases which were reissued in numerous editions. Among the notable publishers of atlases were John Melish (1771-1822), and Henry S. Tanner (1768-1858); Tanner was established in Philadelphia by 1816 as an engraver and by 1819 as a leading publisher.

The firm established by Samuel August Mitchell (1792-1868) operated from about 1831 to 1890, also in Philadelphia. The firm of Joseph H. Colton (1800-1893) and his sons George W. Colton (1827-1901) and Charles B. Colton (1832-1916), was active in New York City from about 1839 to 1884.

A typical work by the Tanner Publishing firm on the description of the area involved in the Mississippi River valley is cited in the bibliography under Robert Baird (ed.), 1832. Unfortunately, many of these early works were printed on poor quality paper and, in conjunction with heavy use by migrants and other travellers, today are scarce and in very fragile condition.

Mitchell's famous *Traveller's Guide Through the United States* was first printed in 1834 and was issued in at least five other editions dating to 1845. In the 1845 edition, this handy booklet of 78 pages, and one folded map, was designed to fit in one's pocket, being only 5 1/4 x 3 1/4 x 3/8 inches; the map measured 17 3/4 x 22 inches when unfolded. The map shows principal towns and cities from the Atlantic coast westward to Iowa, Missouri, Arkansas and Louisiana. The text gives an index of principal localities and other important features such as steamboat mileage from Pittsburgh to New Orleans (2, 003 miles), St. Louis to New Orleans (1, 218 miles), St. Louis to Pittsburgh (1, 145 miles), and mileage to many other river and overland destinations.

A large part of Mitchell's publications were dedicated to serving travellers in the midwestern states centering around Illinois whose area was just then being extensively developed and settled. Mitchell's 1835 Tourist's Pocket Map of the State of Illinois is a quaint representative of his early work. The 3 x 4-3/4 x 3/8 inch booklet contains only one page of text with a map whose size unfolded measures 13 x 15-1/2 inches at a scale of approximately 1 inch equals 30 miles. A copy of this map in the Kansas City Public Library is in good condition, having been printed on thin bankers paper.

In 1837, Mitchell published a fairly extensive text of 142 pages on the State of Illinois; this text is basically a descriptive account of the State and summarizes the physical attributes of then existing Counties as well as principal towns. A half dozen works, dating from 1834 to 1846, are cited in the current bibliography as being typical of the work of the S. A. Mitchell firm. A wealth of detail on 19th century American atlas publishers is given in the more recent 1985 book by Ristrow.

MIDWEST MAP PRINTERS. After about 1850, the publishing and printing of maps was extended westward to include the cities of Cincinnati, St. Louis, Milwaukee, and above all, Chicago; four major cities which were to receive very heavy populations of German immigrants.

During the last part of the 19th century, the map publishing firm of George F. Cram (1841-1928), was very active in Chicago.

The firm of Rand and McNally established Chicago as a center of map publishing in the United States. William H. Rand (1828-ca. 1900) initiated operations about 1856. He was joined a couple of years later by Andrew McNally (1836-ca. 1904). With the printing of their first railroad map in 1872, their firm became a dominant force in map printing lasting through the later part of the 19th century and until the present. Much business was generated also through the printing of train tickets and railroad schedules. One of the many representative early maps printed by the firm was the 1873 map titled *Railroad Map of the United States and Canada*. Another milestone was the introduction in 1924 of the annual series titled *Rand McNally Road Atlas*, which met the demand of the increasingly voluminous automobile traffic.

Typical of other publications of the Midwest was Alfred T. Andreas' 1883 *History of Kansas* (Chicago); the 1869 *Atlas of the State of Illinois* by Augustus Warner and J. Silliman Higgins (Philadelphia & Chicago); and the 1887 *Official State Atlas of Kansas* by L. H. Everts & Co (Philadelphia). All of these publications were used to some extent for background information in the first and last chapters of this book.

REFERENCES

Baird, Robert (ed.), 1832, *View of the Valley of the Mississippi, or the Emigrant's and Traveller's Guide to the West.* H. S. Tanner Publ. Co., Philadelphia, 372 p., 15 maps, 1st ed, (2nd ed.-1834).
The Introduction to the book under the initials R.B. possibly refer to Lieutenant Robert Bache rather than Robert Baird.

Bartlett, R. A., 1962, *Great Surveys of the American West.* Univ. Oklahoma Press, Norman, 408 p., maps, illus.
A concise, illustrated summary of the four mid-19th century geological and geographical surveys of the far West with a lively narrative tone.

Baughman, R. W., 1961, *Kansas in Maps.* Kansas State Historical Soc., Topeka, Kans., 104 p., illus., maps.
A highly illustrated and useful book showing the evolution of mapping in Kansas territory from the earliest 16th century hand drawn maps to 19th century printed maps.

Bond, B. W., Jr. (ed.), 1942, *The Courses of the Ohio River.* Hist. & Philos. Soc. of Ohio, Cincinnati, 77 p., 2 maps.
Documents and reprints 1766 works of Captain Harry Gordon and Lt. H. Hutchins along 1,164 miles of the Ohio River.

Brown, L. A., 1959, *Early Maps of the Ohio Valley.* Univ. Pittsburgh Press, 132 p., 52 pls.
Good for historical background data on the Ohio Valley.

Cappon, L. J., B. B. Petchenik, & J. H. Long, 1976, *Atlas of early American History: the Revolutionary era, 1760-1790.* Princeton Univ. Press, 157 p., 74 maps (oversized publication).

Carrington, D. K., & Stephenson, R. W., 1978, *Map Collections in the United States and Canada, A Directory.* Special Libraries Assoc., N.Y., 230 p. (3rd ed.).
_____, 1985, *Map Collections in the United States and Canada.* Special Libraries Assoc., 180 p., (4th ed.).

Clark, D. S., 1969, *Index to Maps of the American Revolution.* privately printed, Washington, D.C., 288 p.

Ehrenberg, R. E., 1987a, "Exploratory Mapping of the Great Plains before 1800." In Luebke, F. C., et al, *Mapping the North American Plains.* Univ. Oklahoma Press, Norman, p. 3-26, illus.
_____, 1989a, *Mapping the North American Plains. A Catalog of the Exhibition.* ibid, p. 173-230, illus.

Ehrenberg, 1989b, *The Earth Revealed: Aspects of Geologic Mapping. A Catalog of the Exhibition - 28th International Geological Congress*. Library of Congress, Geography and Map Division, Washington, D.C., 36 p.

Goetzmann, Wm. H., 1966, *Exploration and Empire: The Explorer and the Scientist in the Winning of the American West*. A. A. Knopf Co., N.Y., 656 p., + 17 p. index, 45 maps (also paperback reprint, 1978, W. W. Norton Co., N.Y.).
_____, 1982, "Explorer, Mountain Man, and Scientist." In *Exploring the American West, 1803-1879*. U.S. Dept. Interior, Washington, D. C., National Park Handbook 116, 21-99, illus., maps.

Goss, John, 1990, *The Mapping of North America*. The Wellfleet Press, Secaucus, N.J., 184 p., 85 maps
Contains a good selection of early maps, well chosen for representation of maps of North America.

Grim, R. E., 1987, "Mapping Kansas and Nebraska: The Role of the General Land Office." In Leubke, F. C., et al, *Mapping the North American Plains*. Univ. Oklahoma Press, Norman, p. 127-144, illus.

LeGear, C. E., 1950, *United States Atlases - A list of National, State, County, City, and Regional Atlases in the Library of Congress*. The Library of Congress, Reference Dept., Washington, D.C., vol. 1, 445 p.
_____, 1953, ibid, vol. 2, 301 p.

Lunny, R. M., 1961, *Early Maps of North America*. New Jersey Historical Soc., Newark, N.J., 48 p., maps.
Concentrates on early maps along the eastern seaboard.

Makower, Joel & Laura Bergheim (eds.), 1986, *The Map Catalog*. Vintage Books, N.Y., 252 p., illus.
Good introduction to map sources and addresses for ordering U.S. maps.

Martin, J. C., & R. S. Martin, 1984, *Maps of Texas and the Southwest, 1513-1900*. Univ. New Mexico Press, Albuquerque, 174 p., illus.

Martin, R. S., & J. C. Martin, 1982, *Contours of Discovery*. Texas State Historical Assoc., Austin, 66 p., 60 maps.

Mitchell, S. A., 1834, *An Accompaniment to Mitchell's Reference and Distance Map of the United States*. Mitchell & Hinman Publ., 324 p. (1838 edition contains 344 p.).

Mitchell, S. A., 1835, *Tourist's Pocket Map of the State of Illinois*. S. A. Mitchell, Philadelphia, 1 page text; folded map; map by J. H. Young. Text on map margin includes Illinois County population census and steamboat routes along the Mississippi and Illinois Rivers.

———, 1837, *Illinois in 1837*. Mitchell & Grigg & Elliott Publ., Philadelphia, 142 p., map.

———, 1845a, *Mitchell's National Map of the United States of North America*. S. A. Mitchell Publ., Philadelphia, large sheet measuring approximately 39 x 47 inches. Main map measures 25 x 32 1/2 inches at a scale of about 1 inch equals 54 miles; bordered with enlarged views of 32 cities; drawing and engraving by J. B. Young and J. H. Brightly; shows eastern Kansas as "Indian Territory."

———, 1845, *Traveller's Guide through the United States*. S. A. Mitchell, Philadelphia, 78 p., map. Map engravers were J. B. Young and D. Haines.

———, 1846, *A New Universal Atlas of the World*. S. A. Mitchell Publ., Philadelphia, 117 maps, plans, and sections. Atlas size 14 x 17 3/4 x 1 inch; individual State maps are 11 1/4 x 13 5/8 inch at a scale of about 1 inch equals 30 miles.

Moulton, G. E. (ed.), 1983, *Atlas of the Lewis and Clark Expedition*. Univ. Nebraska Press, Lincoln, vol. 1, 24 oversized text pages, 126 mainly manuscript maps.

Pool, W. C., Edward Triggs, & Lance Wren, 1975, *A Historical Atlas of Texas*. Encino Press, Austin, 190 p., numerous sketch maps.

Reid, R. L. (ed,), 1991, *Always a River. The Ohio River and the American Experience*. Indiana Univ. Press, 256 p., illus. This is a series of articles by eight authors narrating settlement and personal experiences encountered in life along the Ohio River. Especially interesting are the articles by D. E. Bigham and by L. R. Johnson which document the history and development of numerous locks along the river in the 19th century.

Robinson, A. H., 1982, *Early Thematic Mapping in the History of Cartography*. Univ. Chicago Press, Chicago, Ill., 266 p., 110 figs. Contains good bibliography.

Ristrow, W. W., 1985, *American Maps and Mapmakers: Commerical Cartography in the Nineteenth Century*. Wayne State University Press, Detroit, 488 p., illus.
Basic reference for historical data concerning major American map publishers.

Schwartz, Seymour I., & Ralph E. Ehrenberg, 1980, *The Mapping of America*. Harry N. Abrams Co., Inc., N.Y., 363 p., 223 pls.
Basic reference; data mainly from the National Archives and the Library of Congress.

Simonetti, M. L., et al, 1976, *Descriptive List of the Map Collection in the Pennsylvania State Archives*. Pennsylvania Historical and Museum Commission, Harrisburg, 178 p.
Comprehensive listing of historic maps for Pennsylvania for period 1681 to 1976.

Sommers, Richard (ed.), 1978, *The Official Military Atlas of the Civil War (reprint of Atlas to Accompany the Official Records, etc., dated 1891-95)*. Arno Press-Crown Publishers, Inc., N.Y., 821 maps, 106 engravings, 209 drawings, text 29 p.

Stephenson, R. W., 1967, *Land Ownership Maps: A Checklist of Nineteenth Century United States County Maps in the Library of Congress*. U.S. Government Printing Office, Washington, D. C., 86 p.
_____, 1989, *Civil War Maps*. Library of Congress, Washington, D.C., 410 p. (2nd ed.), illus.

Tanner, H. S., 1840, *A description of the Canals and Rail Roads of the United States*. T. R. Tanner & J. Disturnell, N.Y., 272 p., 3 maps.
Reprinted by A. M. Kelley, N.Y., 1970; contains three important maps of the eastern part of the U.S.

Tinkcom, H. M., N. B. Tinkcom, & G. M. Simon, 1955, *Historic Germantown*. American Philosophical Soc., Philadelphia, Pa., 155 p., figs., maps.
Good list of early maps of Germantown dating 1683-1943, p. 148-149.

Tooley, R. V., 1973, *A Sequence of Maps of America*. Map Collectors' Circle, vol. 10, no. 92, 12 p., 14 pls.

Tucker, S. J., 1942, *Indian Villages of the Illinois Country. Pt. I, Atlas*. Illinois State Museum, Scientific Papers, text in 18 folio size pages, 54 pls.
Contains a series of reproductions of manuscript and published maps of Illinois, one of the most notable being John Melish's 1819 Map of Illinois.

Wheat, C. I., 1957, *Mapping the Transmississippi West, 1540-1861*. Institute of Historical Cartography, San Francisco.
Elaborate listing of manuscript and printed maps in six oversized volumes as follows:
Vol. I, *The Spanish Entrada to the Louisiana Purchase, 1540-1804*, 264 p., illus.
Vol. II, *From Lewis and Clark to Fremont, 1804-1845*, 281 p., illus.
Vol. III, *The Mexican War to the Boundary Survey, 1846-1854*, 349 p., illus.
Vol. IV, *Pacific Railroad Surveys to the Onset of the Civil War, 1855-1860*, 260 p., illus.
Vol. V, pt. I, *Civil War to the Geological Survey (1860-1879)*, 222 p., illus.
Vol. V, pt. II, *Civil War to the Geological Survey (cont'd)*, p. 223-487, illus.

Wheat, J. C., & C. F. Brun, 1969, *Maps and Charts Published in America before 1800, A Bibliography*. Yale Univ. Press, New Haven, 215 p., illus.

Wokeck, M. S., et al (eds.), 1986, *The Papers of William Penn, Vol. III, 1685-1700*. Univ. Pennsylvania Press, 796 p.
Reprints, in sections, Thomas Holme's important 1687 map of Chester, Philadelphia and Bucks Counties in Pennsylvania.

Wood, W. R., 1983, *Atlas of Early Maps of the Midwest*. Illinois State Museum, Springfield, Ill., double-folio size, text 14 p., 22 pls.; Maps date 1714-1856.

Yoseloff, Thomas, 1958, *Atlas to Accompany the Official Records of the Union and Confederate Armies*. Govt. Printing Office, Washington, D.C., text 29 p., 175 pl.
Reprint edition compiled by Thomas Yoseloff, Inc., N.Y., with 4 pages introductory text by H. S. Commager.

ennonites, Quakers and the Settlement of Pennsylvania

ARLY LIFE OF A DUTCH REFORMER. MENNO Simons was born at the small northern Dutch community of Witmarsum, in Friesland, probably about 1496. Menno's father's name was Simon (last name unknown). Consequently, Menno took as his last name, the name Simons(zoon), or Simon's son, as was the early Dutch custom. In 1524, Menno was ordained a priest in the Catholic Church in Utrecht. His first assignment was that of Vicar at Pingium, near Witmarsum. He remained as a priest at Pingium from 1524-1531 and then went to Witmarsum. During the next few years, he was disturbed by the persecution of early reformers, by the subsequent martyrs' deaths and by the repression of religious freedom at Oldeklooster (at Bolsward, in Friesland) and at Münster in northern Germany. During this time, he made comments on "the abominations of the papal system" and also preached against the warfare of the radical Münsterites, a warfare which occurred from May, 1535 to January, 1536. By early 1536, Menno withdrew as a priest from Witmarsum and went into hiding while he worked as an underground evangelist and otherwise spent time on Bible study.

In early 1536, Menno probably went to the inland harbor city of Groningen in the northeastern part of the Netherlands, where it appears he was baptized by Obbe Philips, an early reformer. He was ordained by Philips in early 1537. In Groningen he also may have married Geertruida (or Geertruydt), last name unknown. This marriage produced at least two daughters and one son, Jan.

ONE STEP AHEAD OF THE AUTHORITIES. At the request of a small group of Anabaptists, Menno became an Elder and started preaching in East Friesland in Germany. Menno stated that he had no permanent home between the years of 1536 and 1544. It appears likely that these years were consumed with constant travel over the northern Dutch provinces of Friesland and Groningen, and the adjacent German province of East Friesland.

One of Menno's most important writings was *Dat Fundament des Christeljcken Leers* (Foundation Book), published in 1539-40. There were a number of other works. Basically, Simons attempted to reconcile the language of the eastern Dutch with Low German in his religious publication in order to increase the area of Mennonite influence. In this he was partially successful. In fact, Menno's writings played the same role for the development of the Low German language, although in a much lesser sense and slightly later, that the numerous publications of Martin Luther played for the development of the High German language.

In 1544, Princess Maria of the Austrian, Catholic Habsburg line asked Anna, German Countess of Ostfriesland (East Friesland), to expel the Anabaptists. Although reluctant, the Calvinist Countess began to enforce the regulations of the higher Habsburg authority. Anna (1501-1575), Countess of Ostfriesland, was Regentess from 1540-1562 after her husband, Count Enno II (1505-1540), had died an early death. In May-June, 1544, Menno went to Köln, along the lower German Rhine, with another reformer, Dirk Philips, who was a brother of the above mentioned Obbe Philips. Menno stayed in the lower Rhine area most of the period of 1544-46. At this time, he made a short trip to the Maas River communities in southern Holland and to Roermond.

Hermann V, Graf von Wied, who became Archbishop of Köln in 1515, had a strong influence over the lower German Rhine. Although in August, 1534, he had issued a severe edict against the Anabaptists of that area, he gradually became more tolerant and in July, l544, he introduced moderate reformation. However, by 1546 he was forced to vacate office and Mennonite ideas were again suppressed in the Lower Rhine.

THE FINAL YEARS IN NORTH GERMANY. During 1546, the Simons family took up residence in the north German province of Schleswig-Holstein, near Lübeck. Other short trips took Menno back to Goch in the lower German Rhine, where he had a disagreement with Adam Pastor over the affairs of the Church. Other special Church meetings occurred in northern Germany in Emden in 1547 and in 1552. Menno was also on the German Baltic Coast at Danzig in 1549.

During the years 1553-54, the Menno Simons family was in the Hanseatic City of Wismar. However, the City Council eventually requested that all Anabaptists leave the City. During the latter part of 1554, Menno moved to Fresenburg near Oldesloe (between the north German coastal cities of Hamburg and Lübeck). In the following years, many of his books were reprinted in Dutch, Frisian, and Low German editions. In 1557, Menno made a final trip to Friesland although he was crippled by arthritis at this time. Menno died in Wüstenfelde (in Holstein, northern Germany) on January 31, 1561.

THE MENNONITE TRADITION. The term "Menisten" (or "Mennisten"), to denote the adherents to the peaceful Anabaptist concept, was officially used in 1545. In English, the term later became Mennonites. In general, the Mennonites followed the main principles of other Anabaptist groups, namely the refusal to swear under oath, the refusal to bear arms, the insistence upon a personal Christian discipleship, and a church made up of adult disciples who were baptized on their own volition. By these means, they were generally apolitical.

Never very large congregation-wise, the Mennonites were to persist in small groups, mainly along the Rhine in German villages such as Krefeld (near Köln, that is, Cologne) and Krisheim (near Worms), as well as in somewhat larger groups in Amsterdam and other Dutch cities. Composed of farmers and small tradesmen, they often formed close communities with even closer family associations. Never having been quite accepted in their native lands, many Mennonites were prone to the ideas of travelling evangelists of the 17th century, such as the Quaker William Penn, who led them to seek a new life in the New World. Among the first of the Mennonites, later converted to Quakerism, were the Hendricks, described in Part 1 of this book.

By some accounts, the first Mennonite colony in America is credited to a group of forty-one "German" Mennonites who, in 1663, settled on the Horekill River where it merges with the Delaware river. Most of the members of this group were actually Dutch Mennonites (see comments on page 252 associated with Pieter Cornelisz Plockhoy). The next group of Mennonites to America were those who joined the Germantown Quakers, settling there in the years after 1683. All during the 18th century, relatively small groups entered Pennsylvania via Philadelphia and Germantown, forming the dominant farmer element at Lancaster and other well-known eastern Pennsylvania communities.

Part 7 of this book will trace the migration of another typical Mennonite family group, the Marzolf family, down the Rhine, across the Atlantic, and into the interior of America.

FIFTY-FOUR YEARS OF PERSEVERANCE AND PRESERVATION. In the early part of this century, Mennonites dedicated to the preservation of their history began producing an encyclopedia, *Mennonitisches Lexikon*, which would become noted for its meticulousness. The German historians Christian Hege (1863-1946) and Christian Neff (1869-1943) coordinated the effort of various local authors to produce the ambitious four volume set. Volume I (A-C) of the *Mennonitisches Lexikon* (in German) was published in 1913, and volume II (D-H) appeared in 1937, each volume containing 720 pages. The two volumes were privately printed in Frankfurt am Main in Germany and in a three-century old Mennonite community called Weierhof (Pfalz), near Worms. Work on the *Lexikon* was interrupted by the two World Wars. After the second World War, the German-American historian Harold S. Bender and the German historian Ernst Crous persevered in the effort to complete the Lexikon; thus, volume III (J-N) appeared in 1958, and volume IV (O-Z) was completed finally in 1967.

Bender acted also as chief editor for an English version, again in four volumes, titled *Mennonite Encyclopedia*. The English version has publishing dates of 1955 (A-F), 1956 (F-M), 1957 (M-R), and 1959 (S-Z); the printer was the Mennonite Publishing House of Scottdale, Pa. More recently, a supplemental fifth volume to the English edition came out. The two editions contain numerous short articles on Dutch, German, and Swiss family names and various subjects related to Mennonite history. In this joint German and American effort, the Mennonite community attained their goal of maintaining historic records which are superior to those kept by any group of comparable size. In the United States, virtually all major libraries have a copy of the English version.

REFERENCES

Funk, J. F., 1983, *The Complete Works of Menno Simons*. Pathway Publishers, reprint of 1871 ed., 455 p.

Gleysteen, Jan, 1984, *Mennonite Tourguide to Western Europe*. Scottdale, Pa.: Herald Press, 340 p., illus.
Contains good reference maps and good summaries of the major Mennonite communities in Europe.

_____, 1986, "Catholic Priest Menno Simons becomes 16th Century Leader of the Mennonites." *Mennonite Family History*, vol. V, no. 1, p. 4-6. Elverson, Pa.
Contains a good pictorial essay of Menno Simons' life.

Horst, I. B., 1962, *A Bibliography of Menno Simons, ca. 1496-1561, Dutch Reformer*. B. de Graaf, Nieuwkoop, Netherlands, 157 p.

Keeney, W. E., 1968, *The Development of Dutch Anabaptist Thought and Practice from 1539-1564*. B. de Graaf, Nieuwkoop, Netherlands, 247 p.
Contains extensive documentation of source material, especially those in the Dutch language.

Klaassen, Walter, 1986, "Menno Simons Research, 1937-1986." *Mennonite Quarterly Review*, vol. 60, no. 4, p. 483-496.

Krahn, Cornelius, 1957, "Menno Simons (1496-1561)." In *Mennonite Encyclopedia*, vol. 3, p. 577-584, Mennonite Publishing House, Scottdale, Pa.
_____, 1968, *Dutch Anabaptism, Origin, Spread, Life, and Thought (1450-1600)*. Martinus Nijhoff, The Hague, 303 p.

Vos, K., 1914, *Menno Simons, 1496-1561*. E. J. Brill, Leiden, 350 p.

HE SOCIETY OF FRIENDS WAS FOUNDED about 1647 in England by George Fox (1624-1691). The popular name Quakers was evidently attached in 1650 after George Fox provided the admonition to "tremble at the word of the Lord." Quakerism was from the very beginning strongly evangelistic and missionary-oriented. The group was further characterized by repudiating violence and warfare, by advocating complete non-resistance, and by refusing to take oaths.

William Penn (1644-1718) became a strong Quaker and did much to foster the rapid growth of membership in the Americas during the latter part of the 17th century. In fact, he was probably the dominant Quaker during the period 1680-1695. Penn's two trips to the European continent in 1671 and 1677, along with the names of accompanying Quakers, are described in some detail in the next essay. In spite of Penn's efforts, the Quaker movement was to remain basically an English phenomena.

ENGLISH MISSIONARIES ON THE CONTINENT. After about 1650, Quaker missionaries traveled among the Mennonite colonies in continental Europe, winning over small groups here and there. The first missionaries, John Stubbs and William Caton, went to Holland in 1653. Others followed, traveling about Holland, Germany, and Austria between 1653 and 1683:

Quaker Missionary	Active
William Ames	1655-1662
William Bale	
Joseph Cal	
William Caton	1653-1665
Jan Claus	1669-1679
Stephen Crisp	1663-1683
John Higgins	
Roger Longworth	1679
William Moore	1661-1663
John Philly	1661-1664
George Rolf	1657
John Stubbs	1653-?

Among this group of missionaries, William Ames first went to Krisheim (then called Griesheim) in 1657, and returned in 1661 with some of the others (perhaps William Caton, George Rolf, and Benjamin Furly). They helped with the harvest and converted some seven or eight families of the local Mennonite community to Quakerism, a number of whom were later inspired by William Penn to migrate to Pennsylvania.

The noted Quaker historian Willem Sewel (1653-1720) was very instrumental in preserving many early records with his publication in 1717, in Dutch, of a monumental treatise on the history of the Quakers. Sewel's work was published in an English version in 1722 and, over the next century in at least fourteen different Dutch, English, and German editions.

Willem Sewel was the grandson of William Sewel who moved from England to the Netherlands in 1589, and the son of Jacob Sewel (or Zeenwel, in some Dutch spellings). The father, Jacob Sewel, and his wife Judith Zinspenning were prominent members of the Utrecht Mennonite Church, and later of the Amsterdam Flemish congregation. About 1656, Jacob and his wife left the Mennonite Church and became ardent Quakers. Judith Zinspenning died in 1664; her husband died about the same time.

REFERENCES

Braithwaite, W. C., 1912, *The Beginnings of Quakerism*. Macmillan & Co. Ltd., London, 562 p.

Croese, Gerhard, 1696, *Historia Quakeriana (etc.)*. Amsterdam, 580 p., 2nd ed.
The first edition was published in Latin in 1695; there was also a 1696 edition published in German in Berlin.

Otto, Heinrich, 1972, *Werden und Wesen des Quäkertums und Seine Entwicklung in Deutschland*. Sensen-Verlag, Vienna, 498 p.

Vipont, Elfrida, 1960, *The Story of Quakerism*. The Bannisdale Press, London, 310 p., illus. (2nd ed.).

 ILLIAM PENN. William Penn (1644-1718) was a son of Sir William Penn. The elder Penn was knighted, held the rank of Admiral in the English Navy by 1656, and was the owner of 10,000 acres of land in County Cork, Ireland. The younger William Penn was born in London, his mother being Margaret, a daughter of the Rotterdam merchant John Jasper. Young Penn went to a variety of private schools for children of monied families. At age 16, he entered Christ Church College at Oxford.

About 1661, while still at Oxford, young Penn came under the influence of Quaker Thomas Loe. Because of religious non-conformance, Penn was expelled from the University, a matter which displeased his father who sent him to Paris in 1663. There Penn was introduced to the Court of Louis XIV, studied for a while at the French Reformed (Huguenot) Church at Saumur, crossed the Alps, and, by 1664, went to Turin in Italy. When he returned to England, he was briefly in the English Navy, and, in 1665, entered Lincoln's Inn in London, a leading law school.

In 1667, Penn attended a Quaker meeting at which Thomas Loe presided and thereafter became a regular attendant at these meetings. Penn began to publish articles upholding the Quaker faith and also to preach the cause. One of his unauthorized publications in 1668 caused his imprisonment. He remained in prison for the better part of a year.

In 1672, Penn, then twenty-eight, was married for the first time, to Gulielma Maria Springett. She was born circa 1643 and died in 1694. By this marriage, Penn had two sons and six daughters.

Penn's second marriage in 1696, was to Hannah Callowhill, who died in 1726, or some six years after Penn. By this second marriage, Penn had four sons and four daughters. Of the total of sixteen children, only seven reached adulthood. Eventually, the Penn family name died out.

PENN'S EUROPEAN TRAVELS. After a second imprisonment in 1670-71, Penn was again released following which he made his first trip (1671) to Holland and to Germany, going as far as Herford. Penn's companions on this evangelical trip were Benjamin Furly and Thomas Rudyard. At Herford, his German hostess was the well-known and influential Countess Elisabeth, Abbess of Herford.

In 1676, Penn became one of the trustees of the western half of New Jersey. By that time there were only a smattering of colonists, mainly Dutch, Swedish, and Danish, in the area that was to become Pennsylvania, Delaware, and New Jersey. Penn began to actively encourage Quakers from England and Wales to go to America. Penn's efforts paid off; in 1677 the ship *Kent* arrived in the Delaware River with two hundred settlers who would found the town of Burlington.

His successes in England and Wales no doubt inspired Penn to visit the Continent again and in 1677 Penn made his second, rather extensive trip to Holland and Germany. His companions as far as Herford in Germany were Robert Barclay (1648-1690), George Keith (1639-1716), and Benjamin Furly (1636-1716).

Robert Barclay, who was a distant cousin of the Countess Elisabeth in Herford, used his increasing influence with his cousin to provide access to other parties along the trip, notably the Countess' brother Karl I, Ludwig, who was Elector Palatine from 1648-1680. The 1677 trip was actually two circular journeys (see Tables 4.1 and 4.2), shown on a sketch map published in the 1981 reference by M.M. Dunn and R.S. Dunn. There are some inaccuracies in the Dunn sketch map, which shows Bacharach on the wrong side of the Rhine and a misspelling of Duisburg. Nonetheless, it is a good index map which one may use to calculate travel times during this period.

ELISABETH (1618-1680), PFALZGRÄFFIN BEI RHEIN. On both of Penn's 1677 circuits the small village of Herford, Germany, was a key stopping point for Penn and his party. On the hill above the village stood the famous Convent of the noted Abbess of Herford, Elisabeth, Pfalzgräffin bei Rhein. The Countess Elisabeth was born in Heidelberg on December 26, 1618, and died in Herford on October 8, 1680. She was the daughter of Friedrich V (1596-1632), the "Winter King," and Elisabeth (1596-1662) of the royal Stuart family of England. Countess Elisabeth was also a granddaughter of Princess Luise Juliane (1576-1644) of the royal Oranien (Orange) family of Holland.

Elisabeth never married although she had several proposals. In at least one case, differences of opinion in religious beliefs prevented the proposal from being accepted. In 1661, Elisabeth's cousin, Friedrich Wilhelm, Prince of Brandenburg, nominated her to be co-regent of the Convent at Herford. Thus, when her cousin Elisabeth Luise, Countess of Zweibrücken, who was Abbess, died in 1667, Elisabeth, Pfalzgräffin bei Rhein, became the sole regent.

In this position of authority, Elisabeth exercised strong influence through family ties over central German politics and religious matters. Although basically of Reformed belief, she was sympathetic toward minority beliefs, notably toward the Labadists and, to some extent, the Quakers. In 1670, a significant number, perhaps 300 to 400 Labadists, in fact moved from Amsterdam and other places to Herford. However, most of them left Herford again two years later in 1672.

Elisabeth was apparently equally fluent in German, Dutch, and English. She carried on much correspondence with such notables as William Penn, the French mathematician Rene Descartes (1596-1650), the Dutch astronomer Christian Huygens (1629-1695), the German mathematician Baron Gottfried Wilhelm Leibnitz (1646-1716), and numerous other prominent academicians.

TABLE 4.1
PENN'S FIRST CONTINENT TRIP, 1677

Approx. Km to:	Penn's Spelling	Modern Day Spelling	Arrival Date	Remarks
0.0	Briel	Briel	26-Jul	by boat
16.5	Rotterdam	Rotterdam	28	by boat
28.8	Leyden	Leiden	31	by boat
27.8	Haerlem	Haarlem	1-Aug.	(probably by boat)
18.5	Amsterdam	Amsterdam	2	(probably by boat)
18.2	Naerden	Naarden	6	by boat
194.2	Osnabrug	Osnabrueck	8	by post-wagon
46.2	Herwerden	Herford	9	
44.8	Paderborn	Paderborn	13	
61.6	Cassel	Kassel	15	by open cart
148.8	Franckfurt	Frankfurt	20	
54.0	Worms	Worms	23	
11.2	Crisheim	Kriegsheim	23	by coach
14.0	Franckenthal	Frankenthal	25	on foot
10.0	Manheim	Mannheim	26	on foot
16.8	Worms	Worms	26	by boat
11.2	Crisheim	Kriegsheim	26	on foot
11.2	Worms	Worms	27	
38.8	Mentz	Mainz	28	by overnight boat
30.8	Franckfurt	Frankfurt	28	by open cart
30.8	Mentz	Mainz	29	by boat
41.0	Hampach	N. Heimbach	29	by boat
84.0	Treissig	Breisig	30	by boat
63.0	Coelln	Koeln	31	(probably by boat)
55.2	Duysbergh	Duisburg	2-Sept.	by boat
10.0	Holton	Holten	3	on foot
17.3	Wesel	Wesel	4	(?post-wagon)
18.8	Rees	Rees	5	(?post-wagon)
13.8	Emmerick	Emmerich	5	(?post-wagon)
10.0	Cleve	Kleve	5	
19.0	Nimmegen	Nijmegen	7	wagon (?post-wagon)
57.5	Utrecht	Utrecht	8	by wagon
35.3	Amsterdam	Amsterdam	8	by wagon?

1259.1 kms (782.3 miles)

MODE OF TRAVEL. Penn's first circuit in 1677 was from July 26 to September 8 and included the cities shown in Table 4.1.

This amazing trip of some forty-four days covered a distance of about 1,259.3 km (782.5 miles). Discounting ten days for extended stops in Amsterdam, Herford, Frankfurt, Köln, and Kleve, Penn averaged more than thirty-seven km (twenty-three miles) per day, using a variety of modes of transportation. In those days, a good average daily speed varied between twenty-seven and sixty kms (i.e., between 16.8 and 37.3

TABLE 4.2
PENN'S SECOND CONTINENT TRIP, 1677

Approx. Km to:	Penn's Spelling	Modern Day Spelling	Arrival Date	Remarks
0.0	Amsterdam	Amsterdam	8-Sept.	
31.8	Horn	Hoorn	10	by boat
17.0	Enck-huysen	Enkhuizen	10	by wagon
32.0	Worckum	Workum	10	by boat
21.3	Harlingen	Harlingen	10	by wagon
25.0	Leuwarden	Leeuwarden	12	by boat
2.8	Wiewart	Wieuwerd	12	by wagon
26.0	Lippenhusen	Lippehuizen	13	
37.3	Groningen	Groningen	14	by wagon
26.8	Delfzyl	Delfzijl	15	by boat
19.0	Emdgen	Emden	16	by boat
22.0	Leer	Leer	n/a	
106.8	Bremen	Bremen	18	?post-wagon
106.8	Herwerden	Herford	21	?post-wagon
171.6	Wesel	Wesel	27	by post-wagon
27.3	Duysbergh	Duisberg	28	?post-wagon
25.2	Dusseldorp	Duesseldorf	29	?post-wagon
32.0	Ceulon	Koeln	30	?post-wagon
32.0	Dusseldorp	Duesseldorf	2-Oct.	by boat
52.5	Wesel	Wesel	3	by boat?
35.2	Cleve	Kleve	5	"post-carr"
30.4	Nimmegen	Nijmegen	6	?post-wagon
92.0	Utrecht	Utrecht	6	?post-wagon
56.4	Amsterdam	Amsterdam	7	by night-boat
59.2	Leyden	Leiden	11	
22.0	Hague	The Hague	12	?post-wagon
31.6	Rotterdam	Rotterdam	12	?post-wagon
16.5	Briel	Briel	n/a	by boat?

1158.5 kms (719.9 miles)

miles) per hour, with the higher speeds being by horseback. Considerable portions of Penn's trip were by barge along the Rhine, traveling, as related elsewhere, about 3.5 km/hr (2.2 miles/hr). Penn's second circuit in 1677 was from September 8 to October 12, and included the cities cited in Table 4.2.

This second circuit of some thirty-five days duration, covered a distance of about 1,158.5 km (719.5 miles). On this trip, Penn averaged more than forty-six km (28.8 miles) per day.

By the late 17th century, there was a fairly elaborate network of postal services across Europe, connecting virtually all of the cities and major towns. No doubt, Penn took advantage of the Imperial postal system in his travels as he mentions using the "post-wagon" in a number of his letters. The postal system was designed initially as a diplomatic courier service and was run on fixed time schedules. For example, the schedule across Europe, between Brussels and Vienna, was 5 1/2 days in the summer and 6 1/2 days in the winter.

Penn also mentions using "night-boats." For trading purposes and the regular transportation of passengers, there was a systematic schedule of special ferries plying the rivers and numerous canals of the Netherlands, as well as the Rhine in Germany. These boats were smallish sailing boats with one or two masts. They often sailed at night. In Germany, it was one thing to sail or float down the Rhine and quite another matter to go up the Rhine against the strong current, particularily upstream from Köln. It has been estimated that for a fairly large boat of 150 tons either ten to twelve horses or eighty to ninety men were required to move the boat upstream. Smaller boats could make some headway sailing against the current as far east as Koblenz by tacking back and forth if a good wind was in their favor, which it normally was.

PENN'S EVANGELICAL ACTIVITIES. William Penn undertook his extensive travels for the dual purpose of evangelicalization and the recruiting of families to settle colonies in New Jersey, and, later, in what were to be named Delaware and Pennsylvania.

However, his evangelical successes on the Continent were limited and restricted mainly to small German villages like Krisheim (Crisheim) and Krefeld (Crevelt) which already had small but flourishing colonies of Mennonites.

No doubt some interest was gained in places like Homburg (near Frankfurt, Germany), and Bacharach, along the Rhine, which had Huguenot refugees, even though Penn did not actually stop at these places. At many villages, he left evangelical books or pamphlets for the local public to read and to disperse.

During his first 1677 circuit, Penn was in Frankfurt on August 20-22, and again on August 28. This stop was ostensibly to make contact with the local Piëtists, some of whose forebearers were refugees from the Low Countries. During the years 1666-1686, the Frankfurt Piëtists were led by Philipp Jakob Spener.

THE SETTLING OF PENNSYLVANIA. In 1680, Penn was part of an association which purchased the province of East Jersey and stimulated further migration to that area. In 1681, Penn gained the rights to the province of Pennsylvania as a credit against large loans by Penn's father to the King of England, who was then Charles II (reigned 1660-1685).

About April, 1681, Penn issued the first public announcement concerning *Some Account of the Province of Pennsilvania,* in London. The first detailed plan for the settlement of Pennsylvania was devised by him in July, 1681. During the months of July to September, 1681, Penn traveled across southern England, selling land in Pennsylvania at a rapid rate: about 300,000 acres to some 250 individual purchasers who were mainly Quaker merchants, tradesmen, and properous farmers from the vicinity of London and Bristol.

The ship *Bristol Factor* sailed from London in December, 1681 with the first load of Penn's settlers. In 1682, at least twenty-three ships sailed from England for Pennsylvania with English, Irish, and Welsh settlers. These ships contained an estimated 800 families or some 1,800 to 2,000 individuals, many of whom were Quakers.

PENN'S TRIPS TO AMERICA. Penn himself went to Philadelphia in late 1682 aboard the ship *Welcome*, arriving there in sixty days. Of the 100 or so Quakers aboard the *Welcome*, some thirty died of smallpox during the trip. Penn's first stay in America lasted only a year and ten months.

By the end of 1684, there were an estimated 7,000 persons in the Delaware and Pennsylvania colonies, mostly from the British Isles, but with significant numbers from Germany, Holland, and Scandinavia.

In 1685, Penn's old friend and mentor, the Catholic Duke of York, succeeded to the throne of England as James II, who reigned only from 1685 to 1688. Having returned to England by this time, Penn used his unlikely influence with the Catholic King to secure the release from prison of some 1,300 Quakers.

Penn's third and final evangelistic trip to Holland and Germany was made in June to August, 1686. Relatively little is known of this trip. It is recorded, however, that he made little publicized visits to Prince Willem III of Oranien in The Hague. Penn also went to Amsterdam, and to Utrecht, and to unspecified places in Germany.

After the reign of James II the mood of the English public was decidedly anti-Catholic and Prince Willem III of Oranien of the Netherlands, who was Calvinistic, succeeded him, reigning simultaneously over the Netherlands and over England as William III (1689-1702).

Penn's alliance with the Catholic James II now created problems for him. In the following several years, Penn was annually brought to trial for "treason" and periodically imprisoned.

By 1690, Penn's personal influence, both in America, England, and in Ireland was waning, as was his financial well-being. Penn's second trip to Philadelphia was in December, 1699, where he arrived after a lengthy ocean voyage of ninety-two days. He stayed in Pennsylvania until late 1701, and then returned to England.

Penn continued his evangelistic activities in England until about 1712, when he became too ill to govern his affairs. He died in 1718.

THE PENN LEGEND. The legend of William Penn, of course, lives on, not only in the name of the state, but more importantly in the introduction of millions of 16th century English, Dutch, and Germans to the possibilities of migration to a new land where there was the promise of religious freedom as well as boundless economic opportunity.

REFERENCES

Anonymous, 1760, "William Penn." In *Biographia Britannica*. London, vol. 5, p. 3317-3324.
This important encyclopedia was reprinted by Georg Olms Verlag, Hildesheim, 1969.

Anonymous, 1888, "William Penn." In *Appleton's Encyclopedia of American Biography*, vol. IV, p. 712-717.

Braithwaite, W. C., 1912, *The Beginnings of Quakerism.*. Macmillan & Co. Ltd., London, 562 p.

Bronner, E. B. & David Fraser (eds.), 1986, *The Papers of William Penn. Vol. V: William Penn's Published Writings, 1660-1726. An Interpretive Bibliography*. Univ. Pennsylvania Press, Phila. 576 p., 135 illus.

Croese, Gerhard, 1696, *Historia Quakeriana (etc.)*. Amsterdam, 580 p., 2nd ed.
The first edition was published in Latin in 1695; there was also a 1696 edition published in German in Berlin.

Dunn, M. M., & R. S. Dunn (eds.), 1981, *The Papers of William Penn, Vol. I, 1644-1679*. Univ. Pennsylvania Press, Phila., 703 p., illus.
_____, & _____, 1982, *ibid*. Vol. II, 1680-1684. Ibid, 710 p., illus.
_____, & _____. 1986, *The World of William Penn*. Ibid, 438 p.

Horle, C. W., et al (eds.), 1987, *The Papers of William Penn, Vol. IV, 1701-1718*. Univ. Pennsylvania Press, Phila., 840 p., illus.

Hull, W. I., 1937, *William Penn, A Topical Biography*. Oxford University Press., London, 362 p., illus., genealogy chart.

Kelsey, R. W., 1934, "William Penn." In *Dictionary of American Biography*, Vol. XIV, p. 433-437.

Otto, Heinrich, 1972, *Werden und Wesen des Quäkertums und Seine Entwicklung in Deutschland*. Sensen-Verlag, Vienna, 498 p.

Rigg, J. M., 1895, "William Penn." In *Dictionary of National Biography*. London, vol. XLIV, p. 311-320.

Roach, H. B., (ed.), 1967, "The Family of William Penn." *Pennsylvania Genealogical Mag.* Vol. XXV, no. 2, p. 69-95
Notes two wives, sixteen children; the Penn name not descended.

Ryerson, R. A., 1981, "William Penn's Commissioners." *Pennsylvania Genealogical Mag.* Vol. XXXII, no. 2, p. 95-117.

Seidensticker, Oswald, 1878, "William Penn's travels in Holland and Germany in 1677." *Penn. Mag. Hist. & Biogr.* Phila., vol. 2, no. 3, p. 237-282,
This is a very succinct account.

Soderlund, Jean (ed.), 1983, *William Penn and the Founding of Pennsylvania. A Documentary History.* Univ. Pennsylvania Press, Phila., 380 p., 25 illus.

Vipont, Elfrida, 1960, *The Story of Quakerism.* The Bannisdale Press, London, 310 p., illus. (2nd ed.).

Wokeck, M. S., et al (eds.), 1986, *The Papers of William Penn, Vol. III, 1685-1700.* Univ. Pennsylvania Press, Phila., 796 p.

RISHEIM. THE FIRST QUAKER MISSIONARY to go to Krisheim (then called Griesheim), was William Ames in 1657. During the grape harvest of 1661, Ames and some of the others (perhaps William Caton, George Rolf, and Benjamin Furly) spent several months there helping with the harvest and converting some seven or eight families of the local Mennonite community to Quakerism, among them the Hendricks Family we discussed in Part I. The names of the other families are listed below and in Table 4.3 on the next page.

THE KRISHEIM QUAKERS OF 1657-1685. In recent historical research, the local German historian Paul Michel (1965/66, 1981) reviewed the primary records of the "Kriegsheim" Quakers. Today, those records, located in the Badisches Generallandesarchiv at Karlsruhe, involve the years 1664, 1670, 1677, 1684, and 1685. Michel quoted names of the following Quakers:

Johann Cassel (Johannes Cassel)
Catharina Ebertsen
Conrad Gebhardts' widow Agnes
Johann Gebhardts
Herderich Girretsen (probably Hendrick Gerrits)
Jan Henderiksen
Gerret Hendricus (Gerhardt Henrich; Gerhardt Hendricks)
Agnes Jakobsen
Hans Plibus Laubauch (Philipp Laubach)
Stoffel Murett (Christoffel Morett)
Joerg Schuhmacher (Schumacher; Georg Schuhmacher)
Peter Schuhmacher (Schumacher)
Hans Peter Umstadt

The Michel lists tally to a great degree with the compilation of the American historian Wm. I. Hull (1935), which is tabulated as Table 4.3 on the next page.

But note that there is considerable variation in orthography, as might be expected from the transcription of 17th century hand-written records. In addition, Hull was prone to translating names into Dutch.

The key archives in Karlsruhe show that the spelling used by Michel may be more reliable insofar as several names (Ebertsen, Girretsen, Henderiksen, and Jakobsen) definitely end with the suffix "-sen". Michel may also be correct in assuming that this suffix could be related to a Dutch origin, although it is common also in certain Low German speaking areas.

TABLE 4.3: MANUSCRIPT RECORDS OF THE KRISHEIM QUAKERS
(taken from Hull, 1935, p. 266, 276, 286, 289, 291-92, et seq.)

Names	1658-60	1663-64	1666	1670	1684	Deceased
Johanes Cassel	o	o	o	o	x	after 1684
(Johannes Castle)						
Velter Eberten	o	x	o	o	o	before 1664
Conrad Gerhard	o	o	o	o	o	unknown
Johannes Gerhard' s widow	o	o	o	o	o	unknown
Hendrick Gerrits	o	x	x	o	x	after 1684
(Hendricsz Gerrits; Henrich Gerhards)						
Jan Hendriks	x	x	x	o	o	after 1666
(John Hendricksz)						
Gerrit Hendricks	o	o	o	x	o	ca. 1691
(Gerhardt Hendricks; Gerret Hendricus)						
Jacob Jansen	x	x	o	o	o	before 1664
(John Johnson, his widow Agnes)						
Hans Philip Laubach	x	x	o	x	o	after 1670
(John Philip Laubeck; Hans Plibus Laubach)						
Christopher Morett (Morrell, Murrett)	x	x	x	x	x	after 1684
(Christoffel Morrell; Stofell Morett)						
Joerg Schumacher	x	x	x	x	x	ca. 1684
(Georg; George Shoemaker)						
Peter Schumacher (the Elder)	x	x	x	x	x	1707
(Peter Shoemaker)						
Hans Peter Umstat	o	o	o	o	o	unknown

Key: x = on record; o = no record

THE KRISHEIM MENNONITES OF 1664-1685. From the primary records of the Badisches Generallandesarchiv at Karlsruhe, Michel (1965/66, 1981) cites also the following Mennonite names for the period 1664-1685:

Gerhard Becker
Heinrich Blom (Henrich Blöhm)
Matthes Bonn (Mathias Bonn; brother-in-law of the Quaker Peter Schumacher)
Peter Buchholts (Peter Buchholtzer)
Gilles Cassel
Johannes Cassel (became a Quaker after 1664)
Simon Cassel
Valtin Eberts
Peter Engers
Johann Gebhard
Hans Gram
Nikolaus Gram
Valetin Hütwohl
Vollmar Janssen
Peter Lüster Erben (Peter Lüster's heirs)
Arnold Schumacher (brother of the Quaker Peter Schuhmacher)
Peter Schuhmacher's foster son Peter (actually Rohr Otto)

The Schuhmacher/Bonn family relationships are obviously taken from Niepoth (1956, 1957), although this source is not cited by Michel. It is interesting to note that others, or perhaps many, of the early Krisheim Quakers were closely related to the Mennonites of the same area.

The relationship between "Gilles" Cassel, Johannes Cassel, and Simon Cassel listed above is not clear. This Gilles Cassel undoubtably is Ylles Cassel who was born ca. 1618 and died ca. 1681. He was a Mennonite minister at Krisheim beginning at least as early as 1665. Descendants of Ylles Cassel went to America about 1717 led by a grandson, Hupert Cassel.

GERMANTOWN IMMIGRANTS FROM KRISHEIM OF 1685-1686. With the Treaty of Westphalia in 1648, three basic religious groups were recognized in the German States, namely: The Catholics, the Lutherans, and the Reformed. The lesser religious minorities were tolerated only in certain states and then to a limited degree.

The Krisheim Quakers, in refusing to pay taxes to support the King's armies, had property confiscated at various times. In addition, they received little support from other religious groups in the area, especially from the Lutherans and from the Catholics, or, on occasion, even from the Mennonites and the Jews. Consequently, the few Quaker families remaining in Krisheim in 1685 decided to emigrate. It was their lucky fate to escape just ahead of the rampaging armies of Louis XIV who began in 1688 the so-called War of the League of Augsburg which lasted until 1697. During this War, virtually all of the Palatinate was decimated and the population greatly reduced.

An interesting article by Roach (1970) reviews the 1685-86 passenger lists cited in the 1884 anonymous publication of the *Pennsylvania Magazine History & Biography*. Roach correctly surmises that these lists were first printed in 1881 in a book titled *The History of Chester County*. Variants of the lists were also printed in 1885 and in 1887. According to Roach, none of the transcripts were "verbatim et literatum." Roach further states that two unequal 17th century manuscript copies exist, both in the handwriting of the English Quaker Phineas Pemberton who went to Pennsylvania in 1682 and died there in 1701. Roach attempts to correct the transcription of Pemberton's handwriting, but makes no allowance for the horrible phonetic English spellings.

Although the records are unclear, it appears that the original manuscript of the passenger lists in question was done by James Claypoole who went from London to Pennsylvania in 1683 and died in Germantown in 1687.

All of the publications listed in the attached bibliography have been reviewed in detail. The list of the Krisheim immigrants to Germantown in America is here interpreted as follows:

October, 1685 (Ship: the *Francis and Dorothy*)
Gerrit Hendricks, wife Maria; sons Willem and Lambert; daughter Sarah
Peter Schuhmacher, wife Sarah; son Peter; daughters Mary, Frances, and Gertrude
Heivert Papen, a bachelor (actually from Mühlheim/Ruhr)
Hans Peter Umstadt, wife Barbara; son Johan; daughters Margaret and Eve
Heinrich Buchholtz, wife Maria (both probably from Krisheim)

March, 1686 (Ship: the *Jeffries*)
Johannes Cassel, wife unnamed; sons Arnold and Peter; daughters Elizabeth, Mary, and Sarah
Sarah Schuhmacher (widow of Georg); sons Georg, Abraham, Isaac, and Benjamin; daughters Barbara, Susanna, and Elizabeth.

Thus, the Krisheim contingent in early Germantown was composed of eleven adults and thirty-three children. This group comprised some 25% of settlers living in Germantown during the period 1683-1690.

THE KREFELD QUAKERS. Another Mennonite community in Germany, the one at Krefeld, near the Dutch-Germany border, eventually came under the influence of the Quaker evangelists.

One of the early leaders of the Mennonite group in Krefeld was Hermann op den Graeff, four of whose grandchildren, Hermann, Abraham, Dirck, and Margrit, converted to Quakerism about 1679-80 and were among the so-called thirteen original Germantown (Pennsylvania) colonists in 1683.

THE THIRTEEN ORIGINAL GERMANTOWN COLONISTS. This much publicized group of "13 Dutch Quakers" from Krefeld arrived in October, 1683, shortly after Pastorius. They were thus considered founders of Germantown, albeit a very small minority as compared to the large numbers of English and Irish Quakers already in Philadelphia and surrounding areas. Most of these so-called "Thirteen Original Founders," but not all, were Quakers. The group is supposed to have contained about thirty-four "full fares."

Table 4.4 on the next page gives the list of the thirteen heads of families. For the record, the spelling of their names is copied from that of four prominent German historians, notably Francis Daniel Pastorius from about 1685, Oswald Seidensticker from 1878, Friedrich Kapp from 1884, and Wilhelm Niepoth from 1953.

Even considering the fact that the umlauts (ä, ö, ü) are replaced by 'ae', 'oe', and 'ue', there is considerable divergence in interpretation even by native Germans as to how these names were, or should have been spelled.

The American historian William I. Hull created quite a discussion in 1935, and subsequent years, when he termed the thirteen original founders of Germantown as being: (1) founders, (2) Dutch, and (3) Quakers. Later German historians never accepted the concept of residents of Krefeld as being Dutch.

Hull's statement was based to a large degree upon a Krefeld marriage certificate of 1681 which confirmed the marriage of Derick Isacks (op den Graeff) and Noeleken Vijten. The certificate, which was signed by the majority of those emigrating to America, was written in Dutch. Hull also noted that virtually all of the group of thirteen had Dutch (sounding) names.

TABLE 4.4
COMPARISON OF SPELLING
"The Thirteen Original Germantown Colonists"

Pastorius' Spelling ca. 1695 (1)	Seidensticker's Spelling 1878	F. Kapp's Spelling in 1884 (1)	W. Niepoth's Spelling in 1953 (2)
Dirck op den Graeff	Dirk op den Graeff	Dietrich op de Graeff	Dirk Isaaks op dem Graeff
Abraham op den Graeff	Abraham op den Graeff	Abraham op de Graeff	Abraham Isaaks op dem Graef
Herman op den Graeff	Herman op den Graeff	Hermann op de Graeff	Hermann Isaaks op dem Graef
Lenerts Arets	Lenert Arets	Leonhard Arets	Leonard Arets
Thones Kunders	Tunes Kunders	Teunis Kuenders	Toenis Kunders
Reinert Tisen	Reinert Tisen	Rheinhard Theisen	Reiner Theissen
William Strepers	Wilhelm Strepers	Wilhelm Strepers	Wilhelm Strepers
Jan Lensen	Jan Lensen	Jan Lensen	Johann Lenssen
Peter Keurlis	Peter Keurlis	Peter Kuirlis	Peter Kurlis
Jan Simon	Jan Simens	Jan Simens	Johann Simons
Johannes Bleickers	Johannes Bleickers	Johann Bleikers	Johannes Bleickers
Abraham Tunis	Abraham Tunes	Abraham Tuenies	Abraham Tunes
Jan Luken	Jan Luecken	Jan Luycken	Johan Lucken

Remarks:
(1) as cited in Learned, 1908, p. 130
(2) as cited in Luken, 1980, p. 192-193

HERMANN OP DEN GRAEFF (1585-1642). The op den Graeff ancestor, Hermann, was born November 26, 1585 at Aldekerk, a small village near the German-Dutch border, but on the German side; although the prefix "op den" indicates a name of Dutch origin. He was a citizen of Kempen (near Krefeld) in 1605 where he married a Mennonite maid whose name was Grietjen Pletjes. Her father's name was Pletjes Driessen; he stemmed from Kempen.

Hermann op den Graeff was in Krefeld by 1608. In Krefeld, a city long noted for its weaving industry, he became a prominent fabric and linen dealer. He was one of the leading Mennonites signing the Dordrecht Confession in 1632.

Hermann sired 18 children, nine of whom died early. The surviving nine children consisted of three sons and six daughters. One of those sons was Isaac op den Graeff (1616-79) who was the father of the four so-called thirteen original Germantown colonists, Hermann, Abraham, Dirck, and Margrit op den Graeff mentioned above.

Hermann op den Graeff the Elder died in Krefeld on December 27, 1642; his wife died on January 7, 1643. In America, his numerous descendants carried multiple versions of spelling of the name. There are still descendants living in Germantown, Pennsylvania, under the spelling of Updegraf.

The semiannual publication *Krefeld Immigrants and Their Descendants* (Sacramento, Ca.) regularly carries short articles on the op den Graeff family in its multiple spellings.

THE MYSTERY OF THE STAINED GLASS WINDOW PANE. There is extant today, a famous stained glass window pane from the house of Hermann op den Graeff, the Elder; its legend was noted in publications by Rembert (1899), Niepoth (1939), Nieper (1940), Hertzler (1981), and by Rotthoff (1981). None of the printed versions, are identical. The original text is in a Lower German Rhine dialect. Professor Klaus Weissenberger of the Department of German & Slavic Studies, Rice University, translated the Rotthoff version into High German and then further into English. The translation, kindly given by Professor Weissenberger, is as follows:

Gottesfuerchtig, fromm	Fearing God, being pious
und gut von Sitten,	and having proper behavior,
lustig, freundlich	being happy, friendly
und wahr im Reden,	and true in speech,
(das) ist christlich und	that is Christian and
gefaellt dem Herrn,	is pleasing to the Lord,
bringt Gunst und setzt	will bring good will and endow
manchen in grosse Ehren.	many a person with great honor.
Hermen op	Hermen op
den Graff	den Graff
und Gretchen	and Gretchen
seine Hausfrau	his wife
Anno 1630.	Anno 1630.

By 1894, the stained glass window pane was in the Kaiser-Wilhelm Museum at Krefeld. In 1940, the pane was in the Krefelder Heimat Museum at Burg Linn. During World War II, the pane mysteriously disappeared, only to turn up a few years ago at an auction in Stuttgart, Germany. Fortunately, the pane was purchased privately and returned to Krefeld.

REFERENCES

Boecken, Charlotte, 1982, "'Dutch Quaker' aus Krefeld, die (Mit) Gründer Germantowns 1683." In *Die Heimat*, Krefeld, Jahrg. 53, p. 15-23, 1 pl.
Repeats the well worn argument that the original Germantown settlers were neither Dutch nor Quaker in contrast to the ideas generated by William I. Hull.
This paper was part of a series published to commemorate the 300th anniversary of the first relatively large group of German settlers migrating to America. See also the 1982 paper by Rotthoff listed below.

Buschbell, Gottfried, 1953, *Geschichte der Stadt Krefeld*. Staufen Verlag, Krefeld. Bd. I (1953), 257 p., illus. (?1104-1794); Bd. II (1954), 498 p., illus. (?1794-1870).
_____, & Carl Müller, 1956, *Krefeld: in Deutsches Städtebuch*. Bd. III, Nordwest-Deutschland. 3, Landschaftsverband Rheinland, p. 278-284, W. Kohlhammer Verlag, Stuttgart.
The above two publications are extensive histories of the City of Krefeld.

Heesch, Albert, 1975, "Die Mennoniten und die Anfänge der Wirtschaft am unteren Niederrhein." In *Die Heimat*, Krefeld, Jahr. 46, p. 65-71, illus.

Hertzler, H. A., 1981, *Mennonitengemeinde Krefeld: Auftrag des Kleinen Konsistoriums der Mennonitengemeinde Krefeld*. 31 p.

Hull, William I, 1970, *William Penn and the Dutch Quaker Migration to Pennsylvania*. Genealogical Publ. Co., Baltimore, 445 p.
This is an oft cited reprint of Swarthmore Coll. Monograph No. 2, dated 1935. It is an extensive documentary of 17th century German Mennonites and Quakers.

Kannegieter, J. Z., 1971, *Geschiedenis van de Vroegere Quakergemeenschap Te Amsterdam*. Schelteman & Holkema N.V., Amsterdam, 350 p.
Contains an English summary on p. 321-327 of the early Quakers in Amsterdam.

Learned, M. D., *The Life of Francis Daniel Pastorius, The Founder of Germarmantown*. W. J. Campbell Co., Philadelphia, 324 p., illus.

Motl, H. J., 1983, *Krefeld und die Mennoniten*. Druckerei Steinbacher GmbH & Co. KG, Krefeld, 85 p., illus.

Nieper, Friedrich, 1940, *Die ersten deutschen Auswanderer von Krefeld nach Pennsylvanien.* C. Brugel & Sohn, Ansbach (Buchhandlung des Erziehungsvereins, Neukirchen Kreis, Moers), 407 p.

Niepoth, Wilhelm, 1939, "Die Mennonitengemeinde in Krefeld und ihre Beziehungen zu ihren Nachbargemeinden." In *Schriftenreihe des Mennonitischen Geschichtsvereins*, Weierhof (Pfalz), Nr. 2, p.131-142, 1 illus.

_____, 1987, (translation of the above article by C. R. Haller): *Krefeld Immigrants and their Descendants*, Sacramento, Calif., Vol. 4, No. 2, p. 43-61
Includes numerous explanatory notes by the translator; see also Errata,1988, vol. 5, no. 1, p. 25-26

_____, 1958, "Evangelische im Kempener Raum." *Schriftenreihe des Landkreises Kempen-Krefeld*, Bd. 6, Thomas Druckerei, Kempen, 130 p.

_____, 1961, "Krefelder Genealogie: Ist in der Erforschung der mennonitischen Familiens Krefelds über das sogenannten Scheutensche Stammbuch hinaus noch weiterzukommen?" *Die Heimat*, Krefeld, Jahrg. 31, p. 116-130
Wilhelm Niepoth has published extensively on the various Mennonite communities in and around Krefeld. His large collection of unpublished manuscripts include several thousand family names and reside in the Stadtarchiv Krefeld.

Pennypacker, S. W., 1880, "The Settlement of Germantown and the causes which led to it." *Pennsylvania Mag. Hist. & Biogr.*, vol. 4, no. 1, p. 1-41.
_____, 1899, *The Settlement of Germantown, Pa.*: Robert A. Tripple, Phila., 416 p., illus.
Samuel Pennypacker, eventually the colorful governor of Pennsylvania, developed an early interest in the early Mennonite communities in Pennsylvania, in part because of his German Mennonite descendancy. His ancestors came from an area northwest of Worms, not far west of the Rhine. The most important of his publications are cited here; see also the National Union Catalogue for holdings.

Rembert, Karl, 1899, *Die "Wiedertäufer" im Herzogtum Julich.* Hermann Heyfelder Verlag (R. Gärtners Verlagsbuchhandlung), Berlin, 632 p.
_____, 1939, "Zur Geschichte der Auswanderung Krefelder Mennoniten nach Nord-Amerika." *Schriftenreihe des Mennonitischen Geschichtsvereins*, Weierhof (Pfalz), Nr. 2, p. 161-183.

Rotthoff, Guido, 1981, "Die Glasgemälde von Hermann op den Graeff." *Die Heimat*, Krefeld, Jahrg. 52, p. 130-131.
_____, 1982, "Die Auswanderung von Krefeld nach Pennsylvanien im Jahre 1683." *Die Heimat*, Krefeld, Jahrg. 53, p. 2-11.

Ruth, J. L., 1983, "A Christian Settlement 'In Antiquam Silvam'." *The Mennonite Quarterly Review*, Vol. 57, No. 4, p. 307-332.
_____, 1984, *Maintaining the Right Fellowship*. Herald Press, Scottdale, Penna., 616 p., illus.
Gives a slightly different translation of the verse of the famous op den Graeff stained glass window pane. Also provides a somewhat different viewpoint on the history of early German migration to America.

Scheibler, H. C., & Karl Wülfrath (eds.), 1939, *Westdeutsche Ahnentafeln*. Verlag Hermann Böhlaus Nachf., Weimar, 650 p., pls. illus.
Contains genealogical tables for leading families in 17th century Krefeld.

 URING HIS FIRST 1677 CIRCUIT, WILLIAM Penn was in Frankfurt on August 20-22, and on August 28. This stop was ostensibly to make contact with the local Piëtists, some of whose forbearers were refugees from the Low Countries. During the years 1666-1686, the Frankfurt Piëtists were led by Philipp Jakob Spener. This group of Piëtists, called the Saalhof group, included ten individuals who would later comprise the "Frankfort Companie," an investment group who would buy large tracts of land in Pennsylvania and thus play an important role in the founding of Germantown.

THE SAALHOF GROUP. During the European religious wars of the mid-16th century, numerous refugees from Flanders decided to relocate. About 1554, many people originally from the Lowlands went to the area of Frankfurt and south along the Rhine to Frankenthal in the Palatinate of Germany. In 1597, a thousand or so of these Flemish refugees moved again, this time from Frankfurt to nearby Hanau. In 1623, many people from Frankenthal also went to Hanau.

It is estimated that by 1660 the population of Frankfurt was comprised of about 14,500 people, of which some 1,200 had ancestors who had originated in the Lowlands. During the period of 1661-98, there was actually a section of Frankfurt called "das Niederländisches Viertel" (Lowlands, or Dutch Quarter).

In the mid 17th century, among these refugees and their descendants a Piëtistic Circle developed, known as the "Saalhof" group. The Saalhof, located on the Saalgasse, was a large building with a half dozen or so residences. (The building was destroyed during World War II; a model is currently in the Historischen Museum in Frankfurt).

The Saalhof group, included, as quoted in the 1908 publication by M. D. Learned, page 122, the following:

Dr. Johann Wilhelm Petersen
his wife Johanna Eleonora von Merlau
Daniel Behagel
Casper Merian
Jakob van der Walle
Abraham Hasevoet
Johann Jacob Schütz
Georg Strauss
Johann Wilhelm Überfeldt
Johann Laurenz

These same ten individuals would later comprise the Frankfort Companie.

Van der Walle, Hasevoet, and Laurenz are Dutch names, probably originally from Rotterdam.

The Behagel family came from West Flanders in the 16th century. Daniel Behagel had been born in Hanau in 1625, but in 1658 was a resident of Frankfurt am Main. In 1661, Daniel Behagel (1625-1698) and his brother-in-law, Jakob van der Walle (d. 1688) received the right to manufacture Fayence (glazed earthenware) in Hanau, and in 1666, they received these same rights in nearby Frankfurt. They had joint interests both in porcelain manufacture and in importing goods of all types.

Caspar Merian (1627-1688) was from the famous Merian Publishing Company. His father, Matthäus Merian the Elder, had been Swiss, but his maternal grandfather, Theodor de Bry, who had laid the foundations of the Merian Publishing Company, had been born in Liege, Belgium. Like the Behagel family, the elder de Bry had left Belgium because of his Protestant beliefs and eventually settled in Frankfurt am Main.

PHILIPP JAKOB SPENER (1635-1705). In 1666, Protestant theologian Philipp Jakob Spener was called to Frankfurt to take leadership of the Saalhof group. About the time William Penn visited Frankfurt in 1677, the Saalhof group included the following:

Dr. Philipp Jakob Spener, spiritual leader
Jakob van der Walle, commercial leader
Johann Jacob Schütz
Christian Fenda, notary
Maximilian Lersner
Eleonore von Merlau
Maria Juliana Bauer

Philipp Jakob Spener was born on January 13, 1635 in Rappottsweiler in Upper Alsace. He attended school in Strassburg (Strasbourg) during the period 1651-53. Subsequently, he was a private tutor to members of the Palatinate nobility, including, among others, the princes Christian II (1637-1717) and his brother Johann Karl (1638-1704).

In the years 1659-62, Spener took courses at the Universities of Basel, Tübingen, and Geneva. About this time he developed a keen interest in heraldry, especially of the noble families in the Palatinate. Spener was a prolific writer whose works included several books on the heraldry of the German nobility.

The year 1663 found Spener occupying various clerical posts in Strassburg. In 1666, he was nominated chief pastor of the Lutheran Church in Frankfurt. In the following years, Spener departed from the main stream of Lutheran thought and was one of the principal promoters of the Piëtistic movement.

One imagines that there was considerable discussion between Penn and Spener in 1677 regarding the comparative results of the Quaker and the Piëtistic movements. At any rate, the Piëtists of Frankfurt supported Penn financially although none of the Piëtists accepted the option of joining Penn's colony in America.

In 1686, Elector Johann Georg, of Saxony, offered Spener the position of first court chaplaincy at Dresden. In 1691, Spener took over the rectorship of the St. Nicolas Church in Berlin and helped found the University of Halle in 1694.

By 1695, the main group of the Lutheran clergy at the University of Wittenberg brought charges against Spener for his involvement in the Piëtistic movement. By the time of Spener's death in 1705, the charges had never been formally brought to court.

THE FRANKFORT COMPANIE. A number of the Saalhof Group went on to organize the Frankfort Companie (later called the German Company and also the High German Company) for the purpose of investing in America. The original members of the Frankfort Companie included:

Jakob van der Walle
Johan Jacob Schütz
Johann Wilhelm Überfeldt
Daniel Behaghel (Behagel)
Georg Strauss
Jan Laurenz
Abraham Hasevoet

Later, Caspar Merian also became a member. However, before long, Merian, Strauss, Laurenz, Überfeldt, and Hasevoet dropped out.

Their shares were bought by:

Francis Daniel Pastorius
Eleonore von Merlau
Balthasar Jawert
Johannes Kemler of Lübeck
Dr. Gerhard von Maastricht (of Duisburg)
Johann Le Brunn (of Wesel)
Thomas van Wijlick (also of Wesel)

Eleonore von Merlau eventually became the wife of the theologian Johann Wilhelm Petersen. Dr. Johann Heinrich Horb married Spener's sister Sophia Caecilia; Horb appears to have been the main initial contact between the Frankfort Companie and its eventual representative in America, Francis Daniel Pastorius. There is, however, no firm evidence that Pastorius, a Lutheran by background, ever formally joined either the Piëtists or the Quakers. None of those listed above for the Frankfort Companie ever went to Pennsylvania except for Pastorius.

Thus, the Frankfort Companie was an alliance of German speaking, Piëtist investors from Frankfurt, Duisberg, Wesel, and Lübeck. Their principal commercial leader was Jakob van der Walle. The Companie eventually was represented in Pennsylvania by Francis Daniel Pastorius (1651-1719) who was resident in Frankfurt in 1682.

In late 1683, Pastorius took a small group of non-investors to Pennsylvania, and thus became a principal founder of Germantown. Under the warrant issued to Pastorius on May 2, 1684, a total of 5,350 acres, constituting Germantown Township, were finally laid out and allotted as shown in Table 4.5. At this time, 200 acres were allotted to Francis Daniel Pastorius, and 150 acres were allotted to Jurian Hartsfelder.

TABLE 4.5
THE GERMANTOWN PURCHASERS AS OF MAY 2, 1684

The Frankfurt Purchasers

Name of Purchaser	Acres
Jacob van de Walle	535
Johann Jacob Schutz	428
Johann Wilhelm Ueberfeldt	107
Daniel Behagel	356-2/3
Georg Strauss	178-1/3
Jan Laurens	535
Abraham Hasevoet	535
	2,675

The Crefeld Purchasers

Name of Purchaser	Acres
Jacob Telner	989
Jan Streypers	275
Dirck Sipman	588
Govert Remke	161
Lenart Arets	501
Jacob Isaacs (van Bebber)	161
	2,675

A more formal agreement establishing the rights of the Frankfort Companie was executed on November 12, 1686. The original acreage was expanded to comprise about 25,000 acres including the 2,675 acres in Germantown Township, 300 acres at Schuykill along the Wissahickon

River, and 22,025 acres in "Faulkners Swamp" (later, around the town of New Hanover). The distribution of the land of the Frankfort Companie members was then as shown in Table 4.6.

TABLE 4.6
FRANKFORT COMPANIE LANDOWNERS AS OF NOV. 12, 1686

Name of Landowner	Acres
Jacob van de Walle	2,500
Jacob van de Walle (formerly Caspar Merian)	833-1/3
Daniel Behagel	1,666-2/3
Johann Jacob Schutz	4,000
Francis Daniel Pastorius (formerly Ueberfeldt)	1,000
Jacob van de Walle	1,666-2/3
Johanna Eleonora von Merlau (formerly Strauss)	1,666-2/3
Daniel Behagel	1,666-2/3
Dr. Gerhard von Maastricht, of Duisberg	1,666-2/3
Dr. Thomas von Wijlick, of Wesel	1,666-2/3
Johannes Lebruen, of Wesel	1,666-2/3
Balthasar Jawert, of Luebeck	3,333-1/3
Johannes Kemler, of Luebeck	1,666-2/3
	25,000

ERMANTOWN, 1683-1709. GERMANTOWN, founded on October 25, 1683, and now a part of the City of Philadelphia, was the first permanent "German" settlement in Pennsylvania. Germantown had Borough status from 1691 to 1707. After 1707, it became a part of Philadelphia for legal purposes, and was incorporated officially into Philadelphia in 1854.

In 1683, the distance between Germantown and Philadelphia was about six miles, or roughly two hours walking through a dense forest. The rocky, hilly terrain of Germantown was bisected by a narrow, crooked Indian trail which eventually became the main, or Germantown Road in the area.

THE FIRST GERMAN COMMUNITY IN PENNSYLVANIA.

Francis Daniel Pastorius (1651-1720) and a small band of six heads of families reached America on August 20, 1683, aboard the ship *America*. They had been dispatched by the "Frankfort Companie" to organize a colony in William Penn's 1681 land grant from the King of England.

The Pastorius group included ten people: five men other than Pastorius, two women, and two children. Their first homes were caves in the banks of the Delaware River. Although Pastorius was the prime organizer of Germantown, he did not actually settle there until almost two years after arriving in America, preferring at first to live in Philadelphia, which was already well populated by English families.

Thirteen families, mostly Quaker families from Krefeld and adjacent Kaldenkirchen in the Lower German Rhine, arrived aboard the ship *Concord* at Chester, near Philadelphia on October 6, 1683. The number of individuals in this group is usually cited at thirty-three full fares, but should actually be counted as forty-two people according to Hocker (1933). There were apparently two births and one death en route or shortly after the group's arrival. Krefeld, about twenty-three kilometers (fifteen miles) northwest of the City of Köln (Cologne in English and French), is noted as being a center of weaving of linen and silk, from the 17th century up to the present time. The technology of weaving was transferred to Germantown by the immigrants.

Thus, the families from the ships *America* with six families, the *Concord* with thirteen families, and the *Francis and Dorothy* with five families, arriving in 1683 and 1685, formed the nucleus of Germantown. They were complemented by twenty-four families from unnamed ships who arrived in 1684 and in 1686. A total of forty-eight families were listed as property owners in Germantown by 1690. Apparent additions to Germantown residents between 1687 and 1691 included about twenty-three heads of families.

In 1684, 5,350 acres of Germantown were laid out and allotted under a warrant issued to Daniel Pastorius (see Table 4.5 on page 138).

In December 29, 1687, a more accurate survey of Germantown Township was made and a patent was granted for the 5,700 acres it was found to contain. The township was then divided into four villages, namely:

Germantown village	2,750 acres
Cresheim	884
Sommerhausen (now Chestnut Hill)	900
Crefeld	1,166

Total	5,700 acres

Although the spelling of the subdivisions is English, the names clearly reflect their common German origin.

The principal individual purchasers of land in Germantown from Krefeld were Jacob Telner, Dirck Sipman, and Jan Streypers, who each purchased 5,000 acres. Jacob Isaacs (van Bebber) from Krefeld is also listed as a "first purchaser" of land in Germantown.

In a survey of the known records, Dunn & Dunn, 1982, vol. 2, p. 630-664, give a list of 589 persons who are cited as having bought 715,437 acres of land in Pennsylvania between July, 1681 and March, 1685. In this list, perhaps 88% were shown as being English with minor numbers being from Ireland, Wales, and Scotland.

The van der Walle (Vandewall) name appears on the well-known map of 1687 by Thomas Holme of the *Province of Pennsilvania* as the "first purchaser" of land in Germantown Township. Van der Walle never went to Pennsylvania himself, nor did any others of the Frankford Companie except for Francis Daniel Pastorius.

Only twenty of these "first purchasers" were from the continent, mainly Germany and the Netherlands. The 1687 map by Thomas Holme shows the location of land owned by about 670 early Pennsylvanians, around Philadelphia. On this map however, names of individuals in Radnor (forty settlements), Haverford (thirty-two settlements), Plymouth, Germantown and Dutch Townships are omitted.

FRANCIS DANIEL PASTORIUS (1651-1720). Pastorius, a Protestant, was attorney for the Frankfort Companie from 1683 to 1700 and it appears that he was largely responsible for the early development of Germantown. In fact, his training and background indicate that he was by far the most literate of the early Germantown settlers.

He had attended four universities (Altdorf, Strassburg, Basel, and Jena) and had command of seven languages: German, Latin, Italian, English, French, Dutch, and Greek. He had also practiced law in Frankfurt am Main before coming to America.

In 1684, Francis Daniel Pastorius was one of three justices in Philadelphia County and he became a member of the Assembly in 1687.

Pastorius was designated Bailiff, or chief officer, of Germantown in 1691-92, and again in 1696-97. Another principal activity was his role as head of the school in Germantown from 1701 to 1718.

GERMANTOWN POPULATION DYNAMICS. In 1689, "Owners of Property" in Germantown numbered forty-seven heads of families (Hocker, 1933, p. 29-30). A second list of Germantown residents is the well-publicized Naturalization List of 1691. Between 1683-1690, about 175 people lived in Germantown, all but eight or ten from either Krefeld or Krisheim. By reference to the third well-known list of early Germantown residents, that is, the Tax List of 1693, there were counted some fifty-two families and about 200 people in Germantown.

By 1701, there were some sixty families, totaling some 230 people (Wolf, 1976, p. 41). Seventy percent of Germantown's original families remained for less than a generation (Wolf, 1976, p. 94). Besides the high mortality rate due to primitive medical facilities, many owners preferred to sell their Germantown holdings for a profit and move to the much larger and more fertile land grants in the western part of what later became Montgomery County. Much of this movement occurred between 1700 and 1710, especially at the time of the large influx of Germans beginning in 1709.

GERMANTOWN RELIGIOUS LIFE. In early Germantown, there were five active religious groups: Quakers, Lutherans, Reformed, Mennonites, and, later, Dunkards.

The earliest of the churches was built by the then dominant Quaker group in 1686, while the Mennonite Meeting House was built in 1708. Quaker meetings began in private homes about 1684. Mennonite meetings were held as early as 1690. During the period 1683-1708, probably no more than 15% of Germantown residents were actually Mennonites.

THE SUSQUEHANNA SUBSCRIBERS, 1696. Beginning about 1682, William Penn (1644-1718) had generated the idea for a second settlement in the Province of Pennsylvania to rival or complement the settlement at Philadelphia. The area Penn chose was the Susquehanna Valley which was strategically located for trade routes. The idea was formally proposed by him in 1690 and again in 1695.

In the spring of 1696, approximately 450 people from Pennsylvania subscribed individual small sums for land on the Susquehanna. This list included twenty-six residents of Germantown whose names read like a horror story in phonetic English spelling. The compiler of the list is uncertain, but may have been the Englishman Samuel Carpenter. The list of Germantown resident-subscribers reads as follows:

TABLE 4.7
SUSQUEHANNA SUBSCRIBERS IN GERMANTOWN, 1696

Spelling as in Wokeck, et al 1986, Vol. III, p. 674-675	More Probable Spelling from Various Sources
Fra: Dannl Pestorus	Francis Daniel Pastorius
Peter Shomaker junior	Peter Schumacher Jr.
Aret Klinken	Arent Klincken
Arnold Cassel	Arnold Cassel
Willm Strepers	Willem Streypers
Johannes Blacker	Johannes Blijkers
Jacob Issac's van bebeme	Jacok Isaacs Van Bebber
Geo: Golschich	Georg Gottschalck
Rinert tisen	Reyner Teissen
Anthony Loofe	Antonij Loof
Jane Luken	Jan Lückens
Geo: Shoemaker	Georg Schumacher
Jemes Kunders	Tünes Kunders
Peter Keurlis	Pieter Keurlis
Abraham Teneson	Abraham Tünes
Walter Simons	Wolter Siemes
Paull Wulfe	Paul Wulff
Isaac Schumaker	Isaac Schumacher
Herfert Pappen	Heivert Papen
Liven Herberkink	Levin Harberdinck
Peter Clever	Peter Klever
Martin Seel	Martin Sellen
Lenart Arets	Lenart Arents
Jan Doeden	Jan Döden
Johannes Kosters	Johannes Kuster
Peter Cassell	Johannes Peter Cassel

At least sixteen of "The Susquehanna Subscribers" were still living in the County of Philadelphia (probably in Germantown) in 1709, with two others known as deceased by 1709. Thus, the Susquehanna Valley was a dismal failure as far as Penn's dream of a new community was concerned. Still, the concept was utilized at a later date in the establishment of the important Pennsylvania communities of Lancaster and Harrisburg.

THE MISSING LINK.

Table 6.8 on page 253 shows documentation for twenty-two ships arriving in Philadelphia in 1682 and twenty-three ships arriving there in 1683. One might assume that similar numbers of ships with passengers arrived on an annual basis during the following four decades. After that immigration substantially increased.

Unfortunately, there are currently known only some scant ship arrival records for Pennsylvania for the period 1684-1727. In the latter year, the Commonwealth of Pennsylvania decreed that, henceforth, lists of "foreigners" (mainly referred to as Germans or Palatines) be recorded. Subsequently, these lists were kept fairly accurately for the period 1727 to 1808 except during and after the Revolutionary War years of about 1776 to 1785.

Thus, for the period of 1684 to 1727, the record of new arrivals in Germantown is very spotty. By deductive reasoning, an approximation of the numbers of arrivals can be made. The often reprinted 1709 Naturalization List of "Germans" is comprised of eighty-two males of which some thirty-seven formed the early Germantown settlers. Of the remaining forty-five on the list, most likely all came to America in the period from 1692-1709. However, there are no known ship's passenger lists to account for this group. The attached references mention early immigrants groups to Pennsylvania as follows:

TABLE 4.8
PARTIAL LIST OF GERMANS TO PENNSYLVANIA, 1684-1719

Year	Remarks
1684	At least one ship, the *Vine*, to Philadelphia.
1685	19 Germans to Philadelphia aboard the *Francis & Dorothy*; at least four other ships to Philadelphia.
1686	15 Germans to Philadelphia aboard the *Jeffries*; at least three other ships to Philadelphia.
1688	At least one ship to Philadelphia, the *Margaret*.
1689-97	No apparent records
1698	Two or more families from Krefeld to Germantown.
1698	Two or more families from Amsterdam to Germantown.
1700	6-8 families (some 30 people) from Hamburg-Altona to Germantown.
1707	At least three adult males from the Palatine to the Germantown/Skippack area (the Kolb brothers).
1709	Two or more families from the Palatine to Germantown, Pa., apparently associated with the large group of "Palatines" numbering about 847 families who settled along the Hudson in N.Y.
1709	"A dozen families," most to Bebbers Town.
1710	Bernese Mennonite refugees to Lancaster Co., Pa.
1717	"3 ships, 363 Palatine German" immigrants to Penna. Most of this group may have been actually from Baden and Württemberg, i.e., east side of the Rhine.
1719	Krefeld Dunkers to Pennsylvania.

By some accounts, 6,000 to 7,000 Palatines arrived in Philadelphia and spread out into the countryside; many probably went to Lancaster County. After 1719, the average rate of "Palatine Germans" is supposed to have been around 2,000 per year. These numbers, however, are not thoroughly documented.

REFERENCES

Anon, 1839, "29 September 1709 Naturalization List, Germans in Pennsylvania." *Colonial Records of Pennsylvania*, vol. 2, p. 493-494

Bender, H. S., 1933, "The Founding of the Mennonite Church in America at Germantown, 1683-1708." *Mennonite Quart. Review*, vol. 7, p. 227-250.

Damon, S. F., 1926, *One line of the Pastorius Family of Germantown, Pa.* Privately published, Cambridge, Mass., 22 p.

Duffin, J. M., 1987-90, "Germantown Landowners, 1683-1714." *Germantown Crier*, Phila., vol. 39, no. 2, p. 37-41; vol. 39, no. 3, p. 62-67; vol. 42, no. 2, p. 37-39; vol. 42, no. 3, p. 63-65; vol. 42, no. 4, p. 85-89 Excellent reference on early Germantown landowners.

Dunn, M. M., & R. S. Dunn (eds.), 1982, *The Papers of William Penn. Vol. II, 1680-1684.* Univ. Pennsylvania Press, Phila., 703 p., illus.

Hocker, E. W., 1933, *Germantown 1683-1933.* Published by the author, Germantown, Pa., 68 p., illus.

Hull, W. I., 1935 (reprinted 1970), *William Penn and the Dutch Quaker migration to Pennsylvania.* Genealogical Publishing Co., Baltimore Md., 445 p., illus. Cites 1691 and 1709 Naturalization Lists, 1693 Tax List; p. 417-418, 420-421.

Keyser, N. H., 1906, *Old Historic Germantown.* Pennsylvania German Society, Lancaster, Pa., 68 p., illus.
_____, Kain, C. H., Garber, J. P., & H. F., McCann, 1907, *History of Old Germantown.* Horace F. McCann Publ., Germantown Pa., 453 p.

Learned, M. D., 1908, *The Life of Francis Daniel Pastorius.* W. J. Campbell Co., Philadelphia, Pa., 324 p., illus.

Lippincott, H. M., 1923, *An account of the People called Quakers in Germantown.* Philadelphia: Burlington, N.J.

Miller, M. L., 1983, "Germantown residents naturalized in 1691." *Mennonite Family History*, vol. II, no. 3, Elverson, Pa., p. 102-104

Michel, Paul, 1965/66, *Täufer, Mennoniten und Quäker in Kriegsheim bei Worms.* Der Wormsgau, Worms am Rhein, Siebenter Bd., p. 41-52

Michel, Paul, 1981, "Täufer, Mennoniten und Quäker in Kriegsheim." In *Chronik von Monsheim*, p. 180-195, Druckerei Kunke GmbH, Monsheim bei Worms.

Niepoth, Wilhelm, 1953, "Die Abstammung der 13 Auswanderer von Krefeld nach Pennsylvanien (1683) in Lichte niederrheinischer Quellen." *Die Heimat*, Krefeld, Jahrg. 24, p. 2-9.

_____, 1980, (translation of the above article by J. B. Lukens): *Pennsylvania Genealogical Mag.*, Vol. 31, No. 3, p. 191-207, map.

_____, 1956, "Die Wanderungen und die Wandlung der Mennonitenfamilie Schuhmacher." *Der Mennonit*, Frankfurt am Main (Feb. 1956), p. 27-28.

_____1957, "From Kriegsheim to Pennsylvania: origin and career of the brothers Peter and George Shoemaker, of Kriegsheim, in the Palatinate." *Germantown Crier*, vol. IX, no. 1, March, 1957, p. 7-9, 26 Translation of the above article was by Edward W. Hocker.

Pennypacker, S. W., 1883, *The Settlement of Germantown, Pa.*. Robert A. Tripple, Philadelphia, Pa., 416 p., illus.

_____, 1899, *The Settlement of Germantown, Pa.* William J. Campbell Co., Philadelphia, Pa., 310 p., illus.

Roach, H. B., 1970, "The Philadelphia and Bucks County Registers of Arrivals." In Sheppard, W. L., Jr., (ed.), *Passengers and Ships Prior to 1684.* Genealogical Publ. Co., Baltimore, p. 159-167. Reprinted 1992 by Heritage Books, Inc., Bowie, Maryland.
Repeats phonetic spellings of "Garret Hendrix" and "Henry Pookeholes."

Seidensticker, Oswald, 1876, *Geschichte der Deutschen gesellschaft von Pennsylvanien von der zeit grundung, 1764 bis zum jahre 1876. I.* Kohler, Phila. 336 p.

_____, 1883, *Die erste Deutsche Einwanderung in Amerika.* Globe Printing House, Philadelphia, 94 p.
The above two publications are rather unusual historical texts, written in German by an individual living in America. Both concern the history of the German migration to Pennsylvania. There were numerous books printed in German, in America, beginning about 1725; these were mainly of a religious nature.

Schweitzer, C. E., 1983, "Francis Daniel Pastorius, the German-American Poet." *Yearbook German American Studies*, vol. 18, p. 21-28

Tepper, Michael (ed.), 1980, *New World Immigrants (A Consolidation of Ship Passenger Lists. . .)*. Genealogical Publ Co., Inc., Baltimore, Md., Vol. I, 586 p., Vol. II, 602 p., Note article "Naturalizations Germantown, Pa 3/7/1691/92", p. 434-435

Tinkcom, H. M., Tinkcom, N. B., & G. M. Simon, 1955, *Historic Germantown*. American Philosophical Soc., Philadelphia, Pa., 155 p., figs., maps.

Ulle, R. F., 1983, *The Original Germantown Families: Mennonite Family History*. vol. II, no. 1, p. 48-51, Elverson, Pa.
_____, 1983, "Sources on Germantown History." *Mennonite Quarterly Review*, vol. 57, pp. 332-338
_____, 1983, "Materials on Mennonites in Colonial Germantown." *Ibid*, p. 354-387, 1 illus.

Wolf, S. G., 1976, *Urban Village: Population, Community and Family Structure in Germantown, Pa., 1693-1800*. Princeton Univ. Press, Princetown, N.J., 361 p., 6 figs.
_____, 1985, "Hyphenated America: The Creation of an Eighteenth Century German-American Culture." In *America and the Germans*, Vol. I, p. 66-84, University of Pennsylvania Press, Phila.

Wokeck, M. S., et al, (eds.), 1986, *The Papers of William Penn, Vol III, 1685-1700*. Univ. Pennsylvania Press, Phila., 796 p.

Part 5

rotes-
tantism
and
Books:
Driving
Forces
Behind the
German
Migration

AMILY GUTENBERG. JOHANNES GUTENberg was born in Mainz about 1397. With the vagaries of 14th and 15th century's records, there remains some doubt about the actual family name as well as about his birth date. Some authors indicate the family name as Gensfleisch, and others as Gensfleisch zur Laden zum Gutenberg. The birth date cannot be documented and speculation revolves around the period of 1393-1403. The father and older brother of Johannes were both named Friele. The family line is fairly well documented several generations prior to the birth of Johannes. The early records of the elder Friele and his two sons and daughter are obscure, but it is thought that the father was associated with the archbishop's mint in Mainz and that he was from a minor patrician clan. An uncle of Johannes was reputed to have been a master of the archiepiscopal mint. The elder Friele died in 1419.

By 1434, Johannes' older brother Friele had moved his family to Eltville in the Rheingau, across the Rhine River from Mainz. In any event, many of the patrician clans of Mainz were forced to leave the city following dissensions with the craftsman guilds. Johannes evidently went to Strassburg about 1428-1430, and he remained there until about 1443. In Strassburg, he had a variety of obscure occupations, trying to earn a living as an inventor and a manufacturer. At one point, he was in the gem cutting business. Later, he was cited as having devised a method of manufacturing mirrors, and still later (possibly 1436) as having experimented with crude printing presses and with the development of alloys necessary for the casting of moveable type, that is, individual letters which can be reused.

In Strassburg in 1436, Johannes was sued by Ennelin zur Iserin Tuer for breach of promise of marriage. There are no firm records that Johannes was ever married.

THE BEGINNING OF THE PRINTING PRESS. By 1448 (possibly as early as 1444), Johannes is recorded as being back in Mainz. The records show that he borrowed 150 Gulden in 1448 to establish a business. In early 1450 he borrowed 800 Gulden from a wealthy Mainz lawyer, Johannes Fust. Gutenberg seems to have been in the printing business at this time. Two years later, Gutenberg asked Fust for another 800 guilders, upon which Fust demanded to become a partner in the business.

At this time, Peter Schöffer of Gernsheim was cited as being Gutenberg's main assistant. One of the first known products of the printing firm was the thirty and thirty-one line (that is, correspondingly thirty or thirty-one lines of print per page) "Letters of Indulgence" ordered by Pope Nicholas V. These appeared about 1454-55.

Gutenberg's talent lay in developing an art rather than in running a business economically. In 1455, Fust brought a lawsuit against Gutenberg for the sum of 2,026 Gulden against the outstanding loans which were being carried at 6% annual interest. The court apparently awarded the lawsuit in favor of Fust who became the sole owner of the firm. Fust then formed a partnership with Schöffer to carry on the printing business. Schöffer became head of the Mainz printing firm and later married Fust's daughter, thus sealing his interest in the business. Between 1462-68, Fust and Schöffer were to play a prominent part in establishing the Frankfurt Book Fair in order to develop a market for their books.

There are European claims that Gutenberg was the inventor of printing. What he actually did was to develop moveable type and thereby substitute machinery for handicraft. Gutenberg applied the principle of replica-casting by pouring molten lead into a die cast in brass; by this means, large quantities of individual letters could be manufactured. He further applied the theory of interchangeable parts to the mass production of letter type. Not only that, he adapted the discoveries of Flemish painters by using inks made from pigments ground in linseed oil-varnish which could be applied to paper with metal type.

Finally, Gutenberg utilized the screw press to save labor and time, thereby speeding up printing. With these methods, the work of 50 or 100 scribes was superseded and it became possible to print ten thousand indulgences in a month. This mass production in turn served to lower the cost of printed matter which thus became available to the public at large and not just to the nobility, the clergy, and the well-to-do.

THE GUTENBERG BIBLES. The much publicized "Gutenberg Bible" is universally cited as being the first printed book. Also known as the 'Vulgate' and as the 'Mazarine Bible', the two-volume set contains forty-two lines per page, and was printed, in Latin, during the years of 1452-55. The letter-type was the so-called Rhenish missal type, which nearly reproduced the letter form of the written manuscripts.

Current estimates suppose that there were originally 150 copies on paper and about 35 copies on vellum (fine calf skin) and that Gutenberg's work contained 1,282 folio pages (641 sheets). It can be surmised that it took six to eight men the better part of two years to print it.

JOHANNES GUTENBERG AFTER MAINZ. After 1455, when he was no longer associated with Fust, the records of Gutenberg's life are again obscure. There is an indication that he obtained a new financial backer, one Dr. Konrad Humery, and that he set up a second press in Mainz. In the political turmoil year of 1461, Gutenberg apparently lived in Eltville and he may have temporarily renewed his printing activities there.

In 1461, Archbishop and Prince Diether von Isenburg was replaced by Adolf II of Nassau. A civil war developed in Mainz and Adolf II sacked the city. Some 400 people were killed out of an estimated population of 5,750. At this time, apprentices and master printers alike left Mainz and scattered up and down the Rhine. Among those departing, the names Peter Schöffer, Ulrich Zell, the Abbot Trithemius, and Jacob Wimpheling are recorded. Undoubtedly there were others. In early 1465, while in Eltville, Gutenberg received a pension and the title of "Hofmann" from the Archbishop of Mainz, Adolf II of Nassau. Gutenberg died in Mainz in 1468 and was buried in the graveyard of the Franciscan Church in Mainz. Gutenberg's association with the printing business was thus a matter of some 18 years.

In recent years, an intensive search by the staff of the Gutenberg Foundation and Museum in Mainz of the scattered records has produced an amazing variety of spellings and misspellings of Johannes Gutenberg's name, among them the ones shown here in Table 5.1.

TABLE 5.1
VARIATION IN SPELLING OF THE NAME GUTENBERG

1430	Hengin zu Gudenberg
	Henne zu Gudenberg
	Henchin zu Gudenberg
1433	Henne Gensfleisch
1434	Johann Gensefleisch, named Gutemberg
	Hengin Gudenberg
1436	Henne Genssefleisse, named Gudenberg
	Hengin Gudenberg
1436	Hannssee Gensefleisch from Mentze, named Gutenberg
	Johann Gutenberg from Mentz
1439	Hans Gutenberg from Mentz
	Johan from Mentze, named Gutenberg
	Hans Genssefleisch from Mentz, name Gutenberg
1441	Johannes dictus Gensefleisch, otherwise named Gutenberg
1442	Johannes dictus Gensefleische alias Guttenberg of Maguncia
1443	Hans Guttenberg
1444	Hanns Guttenberg
	Hanss Gutenberg
	Hans Guttenberg
1444-57	Johannes Gutenberg
1448	Henn Genssefleisch, named Gudenbergk
1453	Johann Gudenberg, of Mencze
1453-55	Johann Guttemberg, named Gensefleisch
1455	Johann Gutenberg
1457	Johannes Gudenberg
1457/58	Johan Guttenberg
1458-74	Johann Guttenberg
1459/60	Johan Guttenberg
1461	Johann Guttemberg

1461/62   Johann Guttenberg
1465   Johann Gudenberg
1468   Johannes Gensfleisch
             Hengin Gudenberg of Mag(untinus) Johann Gutenberg

THE DEVELOPMENT OF PRINTING PRESSES IN EUROPE. Mainz never became a major center of printing. Even through Peter Schöffer, the Elder, was active in Mainz from 1457 until 1502 and his descendants carried on the family printing business until 1559, the City of Mainz was not especially noted as a center of printing when compared to the cities of Augsburg, Nürnberg, Köln, and the like.

In retrospect, there were two driving forces in the establishment of the major printing centers. On the one hand, numerous presses were associated with prominent Protestant Reformers, such as the Lutherans living in Wittenberg, the Zwinglians living in Zürich, the Calvinists living in Strassburg and Geneva, and the Humanists, notably Erasmus, in Basel. On the other hand, the great early universities, such as those in Paris and Köln, required numerous texts for their students.

By 1500, there were presses in more than 250 European cities. In actual numbers of presses during the 16th century, Venice, Milan, Augsburg, Nürnberg, Florence, Köln, Paris, Rome, Strassburg, Basel, and Augsburg, in that order, were well in front of the others. Tiny Wittenberg, population about 3,000 during Martin Luther's prime decade of 1520-29, was also very active as a printing center having at that time eleven presses, all mainly devoted to printing the works of the Reformers. However, with Luther's death in 1546, the main center of Protestant intellectuals was relocated to Magdeburg where printing activities continued until the destruction of the city in 1631. The importance of printing in supporting the Protestant cause is documented in the following two essays.

Strangely enough, the book-fair city of Frankfurt did not have a permanently operating printing press until 1511, and then only for two years. In Frankfurt, the well-known printer Christian Egenolff, originally from Strassburg, established a press during the years 1530-55 which his descendants carried on through the 16th century. The major publishing output of the Merian family of Frankfurt is documented in a later essay.

MAJOR REPOSITORIES FOR INCUNABULA. It has been estimated that there are extant approximately 40,000 incunabula, as the first printed books (those printed from 1450-1500) were called. Some of the primary collections of such books include the Vatican Library in Rome, the Library of Congress in Washington, D.C., The British Museum in London, The Bibliothèque Nationale in Paris, Oxford University's Bodleian Library, the Pierpont Morgan Library in New York, and the Huntington Library in San Marino, California.

REFERENCES

Febvre, Lucien, & Henri-Jean-Martin, 1976, *The Coming of the Book*. Atlantic Highland. Humanities Press, London, 378 p.
Translation from the 1958 edition printed in French by Editions Albin Michel, Paris; a good survey of the history of printing from the French point of view..

Friederichs, H. F., 1968, "Der Erfinder Johannes Gutenberg: in Ahnentafeln berühmter Deutscher. *Genealogisches Jahrbuch*, Neustadt a.d. Aisch, Bd. 8, p. 93-101

Geck, Elizabeth, 1968, *Johannes Gutenberg*. Inter Nationes, Bad Godesberg, 123 p., map
Map shows centers of printing up to year 1500.

Goff, F. R., 1970, *The permanence of Johann Gutenberg*. Univ. Texas Press, Austin, 29 p.

Ing, Janet, 1983, "The Mainz Indulgences of 1454/5: A Review of Recent Scholarship." *The British Library Journal*, vol. 9, no. 1, p. 14-31

Kapr, Albert, 1985, "Johannes Gutenberg und die Kaiser-Friedrich-Legende." *Gutenberg-Jahrbuch*, Gutenberg-Gesell., Mainz, p. 105-114
_____, 1987, *Johannes Gutenberg*. C. H. Beck Verlag, München, 331 p., illus.

Löschburg, Winfried, 1974, *Historic Libraries of Europe*. Druckerei Fortschritt Erfurt, GDR, 140 p., numerous illus. (trans. by Elisabeth Ross)

Putnam, G. H., 1962, "The Invention of Printing." In *Books and Their Makers during the Middle Ages*. Hillary House Publ. Ltd., N.Y., vol. I, p. 348-402
Reprint of the somewhat dated edition of 1896-97.

Ruppel, Aloys, 1955, *Druckte Gutenberg vor seiner 42zeilingen Bibel ein grösseres Werk*. Verlag der Gutenberg-Gesell., Mainz, 18 p.
_____, 1967, *Johannes Gutenberg. Sein Leben und sein Werk*. B. de Graaf, Nieuwkoop (Netherlands), 233 p., 3rd ed.
A very comprehensive work which according to the author has been little altered from the 1st edition of 1947; contains very extensive bibliography through 1967.

Scholderer, Victor, 1970, *Johann Gutenberg*. University Press, Oxford, 2nd ed., 32 p., 18 pls.

Stöckl, A. T., & J. A. Künzer, 1988, *Gutenberg war nicht allein*. Löper Verlag, Karlsruhe, 86 p., illus.

Swierk, Alfred (ed.), 1974, *Beiträge zur Geschichte des Buches and seiner Funktion in der Gesellschaft*. Anton Hiersemann, Stuttgart, 335 p.

Thorpe, James, 1975, *The Gutenberg Bible*. The Huntington Library, San Marino, Calif, 23 p.

Widmann, Hanns, 1965, *Der deutsche Buchhandel in Urkunden und Quellen*. Hamburg.

_____, (ed.), 1972, *Der gegenwärtige Stand der Gutenberg-Forschung*. Anton Hiersemann, Stuttgart, 302 p. Contains 16 articles with subject matter varying according to author. all articles are concerned with the general subject Gutenberg.

_____1973, *Vom Nutzen und Nachteil der Erfindung des Buchdrucks*. Verlag der Gutenberg-Gesell., Mainz, 54 p.

_____, 1975, *Geschichte des Buchhandels, Teil I*. Otto Harrassowitz, Wiesbaden, 308 p., 2nd ed. (reprint of 1952 ed.)

Williams, G. W., 1985, *The Craft of Printing and the Publication of Shakespeare's Works*. Associated University Presses, Cranbury, N.J., 103 p., illus.

ACH OCTOBER, PRINTERS, PUBLISHERS, book dealers, and bibliophiles converge on Frankfurt am Main for the annual six-day book fair. It is a massive show; in 1992 there were more than 8,000 exhibitors. The history of the fair has been long and checkered. By some accounts, the actual book fair, as an outgrowth of the much earlier trade fair, was started between the years 1462-1466. Beginning about 1235, the earliest trade fairs in Frankfurt involved commerce of all types. They were probably religious in origin; after the religious celebration there was time for social and commercial intercourse. Observers and participants from all parts of Germany attended the Frankfurt Fairs as did many travellers from other parts of Europe, especially those from the Lowlands who were able to take advantage of the Rhine waterway.

HISTORICAL OVERVIEW. The earliest known records of Frankfurt am Main (not to be confused with Frankfurt am Oder in the east), dating from 794, show the name as Franconofurd. The subsequent succession of spellings included: Franconofurt (874), Franchonofurt (882), Franconevurt (977), Franchennevort (1112), etc. It was only after 1360 that the spellings of Frankfurt and Frankfort, among other variations, were used.

The first printed record of trade fairs in Frankfurt dates from about 1235. In a document signed by Kaiser Friedrich II, who ruled 1215-37, he permitted an annual fair, probably a Herbstmesse (Autumn Fair). In 1330, Kaiser Ludwig der Bayer (reigned 1314-1346) gave permission for a Fastenmesse (Easter Fair) and the tradition of semi-annual fairs in Frankfurt was firmly established. Kaiser Friedrich III (who ruled from 1440-93), in 1442, confirmed the fair privileges of Frankfurt and attempted to regulate its proceedings, but had little success. Nearly all the Holy Roman Emperors for the period 1330-1726 granted some type of Fair privileges to the citizens of Frankfurt am Main. Eventually, the trade fairs were held three or four times annually.

Frankfurt am Main became a free imperial city in 1372, lasting as such until 1806, and again from 1815 to 1866. Being a free city offered many benefits, one of which was a form of self-government responsible, for the most part, only to the Emperor. Another benefit was the right to mint its own currency, a currency which proved to be one of the most stable in the German speaking world.

A classic document on the history of the Frankfurt Book Fair was edited by J. W. Thompson and published in Chicago in 1911. Thompson cites three periods for the book fairs in the eras before World War I:

1st period	1450-1546
2nd period	1546-1764
3rd period	1764-1939 ·

The periods designated by Thompson show the evolution from a printer's fair to a book dealer's fair.

FIRST FAIR PERIOD, 1450-1546. With the introduction of movable type in Mainz by Johannes Gutenberg (ca. 1397-1468) about 1450, the mass production of books became a reality. Likely, a few handwritten manuscripts were sold at trade fairs from the advent of such fairs. On the other hand, 15th century incunabula (i.e. books printed between 1450-1500) evidently were not sold at trade fairs until a decade or so after Gutenberg's revolutionary ideas.

After the falling out between Gutenberg and his financial partner Johannes Fust in 1455, Fust and an employee, Peter Schöffer, carried on in Mainz the printing business established by Gutenberg. The turmoil in Mainz during the Civil War of 1461-62, in which Prince Diether von Isenburg was replaced as Archbishop by Adolph II of Nassau, upset the fledgling Mainz printing industry and sent apprentices and master printers to more stable cities up and down the Rhine River. Schöffer, as mentioned before, left Mainz, probably for Frankfurt, and the Fust & Schöffer printing business lay dormant from 1462 until 1464.

It was not until this period that the idea of a Frankfurt Book Fair was generated. In 1466, after the death of Johannes Fust, Peter Schöffer, back in Mainz again, issued a printed list of books he had for sale. This action appears to mark the first known systematic effort at selling books and most likely was done in conjunction with the book fair.

Schöffer began to transfer much of his activities to Frankfurt and apparently took residence there by 1479 although he maintained his printing establishment in Mainz. In thirty-six years, Schöffer (who was listed on title pages under the Latin name of Petrus Schoiffer de Gernsheim) printed some thirty-seven separate works. Schöffer died in 1502, but his descendants carried on his business until 1557.

By 1485, the Frankfurt Book Fair was well established. During the 15th century, the book fair in Frankfurt was held in the open area near the St. Leonhards-Kirche - today, this area between the Main River and the Church is called the "Buchgasse," "Book Alley" in English.

In Europe before 1500, about three-quarters of all printed matter was written in Latin with the remaining one-quarter in Italian and in German. These proportions changed gradually with the increased use of German by Martin Luther and other authors. In fact, the proportion of Latin, German and other language titles sold at the Frankfurt and at the Leipzig Book Fairs shows the steady increase of printing in the vernacular, as in Table 5.2. By 1690, books with German titles had exceeded those with Latin titles. Other languages included in Table 5.2 are mainly French, with minor numbers in Italian, Spanish, Dutch (in that order of importance), and perhaps a dozen others.

Also shown in Table 5.2 is the predominance of Protestant theological works with the number of religious works declining drastically in the

TABLE 5.2

PERCENT OF TITLES - FRANKFURT & LEIPZIG BOOK FAIRS

Year	Language			Theology		
	Latin-%	German-%	Other-%	Prot.-%	Catholic-%	Total Th.-%
1564	71	29	0	24	16	40
1570	61	34	5	30	17	47
1580	72	25	3	26	16	42
1590	62	34	4	29	12	41
1600	66	28	6	27	15	42
1610	64	30	6	32	14	46
1620	66	30	4	28	16	44
1630	62	34	4	27	23	50
1640	57	38	5	33	14	47
1650	65	32	5	26	15	41
1660	55	35	10	28	11	39
1670	56	38	6	29	11	40
1680	48	46	6	26	7	33
1690	45	51	4	33	6	39
1700	38	60	2	39	5	44
1710	40	58	2	34	9	43
1720	30	68	2	36	3	39
1730	26	71	3	40	2	42
1740	26	66	8	32	1	33
1750	20	68	12	27	2	29
1760	16	73	11	21	2	23
1770	12	71	17	13	2	15
1780	13	76	11	12	3	15
1790	8	85	7	6	2	8
1800	4	87	9	5	1	6
1810	5	83	12	6	1	7
1820	8	88	4	8	3	11
1830	7	86	7	12	5	17
1840	7	88	5	8	2	10
1846	4	91	5	15	7	22

Data Source: Schwetschke, 1850, 1877
For period 1564-1592, mainly from Frankfurt Catalogues.
For period 1595-1846, mainly from Leipzig Catalogues.

mid-18th century. The 16th century Protestants in the era of Martin Luther had early learned to use the book fair as a strong tool in marketing their beliefs (see also the next essay). This concept was carried on also by the firm of Christoph Froschauer during the years 1521-1590, as outlined in a later essay.

Other changes in the printing industry have been well documented. For instance, book sizes expanded from the larger folio (approx. 25 x 19 inches) editions to include quarto, (about 19 x 12-1/2 inches), octavo (12-

1/2 x 9-1/2 inches), duodecimo (7-3/4 x 5 inches), and, for convenience, even smaller sizes. These are respectively half sheets, quarter sheets, eighth sheets, and twelveth sheets. Martin Luther (1483-1546), resident in Wittenberg, tended to favor octavo and duodecimo sizes.

The Frankfurt Booksellers Association was organized in 1525 in order to promote sales of books and the marketing of book printing equipment. Oddly enough, a printing firm was not established in Frankfurt until 1511 and then lasted only for a few years.

During the late 15th and early 16th centuries, many famous printing names were associated with the Frankfurt Book Fair. Prominent early exhibitors were: Anton Koberger (1445-1513) of Nürnberg, who went to the Frankfurt Fair perhaps fifteen times during the years 1493-1509, and Johann Amerbach (1443-1513) of Basel.

The majority of printers bought type "ready-made." A prominent type-casting foundry, as well as publishing firm, was that of Christian Egenolf (1502-1555) which was established in Frankfurt in 1531. The Egenolf firm conducted much of its type-casting marketing activities during the fair period. This firm became known under the name of Luther (not related to Martin Luther) in 1629.

During the period of 1518-40, the Frankfurt Book Fair became a Mecca of the book trade. The fair became termed loosely "the Protestant book trade" because of the nature of the books for sale. Despite the bans on works by the Reformers imposed by various ecclesiastic and imperial authorities in 1520, 1521, and 1524, a large part of the Book Fair was concerned with the books of Martin Luther. For instance, Luther's controversial address against the German theologian Johann Eck (1486-1543, original surname Mayer) in 1518 sold 1,400 copies at the Frankfurt Book Fair in two days. During the period 1522-46, there were ten versions of the "Vollbibels", i.e., ten complete editions of the Luther Bible in print, and were sold at the Fair by the thousands. Most editions were printed in Augsburg with other editions being printed in the lesser printing centers of Strassburg, Nürnberg, Zürich, and Basel.

The Schmalkaldic War of 1546-47, which was essentially a revolt of the Protestant nobles, culminated in their defeat by the Emperor's forces. The fighting, although occurring mainly to the East around the cities of Regensburg and Augsburg, unsettled the regular participants of the Frankfurt Fair and kept many merchants away. In fact, military forces were encamped at Frankfurt in crowded and unsanitary quarters and a serious epidemic occurred there.

SECOND FAIR PERIOD, 1546-1764. The free Imperial city of Frankfurt had accepted Reformation in 1530. About 1554, some 1,800 Dutch and Walloon Protestant refugees, led by French theologian Valerand Poullain, had settled in Frankfurt and had added to the already dominant Protestant population. The refugees were variously termed "reformed Calvinist" and "Flanders reformed." Estimates of Frankfurt's population for 1560 totaled about 13,000; this figure included the Protestant refugees as well as about 700 Jews. By 1600, the population estimates for Frankfurt was 20,000 total, including approximately 3,000 Protestant refugees, and possibly some 2,500 Jews.

The heyday of the Frankfurt Book Fair was from about 1550 to 1618. The Book Fair of 1569 registered eighty-seven printers and publishers, including seventeen alone from Frankfurt. A prominent participant was Sigismund Feyerabend (1528-1590), publisher in Frankfurt.

During the latter part of the 16th century, a hazard in congested European cities and in army camps was the so-called "pest" (i.e. the plague). While Frankfurt was not directly affected during the pest years of 1563, 1564-65, 1575, and 1586, travel to Frankfurt by participants in the Fair was restricted by outbreaks of these epidemics.

In the non-pest years, the Frankfurt Fair was typically attended by book merchants from Lübeck, Vienna, Lyon, Antwerp, Amsterdam, Strassburg, Basel, Ulm, Nürnberg, and Augsburg, as well as travellers from many lesser cities in Europe.

By 1570, there was universal interest in the book trade business also in other European countries. In France and Switzerland, the main centers were in Paris, Lyon, and Geneva; in Italy, the major centers were Venice, Rome, and Florence. In the Low Countries, active book trade centers were in Antwerp, Amsterdam, and Leiden.

In Germany, in 1579, under the realm of Kaiser Rudolf (ruled 1576-1612), there was once again heavy censorship as a result of the Counter-Reformation. Much of the censorship was directed against the printing of works by the Protestants. The Imperial Book Commission had inherited by default, from the Frankfurt Town Council, the right to regulate the privileges of the printers and to guard against unauthorized copying and translation of books. Coincidentally, at that time, the Imperial Book Commission was controlled by the Jesuits, who were, of course, against any form of Protestant propaganda.

The records from 1595 show the distribution of exhibitors at the Frankfurt Book Fair, in terms of percentages by area and in terms of representation by number of cities, as follows:

Area	Percent	Cities
South Germany	47	36
(including Frankfurt and Basel)		
Rhineland	6	5
North Germany	26	28
Foreign	21	17
	----	----
Totals	100	86

In the above, foreign countries with their respective cities, were represented as follows:

England: Edinburgh, London
France: Lyon, Paris
Italy: Rome, Venice
Lowlands: Amsterdam, Antwerp, Leiden
Switzerland: Basel, Genf (Geneva), Zürich
Miscellaneous: Bohemia, Denmark, Poland, Russia

THE FAIR CATALOGS. Printed lists of publications for sale included those of Peter Schöffer (active 1457-1502) and, about the same time, of Johann Mentelin (active 1458-1478); both issued lists in the 1460's. By 1543, more advanced lists of publications for sale were printed by the firms of Aldus Manutius (active 1450-1515), of Christian Wechel (active 1520-1554), and of Christoph Froschauer (active 1521-1564).

Christoph Froschauer (ca. 1490-1564) had a large influence on the Frankfurt Book Fair. He began printing in Zürich in 1521. His printing shop was biased toward printing the works of the Reformers, notably those of Huldreich or Huldrych (Ulrich) Zwingli (1484-1530), and adaptations from the works of Martin Luther (1483-1546). Froschauer was one of the first printers to issue a "Fair catalog" of his printings. In 1543, his catalog contained thirty-five pages and listed 110 works in German with 106 works in Latin. For many years, Froschauer went twice yearly to the Frankfurt Book Fair. In 1534, he is recorded as taking 2,000 copies of his printing of the book *Epitome trium terrae partium* to the Fair with the expectation that half would be sold in that year and the remaining copies sold in succeeding years.

The real Frankfurt Fair catalog (*Messekatalog*) was issued as early as 1564; it was still unofficial and privately printed by Georg Willer of Augsburg. He printed it in quarto size until 1592. In 1598, the *Rathskanzlei* (Town Council) of Frankfurt undertook the publication of an official catalog which they continued doing until 1749.

As previously noted, the Frankfurt Book Fair catalogs were begun in 1564. Leipzig, was located some 42.5 (German) Meilen (about 320 kilometers, 199 English miles) to the northeast, over a much travelled, but very poor trade route. The first Leipzig catalogs did not appear until 1600 at which time the two fairs were roughly equal in importance. Table 5.3, a tabulation of the combined catalogs for the Frankfurt and Leipzig Fairs, shows the level of activity for the period 1564-1846.

According to some sources, the annual catalogs for the period from 1564 to 1600 contained a composite list of nearly 20,000 different titles of which seventy-three percent were in German; these were published by 117 firms in sixty-one towns and cities. Nearly thirty-one percent of the total titles were printed in countries outside Germany and about five percent of the titles indicated no country of origin.

With the onset of the wars of Louis XIV, and especially with the 2nd Devastation of the Palatinate in 1688-89, the Frankfurt Book Fair became almost dormant.

TABLE 5.3
FRANKFURT/LEIPZIG FAIR CATALOGUES

Year	No. Titles	Year	No. Titles
1564	256	1710	1,368
1570	475	1720	979
1580	493	1730	993
1590	875	1740	1,326
1600	1,059	1750	1,296
1610	1,511	1760	1,198
1620	1,377	1770	1,807
1630	1,346	1780	2,642
1640	730	1790	3,561
1650	948	1800	4,012
1660	811	1810	3,864
1670	698	1820	3,772
1680	687	1830	7,308
1690	907	1840	11,151
1700	978	1850	10,536

Data from Schwetschke, 1850, 1877

Nonetheless, the great Merian Publishing Company upheld the printing of numerous books in Frankfurt during the period 1624-1726. Matthäus Merian, the Elder (1593-1650), developed the publishing house in Frankfurt which was to contribute about 135 new titles to the Book Fair catalog during the years 1626-1650. The Merian firm was especially active from 1635-1656. The history of the firm is outlined in a later essay.

THIRD FAIR PERIOD, 1764-1939. Restrictions to travel along the middle Rhine during the War Years of 1677, 1688-89, 1740-48, and 1756-63 contributed to the long period of decline of the Frankfurt Book Fair and to the increased importance of the Leipzig Book Fair.

After the War of Spanish Succession (1740-48), the Frankfurt Book Fair became a shadow of its former self. During part of the Seven Years War (1756-63), Frankfurt was under French rule and occupied by French troops. The Leipzig trade fair had begun as early as 1165 and eventually was held three times annually. Printing was established in Leipzig by 1479. The Leipzig Book Fair was started by 1495 and a corresponding Booksellers Association began about 1525.

The Leipzig Book Fair also had its ups and downs. During the reign of Duke Georg, Elector of Saxony (he reigned 1524-1533), the Protestant printers of Leipzig fell under heavy censorship and many left Leipzig for Wittenberg and other cities. Later rulers were decidedly more tolerant and the Fair regained its status, especially with the decline of the Frankfurt Fair during the War Period of 1616-48.

By 1764, the center of printing and of book fairs for southern Germany had decidedly shifted to Leipzig. The Leipzig Fair remained a dominant European Fair during the 18th and 19th centuries. Even though Frankfurt's fairs abated, the city itself continued to grow and to expand its commerce in the 19th century, in part because of its favorable location in regards to land and river transportation. Corresponding to this growth was the increase in population between wars and the decrease in population during war years as evidenced below:

TABLE 5.4
POPULATION OF FRANKFURT, 1817-1946

Year	Population	Year	Population
1817	41,458	1875	103,136
1840	55,269	1890	179,985
1864	55,269	1905	334,951
1871	59,265	1939	553,464
		1946	446,065

The 1905 population estimates include 175,909 Protestants, 88,457 Catholics, and 21,974 Jews.

THE INFLUENCE OF THE FAIR ON MIGRATION. As we have seen at this point, there were a number of stepping stones leading up to the great migrations to America. The first, of course was the development of printing and the means of mass communication. The second was the introduction of Protestantism and the generation of religious freedom in the minds of the ordinary citizen. The third step was the development of the book fair and consequent marketing services. These three critical steps took place in the period of about 1450 to 1550. Although Columbus discovered America in 1492, the lands to the west, across the Atlantic, were largely inconceivable without proper guides in the form of 17th century maps, the fourth step. Finally, the really great migrations of the 18th and 19th centuries were at the whim of improved transportation which, in effect came largely with the Industrial Revolution, beginning about the middle of the 18th century.

REFERENCES

Borm, Wolfgang (ed.), 1982, *Catalogi Nundinales 1571-1852. Die Frankfurter and Leipziger Messekataloge der Herzog-August-Bibliothek Wolfenbüttel.* Otto Harrassowitz, Wiesbaden, Reportorien zur Erforschung der frühen Neuzeit, Bd. 5, 139 p., 20 illus. Lists the numerous Book Fair catalogues in the Herzog-August-Bibliothek archives which is a major repository in Germany for such items.

Clair, Colin, 1969, *A Chronology of Printing.* Frederick A. Praeger Publishers, N.Y., 228 p.

_____, 1976, *A History of European Printing.* Academic Press, London, 526 p., illus.

Dietz, Alexander, 1921, *Zur Geschichte der Frankfurter Büchermesse 1462/1792.* Buchdruckerei R. Th. Hauser & Co., Frankfurt am Main, 31 p.

Glaister, G. A., 1979, *Glaister's Glossary of the Book.* George Allen & Unwin Ltd., London, 551 p.

Hirsch, Rudolf, 1967, *Printing, Selling and Reading 1450-1550.* Otto Harrassowitz, Wiesbaden, 165 p.

Kapp, Friedrich, 1886, *Geschichte des Deutschen Buchhandels.* Verlag des Börsenvereins der Deutschen Buchhändler, Leipzig, 880 p. Chapter on "Die frankfurter Messe", p. 448-521.

Keyser, Erich (ed.), 1958, "Frankfurt a M." In *Deutsches Städtebuch.* Bd. IV, Südwestdeutschland. 1, Land Hessen, p. 122-154, W. Kohlhammer Verlag, Stuttgart.

Köttelwesch, Clemens, 1968, *Frühe Frankfurter Buchmesse von 15.-17. Jahrhundert.* Vortrag zur Eröffnung der Ausstellung 19.9.1968, 6 p.

_____, 1973, "Die Frankfurter Buchmesse für den Deutschen Buchhandel." Nr. 81, (12.Okt.1973), *Frankfurter Ausgabe,* p. 1642-1650

Le Roy Ladurie, Emmanuel, 1981, "The Unification of the Globe by Disease." In *The Mind and Method of the Historian.* Univ. Chicago Press, p. 28-83 Translated from the French edition of 1978; this book presents an interesting discussion of the bubonic plague and its effects on the population.

Lübbecke, Friedrich, 1948, *Funfhundert Jahre Buch und Druck im Frankfurt am Main*. H. Cobet Verlag, Frankfurt am Main, 463 p., illus. Chapter on "Die Frankfurter Buchmesse", p. 35-58.

Recke, Bruno, 1951, *Die Frankfurter Büchermesse*. D. Stempelverlag, Frankfurt am Main, 31 p.

Schwetschke, Gustav, 1850, 1877, *Codex Nvndinarvs Germaniae literatae biservlaris*. Mess-Jahrbücher des Deutschen Buchhandels 1564-1846. Halle, 440 folio pages.
Reprinted in 1963 by B. de Graaf, Nieuwkoop, Netherlands. This is a phenomenal compilation of book fair catalog data over a 283 year period for the Frankfurt and Leipzig Book Fairs. The text is in German.

Steinberg, S. H., 1974, *Five Hundred Years of Printing*. Penguin Books Ltd., Harmondsworth, England, 3rd ed., 400 p., illus.

Stephanus, Henricus (Estienne, Henri), 1968, *Francofordiense Emporium*. Frankfurter Buchmesse, Frankfurt am Main (Anniversary edition, 20th Fair), 178 p.
Contains translations of publication dated 1574, i.e., the earliest history of the fair.

Thompson, J. W. (ed.), 1911, *The Frankfurt Book Fair (The Francofordiense Emporium of Henri Estienne)*. The Caxton Club, Chicago, Ill., 204 p., illus.
Reprinted in 1968 by Burt Franklin, N.Y. This is a classic work and high quality collector's item, in English.

Töller, Monika, 1983, *Die Buchmesse in Frankfurt a. Main vor 1560*. Doktorgrades Dissertations, Ludwig - Maximilians - Universität, München, 237 p., illus.

**UTHER'S FORMATIVE YEARS.** MARTIN Luther was born on November, 10, 1483, in Eisleben, province of Thüringen (formerly central Germany, now in eastern Germany). He was the son of Hans and Margarethe (Ziegler) Luther. After moving to Mansfeld in 1484, the father became a small-scale mining entrepreneur. The younger Luther had his early schooling at Mansfeld, at Magdeburg, and at Eisenach. During the years 1501-05, Luther attended the University of Erfurt and received his first degree in the Arts. In these early years, Luther developed into an excellent Latinist.

At Wittenberg in July, 1505, he entered the Augustinian Monastery and was ordained as a priest in 1507 (Wittenberg is also now in eastern Germany, near Leipzig). Luther taught at the University of Wittenberg in 1508-09, and received a second degree. The University had been founded by Friedrich the Wise, Elector of Saxony, in 1505.

In January, 1511, Luther went on a three month trip to Rome, returning via Augsburg and Nürnberg. Back at Wittenberg he continued studies while teaching. At Wittenberg, Luther was awarded the degree of Doctor of Philosophy in October, 1512. At this time, he also preached at the town church. By 1514, Luther began learning the Greek language.

LUTHER IN REBELLION. As we shall see, it was fortunate for Luther that Emperor Maximilian I (1459-1519) was in the waning years of his long reign of 1493-1519. By 1514, Maximilian I suffered from a variety of debilitating ailments including a bad leg from a fall from a horse, hardening arteries, gout, bronchitis or asthma, gallstones, and perhaps stomach cancer. Maximilian had, after all, outlived two wives, and had been involved in an ongoing series of wars, territorial disputes, and uprisings, from 1478 up to 1516.

In 1514, Luther first spoke out publicly against Pope Leo X, although he continued in his position of District Vicar during the period 1515-18. In April, 1517, Luther translated a few sections of the Bible into German. In October, 1517, Luther published his *Critic*, known as the *Ninety-Five Theses*, which expounded on the excesses of the Roman Catholic Church and, in particular, on the economic exploitation of the German people by the Roman Curia. This work was nailed to the door of the Wittenberger Schlosskirche (Wittenberg Castle Church). The public came from far and wide to learn about the blasphemy issuing from the learned "Doktor."

Printed initially under the Latin title of *Disputatio pio Declaratione Vitutis Indulgentiarum*, the Ninety-five theses were reprinted in German in 1518. Subsequently, the theses were reprinted in twenty-two other editions by various printers located in Wittenberg, Leipzig, Nürnberg, Augsburg, Basel and in Breslau.

During 1518, considerable controversy developed over possible charges against Luther and his possible countercharges. At the University of Heidelberg in the spring of 1518, during the meeting of the German Augustinians, Luther expounded on his views and won important followers. Subsequently, Archbishop Albrecht of Mainz took legal action against Luther, which resulted in a hearing in Augsburg in October, 1518. However, through the intervention of Friedrich the Wise, Elector of Saxony, the trial was further delayed and was set for the German City of Worms rather than Rome.

However, with the death of Emperor Maximilian I in January, 1519, the charges against Luther were again delayed pending the selection of a new Emperor. In June, 1519, Karl V became the new Emperor, but still no action was taken against Luther. Karl V (1500-1556), who reigned 1519-1556, was likewise preoccupied with a steady succession of internal and external conflicts, most notably four major wars with France, 1521-26, 1526-30, 1536-38, and 1542-44, and with the commitment by the Hapsburg regime to provide a buffer zone between Vienna and "the Turks" to the southeast.

In June, 1520, the Pope responded by issuing a papal bull against Luther. The bull excommunicated Luther, ordered all his existing publications burned, and prohibited further the printing, sale, distribution and possession of Luther's works. The public virtually ignored the ban; in fact, their curiosity was piqued and sales mushroomed.

LUTHER ON TRIAL FOR HIS LIFE. In December, 1520, Luther made a public display of burning the papal bull mentioned above. On April 17, 1521, Luther went before the Reichstag (Imperial Diet), and again on the following day, to defend his actions. On May 26, 1521, long after Luther's departure from Worms, the Diet issued the Edict of Worms banning Luther from the Church and from the German Empire. Two of the Electors, Friedrich of Saxony and Ludwig of the Palatinate, refused to sign the Edict. In fact, Elector Friedrich sent Luther into hiding at the Castle of Wartburg, near Eisenach, about mid-way along the ancient trade route between Frankfurt am Main and Leipzig.

THE PUBLISHING EXPLOSION. While in hiding, from May, 1521 to March 1522, Luther completed his translation of the New Testament from Greek (and in part from Latin) into German following mainly the 1516 texts of the Dutch theologian Desiderius Erasmus (?1466-1536; original name Geert Geerts). Its simple title was *Das Neue Testament, Deutsch, Vuittenberg*. Three presses were occupied with the printing. Luther's translation of the New Testament was published in May, 1522; it is estimated that from 3,000 to 5,000 copies were printed and these were sold out within three months. A second edition of the New Testament was printed by September, 1522. In the same year, Luther authored some 130 other articles or books.

Censorship against Luther was confirmed and extended by the Edict of Nürnberg of 1524 and public indignation was further inflamed. Luther's printed works date from 1516. Many of the earliest were "Flugschriften" or pamphlets. A typical early publication was a tract titled *Die Deutsche Theologie*, first printed in 1518. In the succeeding four year period, it went through seventy-five to eighty different editions by publishers scattered through Europe.

Johann Froben (1460-1527) of Basel was the first publisher to launch a collected edition of Luther's Latin tracts. He published four editions between October, 1518 and July, 1520. In 1520, Luther wrote some sixteen new treatises totaling about 400 printed pages.

In August, 1520, some 4,000 copies of Luther's treatise *An den christlichen Adel deutscher Nation von des christlichen Standes Besserung* (Address to the German Nobility on the Improvement of Christian Standing) were printed in Strassburg by the firm of Martin Flach, and shortly thereafter it was necessary to have a second printing.

A phenomenal increase in the printing of books in German, rather than in Latin text, especially of the works by Luther, developed. His writing during the notable years of 1520-24 were printed in fifty different cities of the German speaking areas.

Over the twelve year period of 1522 to 1534, eighty-seven editions of the New Testament in High German and nineteen editions of the New Testament in Low German, totaling some 200,000 copies, were printed by various presses scattered throughout northern Europe. With this massive printing by Protestant publishers of the New Testament in the vernacular, Luther had effectively initiated the Book War, that is, the use of books to spread religious propaganda among the public.

During Luther's prime decade of 1520-29, there were eleven presses active in Wittenberg. Among them, Johann Rau-Grunenberg (active 1508-1525) was the first to print Luther's works. He was followed by Melchoir Lotter the Younger (active 1519-25) who printed many of Luther's publications including his translation of the New Testament. Another Wittenberg printer, Hans Lufft (active 1523-84), was the most prominent of the so-called Luther printers by virtue of volume and longevity. Nichel Schirlentz (active 1521-47) printed numerous publications not only of Luther, but also of other Reformers.

By 1523, Luther had some 1,300 works in print, including pamphlets, broadsides, open letters, satires, dialogues, sermons, and discourses; all told perhaps a million copies. In 1525, there were 498 books printed in German of which 183 publications were written by Luther himself. Eventually, Luther's works amounted to about 60,000 pages of manuscript and filled 102 volumes of his collected works in the famous Weimar edition.

Actually, there had been eighteen different early versions of the complete Bible in German, beginning with that of Johannes Mentelin in Strassburg in everyday common language which could be understood by the man on the street. His translation was at a time when there were no dictionaries in the German language. Luther and his co-workers fused together the various German dialects and produced a High German language upon which modern German literature is based. In 1537, Luther even completed a treatise on German names. Luther's works, in their greatly simplified German, had a tremendous impact on the literacy of the German people. And for those who could not read, in many towns, the message was spread by reading Luther's works aloud in the town square.

One of the better known printings of the Luther's translation of the New Testament was that by Christoph Froschauer in 1524 in Zürich. The last "Luther Bible" appeared in 1545. Among other works, Luther had also completed the Wittenberg *Book of Hymns* in 1524, as well as other Church related materials, in order to meet the rapidly changing needs of Protestant ideas. The translation of the New and the Old Testaments, the large printing runs and the wide distribution was the key to bringing together the profusion of German dialects existing in the early 16th century. This fusion of dialects produced Modern High German (Lutheran German). Later, a marked contrast developed between the High German of southern Germany and northern Switzerland, and the similar Germanic language of the Dutch peoples, namely Nederlands.

CONFLICT AMONG THE REFORMERS. As an outgrowth of the Reformation in general, civil war erupted in 1524-25, the so-called Bauernkrieg (Peasants Revolt). This began in the Schwarzwald (Black Forest) in Württemberg and rapidly spread over southern Germany. Luther immediately dissociated himself from the more radical leaders of this revolt, among whom Thomas Münzer (or Müntzer) was prominent.

Shortly after the Peasant's Revolt was brutally suppressed, Luther, then forty-two, married on June 27, 1525, a former nun, Katharina von Bora. She was born 1499, died 1552. They eventually had six children.

Luther returned to teach at the University of Wittenberg. After the death of Elector Friedrich, the Wise, of Saxony, in May, 1525, Luther's main protector and supporter was Prince Philip I, the Magnanimous, of Hesse, who lived 1504-67.

In the years after 1525, there were notable conflicts with the Swiss and southern German theologian reformers. One dispute, in 1527-28, over Communion, involved the noted reformer from Zürich, Ulrich (Huldrych) Zwingli. In 1529, the debate carried over to a conference at the castle of Philip of Hesse at Marburg. The major controversies with the south German reformers were finally settled by the Wittenberg Concord in 1536.

Luther died on February 22, 1546, while on a trip with his three sons to Eisleben to settle a dispute between the Counts of Mansfeld. Luther was perhaps fortunate to be at the end of his life in 1546 for his primary mentor of the time, Prince Philip of Hesse, was deeply involved in territorial disputes and was in fact taken prisoner in 1547, in which status he remained for some time. Luther was buried at the Castle Church in Wittenberg.

LUTHER'S IMPRINT ON CIVILIZATION. During his busy lifetime, Luther led the German Church reform movement, a movement which precipitated Lutheranism in Germany, the Mennonites and the Calvinists in Holland, the Huguenots in France, and Protestantism in general. Some of his major accomplishments were to standardize the German language through the widespread printing of his bible translations and through the writing of hymns and other church related material. In addition, he revolutionized church music and also provided Germany with its central political issue: the reform movement. The reform movement lasted until 1648 when, by the Treaty of Westphalia, certain rights of Protestants, Catholics, and other religions were recognized. In this latter matter, Luther acted as the voice of a growing German national spirit. Unfortunately, Luther's desire to achieve a German national unity was not fully accomplished until much later, in 1871.

Luther could easily have become directly involved in the numerous territorial and religious wars which swirled through the German States during the first half of the 16th century. He preferred, however, to direct his actions through the Book War whereby Protestant theological works dominated for more than two centuries all other types of books offered at the Frankfurt and Leipzig Book Fairs.

After 1525, the Book Fairs offered a form of mass marketing unknown to earlier generations. Ideas of reform were generated and spread among the people. The rate of literacy took a dramatic increase and new philosophical ideas were generated. Among these ideas was the desire and hope of the common man for a better life through association with the Protestant movement. In the next century, the Protestant movement became a physical as well as a mental movement. The 16th century Reform movement spread to all parts of Europe and in the 17th century became a trans-Atlantic movement.

CONTEMPORANEOUS REFORM GROUPS IN EUROPE. Even during Luther's lifetime, new and sometimes strange religious sects sprang up everywhere in western Europe. Some, such as the Lutherans and the Calvinists, became dominant forces in the theological world. Most of the smaller groups maintained low profiles, although some were radical (such as the Münster group of 1532-35) and promoted the use of force to achieve their ideas. Moderately radical groups went under the collective name of Anabaptists - these included the Swiss Brethren (Wiedertäufer or Täufer) of Switzerland and southern Germany, and the Menists (later to become Mennonites), Wederdopers, and Doopsgezinden of Holland and northwestern Germany. Another significant group were the Huguenots of France.

Many of the radical and not-so-radical reformation groups were decimated by mass executions ordered by local government authorities. These executions began in Brussels in 1523 and in Switzerland in 1525, giving rise to the name Martyrs. Two early leaders of the Swiss Brethren movement, namely Felix Manz (ca. 1498-1527) and Georg Blaurock (ca. 1492-1529) died by the hands of the authorities. Another Swiss Brethren leader, Conrad Grebel (ca. 1498-1526) died from the plague following periods of imprisonment. The southern German Anabaptist leader Henk Denk (ca. 1500-1527) also died from the plague while in Basel. Some smaller ultra-radical groups were wiped out by wholesale warfare as in the case of the infamous Münster Anabaptist movement of 1532-35 in northern Germany. None of these religious minority groups had the phenomenal success of the Lutheran movement.

LUTHER'S PERSONAL LEGACY. Martin Luther was fortunate to escape an early death from the hands of the authorities and from the various periodic epidemics raging through Europe.

Luther married past the prime of life at age forty-two, and even so left a fair number of descendants. Luther's death in 1546, at the age of sixty-three, closed a remarkably productive period and went well beyond the life expectancy of the day.

The six children of Martin Luther and his wife Katharina, were Johannes (1526-75), Elisabeth (1527-28), Magdalena (1529-51), Martin (1531-65), Paul (1533-93), and Margareta (?-1556). Descendants bearing the name Luther exist today in a very thin line only through his son Paul Luther. Some of these descendants still reside in the area of Wittenberg to this day.

Over the years, the Luther name was relatively unchanged showing only minor variations such as Lutter and Lutther. Luther's publications used several variants on the name including the Latinized form Lutherii. Luther's Catholic opponents derogatorily referred to the name in print as Luder, a name which translates as poor devil, or even worse.

REFERENCES

Bainton, R. H., 1970, "Martin Luther." In *Colliers Encyclopedia*, vol. 15, p. 111-116.

Bender H. S., (ed.), 1957, "Luther, Martin." In *Mennonite Encyclopedia*, vol. 3, p. 416-422, Mennonite Publishing House, Scottdale, Pa.

Benecke, Gerhard, 1982, *Maximilian I (1459-1519)*. Routledge & Kegan Paul, London, 205 p., 19 pls., 4 maps, 1 Table.

Brecht, Martin, 1983, *Martin Luther, 1483-1546*. Goethe-Institut, München, 96 p. (in 4 languages).

Edwards, Mark U., 1982, "Martin Luther." In *Reformation Europe: A Guide to Research*. Center for Reformation Research, St. Louis, p. 59-83 Contains good reference list.

Eichenberger, Walter, & Henning Wendland, 1977, *Deutsche Bibeln vor Luther*. Friedrich Wittig Verlag, Hamburg, 159 p., numerous illus.

Estep, Wm. R., 1986, *Martin Luther: in Renaissance and Reformation*. Wm. B. Eerdmans Publ. Co., Grand Rapids, MI, p. 112-160, illus. Good general life account and good bibliography.

Krahn, Cornelius, 1968, *Dutch Anabaptism, Origin, Spread and Thought (1450-1600)*. Martinus Nijhoff, The Hague, 303 p.

Kratzsch, Konrad, 1986, *Verzeichnis der Luther Drucke 1517-1546*. Nat. Forschungs- u. Bedenstätten der Klass. Dt. Literatur in Weimar, 213 p. Lists 980 of Luther's books including different editions of the same book dating from 1520-1546. Also refers to the similar extensive compilation of Josef Benzing, dated 1966.

Lang, August, 1913, "Zwingli und Calvin." In *Monographien zur Weltgeschichte, Nr. 31*. Verlag von Velhagen & Klasing, Bielefeld, 152 p., 161 illus. Note the many illustrations concerning the two subjects.

Maurer, Friedrich, 1929, *Studien zur Mitteldeutschen Bibelübersetzung vor Luther*. Carl Winters Universitätsbuchhandlung, Heidelberg, 144 p.

Mortzfeld, Peter (ed.), 1989, "Luther." In *Die Porträtsammlung der Herzog August Bibliothek Wolfenbüttel*. K. G. Sauer, München, Reih A, Bd. 15, nos. A13009 to A13147. Reproduces 138 engravings, mostly copperplate, of Martin Luther.

Reinhardt, Kurt F., 1961, "Martin Luther: His personality and his work." In *Germany: 2000 years*, vol. I (revised edition). Frederick Ungar Publishing Co., N.Y., 428 p. (Luther, p. 215-237).

Roemer, Gerhard & Gerhard Schwinge (eds.), 1983, *Luther und die Reformation am Oberrhein*. Badischen Landesbibliothek, Karlsruhe, 208 p., illus.

Schmidt, Ludwig, 1984, "Luther's Seitenverwandte." In *Genealogie und Landesgeschichte*, Bd. 38. Frankfurt am Main, 567 p.
Lists 8,358 descendants of Luther, most of them bearing a different family name.

Schwiebert, E. G., 1950, *Luther and His Times*. Concordia Publ. House, St. Louis, Mo., 892 p., illus.
Good general survey of Luther's life.

Severy, Merle, & James L. Amos, 1983, "The World of Luther." *National Geographic Mag.*, Washington, D.C., vol. 164, no. 4 (Oct. '83).
A popular account of Luther's life with numerous contemporary illustrations of his environment (p. 418-463).

Strand, K. A., 1966, *German Bibles before Luther. The Story of Fourteen High German Bibles, 1466-1518*. Wm. B. Eerdmans, Grand Rapids, MI, 64 p., illus.
Contains a good bibliography.

_____, 1967, *Early Low German Bibles. The Story of Four Pre-Luthern Editions*. Wm. B. Eerdmans Publ. Co., 48 p., illus.

Tumbült, Georg, 1899, "Die Wiedertäufer." In *Monographien zur Weltgeschichte*, Pt. VII. Verlag von Velhagen & Klasing, Bielefeld, 96 p., 95 illus.
Contains many good illustrations of the subject matter.

Volz, Hans, 1978, *Martin Luthers deutsche Bibel*. Friedrich Wittig Verlag, Hamburg, 255 p., numerous illus.

Walther, Wilhelm, 1966, *Die Deutsche Bibelübersetzung des Mittelalters*. B. de Graaf, Nieuwkoop, South Holland, The Netherlands; reprinted from the three parts of the 1889-1892 edition, 766 p.

Zopby, J. W., (ed.), 1980, *The Holy Roman Empire: A Dictionary Handbook*. Greenwood Press, Westport, Conn., 551 p., 8 maps
Basic subject listing for period the 843-1810, i.e., Charlemagne to Napoleonic dissolution of the Empire.

HE FROSCHAUER FIRM. CHRISTOPH Froschauer was born at Neuburg, near Öttingen, Bavaria, in the latter part of the 15th century, probably about 1490. Froschauer apparently was born out of wedlock and possibly took the name of his stepfather. There is speculation that Christoph Froschauer was related to Johannes, or Hans, Froschauer, who was active as a printer in Augsburg from 1494-1523. Likely, Christoph started his apprenticeship with the Augsburg Froschauer and possibly spent several years in the shops of the great Basel printers of the time, namely Adam Petri (active 1507-1527) and Johann Froben (active 1491-1527).

Documents show that Christoph Froschauer was in Zürich by 1517 (perhaps by 1515-16) and in the employment of the printer Hans Rüeger (active 1503-1517) who died in 1517. Upon the death of Rüeger, Froschauer assumed the leadership of the Zürich printing shop. By 1519, Froschauer had obtained citizenship in Zürich, Switzerland.

In 1521, Froschauer married the widow Elsa Rüeger and thereby became owner of the "Wyngarter" printing establishment. From 1521-1564, he acquired renown as a printer. During the years 1522-1552, he was associated with Eustachius Froschauer, who was apparently a younger brother or stepbrother. By 1535, it seems that Eustachius worked mainly in a paper mill in Zürich which supplied most of the paper for the local printing operation.

From the great volume of printed matter emanating from the Froschauer presses, one imagines that the size of the establishment rivaled the earlier printing organization of the famous Anton Koberger (1445-1513) of Nürnberg. Records show that Koberger controlled some twenty-four presses and had more than 100 employees during his heyday, not all of which were in Nürnberg.

In Zürich, the records indicate that the Froschauer establishment ran between four and six presses, more or less continuously during peak years, and had at least thirty employees.

Christoph Froschauer, or Christoffel Froschouer (also Froschower and Froschouwer) as the name appears on various printings, was childless by both his first marriage (Elsa died in 1550) and by his second marriage in 1550 to Dorothea Löher. Froschauer died in 1564 of the pest which raged over Europe during the epidemic years of 1564-65.

A nephew, Christoph Froschauer II, son of Eustachius, carried on the family name and the business after 1564 and until about 1585. Christoph Froschauer II died in 1585 shortly after having sold the printing firm. Later owners of the firm included the Hans Einrich Escher (active 1585-1591) and Johannes Wolf (active 1591-1626). The firm lives on in the present day house of Orell, Füssli & Co. of Zürich.

MAJOR PRINTED WORKS, 1521-1590. During the era of 1517-1521, the Froschauer shop printed a few anonymous books in addition to broadsides, calendars, and the like. During this formative period, Christoph Froschauer became acquainted with Huldrych Zwingli (1484-1531), and the two began working for the Reformation, then in its infant stages. Froschauer's first known printing, bearing the printer's name, was dated 1521. This consisted of three articles by the humanist Desiderius Erasmus of Rotterdam (c. 1466-1536), the works having been translated from Latin to German by Leo Jud (1482-1542). Other famous names whose works were printed by the Froschauer firm were the French theologian John Calvin (1509-64), the German theologian Philipp Melanchthon (1497-1560), and the Swiss naturalist Konrad von Gesner (1516-65). The earliest religious printings by Froschauer apparently were issued without a publisher's name. However, by 1524, Froschauer tended to use his name on the title page of almost all editions; this assisted him in developing and maintaining a strong marketing position of quality work.

Of the more than 900 titles printed by the two Froschauers, 500 were religious items. By some estimates, more than 800,000 copies of these 900 titles were issued from the Froschauer presses. That was an enormous number of copies for 16th century presses. Recent calculations indicate that 4,000 and more copies of the same book were printed by the larger printing firms existing in the first half of the 16th century.

The Froschauer shop printed all kinds of books, pamphlets, calendars, booklets, broadsides, pictures, hymnals, and playing cards.

During the years 1524-29, Froschauer printed the small folio "Luther Bible" in six parts and in three volumes. This first Bible edition retained the New Testament of Luther's translation with minor Swiss dialect substitutions; the three volume edition was comprised of four parts by Luther and two parts by Leo Jud and other theologians of Zürich.

In 1530, Froschauer printed Zwingli's version which was the first complete edition of the Bible and which appeared in one volume, being of octavo size (or small quarto size). Huldreich Zwingli was to die a violent death in 1531 in a Swiss civil war.

Froschauer's third edition of the complete Bible was a 1531 folio edition richly illustrated with 118 woodcuts in the Old Testament and twenty-one woodcuts in the New Testament. The woodcuts were attributed to the German painter Hans Holbein, the Younger (1497-1543). This limited edition was designed to fit the more expensive tastes of the nobility, the patricians, and the clergy, many of which were University trained. The text translation was three parts Luther and three parts Zürich theologian. Many of the woodcuts were used in later folio editions dated 1536, 1539-40, 1540, 1541, and 1543. One of the most richly illustrated Bibles published anywhere, and the best of the Zürich Bibles, was Froschauer's 1545 folio edition which contained many of the woodcuts by Holbein and some 57 new woodcuts by the Strassburg woodcarver Heinrich Vogtherr, the Elder (1490-1556).

Altogether, between the years 1524-1585, the Froschauer family printed at least thirty-nine editions of the complete Bible as well as fifty versions of the New Testament and six versions of the Old Testament. Reprints and size variations between folio, quarto, octavo and smaller sizes of these various editions brought the total Bible printings to more than ninety-five. The New Testament appeared mainly in German and Latin with one edition in English, and several editions in Greek.

Two well-known English translations were printed by Froschauer in 1550. The English edition of the complete Bible appeared in octavo size; there was apparently also a one-sixteenth size edition of the New Testament, possibly in condensed form. The printing of these translations appears to be related to the stay in 1547-49 in Zürich of John Hooper (c. 1500-1555), later to become bishop of Gloucester and Worcester. For his efforts in promoting the Reformation, Hooper spent almost two years in a London jail before being hanged as a result of repression of religious activities during the conservative reign of Queen Mary I (reigned 1553-1558).

Christoph Froschauer was also known for the monumental printing of the "Latin Bible" in seven volumes in 1532-37. His printing of a folio Bible in Latin in 1543 was considered a "technical jewel."

Froschauer the Elder, was one of the first printers to issue a catalog of his printings. In 1543, the catalog contained thirty-five pages and listed 110 in-print works in German with 106 works in Latin. The catalog contained twelve categories of books including religious, technical, and other fields.

FROSCHAUER'S TRAVELS. In 1522, Zürich's population consisted of perhaps 5,000 or 6,000 individuals, that is, discounting the plague epidemics of the 1520's when an estimated one quarter or so of Zürich's population died from the plague. Obviously, the local market quickly became saturated with books from the Froschauer presses.

In 1522, Froschauer went for the first time to the Frankfurt Book Fair. Subsequently, the Book Fair became a prime outlet for his printings. The Bavarian cities of Augsburg, Nördlingen, and Ingolstadt also were important outlets for his printings as were the Swiss cities of Basel and Zurzach. In Basel, Froschauer bought and sold printing supplies of all types. In the Alsace, the city of Strassburg formed an important market on the trips along the Rhine. Beginning in 1522, Froschauer went twice yearly to the famous Frankfurt Book Fair, a distance of over 400 kms (250 miles), and was a well-known exhibitor there. Like many prominent printers of the day, Froschauer has a depot on the Buchgasse. The Fairs lasted eight to ten days.

One may calculate that 16th century travel by horse drawn wagon (six to eight horses) averaged thirty to forty kms per day (eighteen to twenty-five miles per day); thus, the one way trip to Frankfurt took from ten to thirteen days. Consequently, the strenuous trips to Frankfurt kept Froschauer away from his home a month or more at a time. Under the Habsburg reign of Emperor Maximilian I (1493-1519), the German postal service was officially initiated about 1494. J. B. Homann's 1714 map of German postal routes (titled *Post Charte durch gantz Teutschland*) shows that Froschauer most likely travelled two routes by horse and wagon north from Zürich to Frankfurt. The route east of the Rhine included the following major cities: Schaffhausen, Stuttgart, Heilbronn, Heidelberg, and Darmstadt. The route west of the Rhine probably went through the cities of Zurzach, Basel, Strassburg, Hagenau, Landau, Speyer, and Mainz. Doubtless, Froschauer left broadsides in all of these cities advertising his wares.

On most of his trips, Froschauer was accompanied by well-known personalities and various servants and guards. On one famous trip which occurred in the Fall of 1529, the group included Huldrych Zwingli who was going to Marburg for the historic disputation between him and Luther. Froschauer left Zürich on September 3 and joined Zwingli in Basel. After some delay in waiting on others, they arrived in Strassburg on September 18, and then travelled through Herschen, Hornback, Zweibrücken, Lichtenberg, Meisenheim, Rheinfels, and St. Goar. Arriving in Brechen on September 24, the group split with Froschauer hurrying east to meet the Fair, which was to start on September 29, and Zwingli going north to Giessen and finally Marburg.

FROSCHAUER BIBLES IN AMERICA. Numerous versions of the Froschauer Bibles made their way to America with the immigrant ancestors of German- and Swiss-American families.

Nearly 120 copies of Froschauer Bibles are known to exist in public institutions in the United States, most having been donated by heirs of their former immigrant owners. Ten libraries have from four to fourteen copies of the Froschauer Bibles, with the greatest concentration being in the New York City Public Library which has fourteen copies. Other institutions having four or more copies include Johns Hopkins University, the Lancaster Mennonite Society (Pa.), Huntington Library, Harvard University, Cornell University, the Mennonite Historical Library (Goshen College, Ind.), Union Theological Seminary, Yale University, and the Library Company of Philadelphia. Twenty-six other organizations are recorded as possessing one to three copies of the Froschauer Bibles. A few editions in private hands are documented in the *Quarterly Mennonite Family History* (Elverson, PA); these, which typically are known by a former owner's name, include the following:

"Gerhard Hendricks' Family Bible" of 1538, (MFH, vol. IV, no. 2, p. 59)
"Buckwalter-Froschauer Bible", of 1551, (MFH, vol. VII, no. 3, Editor's page),

"Schneider-Froschauer Bible" of 1560, (MFH, vol. III, no. 2, p. 66),
"Schnebelli-Bachmann Bible", of 1536, (MFH, vol. XI, no. 1, p. 24).

Another copy in private hands of the Froschauer Bible is the
"Schneck-Moser-Amstutz" folio edition dating from 1580. This copy
became a cornerstone of church services about 1818 in the Swiss dominated Sonnenberg Mennonite Church near Kidron in Wayne Co. of
northeast Ohio. As transmitted by I. Glenn Amstutz of Dillon, Co, a
short description by J. O. Lehman of this copy was published in the
Mennonite Historical Bulletin in 1969. Lehman mentions the existence of
three other Froschauer Bibles in private hands in Ohio; these copies bear
the typically Swiss names of their owners Gerber, Nussbaum, and
Neuenschwander.

A copy of the 1556 edition of the Froschauer Bible, formerly belong-
ing to the Basinger family, was deposited about 1952 in the archives of
the Bluffton College Mennonite Historical Library (Allen Co., west
central Ohio).

REFERENCES

Alderfer, J. D., 1992, "1536 Froschauer Bible with Schnebelli-Bachmann Family Records." *Mennonite Family History*, Elverson, PA., Vol. XI, no. 1, p. 24-27.

Anonymous, 1978, *The National Union Catalog Pre-1956 Imprints*. Mansell Information/Publishing Ltd, London/American Library Association, Chicago, 754 vols.
This massive multi-volume publication is essential in locating and defining the existence of older works in American libraries. There is a series of updates.

Bender, H. S., (ed.), et al, 1956, "Froschauer, Christoph." In *Mennonite Encyclopedia*, vol. 2, p. 416

Benzing, Josef, 1952, *Buchdruckerlexikon des 16. Jahrhunderts*. Vittorio Klostermann, Frankfurt am Main, 215 p.
_____, 1963, *Die Buchdrucker des 16. und 17. Jahrhunderts im Deutschen Sprachgebiet*. Otto Harrassowitz, Wiesbaden, 528 p.
The author has long been recognized for his extensive research and documentary concerning German printers.

Bruckner, Albert, 1943, *Schweizer Stempelschneider und Schriftgiesser*. Haas'schen Schriftgiesserei A.G., Münchenstein, Switzerland, 223 p.

Goff, F. R., 1964, *Incunabula in American Libraries (Third Census)*. Bibliographical Soc. America, N.Y., 7, 798 p.
_____, 1972, *Incunabula in American Libraries (Supplement to Third Census)*. ibid, 104 p.

Haller, C. R., 1989, "Froschauer Bibles." *Mennonite Family History*, Elverson, PA, vol. VIII, no. 2, p. 64.

Hirsch, Rudolf, 1974, *Printing, Selling and Reading 1450-1550*. Otto Harrassowitz, Wiesbaden, 165 p.
Contains many little known facts concerning German bookprinting, in English.

Kapp, Friedrich, 1886, *Geschichte des deutschen Buchhandels bis in das siebzehnte Jahrhundert*. Börsenverein, Leipzig, Bd. 1, 880 p.
A pioneering effort concerning the history of German printers.

Leemann-Van Elck, Paul, 1940, *Die Offizin Froschauer, Zürichs berühmte Druckerei im 16. Jahrhundert*. Orell Füssli Verlag, Zürich/Leipzig, 215 p., illus.

Leemann-Van Elck, Paul, 1950, Druck, Verlag, *Buchhandel im Kanton Zürich von den Anfängen bis um 1850*. Mill. Antiquarischen Gesell., Zürich, Bd. 36.

Lehman, J. O., 1969, "An Old Bible in the Community." *Mennonite Historical Bulletin*, Goshen, Ind., Vol. XXX, p. 5-6.

Lupton, Lewis, 1986, *Tyndale, the Translator*. The Olive Tree, London, Pt. 1, 176 p., numerous illus.
_____, 1987, *Tyndale, the Martyr*. ibid, Pt 2, 161 p., numerous illus.
A very curious pair of books in handwritten text; they describe the life of William Tyndale and, in part, of Miles Coverdale.

Metzger, J. J., 1967, *Geschichte der Deutschen Biblübersetzungen in der schweizerisch-reformierten Kirche*. B. de Graaf, Niewkoop (South Holland, The Netherlands), 428 p. (reprint of 1876 edition).

Mozley, J.F., 1937, *William Tyndale*. Macmillan Publ. Co., N.Y., 364 p., 5 illus. (reprinted 1971 by Greenwood Press, Westport, CT).
_____, 1953, *Coverdale and his Bible*. Lutterworth Press, London, 359 p. Includes text on Froschauer's first printing of the Bible.

Roberts, M. T. & Don Etherington, 1982, *Bookbinding and the Conservation of Books*. Library of Congress, Washington, D.C., 296 p.
One of the better known references which describe book sizes.

Rudolphi, E. Camillo, 1963, *Die Buchdrucker-Familie Froschauer in Zürich, 1521-159???*. B. de Graaf, Niewkoop (South Holland, The Netherlands), 93 p.
This is a reprint of the 1869 edition which is one of the oldest and most thorough documents on the Froschauer family, see also Vöglin, 1840.

Schmidt, Rudolf, 1979, *Deutsche Buchhändler - Deutsche Buchdrucker*. Georg Olms Verlag, Hildesheim, 1155 p.

Sheppard, L.A., 1953, "The Printers of the Coverdale Bible, 1535." *The Library*, London, NS, vol 16, p. 280-289.

Shelley, Patricia, 1989, "The Bible as Canon." *Mennonite Life*, North Newton, Kansas, vol. 44, no. 3, p.4-11.
Shows an elaborate title page of a Froschauer Bible dated 1536/38. The copy is in the Mennonite Library and Archives in North Newton, Kansas.

Slack, Paul, 1985, *The Impact of Plague in Tudor and Stuart England*. Routledge & Kegan Paul Plc., London, 443 p.
A good recent discussion of the consequences of the plague in Europe for the period of about 1400-1700.

Staedtke, Joachim, 1965, *Anfänge und Erste Blütezeit des Zürcher Buch Drucks*. Orell Füssli Verlag, Zürich, 118 p., illus.
The publication by Staedtke is one of the most comprehensive on the life of Christoph Froschauer.

Steinberg, S. H., 1974, *Five Hundred Years of Printing*. Penguin Books Ltd., Harmondsworth, England, 3rd ed., 400 p.
A standard handbook on the history of printing in Europe.

Twigg, Graham, 1984, *The Black Death: A Biological Appraisal*. Butsford Academic and Educational, London, 254 p., illus.

Vöglin, S., 1840, *Christoph Froschauer, erster berühmter Buchdrucker in Zürich*. J. J. Ulrich, Zürich, 24 p.

 EGINNINGS OF THE MERIAN FIRM. MATthäus Merian the Elder, the famous engraver and publisher, was born in Basel, Switzerland on September 22, 1593. He died in Bad Schwalbach (near Bad Soden, Taunus, in Hessen, Germany) on July 19, 1650. Merian showed artistic talent at an early age, working in Basel and Zürich during the years 1606-09. One account indicates that he worked in Strassburg during 1610. The period 1612-15 is known as his Parisian period during which time he also worked in Nancy. The years 1615-16 are cited as his first Basel period. During 1616-17, Merian travelled over much of Germany with recorded stays at Augsburg, at Stuttgart, at Nürnberg, and apparently down the Rhine to Holland. In the era 1616-20, his residence varied between Oppenheim and Heidelberg. The years 1620-24 (early part of the Thirty Years' War) was known as Merian's second Basel period.

About 1617, Merian was in Frankfurt, where he married, in 1619, the eldest daughter of engraver Johann Theodor de Bry (1561-1623), Maria Magdalena.

The leader of the de Bry family was Theodor de Bry (1528-98) who was born in Liege, Belgium, and because of his Protestant religious beliefs left Belgium in 1586 to work in England. In 1588, the family moved to Frankfurt am Main, Germany. Theodor de Bry, the Elder, was a goldsmith and copper plate engraver. Two sons, Johann Theodor, mentioned above, and Johann Israel (ca. 1565-1609) carried on the family business in Frankfurt and in Oppenheim, on the Rhine.

The Family de Bry became famous for the series *Collectiones peregrinationum, etc.* which was a series of twenty-eight volumes of "travel books", that is, illustrations with short text which through the medium of copper plate engravings, showed views of localities, some highly artificial, in many parts of the world, including the Americas. The *Collectiones* were published over a period of forty-four years (1590-1634) with six volumes being printed during the lifetime of the elder de Bry. This series stimulated the imagination of early travellers and created an interest in the lands lying across the Atlantic.

THE MERIAN FAMILY. The children of Matthäus Merian the Elder, were Matthäus the Younger (1621-87), and Caspar (1627-1688). By a second marriage, about 1646, a daughter, Maria Sibylla (1647-1717), and a son (1649) whose name is not known, were born. After the death of Merian in 1650, his second wife, Johanna Sybille Heim, married Jacob Marell (1614-1681). All of the children except the youngest son were involved with the family printing business and eventually developed careers of their own as engravers, etchers, and illustrators.

After the death of Johann Theodor de Bry in 1623, Merian returned to Frankfurt (1624) to carry on the de Bry business. He took over the family business on a permanent basis in 1626 and started the famous publishing house of Merian. From 1626 to 1650, the Frankfurt Book Fair catalog lists about 135 new books by the Merian firm. Caspar Merian, as related in Part 4, was a member of the Piëtist Saalhof group in Frankfurt and, consequently, also of the Frankfort Companie. In about 1682, he, through the Frankfort Companie, subscribed to land offered by William Penn in Pennsylvania part of which would later be known as Germantown. Shortly thereafter, he dropped out of the subscription. One report indicates that Caspar died in 1688 at a community of Labadists at Bosch, in Friesland, in the Lowlands.

Maria Sibylla Merian eventually set up residence in Nürnberg where she published, in 1679, her first book on insects. Later, she took her daughter to Holland where she joined a piëtistic community of Labadists. In later years, she established residence in Amsterdam, from which, about 1699, she made her famous trip to Surinam, in South America. Collections of insects and flowers on this trip formed the basis for later manuscripts.

After the death of his father in 1650, Matthäus the Younger, with his younger brother Caspar and Matthäus' son, Johann Matthäus (1659-1716), carried on the family tradition of sumptuously illustrated folios. The Merian business was carried on until 1726 when a great fire destroyed most of the printing stock.

MAJOR PRINTED WORKS, 1626-1656. The Merian enterprise published numerous books, not only those written by the elder Merian, but also by many others. Two series of Merian's authorship deserve special mention. The so-called *Theatrum Europeaum* was published in twenty-one volumes from 1635-1738, of which five volumes were printed prior to Merian's death in 1650. It contained an enormous chronicle of contemporary events with innumerable copperplate engravings.

The so-called *Topographia Germaniae* was published in seventeen (of a total of twenty-nine volumes) in the years from 1642-1656. Twelve of these volumes were published prior to 1650. The entire set of twenty-nine volumes contained 2,142 illustrations, mainly city views, and ninety-two early maps. The series went through seven printings up to 1736. The *Topographia Germaniae* was a fantastic chronology of German and Swiss cities and towns.

Related, but much smaller, series were titled *Topographia Galliae* (France) and *Topographia Romae*. Part of the numerous copper plate engraving illustrations, especially those of southwest Germany and Switzerland, prior to 1650, was done by Matthäus, the Elder, with contributions by various other individuals. The maps were mainly copied from the well-known Dutch map-makers Joan Blaeu (1595-1673), Jan Jansson (1588-1664), and the father and son team of Claes Janszoon Visscher (1587-1652) and Nicolaes Visscher I (1618-79).

FROM WOOD CUTS TO COPPER PLATE ENGRAVING. The use of paper arrived in Europe supposedly in the 12th century. Paper slowly replaced vellum (fine calf skin) as a medium for manuscripts, but by the late 14th century, paper was in general use.

In fact, early paper making in Europe was largely confined to the countries near the Mediterranean, in particular to Italy. There are records dating from the early 14th century of paper mills near Fabriano, Italy. Through most of the 15th century, Italy was the prime manufacturer and distributor of paper to the rest of Europe. In Germany. the early Mainz printers imported their paper from Italy. In the late 15th century, France developed its own paper making industry, especially in the area of Champagne.

It was not until the mid-16th century, after the surge of voluminous writing by Martin Luther and other key Reformers, that the German states became self-sufficient in paper making. Through their efforts at independence, about 1671, the Dutch were forced to develop their own paper mills.

Almost contemporaneous with the rise of paper making in the late 14th century, the use of block prints for devotional images became commonplace, particularly along the Rhine and in certain parts of France, notably in Burgundy. Paper was much superior than vellum for printing the religious iconography which then came into vogue.

In 1461, a notable printer of Bamberg, Albrecht Pfister, conceived the idea of illustrating books with block prints. The idea quickly spread to many parts of Europe. In 1477, an Augsburg printer, Anton Sorg, finished a work requisitioned by the town council of Constance. The work was titled *Das Concilium buch geschehen zu Contencz* and is generally considered to be the first printed armorial; this monumental publication contained woodcut illustration which showed 1,156 coats-of-arms, most real, some imaginary, representing various parts of Europe. In 1491, Anton Koberger, the famous Nürnberg printer, used 91 woodcuts of Bible scenes to illustrate his *Schatzebehalter* (freely translated as the Treasure Chest).

Several other German publishers had established a long history of using wood cuts for town views and maps, among which were Anton Koberger's printing of Hartmann Schedel's 1493 *Weltchronik* (also known at the *Liber Chronicarum* and as the *Nürnberg Chronicle*), as well as Sebastian Münster's 1544 *Cosmographia*, and the 1573-98 *Civitates Orbis Terrarum* by Braun & Hogenberg.

However, the transition included Schedel's 15th century wood-cuts (645 woodcuts with thirty-two town views) and the 16th century woodcuts of Froschauer's folio Bible (dated 1545; more than 200 woodcuts) and Johannes Stumpf's *Schweizerchronik* of 1548 (some 4,000 illustrations, mostly woodcuts).

Of course, Merian's 17th century town views and maps were not the first of their kind. One of the earliest use of copper plate engraving was a 1478 edition, printed in Bologna, of the *Cosmographia* by Ptolemy (ancient Greek astronomer) which contained a series of maps destined to become a model for many later map makers.

Thus, copperplate engraving is supposed to have originated in Florence, Italy, about 1477 (perhaps as early as 1446 according to some authors). Engraving on copper and iron plates was used only sparingly during the 16th century by German map makers who preferred woodcuts. Printers in Italy, however, were considerably more receptive to the use of copper plate engraving.

By the 17th century copper plate engravings in Merian's *Topographae Germaniae* (more than 2,000) show the vastly superior quality in this type of printing. Particularly impressive is Merian's 1645 view of Heidelberg with its famous castle.

The last half of the 17th century saw copper plate engraving brought to a fine art by Dutch and French map makers, as documented in an earlier essay.

REFERENCES

Falk, Tilman (ed.), 1989, *Hollstein's German Engravings, Etchings, and Woodcuts, 1400-1700*. Koninklijke van Poll, Rosendaal, Netherlands, especially Vol. XXV, p. 89-217, and Vol. XXVI, p. 9-230, numerous illus.

Kapp, Friedrich & J. Goldfriedrich, 1886-1913, *Geschichte des deutschen Buchhandels.* Verlag des Börsenvereins der Deutschen Buchhändler, Leipzig, Bd. I, (up to 17th century; 1886), 880 p., 3 pls; Bd. II, (1648-1740; 1908), 552 p.; Bd. III, (1740-1804; 1909), 673 p.; Bd. IV, (Register; 1912), 495 p. + 142 p.

Kirchner, Joachim, 1952, *Lexikon des Buchwesens.* Hiersemann Verlag, Stuttgart, Bd. I, (A-K), 405 p.
_____, ibid, Bd. II (L-Z), p. 406-927.

Merian, Matthäus, 1645, *Topographia Palatinatus Rheni et Vicinarum Regionum.* Franckfurt am Mayn, 67 p., 1 map, numerous town views + other illus. Nahmen Register, 5 p. (Zügab, 17 p., French cities in Lorraine & Savoy, illus.; Zügab printer, Wolffgang Hofmanns).
_____, 1646, *Topographia Archiepiscopatum Moguntinensis Treuirensis et Coloniensis.* Franckfurt am Mayn, 54 p. + 3 p. (Register), 3 maps, numerous town views and other illus.
These two major works are representative of Merian's primary publications and illustrate the areas and cities along the left bank of the German Rhine and along the Mosel.

Rücker, Elisabeth, 1967, *Maria Sibylla Merian.* Druckhaus Nürnberg, 60 p., 34 pls.
_____, 1973, *Die Schedelsche Weltchronik.* Prestel-Verlag, München, 144 p., illus.
_____, 1988, *Hartmann Schedels Weltchronik.* Prestel-Verlag, München, 240 p., illus.

Salloch, S. W., 1935, *Deutsche Städte im siebzehnten Jahrhundert: Kupferstiche von Matthäus Merian and Berichte von Zeitgenossen.* Amthorsche Verlagsbuchhandlung, Leipzig, 61 p., 21 illus.
The title translates as 17th century copper plate views of German cities as printed by Matthäus Merian.

Wütherich, L. H., 1966, *Das Druckgraphische Werk von Matthäus Merian d.Ä.*. Im Bärenreiter Verlag zu Basel, Bd. I, 245 p., 408 illus.

_____, 1972, ibid, Bd. 2, 189 p., 104 illus.

_____, 1967. *Register zu Merians Topographia Germaniae.* Bärenreiter Verlag, Kassel und Basel, 108 p.

The above three volumes comprise an essentially complete summary of the works of the Merian publishing firm for the period of about 1626 to 1726.

N TODAY'S WORLD OF THE WELL-KNOWN Baedekers' and Michelin series of travel guides of various countries, these books are taken for granted. Such travel guides have evolved through the centuries. Indeed, the Romans, about the 3rd century A.D., apparently had a road map showing some of the principal roads of the Roman Empire. This is documented by the so-called *Peutinger Table* which is actually a scroll about twenty-two feet long and one foot wide. The *Peutinger Table* takes its name from an Augsburg humanist and antiquarian, Konrad Peutinger (1465-1547), who had a 13th century copy of the Roman map.

The earliest travel book to appear in print is attributed to one Bernhard von Breydenbach, a wealthy canon of Mainz. Breydenbach visited Palestine in 1483-4 and shortly thereafter promoted the book called *Peregrination in terram sanctum* which contained a map of Palestine and views of the six town he visited. The multi-sheet map was a wood cut printed on four blocks.

TRAVEL GUIDES IN GERMANY. In Germany, during the Middle Ages, Erhard Etzlaub, about 1492, printed decorative woodblock maps showing Nürnberg as a German commercial center with roads leading outward in all directions. In 1500-01, Etzlaub produced a similar, but much larger map titled "Das is der Rom Weg", etc. (The Roman Road). This map shows major roads leading in nine directions, as for instance, to Denmark, to Paris, to Poland, to Vienna, to Rome, etc. The significance of this map is the use of dotted lines with each point being equivalent to one German "Meile" (about 7.5 km or 4.7 U.S. statute miles). At that time, a public transportation or postal carriage could cover one German Meile in about one hour. Horses were normally changed every five German Meilen.

The first public transport on the Continent developed as an outgrowth of the postal service commission which was granted to the Familie Tassis (later Taxis, and then Thurn und Taxis) under the Habsburg reign of Emperor Maximilian I (reigned 1493-1519). This postal service was officially initiated about 1494 and covered an overland route joining royal houses in Mechelen (near Brussels, Belgium) with those in Innsbruck (Austria) by way of the German cities of Köln, Mainz, Worms, Speir (Speyer), and Lindau.

One of the earliest known route books covering Germany was that by Jörg Gail of Augsburg; this booklet is dated 1563. The 272 text pages, being of small size, comprise what might be termed a primitive Baedeker. The pages list travel routes over much of Germany. The first comprehensive road map of Germany, and perhaps the first German travel guide, in the modern sense, was produced in 1641 by Johann Jung and Conrad Jung, and was titled *Deutsche Reisekarte* (German Travel Map).

Early itineraries gave only routes and distances. At the beginning of the 17th century, there was a publication titled *Delitiae Galliae*, and another titled *Delitiae Germaniae*, both written in Latin, mainly for the benefit of gentlemen of means, diplomats, and students.

Martin Zeiller (1589-1661), the well-known German geographer, issued in 1651, his *Fidus Achatu* which is considered by some to be the "first Baedeker" in the German language. Zeiller's travel guides covered many foreign countries. These guides gave a variety of advice to the traveller.

In 1686, Edward Brown printed a popular travel book (in German) about travels through Holland, Hungary, Bulgaria, Austria, and Germany. By the end of the 17th century, there was a veritable flood of early travel guides and maps.

In 1692, Johann Ulrich Müller, and in 1709-11, Johann Peter Nell, both produced similar travel maps. The noted German cartographer Johann Baptist Homann printed a well-known map showing central European postal routes in 1714, this map being apparently a copy of the map by Nell dating a few years earlier.

Along the west side of the Rhine, Homann's famous 1714 postal map shows a "Reittende Posten" route (horseback route) connecting major cities. These cities include Speir (Speyer) in the south, extending northwards to Maintz (Mainz), westward to Bingen, then northwest to Coblentz (Koblenz), Bonn, and Coeln (Köln), where the route becomes a "Fahrende Posten" (carriage post route), and then westward to Cleve (Kleve), and on to the Dutch city of Utrecht.

In Germany, the noted author Alois Wilhelm S. Schreiber (1763-1841) wrote his *Handbuch für Reisende am Rhein* (Handbook for Travellers on the Rhine), with the first edition by 1816. In this historic work, Schreiber gives a short description of the numerous cities, towns, and villages along the Rhein from about Strassburg north to the German/Dutch border, as well as a description of adjacent larger cities, such as Achen (Aachen) and Frankfurt. To provide entertainment for the traveller, an appendix to Schreiber's 1816 edition printed fourteen of the better known legends of the Rhine. The third edition of Schreiber's book, published about 1825, gives in addition to an expanded list of seventeen legends, a good bibliography which had formed a partial source for his earlier publication.

TRAVEL GUIDES IN ENGLAND AND FRANCE. The first well-documented road books in England and in France date from the early part of the 16th century. There was, for instance, a road book by John Leland dating from about 1535-45, called the *Itinerary*.

In 1577, the English author Raphael Holinshed produced a sort of a travel guide named *Chronicles of England and Scotland*.

In Paris, in 1579, Jean Bernard produced a road book titled simply *England and Scotland*.

During the years 1593-98, the Englishman John Norden made road maps of various English counties. In 1625, Norden wrote the book titled *An Intended Guide for English Travailers*. About 1596, the Englishman Philip Symonson also produced road maps of various English counties. In 1635, Mathew Simons wrote *A Direction for the English Traviller*.

In France in the meantime, in 1632 Melchoir Tavernier produced a map showing the postal routes of France. The Tavernier map was copied by the well-known cartographer Nicholas Sanson in 1654, and in succeeding years.

In England, travel guides and maps continued to evolve through the 16th and 17th centuries. Other notable examples are those in 1675 by John Ogilby who printed a series of about 100 maps of the principal roads of England and Wales.

In the years 1790-1828, John Cary published a series of editions of his *Traveller's Companion* which became immensely popular. These editions form a further basis for the modern day Baedekers' and the Michelin guides.

John Murray (1802-1892) was the third of the Murray line in the well-known London publishing family. Likewise, John Murray's publishing of the *Guide for Traveler on the Continent* in 1820 proved very popular with the English reading public. In 1836, Murray issued his *Red Book* about the sights of Holland, Belgium, and Germany. With regular steamship service along the Rhine starting in 1827, travel here had become very popular with those from England. Murray collaborated with Karl Baedeker on at least one of the early Baedekers' travel guides; there was in fact some degree of collaboration between Murray and the Baedekers over the lengthy period of about 1836 to 1862.

THE HOUSE OF BAEDEKER. The famous House of Baedeker was formed by Karl Baedeker (1801-1859). This firm was founded in 1827 in Koblenz, Germany. In fact, a large part of Baedeker's early business evolved around a travel guide for the Rhine as a response to demand for regular steamship passenger service between Mainz and Köln (Cologne) which started also in 1827. Baedeker's first guide was actually an extensively revised version of the guide written by J. A. Klein in 1828. In 1832, Baedeker printed with a yellow cover, his *Rheinreise von Mainz bis Coeln* (Rhine travel from Mainz to Köln); a second edition was printed in 1835 and a third edition in 1839. By 1842, Baedeker had adopted the familiar red cover with gold lettering for handbooks on Germany and on Austria; about this same time numerous town plans were included in the travel guides. In 1844, his handbook on Switzerland was published.

In the early days, Baedeker used various printing establishments in Koblenz, Mainz, Darmstadt, and in Essen, especially for lithography work on the maps.

The second generation of Baedekers included Ernst (1833-1861), Karl (1837-1911), and Fritz (1844-1925).

Long after Karl Baedeker's death, son Karl Baedeker II, moved the business to Leipzig in 1872. The Baedeker travel guides continued to be issued in German, in English, and in French. A great-grandson, Karl Friedrich Baedeker (1910-1979), picked up the remains of the business after World War II and renewed activity in a small city north of Hamburg and in Leipzig, all the while retaining the familiar red cover.

THE MICHELIN GUIDES. The Michelin Guides, also in red covers, began in 1900. Working in Paris, the two Michelin brothers, Edouard and Andre, invented the world's first detachable pneumatic bicycle tire in 1891. The ever increasing tire business prompted demand for travel guides, at first in southern Europe and then, by 1911, for guides of Germany and the Rhineland. By the late 1930's, the familiar red cover of the Michelin guides was reserved for rating of restaurants in France, while the Michelin travel guides adopted a green cover.

The Michelin guides and atlases continue to be published today and are much in demand because of their fine quality and readability.

LEGENDS, SAGAS, AND FAIRY TALES. The modern story of the German "legends, sagas, and fairy tales," many associated with the Rhine, date from a host of poets and writers. Among the better known of the early German writers are Jacob Ludwig Carl Grimm (1785-1863), and his brother Wilhelm Carl Grimm (1786-1859), Karl Simrock (1802-1876), Karl Joachim Friedrich Ludwig v. Arnim (1781-1831), Bettina Brentano (1785-1859) and Clemens Wenzel Maria Brentano (1778-1842), and, of course, Johann Wolfgang von Goethe (1749-1832).

The famous printings of the legends by the Grimm brothers began in the period 1812-15 under the title *Kind- und Hausmärchen* (Children's and House Fairy Tales).

The early English Romantics, who did much to popularize travels along the Rhine, include Thomas Cogan (1736-1816), William Beckford (1760-1844), John Gardnor (1726-1808), and Lord Byron (George Gordon Byron; 1788-1824).

On the Rhine today, passenger boats travel several times an hour, in both directions, between Mainz and Köln (Cologne), during the season. Along every few kilometers, the banks are marked by the remains of a castle or other historic point around which a legend has risen. In fact, a 1985 English edition titled *Legends of the Rhine* by the German author Wilhelm Ruland gives almost fifty of these legends. German and English school children are well acquainted with outstanding tales such as the *Nibelungen Lied, Charlemagne and Johannisberg, Bingen and the Mouse Tower, The Lorelei, The Doctor's Wine of Bernkastel*, and many other bedtime stories. Doubtless, 17th and 18th century migrants travelling along the Rhine were equally fascinated by the many natural wonders and also the man-made features associated with the Rhine.

A natural wonder, *The Lorelei*, was immortalized in 1827 when Heinrich Heine (1797-1856) wrote the following poem:

Die Lore-Lei	The Lorelei
Ich weiss nicht, was solls bedeuten,	What does it mean
Dass ich so traurig bin?	that I should be so sad?
Ein Märchen aus alten Zeiten,	a fairy tale from long ago,
Das kommt mir nicht aus dem Sinn.	which is always on my mind.
Die Luft is kuhl und es dunkelt,	The air is cool in the dusk,
Und ruhig fliesst der Rhein;	and quietly flows the Rhine;
Der Gipfel des Berges funkelt	The summit of the mountain sparkles
Im Abendsonnenschein;	in the evening sunshine;
Die schönste Jungfrau sitzet	The wondrous maiden sits
Dort oben wunderbar,	marvelously up above,
Ihr goldnes Geschmeide blitzet,	her golden form glistening
Sie kämmt ihr goldnes Haar.	as she combs her golden locks.
Sie kämmt es mit goldnem Kamme,	She combs with a golden comb
Und singt ein Lied dabei,	as she sings a song
Das hat eine wundersame,	a haunting,
Gewaltige Melodie.	overwhelming melody.
Den Schiffer im kleinen Schiffe	The sailor in his small boat
Ergreift es mit wildem Weh;	listens with wild desire
Er schaut nicht die Felsenriffe,	and he sees not the sunken rocks,
Er schaut nur hinauf in die Höh.	he sees only the sights above.
Ich glaube die Wellen verschlingen	I believe that the waves devour
Am Ende Schiffer und Kahn;	sailor and boat forevermore;
Und das hat mit ihrem Singen	that which with her singing
Die Lore-Lei getan.	the Lorelei has caused.
H. Heine (1827)	C. R. Haller-translation

REFERENCES

Ambrosi, Hans & K. B. Stewart, 1990, *Travellers Wine Guide - Germany*. Sterling Publ. Co., N.Y., 144 p., maps, illus.
A good modern tourist guide of the Rhine; the senior author is an authority on German wines.

Baedeker, Karl, 1864, *Deutschland nebst Theilen der Angrenzende Länder*. Erster Theil: Österreich, Sud- und West-Deutschland, Zweiter Theil: Mittel- und Nord-Deutschland. Karl Baedeker, Coblenz, 486 p. & 284 p., maps.

Baedeker, Karl II, 1886, *Die Rheinlande*. Verlag von Karl Baedeker, Leipzig, Leipzig, 32 ed., 438 p., 31 maps.

Baumgarten, M. I., 1984, *Baedeker's Rhine*. Prentice Hall, Inc., Englewood Cliffs, N. J., 288 p., map., illus. (English translation by James Hogarth)

Campbell, Tony, 1987, *The Earliest Printed Maps, 1472-1500*. University of California Press, Berkely, 244 p., 69 map reproductions.

Dreyer-Eimbeke, Erika, 1989, *Alte Strassen in Herzen Europas*. Umschau Verlag, Frankfurt am Main, 280 p., 19 sketch maps.
The wealth of historic detail deals mainly with selected, well-known roads, many of Roman origin, in the northern part of Germany. Contains good reference list.

Graves, William (ed.), 1991, *A Traveler's Map of Germany*. National Geographic Soc., Washington, D.C., map.
Shows reunited Germany with touristic text overlay, map scale, 1:200,000.

Hinrichsen, A. W., 1988, *Baedeker-Katalog*. Ursula Hinrichsen Verlag, Holzminden, 111 p.
Includes a listing of of the Baedeker works printed prior to World War II and their 1988 market values.

_____, 1989, *Baedeker-Katalog*. Ursula Hinrichsen Verlag, Holzminden, 46 p.
Translation by Michael Wild; a somewhat uneven history of the Baedeker firm.

Krüger, Herbert, 1974, *Das Ältest Deutsche Routenhandbuch, Jörg Gails "Raissbüchlin"*. Akademische Druck- u. Verlagsanstalt, Graz, 354 p., plus Facsimile pages 357-424, 6 maps.

Reproduces and elaborates on the 1563 booklet by Jörg Gail, resident of Augsburg. The six modern route maps refer to ancient maps dating 1500 to 1650.

Löschburg, Winfried, 1982, *A History of Travel*. Hippocrene Books, Inc., 190 p., numerous illus.
This is one of few histories dedicated to the history of travel in Europe.

Moreland, Carl & David Bannister, 1983, *Christie's Collectors Guides: Antique Maps*. Phaidon/Christies Ltd., Oxford, 314 p., numerous maps
Note especially Chapter 5, p. 25-31, titled "Road Maps, Atlases, and Road Books."

Rees, Goronwy, 1967, *The Rhine*. G. Putnam's Sons, N.Y., 186 p.

Ruland, Wilhelm, 1925, *Rheinisches Sagenbuch*. Verlag von Hoursch & Bechstedt, Köln, 41st printing, 320 p.,
_____, 1975, *Legends of the Rhine*. Hoursch & Bechstedt, Bonn, 286 p.,
_____, 1985, *Legends of the Rhine*. Stollfuss Verlag, Bonn, 3rd ed., 284 p.

Sagar, D. M., J. M. Morris, & Persephone Weene, 1987, *Thomas Jefferson's European Travel Diaries*. Isodore Stephanus Sons Publishing, Ithaca, N.Y., 140 p., illus.
Noted traveller, later president, Jefferson went to principal wine growing regions of France in 1787 and of Germany in 1788.

Schneider, Hermann (ed.), 1914, *Die deutschen Sagen der Brüder Grimm*. Deutsches Verlagshaus Bong & Co., Berlin, Erster Teil-Ortssagen, 278 p., Zweiter Teil-Geschichtliche Sagen, 229 p.
First published in Berlin in 1816-1818.

Schreiber, Aloys, 1816, *Handbuch für Reisende am Rhein von Schafhausen bis Holland*. Verlag Joseph Engelmann, Heidelberg, 488 p (lst edition).
_____, ca. 1825, *Ibid*. 528 p. (3rd edition).

Steinfeld, Ludwig, 1991, *Chronik einer Strasse. Die alte Strasse von Frankfurt nach Leipzig*. Geiger-Verlag, Horb am Neckar, 179 p., map on cover, illus.
An interesting summary of travel on the famous trade-route between Frankfurt am Main and Leipzig. It contains extracts from manuscripts and books over a period of 1,000 years. As late as 1790, portions of the route were of a very primitive nature.

Part 6

he
Push
and
the Pull

VER THE YEARS, BEGINNING FROM ABOUT 1683, the so-called German Americans have been one of the largest foreign groups to migrate to the America. Successive waves of peoples came from all over Germany, but the bulk came from along the Rhine and from the southern portion of Germany, an area universally called "the Palatinate." They migrated in response to various political, economic, and religious factors. Many were motivated to migrate either by impending war or following the end of a conflict, in search of better living conditions.

Just as the Catholic Hapsburg regime (Table 6.4 on page 228) had its "Drang nach Osten" (push towards the East, i.e., the Slavic countries; ostensibly to provide a buffer zone between Vienna and "the Turks") as early as 1480, the Protestant push towards the West after 1683 effectively replaced the eastward migration of German-speaking peoples.

Equally important, perhaps, was the pull of strong interest groups who were committed to populating large blocks of land in America. For instance, most of the colonial German settlers apparently migrated in order to obtain religious freedom (the push). However, William Penn and the Frankfort Companie actively promoted the settlement of their large land holdings in eastern Pennsylvania (the pull) beginning about 1682. There are numerous other examples of the push and the pull in the following paragraphs.

IMMIGRATION ESTIMATES - COLONIAL YEARS. Various learned scholars have attempted to estimate the actual number of German-speaking peoples migrating to America. Nearly all begin with the arbitrary date of 1683, which historically represents the first permanent German settlement.

The year 1683 was the year that Pastorius and his group of Quakers and others from Germany arrived to populate Germantown in Pennsylvania, as told in Part 4. The early group settled in Germantown outside Philadelphia with later arrivals moving to Montgomery Co., Pa.

The records to about 1710 are very spotty. After 1710, there was a large movement of Swiss and Germans to Conestoga along Pequa Creek in Lancaster Co., Pa. The first large influx of Germans and Swiss had begun in 1709 partly as a response to the especially bad winter of 1708-09 in Europe. In September, 1710, some half dozen Swiss Mennonite families arrived in Philadelphia aboard the ship *Maria Hope* and travelled overland thence to Lancaster Co. Their leader, Martin Kendig, returned to Europe a few years later and organized a much larger group of 363 emigrants. This larger group, including many Mennonites from the Palatinate, arrived in Philadelphia in 1717 in three ships. Most followed their leader to Lancaster County. Over the four decade period of 1710 to 1750, possibly 4,000 Swiss went to Lancaster Co.

Descendants of Lancaster Mennonites provided one of America's more spectacular business success stories. The ubiquitous Hershey candy bar was named after the family of Milton S. Hershey (1857-1945), whose ancestors arrived in Pennsylvania about 1717. The family included the patriarch Christian Hershey, his son Benjamin Hershey (1697-1789), who became a bishop of the Mennonite Church, and two other sons. The family group had made the long journey from Friedelsheim, a small village on the eastern edge of the German wine growing district of Rheinland-Pfalz, not far west of the City of Ludwigshaven and the Rhine River. Documents of the family name in Friedelsheim dating from 1716 show the spelling as Hirschi, a name which originated in the Emmenthal of Switzerland in the early 1670's.

The German Reformed Church in eastern Pennsylvania had its start about 1725 under the direction of Johann Philipp Boehm (1683-1749). Another German, Michael Schlatter (1716-90), who arrived in 1746, carried on the work of Boehm. The comparatively rapid expansion of the Reformed Church, which totaled 159 churches by 1775, was due mainly to the influx of the so-called Palatines.

The expansion of the Lutheran Church in America was due in large part to the efforts of another German, namely Henry Melchior Mühlenberg (1711-87), who went to America in 1742.

Up until 1727, few shipping and passenger arrival records were kept. Beginning in 1727, fairly accurate passenger records for arrivals in Philadelphia exist. From these passenger records, the German-American historian Oscar Kuhns (1912) made one of the earliest and most authoritative estimates of German immigrants. Kuhns was concerned basically with the period from about 1683 to the beginning of the Revolutionary War around 1775. He distinguishes three immigration periods, namely 1683-1710, 1710-1727, and 1727-1775. For the first two periods, Kuhns gives no firm estimates, however, we may suppose the number of immigrants totaled about 5,000 people for the years 1683-1727. For the third period, 1727 to 1775, Kuhns estimated that about 69,000 individuals arrived. Wokeck (1981) reviewed the same records, and by different calculations, estimated a similar number.

The peak immigration period was the five year period 1749-54 when about 32,000 people came to America, according to Kuhns, or about 35,000 according to Wokeck. In 1754, the Palatine immigrants brought typhus to Philadelphia, thereby creating an epidemic. Philadelphia also recorded a measles epidemic in 1747 and a yellow fever epidemic in 1788, which although not so virulent as typhus, were especially detrimental to the younger generations.

It is apparent that these colonial German immigrants were overwhelmingly Protestant. Data from Paullin & Wright, 1932, shown here as Table 6.1, give important clues to the relative sizes of the different church affiliations of Germans in America by the year 1775. In Table 6.1 two churches, German Reformed Church and the Lutheran Church, being mainly German, comprise about 9.7% of the total number of 3,195 churches. Of the total number of 3,195 churches, Catholic churches account for less than 2%.

TABLE 6.1
CHURCHES IN THE THIRTEEN ORIGINAL COLONIES, 1775-1776

Faith	No. Churches	Faith	No. Churches
Congregational	668	Lutheran	150
Presbyterian	558	Dutch Reformed	120
Episcopal	495	Methodist	65
Baptist	494	Catholic	56
Friends	310	Miscellaneous	120
German Reformed	159		

*Data from Paullin & Wright, 1932

THE IMMIGRATION PERIOD 1775-1816. For the period of 1775 to 1816, there are few definitive records. One often cited source is the possible number of Germans conscripted for service by the English army in the Revolutionary War. Some interesting statistics given by Radloff & Coyle (1975) are as follows:

TABLE 6.2
GERMAN CONSCRIPTS, 1776-80

German State Origin	Sent to America	Returned to Germany
Ansbach-Bayreuth	2,353	1,183
Brunswick	5,723	2,708
Hesse-Cassel	16,992	10,492
Hesse-Hanau	2,422	1,441
Waldeck	1,225	505
Zerbst	1,152	984
totals	29,867	17,313

*Data from Radloff & Coyle, 1975

Of the 12,554 remaining in America, about 1,500 were killed, another 6,000 died of illness, and some 5,000 deserted. Many deserters are supposed to have either remained voluntarily in America or returned not long thereafter where they were joined by non-deserters. Apparently at least 2,400 of the German mercenaries of the Revolutionary War eventually went to the more hospitable settlements under English control in Canada (see, for instance, Wilheney, 1985).

Various estimates have been made of the number of Germans counted in 1790 during the first U.S. census. The estimates generally range from about 8.6 to 9.0% of the total population although some sources claim the estimates are far too high. If one assumes that the figures are reasonably correct, then roughly 350,000 individuals of German background were counted in the 1790 Census. Other estimates state that 33 to 38% of the 1790 population in Pennsylvania were of German origin. For Maryland, the figure is 12%; for New Jersey, 9%; and for New York, the estimate is about 8%.

POST-REVOLUTIONARY WAR RECORDS. Another source of information, not yet fully developed, are the records of the Holland Land Co. During the first half of the 19th century, the company was actively promoting settlement of its large land holdings in western New York and western Pennsylvania.

During the War of 1812 (1812-15) there appear to have been few immigrants. However, in the period of about 1816 to 1861, there were increasingly larger waves of German-speaking immigrants. The radical student movement in Frankfurt during the years 1830-33 led to armed clashes between students and police, and a gradual unrest spread to Rhenish-Prussia, Rhenish-Bavaria, Nassau, Hessen, and other states along the Rhine. The movement finally culminated in a popular uprising, the so-called 1848 Revolution, in Germany and in many other parts of Europe.

Beginning in 1833, a number of intellectuals and technical experts left Germany. Notable individuals departing for America included Julius Bien (1826-1909), map maker; George Engelmann (1809-1884), physician and botanist; Meyer Guggenheim (1828-1905), mining entrepreneur; August Hoen (1817-1886), formerly spelled Höhn, lithographer and map-printer; Gustav Philip Koerner (1809-1896), politician and newspaperman; Ferdinand Jacob Lindheimer (1807-1879), botanist and newspaperman; Carl Schurz (1829-1906) politician and diplomat; Henry Engelhard Steinway (1797-1871), i.e., Heinrich Engelhard Steinweg, concert piano maker; Levi Strauss (1829-1902), pants manufacturer; and many, many others. Most of the above group belonged to "the 48'ers," or those refugees who left Germany during the social unrest of 1848.

In fact, the prestigious 1928-37 Dictionary of American Biography listed, for the period 1800-1907, some 320 German-born Americans; some 103 of these well-known personalities had arrived in America during the peak transition period of 1846-1855. This group of 320 became men and women of distinction after they seized the golden opportunities awaiting foreign dissidents travelling to America.

Immigration lists peak during 1854, which year saw more than a quarter of a million Germans arriving, mainly farmers and laborers. In the U.S. census year of 1860, 30.83 % of the foreign born population were German-speaking. Only the Irish, who were impelled by the potato famine of the 1840's to migrate, contributed a higher number, namely 38.93% of the foreign born population. The Irish migrants were dominantly Catholic as were many of the mid-19th century German migrants.

For the entire period of 1816-70, Kloss (1971) estimates that about 1,500,000 German-speaking immigrants came to America; this figure was revised by Kloss in 1974 to approximately 7,000,000 immigrants for the expanded period of 1816 to 1914.

Immigration to America during the Civil War (1861-65) slowed somewhat, but picked up rapidly at the end of the War.

The Prussian-Franco War (1870-71) caused a further disruption of passenger arrivals, but afterwards German-speaking immigrants were again on the move. In fact, the records for the period 1872 to 1917 suggest that about 3,100,000 Germans came to America. Two powerful forces were acting to entice people to come to America. The railroads were especially aggressive in attempting to settle their vast land holdings in the mid-West, while various industrial powers were anxious to develop cheap sources of labor in the cities. The year 1882 was another peak immigration year with about 250,000 German immigrants arriving; for the decade 1880-89, about 1,445,000 arrived.

Estimates of 19th century German immigrants to America suggest that perhaps one third were Catholics and two thirds were Protestants.

After World War I (1914-18), more waves of immigrants came. Moltmann (1985), and others, estimate that possibly 1,500,000 German-speaking individuals came during the period 1920-85.

Reviewing all these estimates and records, it appears that approximately 7,000,000 to 8,000,000 "Germans" left their homeland and came to America on a permanent basis. Of course, even though the bulk were from the various German States, large numbers came from Switzerland, from Austria, from the German-speaking lands of the old Austro-Hungarian Empire, and from southern Russia. Data from the 1920 U.S. Census indicate that those claiming a German mother-tongue were subdivided as follows: Germany - 85%, Austria-Hungary - 7.6%, Russian Empire - 3.9%, and Switzerland - 3.5%.

Table 6.3 on the next page shows German immigration by decade for the period 1820-1970. The remarks column shows only a few of the major "push" and "pull" factors. In the war years of 1812-1815, 1861-1865, 1914-1918, and 1939-1945, the push was away from America. The same is true of the depression years of the 1890's and 1930's. The total of almost seven million does not account for the large number of returnees, which may have been as high as twenty percent, especially with the development of modern transportation in the decades after the Civil War.

TABLE 6.3

GERMAN IMMIGRATION BY DECADE, CENSUS RECORDS, 1820-1870

Decade	No. Immigrants	Remarks
1820-29	5,753	x
1830-39	124,726	x
1840-49	385,434	German Revolution of 1848
1850-59	976,072	Rapidly expanding railroad/steamship systems
1860-69	723,734	American Civil War, 1861-65
1870-79	751,769	Prussian-Franco War, 1870-71
1880-89	1,445,181	Railroad and industrial development in U.S.
1890-99	579,072	Depression in U.S.
1900-09	328,722	x
1910-19	174,227	World War I, 1914-18
1920-29	386,634	Rampant inflation in Germany
1930-39	119,107	Depression in U.S.; dust bowl in Midwest
1940-49	117,506	World War II, 1939-45
1950-59	576,905	Economic recovery in Germany
1960-69	209,616	x
1970	10,632	x
total	6,917,000	equals 15.3 % of all immigrants

*numerical data source: U.S. Bureau of the Census, 1975

THE GERMAN BELT. Two factors were dominant in deciding where Germans would settle in America. The first factor was that the primary port of entry was Philadelphia during the 17th and 18th centuries, while by 1820, New York had become the main port of entry: immigrants tended to go due west from these points of entry. The second factor was that the latitude and climate of the northern States were similar to that of Germany. Word of the highly fertile soils to be found in Ohio, Indiana, and Illinois spread rapidly.

Thus a rather well defined "German Belt" developed. It included, first of all, the States of Connecticut, New York, New Jersey, Delaware, Maryland, Pennsylvania, Ohio, and Indiana. Further inland migration of the farmers brought them to Illinois, Wisconsin, Michigan, Minnesota, Iowa, South Dakota, Nebraska, Kansas, Missouri, and Arkansas. There were spotty, concentrated settlements also in Louisiana, Texas, Colorado, California, Washington and some southern States. In general, however, Swiss and German migrants of the 19th century were advised by various travel guides not to settle in the unhealthy climates south of the Ohio River. And for good reason; malaria and other diseases typical of subtropical climates were common, if not prevalent, even as far north as central Illinois which had its last major malaria season in 1872.

In the interior of the United States, virtually no malaria had been recorded for the years 1670 through 1760. Thereafter, the increasing number of migrants brought with them malaria and other diseases. In Illinois, the number of cases of malaria increased at alarming rates, so that by 1800 the southern portion of the State had developed a reputation for being decidedly unhealthy. In the 1820's, in Pike Co., Illinois, adjacent to the Mississippi River, above St. Louis, 80% of the settlers fell ill with malaria. In the swamps and poorly drained farmlands across central and southern Illinois, high rates of malaria incidence continued until the 1870's with malaria disappearing only by about 1890.

Although physicians of the 19th century somehow associated malaria with wooded, swampy areas, they tragically failed to associate it with its real cause and often were unable to disassociate the symptoms of malaria from other virulent diseases such as typhoid and dysentery. At that time, the universal cure and initial preparative treatment usually involved either bloodletting or the administration of emetics and cathartics, all of which did little to enhance the health of the patient. A massive dose of the bitter tasting calomel (mercurous chloride), in combination with jalap and tartarized antimony was designed to flush the intestines and perhaps unknowingly diluted the effect of concurrent typhoid or dysentery. The equally distasteful curative treatment of quinine sulfate, arsenious acid, and opium counteracted to some extent the effects of malaria itself. The last ingredient at least provided some temporary benefit in stimulating a feeling of wellness.

A very interesting map of the United States published by Eichoff (1985, p. 224) shows the *Distribution of Persons born in Germany, 1890*. New York City had the largest concentration, followed by Chicago, Philadelphia, Milwaukee, etc. Thus, many immigrants preferred to live in the larger cities after their arrival. Table 4 in Conzen, 1980, gives more details on the proportion of Germans in U.S. city populations.

The great mass of 19th century German immigrants remaining in the larger cities of the north were subject to all the horrors of poor sanitation involving haphazard waste disposal, open sewers, crowded tenements, and minimal personal cleanliness. In such circumstances, it is little wonder that cholera outbreaks occurred in the United States during 1832-34, 1848-49, 1849-54, 1866, and 1873. For instance, of New York City's half million inhabitants in 1849, 5,017 died from disease, many from cholera. In 1849 also, the much smaller city of St. Louis lost 1,182 from diseases, mostly from cholera.

Typhoid, typhus, dysentery, pneumonia, and tuberculosis were other normal hazards of tenement life in 19th century America. Often diseases occurred concurrently or in unison with malnutrition and poor climatic conditions.

Preventive medicine in the form of sanitation, and especially in the purification of water was virtually unknown. Likewise, causes and carriers of nearly all diseases became known only in the era of advanced microscopic research extending from about 1875 to 1906.

GERMANS IN TEXAS. Although German immigrants had first arrived as permanent settlers in Texas in 1831, during the 1835-36 Texan struggle for independence, Mexican authorities tried to stop European immigration to Texas. At this time, there were some 3,000 settlers of European background in Texas. San Antonio became the initial focus of the Mexican-American conflict.

In 1833 (and more importantly in 1848), cholera swept the south Texas area.

In late February and early March, 1836, the battle for Texas territory was temporarily won by the Mexicans at the Alamo. After the peace treaty of April, 1836, the Americans reclaimed the area and naturally saw the need to build up the local population as rapidly as possible.

In 1842, an "Adelsverein" (nobility society) was formed by fourteen German noblemen to promote migration and alleviate overcrowding in Rhenish districts. The Society, more properly called the "Verein zum Schutze deutscher Einwanderer in Texas," was at first under the supervision of Prince Carl von Solms-Braunfels, and later of Baron von Meusebach. Thus, the Germans came to Texas from various German areas, but mainly from the central German states of Hesse-Nassau and Hesse-Darmstadt.

About 1844, Henri Castro led another group of 2,134 settlers to Texas. Most people of this group were from Alsace with components from other parts of Germany and from Switzerland.

The Adelsverein provided one of the more unusual of the local concentrations: 5,247 German immigrants who landed at Galveston, Texas in late 1845 and early 1846. Most of this group were farmers who came en masse from areas along the Rhine. Altogether, the Adelsverein group totaled about 7,380 individuals migrating to Texas during the years 1844-47.

The 1846 arrivals, numbering some 3,000, were stranded at Lavaca Bay for some months, pending the arrival of inland transportation. During this year, estimates of mortality rates at Lavaca Bay, at New Braunfels, and at Fredericksburg, as well as along the inland route, range as high as 20 to 25%. The main factors contributing to this high rate appear to have been malaria, various types of dysentery, and scurvy. Today, one imagines that the commonly cited "virulent fever" was actually typhoid (water borne) or typhus (louse and flea borne).

Unfortunately, the Adelsverein declared bankruptcy in 1847 and many immigrants were stranded in Texas in transit. To compound problems, the large land grant negotiated by the Adelsverein, in addition to being poorly located far inland away from the market centers of San Antonio, Houston, and Galveston, was also in the poor agricultural area of the Hill Country astride the Edwards Plateau. These Texas Germans were on the forefront of westward expansion.

One prominent German to visit Texas was Ferdinand Roemer (1818-1891). His trip of some fourteen months in 1845-47 resulted in an important book and topographic map of Texas dating 1849. Major trails across south Texas, parallel to the coast, are clearly indicated on Roemer's map as are broad geologic features. Roemer, in his major documentation of early Germans in Texas noted that the main port of disembarkation was New Orleans. From New Orleans, travel was by steamboat to Galveston. Thereafter, most travelled by a small steamer down the coast to a camp at Lavaca Bay (near Victoria). From Lavaca Bay, the trip inland to New Braunfels was 160 miles with ox drawn wagons averaging ten to fifteen miles per day.

Roemer comments upon the insect world (probably lice, fleas and cockroaches) inhabiting virtually all dwellings of the native Indians. Doubtless, diseases like typhus were for all practical purposes endemic in such communities. Naturally, transplanted Americans tended to avoid any invitation to camp overnight in Indian settlements, however well-meant.

Like many immigrants to Texas, Roemer spent several months combating alternating bouts of malaria (mosquito borne) and typhus (louse borne) with perhaps also concurrent dysentery (water borne).

After the collapse of the Adelsverein, the immigrant Germans eventually tended to occupy the transition zone between the humid, subtropical Coastal Plain and the inland Hill Country of Texas. Concentrations of Germans formed well-known settlements at Castroville, New Braunfels, and at Fredericksburg. In addition, many remained in the then relatively populous areas of Galveston, Houston, and San Antonio.

The 1844-47 arrivals must have suffered some anxious moments during the following Mexican War (May, 1846 - Feb., 1848). During this war, however, the bulk of the heavy fighting took place on Mexican soil, culminating in a last ditch effort and in the defeat of the Mexican Army at Mexico City.

Not only was the subtropical climate of Texas alien to the newcomers, but the Lipan, Comanche, and Delaware Indians were active until 1872 although an 1847 treaty between the Germans and the Comanches eased the Indian threat of attack somewhat.

Ironically, many of the Americanized Germans in Texas who missed the Mexican War of 1846-48 were caught up in the Civil War of 1861-65, fighting on the side of the Confederacy.

The present day distribution of individuals of German background in Texas, although relatively minor, forms the curious pattern of a rough triangle marked by the three cities of San Antonio, Austin, and Houston. By 1860, an estimated 30,000 Germans, Czechs, and other European nationalities had migrated to Texas.

THE GERMANS FROM RUSSIA. Nearly 120,000 Germans from Russia emigrated to the United States between 1870 and 1920. Between 1874 and 1879, some 15,000 Mennonites settled also in the Canadian province of Manitoba.

The curious tale of the massive exodus of Germans to Russia is superbly summarized in the 1974 work of Rippley and Bauer. According to them, the first emigration of Germans to Russia occurred during the reign of Ivan the Terrible (1533-1584). At that time, German military officers, technicians, craftsman, merchants, scholars, and other middle-upper class personnel were called to Russia to help build the city of Moscow. The second wave of Germans to Russia was during the reign of Peter the Great (1672-1725). A similar group of Germans, possibly as many as 50,000, went to help with the development of St. Petersburg.

The third wave, and by far the most important in terms of numbers, occurred during the reign of Catherine the Great who reigned from 1762 to 1796. Catherine as well as her husband, Peter III, were of north German descent. The initial open invitation of 1762 to Germans received little response. The second invitation of 1763 provided a clear cut nine-point program which was very advantageous for those who had farming experience. Under the nearly ideal conditions of the second invitation, the Germans transferred virtually intact their language, their religions, and their culture to the area later known as the Ukraine.

Two large concentrations of Germans developed in Russia over the period of 1763 to about 1815, one in the region north of the Black Sea, and the other along the Volga River.

Large groups from Danzig (Prussia), the Palatinate, Alsace, North Baden, and Württemberg were the main sources of inhabitants of the Black Sea area. Evangelical, Catholic and smaller Protestant groups migrated en masse and tended to form similar religious groups wherever they settled. The Germans of the Black Sea area eventually occupied about eleven million acres.

In the Volga area, principal population sources were Hessen, the Rhineland, Baden, Württemberg, Alsace, and the Palatinate. In the Volga region, the Germans occupied about 2,700,000 acres.

By the mid-19th century the Germans had founded some 300 mother colonies in Russia, including 105 colonies in the Volga region and 181 colonies in the Black Sea district. A census in the year 1897 showed a total of 1,790,489 Germans in Russia of which Lutherans comprised about 76%, Catholics about 13.5% and Mennonites about 3.7%. The much-publicized Mennonites tended to be concentrated in the Black Sea district where they comprised about 20% of the overall population in that area.

In 1871 attempts were begun to Russianize the Germans. The right of exemption from military service was annulled and in 1880 the order was given that children should be educated in the Russian language. This led many Germans to migrate from Russia to the United States, beginning about 1874. Migration became increasingly strong especially for the six year period from 1898 to 1904 when some 41,598 Russian-Germans came to America. Most Russian-Germans spread across the upper Midwest.

Large concentrations of Evangelical Volga Germans settled in Chicago and in Lincoln, Nebraska. A large settlement of Catholic Germans developed in Topeka, Kansas. Groups of farmers spread across the northern Great Plains, North and South Dakota, Nebraska, Kansas and eastern Colorado, forming vital communities in the all-important wheat growing grain belt from Kansas north to southern Manitoba.

THE LEGACY OF GERMANS IN AMERICA. The great wave of 19th century Germans brought to America many remarkable items. In the realm of fast food, for instance, where would American baseball without frankfurters and hamburgers. The frankfurter (the ubiquitous Oscar Mayer hot dog) had its origin in the butcher shop of Heinrich Schmidt, opened in Frankfurt in 1875. By 1890, Schmidt had developed a "wurst" factory. Schmidt advised his customers to cook the wurst in steam or hot water instead of boiling it, to avoid bursting the seams.

Another baseball favorite is the German Brezel, better known as the American pretzel, which goes so well with beer.

In 1852, Adolphus Busch, an immigrant from Hessen, founded in St. Louis the Anheuser-Busch brewery. The prohibition years of 1920-33 barely served to slow the thirst of Americans for cold beer. Today, the Anheuser-Busch brewery, with Budweiser beer as its most famous product, is the world's largest brewery.

Along with hotdogs and hamburgers, Americans developed a taste for two other foodstuffs developed by a German descendant. In 1888, Heinrich Johann Heinz (born 1844), son of an immigrant, founded in Pittsburgh the Heinz Food Co. which developed such necessary fast food condiments as relish and ketchup.

The German holiday Weihnachten, in America called Christmas, has become one of America's favorite holidays, complete with all the originally German trimmings: the Weihnachtsbaum or Christmas tree, Sankt Nikolaus who became Santa Claus, and *Stille Nacht, heilige Nacht* which was translated into *Silent Night, Holy Night*. This song had its origin in Wagrain, Austria, when in 1818 the preacher Joseph Mohr (1792-1884) translated the ancient Latin text into German; the music was composed by Franz Xavier Gruber.

One term that resisted translation was the German Kindergarten. The Kindergarten for pre-school age children was developed in Bad Blankenberg, Thüringa, in 1840 by educator Friedrich Fröbel (1772-1852) and eventually found its way across the Atlantic essentially unaltered in concept.

Among American artists, two Germans stand out. Emanuel Gotlieb Leutze (1816-1868), born in Gmünd, Württemberg, was a history and portrait painter who became famous for his 1850 painting *Washington Crossing the Delaware*, while the paintings of Albert Bierstadt (1830-1902, born in Solingen, Westphalia), depicting the American West, can be found in many American museums.

In the 20th century, Germans also made their mark on Hollywood, among them Emil Jannings (1884-1950), Lilian Harvey (1907-1968), Ernst Lubitsch (1892-1947), Fritz Lang (1890-1976), Conrad Veidt (1893-1943), Friedrich Wilhelm Murnau (1888-1931), Peter Lorre (1904-1964), and Billy Wilder (born 1906). But perhaps the most famous of them was Maria Magdalena von Losch, from Berlin, better known to her vast public as Marlene Dietrich (1901-1992).

Two men who helped lay the foundations for this modern world of computers and space travel were Hermann Hollerith and Wernher von Braun. Hermann Hollerith (1860-1929) was born in Buffalo, N.Y., from German immigrant parents. Hollerith's company was a precursor of that data processing giant IBM. More recently, Wernher von Braun (1912-1977), born in Wirsitz, Posen (now Poland), developed, with his team of German scientists, the rockets that put America in space.

REFERENCES

Ackerknecht, E. H., 1982, *A Short History of Medicine*. John Hopkins Univ. Press, Baltimore, 277 p.

Allen, J. P. & E. J. Turner, 1988, *We the People, an Atlas of America's Ethnic Diversity*. Macmillan Publ. Co., N.Y., 315 p., 115 maps, illus. In the statistics for 1980, nearly 18 million Americans claimed "single German ancestry" while more than 31 million claimed a "multiple German ancestry". The counties with the largest German ancestry population were Cook Co. (Chicago), followed by Los Angeles, New York, Milwaukee, and Hamilton (Cincinnati) Counties.

Benson, E. A., 1975, "Martin Kendig, 1710 Mennonite Pioneer leader." *Mennonite Research Jour.*, Lancaster, Vol. XVI, no. 2, (April, 1975), p. 13, 15-17, 23, and Vol. XVI, no. 3 (July, 1975), p. 27-28.

Biesele, R. L., 1987, *The History of German Settlements in Texas, 1831-1861*. German-Texan Heritage Soc., San Marcos, Tx., 261 p., maps, illus. Originally published in 1930, this work is recognized as a standard and contains many names.

Bittinger, L. F., 1901, *The Germans in Colonial Times*. J. B. Lippincott Co., Phila., 314 p. See also recent reprint edition by the Genealogical Publ. Co., Baltimore.

Bötte, Gerd.-J., & Werner Tannhof, 1989, *The First Century of German Language Printing in the United States of America*. Niedersächsische Staats- und Universitätsbibliothek, Göttingen, Vol. 1, (1728-1807), 594 p., Vol. 2 (1808-1830), p. 595-1245. Gives an impressive list of more than 4,000 titles of German language items printed in the United States. Many of the early items were Bibles, hymnals, and other religious articles. Famous names include Christoph Saur (1693-1758), of Germantown, Pa., and two generations of descendants; often the name was recorded under the English spelling of Sower.

Conzen, K. N., 1976, *Immigrant Milwaukee, 1836-1860*. Harvard Univ. Press, Cambridge, Mass., 300 p., illus.
_____, 1980, "Germans." In *Harvard Encyclopedia of American Ethnic Groups*. Ibid, p. 405-425.

Cunz, Dieter, 1966, *They came from Germany. The Stories of famous German-Americans*. Dodd, Mead & Co., N.Y.
Describes the activities of nine prominent German immigrants, namely: Zenger (printer), von Steuben (soldier), Follen (teacher), Astor (merchant), Schurz (statesman), Roebling (engineer), Nast (cartoonist), Mergenthaler (inventor), and von Braun (scientist).

Duden, Gottfried, 1980, *Report on a Journey to the Western States of North America (1824-27)*. Univ. Missouri Press, 372 p., map
Translation from German of one of the numerous imaginative 19th century German propaganda pieces written by Rhinelanders. The 1829 first edition of 1,500 copies, and three later editions, were instrumental in persuading 88,487 Germans to settle in Missouri, mainly St. Louis, by 1860.

Eichhoff, Juergen, 1985, "The German Language in America." In *America and the Germans*. Univ. Pennsylvania Press, Phila., Vol. 1, p. 223-240.

Faust, A. B., 1909, *The German Element in the United States*. Houghton Mifflin Co., Boston, Vol 1, 591 p., 5 maps; Vol. 2, 695 p.
Universally cited by writers on the subject, this work is very comprehensive and well written and includes an enormous bibliography; reprinted 1969 by Johnson Reprint Corp., N.Y.

_____, 1927, *The German Element in the United States*. The Steuben Society of America, N.Y., 2 vols. in 1, 736 p. (2nd ed.).

Furer, H. B., 1973, *The Germans in America, 1607-1970*. Oceana Publications, Inc., Dobbs Ferry, N.Y., 156 p.
An unusual compendium of trivia about Germans in America, some comical, some serious. Notes arrival date of first Germans in America as 1607.

Geiser, S. W., 1954, *Naturalists of the Frontier*. Southern Methodist Univ. Press, Dallas, 296 p. (revised edition, 1st edition printed in 1935).
Good review of 19th century naturalists in Texas and their contribution to scientific knowledge in America.

Gerlach, R. L., 1976, *Immigrants in the Ozarks: A Study in Ethnic Geography*. Univ. Missouri Press, Columbia, 206 p., illus.
_____, 1986, *Settlement Patterns in Missouri*. ibid, 88 p., map
Map shows German settlements along the Missouri and the Mississippi rivers.

Gratz, D. L., 1953, *Bernese Anabaptists*. Herald Press, Scottdale, Pa., 219 p., map.
Good description of selected Amish and Mennonite settlements during the 18th and 19th centuries across the Swiss Belt from Pennsylvania west to Kansas. Contains many typically Swiss family names.

Hoerder, Dirk & Diethelm Knauf (eds,), 1992, *Fame, Fortune and Sweet Liberty, The Great European Emigration*. Edition Temmen, Bremen, 208 p., numerous illus.
The seven authors cover a variety of little known aspects of the various European migrations, both within Europe and to America. The primary emphasis is on 19th and 20th century European migrations with secondary emphasis on German migration.

Jones, H. Z., 1985, *The Palatine Families of New York 1710*. Privately printed, Universal City, Ca, 2 vols., 1298 p., illus. map
A good, recent tabulation of the often cited 13,500 "Palatines" who went to England in 1709. About one fourth went on to New York, a lesser number to the Carolinas and a few to Pennsylvania.

Jordan, G. J., 1980, *German Texana*. Eakin Press, Burnet, TX, 164 p.
An interesting collection of German poems, songs, and the like which were transferred to America.

Jordan, T. G., 1966, *German Seed in Texas Soil: Immigrant Farmers in Nineteenth-century Texas*. Univ. Texas Press, Austin, 237 p., 14 figs.

Kamphoefner, W. D., 1987, *The Westfalians from Germany to Missouri*. Princeton Univ. Press, 216 p.
Concentrates on approximately 6,500 Westfalians who settled in St. Charles and Warren Cos., Mo., during the period of about 1840-1870.

Kloss, Hans, 1974, *Atlas of 19th and early 20th Century German American Settlements*. N. G. Elwert Verlag, Marburg, text 17 p., 96 oversized maps
Cites about 7,000,000 German immigrants for the period 1816-1914.

Kuhns, Oscar, 1912, "The German and Swiss Settlements of Colonial Pennsylvania." *The Penn Germania*, Vol. XIII, no. 4, p. 289-320; no. 5, p. 385-416; no. 6, p. 481-509; no. 7, p. 577-583 (index).

Lambert, M. B., 1923, *A Dictionary of the Non-English Words of the Pennsylvania Dialect*. Lancaster Press Inc., Lancaster, Pa., 193 p. + Introduction 21 p.
This interesting publication deals with the language called "Pennsylvania Dutch". The language is a peculiar dialect which developed in Pennsylvania, especially in the area around Lancaster County. It is neither Dutch nor German, but a corruption of Rhenish dialects with a strong English overprint.

Learned, M. D., 1912, *Guide to the Manuscript Materials relating to American History in the German State Archives*. Carnegie Inst. Washington, 352 p.
Reprinted recently by Kraus Reprint Corp.; an important source for locating original 17th and 18th century records for the Palatinate.

Levine, N. D., 1964, *Malaria in the Interior Valley of North America*. Univ. Illinois Press, Urbana, irregularily numbered pages.
Partial reprinting of massive, two volume work by Daniel Drake dated 1850 with new, introductory pages and summaries by Levine.

Luebke, F. C., 1969, *Immigrants and Politics: The Germans of Nebraska, 1880-1900*. Univ. Nebraska Press, Lincoln, 220 p., illus.
_____, 1990, *Germans in the New World: Essays in the History of Immigration*. Univ. Illinois Press, Urbana, 198 p.

Malone, Dumas (ed.), 1928-37, *Dictionary of American biography*. Charles Scribner's Sons, N.Y., 20 volumes text plus one volume index.
This is a standard treatise available in nearly all large libraries.

McGrew, R. E., 1985, *Encyclopedia of Medical History*. McGraw-Hill Book Co., N.Y., 400 p.

McMaster, R. H., 1985, *Land, Piety, Peoplehood*. Herald Press, Scottdale, Pa., 340 p., illus.
Good book on land ownership in Lancaster Co., Pa with its concentrations of Swiss and Germans ancestry; unfortunately poorly indexed.

Moltmann, Guenter, 1985, "The Pattern of German Emigration to the United States in the Nineteenth Century." In *America and the Germans*. Univ. Pennsylvania Press, Phila Vol 1, p. 14-24, .

O'Connor, Richard, 1968, *The German-Americans*. Little, Brown & Company, Boston, 484 p., illus.
A well-written, entertaining and nearly comprehensive survey of 19th century German-Americans. Notes that late 19th century

German-Americans included August Belmont (financier), Oscar Hammerstein (musician), Ottman Mergenthaler (inventor of linotype), Claus Spreckels (sugar magnate), Henry Villard, i.e., Heinrich Hilgard, (financier), George Westinghouse (of railroad fame), and Frederick Weyerhauser (lumber). Also mentions 20th century baseball stars: Frank Frisch, Lou Gehrig, Babe Ruth (i.e., George Herman Erhardt), Casey Stengel, Rube Waddell, and John Peter "Honus" Wagner.

Radloff, Herman, & Alexander Coyle, 1975, *Hessians in the Revolution*. St. Louis Genealogical Soc., St. Louis, Mo., 27 p.

Rippley, LaVern, 1980, *Of German Ways*. Barnes & Noble Books, N.Y., 301 p., illus. (originally published in 1970).
_____, 1984, *The German-Americans*. University Press of America, Lanhan, Md., 271 p. (originally published in 1976).
_____, & Armand Bauer, 1974, *Russian-German Settlements in the United States*. North Dakota Inst. Regional Studies, Fargo, 207 p., illus., maps.
Translation and supplement to Richard Sallet's 1931 book *Ruslanddeutsche Siedlungen in den Vereinigten Staaten von America*, 126 p.

Roemer, Ferdinand, 1967, *Texas with Particular Reference to German Immigration and the Physical Appearance of the Country*. Texian Press, Austin, 301 p., map
Reprint of 1935 translation by Oswald Mueller of the original 1849 edition; the 1935 edition was printed by Standard Printing Co of San Antonio, TX, while the 1849 German edition was printed by Adolf Marcus in Bonn.

Rosenberg, C. E., *1987, The Cholera Years, The United States in 1788, 1849, and 1866*. Univ. Chicago Press, 265 p. (revised ed., originally published in 1962).

Rubincam, Milton, 1961, "The Rubenkam Family of Hessen." *Pennsylvania Gen. Mag.*, vol. XXII, no. 3, p. 85-112, map.
_____ 1968, "Researching European Origins of Pennsylvania German Families." *Pennsylvania Genealogical Mag.*, Vol. XIV, no. 4, p. 227-245.
_____, (ed), 1980, *Genealogical Research: Methods and Sources*. American Soc. Genealogists, Washington, D.C., Vol. I, 579 p. (revised ed.).

_____, 1987, *Pitfalls in Genealogical Research*. Ancestry Publ., Salt Lake City, Utah, 74 p., illus.
The author has long been recognized for his Pennsylvania German research.

Rydjord, John, 1972, "Deutsch and the Dutch." In *Kansas Place Names*. Univ. Oklahoma Press, Norman, p. 172-184.

Schelbert, Leo, 1980, "Swiss." In *Harvard Encyclopedia of American Ethnic Groups*. Harvard Univ. Press, Cambridge, Mass., p. 981-987.
Cites estimate of about 400,000 Swiss immigrants to America for period of 1700 to 1970 and immigration data of 346,468 Swiss immigrants for period 1820 to 1975.

Smith, C. N. and A. P.-C. Smith, 1978, "Bibliography of Published Emigration Lists." In *The Encyclopedia of German-American Genealogical Research*. R. R. Bowker Co., N.Y. p. 207-232.
An important list of little known publications with places of origin in Germany.

Thode, Ernest, 1983, *Atlas for Germanic Genealogy*. Heritage House, Indianapolis, Ind., 2nd-revised ed., 74 p.
Numerous sketch maps, some maps show foreign born population in America in 1880, 1890, 1930.

Tiling, Moritz, 1913, *History of the German Element in Texas*. Privately published, Houston, 225 p.
Contains good bibliography and other documentation.

Trommler, Frank, & Joseph McVeigh (eds.), 1985, *America and the Germans: An Assessment of a Three Hundred Year History*. Univ. Pennsylvania Press, Phila., Vol. I, Immigration, Language, Ethnicity, 376 p., Vol. II, The Relationship in the Twenthieth Century, 369 p.
A spectrum of twenty-four articles in each volume.

Turk, E. L., 1983, "The German Newspapers of Kansas." *Kansas History Quart.*, Vol. 6, p. 46-64.
Deals with the history of the many newspapers printed in the German language in Kansas during the last part of the 19th and the early 20th century. In the late 1800's there were several hundred papers printed in the German language in the United States; most ceased publication by the time of the 1st World War.

U.S. Bureau of the Census, 1975, *Historical Statistics of the United States, Colonial Times to 1970*. Bicentennial Edition, Parts 1 and 2. U.S. Govt. Printing Office, Washington, D.C., 1200 p., index (numerous tables).

Wellauer, Maralyn A., 1985, *German Immigration to America in the Nineteenth Century*. Roots International, Milwaukee, Wisc., 87 p., illus.

Wilheney, J. P., 1985, *German Mercenaries in Canada*. Maison des Mots, Beloeil, QC., 332 p.
Refers to German mercenaries who fought in the American Revolutionary War.

Wokeck, Marianne S., 1981, "The Flow and Composition of German Immigration to Philadelphia, 1727-1775." *Pennsylvania Mag. Hist. & Biog.*, Vol 105, p. 247-278.
_____, 1985, "German Immigration to Colonial America: Prototype of a Transatlantic Mass Migration." In *America and the Germans*. University of Pennsylvania Press, Phila., Vol. I, p. 3-13.

Yoder, Don, 1979, "Problems and Resources in Pennsylvania German Genealogical Research." *Pennsylvania Genealogical Mag.*, Vol. XXXI, no. 1, p. 1-26.
Contains good bibliography.

Zelinsky, Wilbur, 1973, *The Cultural Geography of the United States*. Prentice-Hall, Inc., Englewood Cliffs, N.J., 164 p., illus.

Zucker, A. E. (ed.), 1950, *The Forty-Eighters*. Columbia Univ. Press, N.Y., 379 p.
A learned discussion of German intellectuals caught up in the 1848 German Revolution, many of whom migrated to the United States.

 AR, FAMINE AND DISEASE. IF ANY AREA IN the world has the right to be called the Land of Wars, then the Palatinate, or the left bank of the Rhine from about Strassburg north to Mainz, may use this title.

Beginning in the early 16th century, the Rhineland was subject to death and destruction on the average of about once every thirty years. Indeed, some of the wars themselves lasted thirty years. In particular during the 17th century, the Rhineland inhabitants had to combat the forces of war, famine, and disease, all three periodically occurring together and so complexly interrelated that depopulation was a mixed blur of the three overwhelming forces. The clash of one raw armed force against another in hand-to-hand combat gave enormous battle casualties. At the same time, the crowded conditions in unsanitary army camps provided for even greater casualties through the occurrence of diseases for which no known treatments were available. Typhus fever (mainly louse borne) was prevalent during the winter months while bubonic plague (mainly flea borne) was a relatively common summer phenomena.

From the time of the Reformation early in the 16th century, there was a growing and nearly constant rebellion in the Holy Roman Empire against the rulers of the Catholic Church seated in Rome and against their local German representation vested primarily in the Hapsburg Emperors of Vienna and the Electors of Mainz, Trier, and Köln.

The growing rebellion embraced both the Lutherans and the Calvinists, principally in the German States, as well as other, smaller groups in neighboring countries, most notably the Huguenots in France, the Anabaptists in Switzerland, and the Mennonites in the Lowlands. The various Protestant groups were above all, mutually independent, and periodically in verbal conflict among themselves. Notably, there was a fine distinction between the adherents of Martin Luther (1483-1546) and those of the somewhat more conservative John Calvin (1509-1564), whose original French name was Jean Chauvin or Caulvin.

THE INFLUENCE OF PRINTED MATERIALS. From the time of Martin Luther, the Protestants recognized the enormous value of printed materials for propaganda purposes in reaching the masses. This material eventually created a groundswell of public opinion against errant rulers, which finally snowballed to the point of no return.

For instance, the Gustav Freytag collection at Frankfurt contains, for the period 1618-1621, more than 1,000 broadsheets (handbills, often of folio size) describing unpopular political events in the German States. Most of the broadsheets adhered to the Protestant cause and contributed to the extension of the Bohemian War beyond the year of 1621. Another example of the power of printed matter occurred in May, 1631, following the sack of Magdeburg and the annihilation of its 20,000 citizens by the Hapsburg forces. On this occasion, more than 205 pamphlets, forty-one broadsheets, and twenty newspapers, scattered across Europe, documented the ultimate crime. Public opinion was widely influenced against the Catholic Hapsburg forces.

By contrast, the Catholics never seemed to realize fully the value of printed materials. In any event, the conservatism of the Catholic Church doggedly adhered to the printing of religious materials in the Latin language. These publications were available in limited quantities and largely reached only the hands of the nobility, the clerics, and the university trained citizens. Very late in the 16th century, the Catholics formed the Jesuit Order, a group designed especially to infiltrate key positions in Universities and in city governments. The Jesuits, whose policy it was to promote Catholic ideals, achieved notable successes, however temporary and local. The development of the Order in the German States is indicated by the fact that they controlled four colleges in 1561, but some fifty colleges by 1650.

Nationalism was another factor leading to conflicts in the Palatinate. On a periodic basis, this pitted German against Frenchman, the Dutch against the Spaniards, the French against the Spaniards, the Swedes against the Poles, and the like. On both greater and smaller scales, territorial and dynastic questions were other primary factors; the scale ranged from the Emperor down to the lowest princeling of the 150 or so German States. The conflicts were not for an economic advantage as the area of the Rhineland does not contain exceptional mineral deposits nor agricultural resources, nor for that matter, in the 17th century, any other apparent special advantage other than territorial control.

Each of the wars left its mark. In many cases, local populations were depleted. Subsequently, the rulers of the area appealed for people from other areas and other countries to repopulate the area. Notable were the influxes of reformed Calvinists, Huguenots, and Mennonites who took advantage of various incentives and repopulated the Rhineland and larger nearby cities, such as Frankfurt, in the late 16th century and periodically through the 17th century.

THE THIRTY YEARS' WAR, 1618-1648. Two wars in particular left their marks upon the Palatinate. One of the more devastating was the Thirty Years' War. Many sections of the Palatinate had an estimated 75% of the population annihilated, an estimated 66% of the houses were destroyed, and 85% of the horses plus 82% of the cattle were carried away. The city of Mainz, during the period of occupation by the Protestant Swedish army from 1631-1636, lost an estimated 25% of its dwellings, 40% of its population, and 60% of its wealth. Naturally, many Catholics and some minority groups left the city for more favorable areas along the Rhine.

The Thirty Years' War has been described as not one but three wars, with six or more principal parties. What started out as a local squabble between the Catholic Hapsburg Emperor Ferdinand II (reigned 1619-1637) on the one side and the Bohemian, Hungarian and German Protestant principalities on the other side, mushroomed into a much broader European conflict.

The Dutch became directly involved in 1621, the Spanish in 1622, the French in 1624, 1628, and 1635, the Danes in 1625, and, above all, the Swedes in 1630. The Dutch, Danes, and Swedes were, of course, the primary Protestant proponents in addition to the German States of Saxony, Brandenburg, and the Palatinate. The Hapsburgers of Austria, along with the Spanish and the French, were the basic Catholic parties.

In 1618, during the turmoil caused by the Bohemian War, Elector Friedrich V (reigned 1610-1620) vied with Ferdinand II for the title of Holy Roman Emperor. Eventually Ferdinand II gained the upper hand. Friedrich V went into exile in The Hague in April, 1621, but continued to foment revolt from that vantage point until his death in the fall of 1632.

During the first decade of the Thirty Years' War, the Protestants were poorly organized and gained few victories in actual battle. However, what the Protestants lost on the battlefield, they seemed to regain in the massive propaganda war which emanated from the printing establishments associated with the Frankfurt-Leipzig publishing axis.

The Protestant forces continued to rejuvenate after each major victory won by the stronger Catholic military forces. The Swedish forces entered the war in 1630, but the first major victory of the Protestant forces was not until 1631. Unfortunately, the strong Protestant leader, King Gustavus II Adolphus of Sweden was killed in battle at Lützen in 1632 and the advantage went to the Catholic forces who achieved a major victory in 1634. Axel Oxenstierna (1583-1654), who was chancellor of Sweden from 1612 until 1654, played a major role in keeping the Protestant forces together.

By 1635, the Catholic forces of France, which had played a passive role during the years 1618-1635, were convinced by the Protestants to enter the dispute against the Hapsburg Catholics. France provided a much needed war fund and eventually also sent its troops.

In the end, the ideals and goals of the Reformation were preserved through the Treaty of Westphalia of 1648, a treaty which outlined the relationship between Catholic and Protestant. It took more than five years of haggling to settle the Thirty Years' War as the negotiating period lasted from January, 1643 until October, 1648. The 176 negotiators, about half of them lawyers by profession, a profession always prone to move slowly, represented 194 separate interests. The group of negotiators was nearly evenly divided between Catholics and Protestants. For the period from November, 1645 to June, 1647, the Catholic group convened in Münster while the Protestants occupied Osnabrück some forty-five km (thirty miles) to the northeast.

Even after the signing of the treaty, demobilization was slow. Spanish troops remained in Frankenthal, near the Rhine, until 1653. The last Swedish troops did not leave northern Germany until 1654. But resettlement was rapid. Beginning about 1650-55, there was a large influx of people from the Lower Rhine and from the Upper Rhine, including much of western Switzerland, into the Palatinate. It was to be a short two decades before the area was once again consumed in war.

THE WARS OF LOUIS XIV, 1676-1697. Other equally destructive, although more localized, wars in the Rhineland during the 17th century were the Wars of Louis XIV, starting in 1676-77, and peaking in 1688-89. The effects of these wars were felt along the Middle Rhine until well into the 18th century.

Following the death in 1685 in Mannheim of·Elector Palatine Karl II, son of Karl I Ludwig (ruled 1648-1680), the rule of the Wittelsbach-Pfalzer line in the Palatinate ended. At that time, King Louis XIV attempted to appoint his sister-in-law, Elizabeth Charlotte von Orleans (popularly known as "Liselotte"), to the rule of the Palatinate. Elizabeth Charlotte (1652-1722) was a daughter of Karl I, Ludwig, Elector Palatine from 1640-80. She was also sister to Karl II, who was Elector Palatine from 1680-85. She married Philip I, Duke of Orleans, in 1671. The Duke, in turn, was a brother to King Louis XIV of France.

When Liselotte's brother died in 1685, she became pretender to the rule of the Palatinate at the urging of her brother-in-law, the French King Louis XIV. When Louis XIV was denied a golden opportunity to legally acquire the Palatinate, he vented his rage by having his armies level its cities to the ground.

Liselotte von der Pfalz was a prolific letter writer, having written an estimated 60,000 letters to various important personalities of the day, of which about 7,000 letters survive. These letters fill six volumes and record critical events of the times.

However, the rule over the Palatinate passed to the House of Neuburg. The Neuburg House then came under extreme pressure from the French, and in a few years, a general war (the Third Pfalz, or Orleans War, 1688-97; also called the Second Devastation of the Palatinate) broke out. All cities on the Left Bank of the middle Rhine, including Mainz, Worms, Mannheim, Speyer, Heidelberg, Oppenheim, Bingen, Kreuznach, Alzey, Frankenthal, Rastatt, Pforzheim, Offenburg, and many others, were burned to the ground by the scorched earth policy of the French armies under the command of General Ezechiel de Melac. The Third Pfalz War finally ended in 1697 with the Peace of Rijswick.

As we have seen, the period of 1677-1682, marked by the evangelistic activities of the Quakers in Krisheim (in the Palatinate) and in Krefeld (in the Lower German Rhine), had a marked effect, in conjunction with the threat of war, in convincing minority groups to migrate to America. This migration was the first of an ever increasing mass movement to the little known lands across the Atlantic.

THREE CENTURIES OF WARFARE IN THE PALATINATE. The many lesser conflicts directly involving the Palatinate may best be summarized in tabular form as follows:

1524-25: The **Peasants War**
   The armed beginning of the Reformation. Uprisings in Swabia and Franconia spread to other German States.

1562-98: The **Religious Wars**
1st War of Religion: 1562-63.
   French Huguenots and English Protestants vs. French Catholics. Some Huguenots migrated northwards.
2nd War of Religion: 1567-68.
   French Huguenots vs. French Catholics.
3rd War of Religion: 1568-70.
   French Huguenots and German Protestants vs. French Catholics.
4th War of Religion: 1572-73.
   French Protestants vs. French Catholics.
5th War of Religion: 1575-76.
   French Protestants vs. French Catholics.
6th War of Religion: 1576-77.
   French Protestants vs. French Catholics.
7th War of Religion: 1580.
8th War of Religion: 1585-89.
   French and German Protestants vs. French Catholics.
Wars of Henry of Navarro: 1589-98.
   French Protestants vs. French and Spanish Catholics.

1618-48: The **Thirty Years' War**
   Roman Catholics vs. Protestants in Germany. Hapsburg Catholics and German Catholic princes vs. German Protestant princes and Protestants of Denmark and Sweden. In the Palatinate, notable events were:
1620:   Mainz, Kreuznach, Oppenheim plundered.
1621:   The Rhine Valley and the Palatinate plundered; Frankenthal occupied by the Spanish (1621-53).
1626-27: The Rhine Valley and the Palatinate plundered.
1631:   The capture of Mainz; occupation by the Swedish to 1636.
1635:   Maneuvering in the Rhine and Main Valleys.
1644:   Fortresses of the middle Rhine captured.
1646-47: Barren countryside in the Palatinate as the result of systematic plundering.

1676-77: **1st Devastation of the Palatinate**, also called the War of Louis XIV. The French laid waste to the land between the Meuse and the Moselle. Zweibrücken plundered.

1688-89: 2nd Devastation of the Palatinate, by armies of Louis XIV.
Totally destroyed: Mannheim, Heidelberg.
Heavily damaged (south to north):

Offenburg	Dirkheim	Mainz
Baden	Frankenthal	Bingen
Rastatt	Worms	Simmern
Pforscheim	Alzey	Montroyal
Durlach	Kircheimbolanden	Cochem
Phillipsburg	Oppenheim	Mayen
Speyer	Kreuznach	Coblenz
Neustadt	Andernach	

1688-97: War of the Grand Alliance, also called War of the League of
Augsburg, 3rd Pfalz War, Orleans War, War of Louis XIV, etc.
This was actually an extension of the 1688-89 2nd Devastation of the
Palatinate. It finally ended with the Treaty of Rijswick.

1701-14: War of Spanish Succession, also called the War of Louis XIV.
1702: Siege of Landau.
1703: Landau and Speyer recaptured.
1713: Speyer, Landau, Freiburg captured.

1733-38: War of Polish Succession, also called the War of Louis XV.
Overrunning of Lorraine.

1740-48: War of Austrian Succession, also called the War of Louis XV.
1743: Main River blockaded. Operations along the middle Rhine.
Encampment west of the city of Worms.
1744: Fighting at Weissenburg (Wissembourg)

1756-63: Seven Years War, also called the War of Louis XV.
1758: French defeated at Crefeld.
1759: Frankfurt under French rule.

1792-00: Wars of the French Revolution
1792-93: French occupy Mainz and Frankfurt.
1794-95: Mainz under siege.
1797: Battle of the Lahn.
1799: Army of Mayence (Mainz).

1800-15: Napoleonic Wars
1807: French capture all Prussian lands between Rhine and Elbe.
1811: All land west of Rhine under French control.

1848: German Revolution
Numerous towns and villages suffer some damage.

1870-71: Franco-Prussian War
1870: Battle of Weissenburg (Wissembourg).
German States unified for the first time.

1914-18: 1st World War

1918-30: Mainz under French rule.

1939-45: 2nd World War
City center of Frankfurt 80% destroyed as were most other German large cities.

1945-49: Mainz under French rule.

MIGRATION IN THE ERA OF CONFLICT. With such instability and devastation along the Rhine, especially along the Middle Rhine, there was an enormous mass movement of human beings. On the one hand, those who were lucky enough and had means to escape seized the opportunity to seek their fortune in more stable lands. After 1683, the escape route increasingly led to America. The more adventurous accepted this choice.

On the other hand, after each brutal conflict, local rulers offered special incentives to foreigners who were willing to risk their well-being in attempts to repopulate the lands. The more conservative or more short-sighted took this choice.

REFERENCES

Dunn, R. S., 1970, *The Age of Religious Wars, 1559-1689*. W. W. Norton & Co., Inc., N.Y., 244 p., illus.

Dupuy, R. E., & T. N. Dupuy, 1986, *Encyclopedia of Military History*. Jane's Publ. Co., London, 1500 p.
One of two such nearly comprehensive encyclopedias; see also Kohn, 1986.

Gutmann, Myron P., 1988, "The Origins of the Thirty Years' War." *Jour. Interdisciplinary History*. Cambridge, Ma., Vol. XVIII, no. 4, p. 749-770.
This article is an excellent overview of the lengthy book by Parker, 1984, cited below.

Koch, H. W., 1981, *The Rise of Modern Warfare, 1618-1815*. Hamlyn Publ. Group Ltd., London, 256 p., maps, illus.

Kohn, George C., 1986, *The Dictionary of Wars*. Facts of Life Press, N.Y., 598 p.

Parker, Geoffrey (ed.), et al, 1984, *The Thirty Years' War*. Routledge & Kegan Paul, London, 340 p., maps., illus.

Parker, N. G., 1979, *Europe in Crisis, 1598-1648*. Fontana Publ. Co., London, 384 p.

Raumer, Kurt von, 1982, *Die Zerstörung der Pfalz von 1689*. Verlag Dietrich Pfähler, Bad Neustadt a.d.Saale (reprinted from 1930 ed.), 371 p.

Schribner, R. W., 1982, *The German Peasants War*. Center for Reformation Research, A Guide to Research, St. Louis, Mo., p. 107-133
Refers to the war of 1524-25, at the beginning of the Reformation.

Steiner, J., 1985, *Die pfalzische Kürwarde des Dreissigjahrigen Krieges (1618-1648)*: Heimatkundliche Veroffentlichungen, Pfalzer Heimat, Speyer.

Stuke, Horst & Wilfried Forstmann, 1979, *Die Europaischen Revolutionen von 1848*. Verlagsgruppe Athenaum Hain, Scriptor, Hainstein, Konigstein/Ts., 235 p.

HE MODERN GERMAN EMPIRE IS LARGELY an outgrowth of the Holy Roman Empire which lasted from about 843 to 1806. This period in Germany was loosely called the First Reich - it extended from the coronation of Charlemagne in A.D. 800 until the time of Napoleon. There were some 300 semi-independent principalities with about one third being ecclesiastical. The Emperor, resident in Vienna, ruled directly over Bohemia, Austria, the so-called Austrian Netherlands and "Further Austria" (southern Baden and the Black Forest), and was nominal overlord of all these territories.

There was a permanent Diet at Regensburg, in Bavaria, which included representatives of all the territories. For convenience in this and other chapters, a list of the Emperors of the Holy Roman Empire is given as Table 6.4 on the next page.

THE ELECTORS. The German States during the time of Martin Luther (1483-1546) were a patchwork of numerous territories nominally under the Holy Roman Emperor. The seven most powerful magnates in the realm consisted of four secular princes and three archbishops. They elected the Emperor who normally reigned until death. Periodically, the Emperor called these seven electors and the other princes, prelates, and city magistrates to a Diet, usually at an Imperial city such as Regensburg, Nürnberg, Augsburg, Frankfurt, or Worms. In this assembly, the Emperor heard petitions and grievances, and asked for money to war against the Turks, or in many cases, money for war against aggressive forces in southern Europe, notably France.

Seven, and later nine, Electors, three of them ecclesiastical princes, had the right to elect the Emperor. These Electors were:

The Elector of Saxony (King of Poland from 1697-1763).
The Elector of Brandenburg (King of Prussia since 1701)
The Elector of the Palatinate.
The Emperor, himself, as King of Bohemia.
The Archbishop of Mainz.
The Archbishop of Köln (Cologne).
The Archbishop of Trier.

and later:
The Elector of Bavaria (Duke of Bavaria since 1623)
The Elector of Hannover (Duke of Hannover since 1692).

In 1777, the electoral office of Bavaria and of the Palatinate were combined. The electoral office of Bavaria was established in 1648 while that of Hannover (or Brunswick-Lüneburg) was granted in 1692.

TABLE 6.4
EMPERORS OF THE HOLY ROMAN EMPIRE

House/Emperor	Rulers of Germany	Holy Roman Emperors
Early Kings (Carolingians)	A.D. 800-911	n/a
Saxon House (Liudolfings)		
Heinrich I	919-936	*
Otto I, der Grosse	936-973	926-973
Otto II	973-983	976-983
Otto III	983-1002	996-1002
Heinrich II, der Heilige	l002-1024	1014-1024
Salians		
Konrad II	1024-1039	1027-1039
Heinrich III, der Schwarz	1039-1056	1046-1056
Heinrich IV	1056-1106	1084-1106
Heinrich V	1106-1125	1111-1125
Suepplinburg House		
Lothar III	1125-1137	1133-1137
House of Hohenstaufen (Staufer)		
Konrad III	1138-1152	*
Friedrich I (III) Barbarossa	1152-1190	1155-1190
Heinrich VI	1190-1197	1191-1197
Philipp v. Schwaben	1198-1208	*
Welfs		
Otto IV, der Welfe	1208-1215	1209-1215
House of Hohenstaufen (restored)		
Friedrich II	1215-1237	1220-1237
Konrad IV	1250-1254	*
INTERREGUM	1255-1272	
House of Habsburg		
Rudolf I	1273-1291	*
House of Nassau		
Adolf von Nassau	1292-1298	*
House of Habsburg (restored)		
Albrecht I	1298-1308	*

TABLE 6.4 (cont'd)

House/Emperor	Rulers of Germany	Holy Roman Emperors
House of Luxemburg		
Heinrich VII	1308-1313	1312-1313
House of Bavaria (Wittelsbach)		
Ludwig IV, der Bayern	1314-1346	1328-1346
House of Luxemburg (restored)		
Karl IV	1346-1378	1355-1378
Wenzel IV, v. Bohmen	1378-1400	*
House of Wittelsbach (restored)		
Ruprecht I, von der Pfalz	1400-1410	*
Jodokus (Jobst v. Mahren)	1410-1411	*
Sigismund v. Luxemburg	1411-1437	1433-1437
House of Habsburg (restored)		
Albrecht II	1438-1439	*
Friedrich III	1440-1493	1452-1493
Maximilian I	1493-1519	a
Charles V (I)	1519-1556	a
Ferdinand I	1556-1562	a
Maximilian II	1562-1576	a
Rudolf II	1576-1612	a
Matthias	1612-1619	a
Ferdinand II	1619-1637	a
Ferdinand III	1637-1657	a
Leopold I	1658-1705	a
Joseph I	1705-1711	a
Karl VI	1711-1740	a
House of Wittelsbach (restored)		
Karl VII (Albrecht)	1742-1745	a
House of Habsburg (restored)		
Franz I	1745-1765	a
(Maria Theresia, Austria)	(1740-1780)	
Joseph II	1765-1790	a
Leopold II	1790-1792	a
Franz II (last Emperor, d. 1835)	1792-1806	a

Remarks:

Key to Symbols: * = never crowned as Emperor

a = After 1493. title of Emperor was assumed

LESSER NOBILITY. As shown by Benecke (1974), the Federal tax schedule of the Imperial Assembly held at Worms in May, 1521 gives a superb overview of the complexity of the territories in the realm. Although the list is not complete, at least 392 parties were involved. This tax schedule is summarized here as Table 6.5. The primary contributions were about 4,000 horsemen, some 20,000 foot soldiers, and over 50,000 gulden.

TABLE 6.5
FEDERAL TAX SCHEDULE, MAY, 1521

Rulers	Horsemen	Foot Soldiers	Money (in Gulden)
Electors (7)	622	5,542	15,585
Archbishops (4)	451	2,022	6,626
Bishops (45)	12	52	1,201
Secular ruling princes (28)	11	178	840
Foreign ruling princes (3)	183	1,081	6,451
Prelates (65)	102	506	840
Abbesses (13)	1,042	4,479	9,281
Commendories (4)	645	2,843	5,781
Counts and lords (138)	177	764	1,211
Free and Imperial towns(85)	760	2,262	3,601
totals	4,005	19,898	51,416

*Data from Benecke, 1974

Most of the Princes from the lesser territories had absolutely no chance of becoming an Elector. In fact, few of the Princes had much say in the ruling of the German territories.

THE DIETS. Below is a partial listing of Diets during the critical formative period of 1521 to 1530:.

1521	Diet of Worms: Edict of Worms against Luther
1522	Diet of Nürnberg (1st session)
1522/23	Diet of Nürnberg (2nd session)
1524	Diet of Nürnberg (3rd session)
1526	Diet of Speyer
1529	Diet of Speyer
1530	Diet of Augsburg: Lutheran Confession

During the Diet of Augsburg, the Lutheran Confession (an article of faith), which was written by Philipp Melanchthon, was submitted. This was the first official documentation of the Reformation. This confession, also called the 1530 "Augsburg Confession", was submitted by the Protestants to Emperor Karl V. The term "reformation" dates from this time and was the first general recognition of the principles it involved.

By the middle of the 17th century, the Diet was composed only of about 76 Princes of which forty-three were from lay principalities and thirty-three were from ecclesiastical principalities.

THE HIERARCHY. The fairly well-defined hierarchy included the following masculine titles:

English	German
Emperor	Kaiser
King	König
Elector	Kürfurst
Prince	Fürst, Prinz
Duke	Herzog
Count, Earl	Graf
Lord	Herr
Baron	Baron, Freiherr
Noble	Elder
Knight	Ritter

At the same time, there were ecclesiastical rankings which included the following: Archbishops, Bishops, Prelates, and Abbots. Individuals could hold more than one title. For instance, Archbishops were normally chosen from the ranks of Princes.

Other terms which are difficult to place in the above sequences include Markgraf, Pfalzgraf (Count Palatine), etc.

THE LEGACY OF JOHANN SIBMACHER. Johann Sibmacher (or Siebmacher), noted coat-of-arms painter and copper plate engraver, was active in Nürnberg during the latter part of the 15th century. His date of birth as well as most of his life history is unknown.

Sibmacher was just one of the numerous individuals active in the literary centers of Nürnberg and Augsburg, who followed the tradition of the famous printer Anton Koberger (1440-1513) and the historian Hartmann Schedel (1440-1514). For instance, at its peak, Koberger's printing establishment ran twenty-four presses simultaneously and employed more than 100 illustrators, printers, binders, and the like. Active at the same time Anton Sorg, one of several early Augsburg printers, in 1477, issued the first printed armorial.

The first known work of Sibmacher was printed in 1591, with a second printing in 1597. His 1596 *Kleines Wappenbuch* (small coat-of-arms book) was a primitive sort of publication compared to his later works. Sibmacher published another essay on heraldry in 1601 which had a second printing in 1604. The major work of Sibmacher, titled *Neu Wappenbuch*, appeared as part 1 in 1605. This part contained 3,320 coats-of-arms. The second part of the same book appeared in 1609; this second part contained an additional 2,400 coats-of-arms.

After Sibmacher's death in 1611, his widow, in conjunction with the merchant Leonhard Steirer, had both parts reprinted in 1612, and again in 1630. A fourth edition appeared in 1657-1668; the fourth edition contained two additional parts. A fifth edition in 1657-1668 added another part and another supplement.

A greatly expanded sixth edition appeared in 1695 under the title *Erneuert-verbessertes Wappenbuch*. The sixth edition went through five printings by 1734; by this time, 14,767 coats-of-arms were illustrated. In the years 1753-1806, a second expanded version contained an additional eleven supplemental volumes. By 1772, twelve printings of the 1695 version with supplements were issued. These early editions, embracing the period 1605-1806, were termed "Der Alte Siebmacher." "Der Neue Siebmacher" editions were printed during the years 1854-1961.

In the years 1855-1936, the famous Nürnberg printing firm of Verlag Bauer und Raspe contracted Otto Titan v. Hefner and a series of other scholars to do a *Neue Siebmacher*. This new revision eventually contained 340 parts in 101 volumes; this set included five volumes dealing with bürgerlich (ordinary citizen) coats-of-arms. Virtually all of the Bauer und Raspe physical assets were destroyed during World War II.

By 1970, the firm of Verlag Degener & Co, located in Bavaria at Neustadt an der Aisch, acquired the rights to *Siebmachers Wappenbücher*. The entire set was physically reordered and condensed into eighty-six volumes which were printed during the years 1978-86. The arms of virtually every noble family in German-speaking lands were illustrated. The five volumes of bürgerlich coats-of-arms were condensed into four.

The famous 1605-1609 opus of Sibmacher has become an exceedingly rare book. In fact, the 1978 *National Union Catalog* (itself composed of 754 volumes) lists only one copy in the United States, that being located at Harvard University. Nearly every major library, however, has a copy of the more recent, expanded version of Siebmacher's *Wappenbuch*.

TRACING YOUR NOBLE ANCESTOR. For individuals fortunate to establish a connection with noble lines, there exists today a vast literature which provides a wealth of documentation. The key references to this literature were neatly discussed in a series of essays by Dorothy L. Behling. This series of eight, short quarterly essays was published under the broad title of "Nobly Speaking" in the *German Genealogical Digest* from 1985 through 1987.

Fortunately, there are a series of key indices which expedite what might have been a very bulky search. Notable among these indices are the following: Hanns Jäger-Sunstenau's 1964 index to the massive *Siebmacher Wappenbücher* volumes (dating 1856-1936); Thomas Freiherr von Fritsch's 1968 index to the numerous *Gothaisches genealogisches Taschenbuch* (Gotha genealogical pocketbooks; dating 1764-1942); and the comprehensive indices to the more recent ninety or so volumes of *Genealogisches Handbuch des Adels* (genealogical handbook of the noble families) edited by Hans Friedrich von Ehrenkrook and Walter v. Hueck, which began in 1946.

Royalty aside, nearly every family with a German sounding name can relate to the spelling of one of the 130,000 names in the index compiled by Jäger-Sunstenau, 1964. In many cases, it is possible to get a clue as to area of origin. For instance, the name Haller most likely comes from Bavaria although it occurs also in certain areas in Switzerland and Austria. This would place the name in the southeast Germanic linguistic quadrant. Moreover, it happens that the name was carried to Hungary in the late 15th century, and further south to Croatia by the 19th century, and to America in the very early 20th century.

REFERENCES

Benecke, G., 1974, *Society and Politics in Germany 1500-1750*. Routledge & Kegan Paul, London, 436 p.

Beumann, Helmut (ed.), 1984, *Kaisergestalten des Mittelalters*. Verlag C. H. Beck, München, 386 p., illus.
Covers royal personalities for period 768-1519.

Burke's Peerage Ltd., 1952, *Burke's Landed Gentry*. Burke's Peerage Ltd., London, 17th ed., 2840 p.

_____, 1963, *Burke's Peerage. Baronetage and Knightage*. ibid, 103rd ed., 2987 p.

_____, 1967, *Burke's Royal Families of the World*. ibid, Vol. I, Europe and Latin America, 594 p., vol. II, Africa and the Middle East, 320 p.
The three volumes listed above are representative of a whole series of the "Burke's" publications on European royalty. Nearly every library has part of the series.

Coddington, J. I., 1980, "Royal and Noble Genealogy." In *Genealogical Research: Methods and Sources*. American Soc. Genealogists, Washington, D.C. Vol I (revised ed.), p. 402-422
Good, concise summary of source materials dating before 1970.

Ehrenkrook, Hans Friedrich von (ed. until 1965) and Walter v. Hueck (ed. from 1966), *Genealogisches Handbuch des Adels*. Adelige Häuser, 35 vols., Adelskexikon, 5 vols., Freiherrliche Häuser, 22 vols., Gräfliche Häuser, 15 vols., Fürstliche Häuser, 13 vols. C. A. Starke Verlag, Limburg a.d. Lahn (90 vols. as of 1987)

Epen, J. C. P. v., 1900, *Naamregister op het Stam- en Wapenboek van Aanzienlijke Nederlandsche Familien*. Heraldisch Genealogisch Archief, Brussels, 137 p.
Every name index to Vorsterman van Oyen, 1885-90.

Fox-Davies, A. C., 1970, *Armorial Families*. David & Charles Ltd., Newton Abbot, Devonsh., Vol. 1, 1020 p., Vol. 2, p. 1021-2190.

Frank, Karl Friedrich von, 1967 et seq., *Standeserhebungen und Gnadenakte für das Deutsche Reich und die Österreichischen Erblande bis 1806*. Privately printed, Schloss Senfteneeg, Niederösterreich, Vol. 1, A-E, 289 p.(1967), Vol. 2, F-J, 267 p. (1970), Vol. 3, K-N, 309 p. (1972), Vol. 4, O-Sh, 310 p. (1973), Vol. 5, Si-Z, 288 p. (1974)
One of the most comprehensive lists of names of nobility of the Hapsburg empire.

Fritsch, Thomas Freiherr von, 1968, *Die Gothaischen Taschenbücher, Hofka-lender und Almanach*. C. A. Starke, Limburg. Vol. 2 of Aus dem Deutschen Adelsarchiv.
Pages 187-349 indexes the circa 179 volumes of the *Gothaisches genea-logisches Taschenbuch*.

Henning, Eckart & Gabriele Jochums, 1984, *Bibliographie zur Heraldik*. Bühlau Verlag, K+ln, 546 p.

Hüber, Lotte, 1984, *Rudolf von Habsburg und seine Nachfolger 1273-1918*. Conzett + Hüber AG, Zürich, numerous pages, charts.
Not actually a book, but a fine compilation in loose-leaf and table form of all the important personalities in the Habsburg regime.

Isenburg, Wilhelm Karl Prinz von, 1975, *Europäische Stammtafeln. Bd. I, Die deutschen Staaten*. Verlag von J. A. Stargardt, Marburg,rg, 197 tab., Register (Bd. I-II), 32 p.
_____, 1976, ibid, Bd. II, *Die ausserdeutschen Staaten*. ibid, 144 tab., Register (Bd. I-II), 32 p.

Jäger-Sunstenau, Hanns, 1964, *General-Index zu den Siebmacher'schen Wappenbüchern, 1605-1961*. Akademische Druck- u. Verlagsanstalt, Graz, Austria, 586 p.
Virtually indispensable index to the 130,000 coats-of-arms in the massive Siebmacher series of volumes; reprint of 1984 includes 13 p. appendix.

Kneschke, E. H., 1959/70, *Deutsches Adels-Lexikon*. Verlag von Friedrich Voigt, Leipzig, 9 vols.

Kühne, C. E., 1979, *Sie Trugen die Krone*. C. A. Starke Verlag, Limburg a.d. Lahn, 340 p., 140 illus.

Loringhoven, Frank Baron Freytag von, 1956, *Europäische Stammtafeln*. *Bd. III*. Verlag von J. A. Stargardt, Marburg, 159 tab., Register, 9 p.
_____, 1975, *Ibid. Bd. IV*. ibid, 160 tab., Register, 11 p.
_____, 1978, *Ibid, Bd. V*. ibid, 160 tab., Register, 5 p.

Louda, Jiri, & Michael MacLagan, 1981, *Heraldry of the Royal Families of Europe*. Clarkson N. Potter, Inc., N.Y., maps, 150 tables, in color.

McNaughton, Arnold, 1973, *The Book of Kings*. Garnstone Press, Ltd., London, Vol. 1, The Royal Houses, 511 p., Vol. 2, The Families, p. 513-1086 , Vol. 3, 394 p., 118 figs (Plates, Indexes).

Neubecker, Ottfried, 1985, *Der bürgerlichen Geschlechter Deutschlands, Österreichs und der Schweiz (Grosses Wappen-Bilder Lexikon)*. Ernst Battenberg Verlag, München, 1147 p.
Large format, mainly plates of coats-of-arms, condensed, indexed, and catalogued. The coats-of-arms deal with ordinary citizens of Germany, Austria, and Switzerland.

Rietstap, J. B., 1884/87, *Armorial General. G. B.* van Goor Zonen, Gouda, 2nd ed., Vol. 1, 1884, (A-K), Vol. 2, 1887, (L-Z).
_____, 1883/87, *Wapenboek van den Nederlandschen Adel.* J. B. Wolters, Groningen, Pt. I, 239 p., 50 pls., Pt. IIa, 148 p., 48 pls., Pt. IIb, p. 149-334.
Large format with plates of Dutch coats-of-arms in color.

Rolland, V. & H. V. Rolland, 1903/26, *Planches de l'Armorial General de J. B. Rietstap.* Paris/The Hague, 3 vols.
Contains 112,600 arms in black & white.

_____, *Ibid.* (reprint ed.), 1967, Hollen Street Press Ltd., Slough, Buckssh. ibid.

Ross, Martha, 1978, *Rulers and Governments of the World.* Bowker Co., London, Vol. I, Earliest Times to 1491, 735 p., Vol. II, 1492-1929, 779 p., Vol. III, 1929-1975, 687 p.

Schwennicke, Detlev, (ed.), 1960/85, *Europäischen Stammtafeln: Stammtafeln zur Geschichte der europäischen Staaten. Neue Folge.* C. A. Starke Verlag, Limburg a.d. Lahn, 13 vols.
Numerous genealogical tables of virtually all the ruling families in Germany, indexed; essentially a revision of Isenburg and Loringhoven above.

Siebmacher, Johann, 1856-1936, *J. Siebmacher's grosses und allgemeine Wappenbücher.* Originally printed 1856-1936. Verlag von Bauer und Raspe, Nürnberg, reprinted 1951-86 by Verlag Degener & Co., Neustadt/Aisch, 86 vols.
A massive, folio size, authoritative work by numerous area specialists in the former German-speaking areas.

Taddey, Gerhard (ed.), 1977, *Lexikon der Deutschen Geschichte.* Alfred Kröner Verlag, Stuttgart, 1352 p.

Vorsterman van Oyen, A. A., 1885-90, *Stam- en Wapenboek van aanzienlijke Nederlandsche familien.* J. B. Wolters, Groningen, Vol I, 359 p., Vol. II, 415 p., Vol. IIIa, 264 p., Vol. IIIb, p. 265-521
Large format of Dutch coats-of-arms.

Wilberg, Max, 1962, *Regenten-Tabellen*. Akademische Druck- u. Verlag-sanstalt, Graz, Austria, 336 p. Reprint of 1906 publication by Paul Beholtz, Frankfurt a. Oder, it includes tables of ruling personalities, such as kings, princes, popes, etc. in Europe.

Zopby, J. W., (ed.), 1980, *The Holy Roman Empire, A Dictionary Handbook*. Greenwood Press, Westport, Conn., 551 p., 8 sketch maps.

IVER OF DESTINY. AMONG THE FAMOUS rivers in Europe, the Rhine attained the well-developed reputation of being the "Schicksalsfluss," the River of Destiny. Hundreds of thousands of Germans floated or sailed down the river to an unknown destiny, beginning in 1683 and lasting until the mid-1800's when other methods of transportation replaced the slow Rhine barges. Since the time of the Romans, the Rhine has served both as a boundary and as an important travel way. And not surprisingly. This world famous migration and shipping route cuts through five countries: Austria, Switzerland, France, Germany, and the Netherlands (Figures 3 and 4 on the next two pages).

The Romans occupied the Middle Rhine over a period of about six centuries from about 100 B.C to A.D. 486, and in fact, Caesar built a bridge across the Rhine in a narrow stretch between Koblenz and Andernach. The famous "Limes Imperii Romanii" was a line of fortifications straddling a stone wall of some 548 km (341 miles) between the Rhine-Main River area and the Danube. In this period, the wall helped the Romans maintain effective control to the south of the left bank of the Rhine. Nearly all major cities along the Rhine, Strasbourg (Strassburg), Mainz, Koblenz, Bonn, Köln, and Düsseldorf, are of Roman origin, and most of them are located on the left bank.

Before 1830, the Rhine was the most obvious route of migration: by barge or boat down the Rhine to Rotterdam, and then across the Atlantic to the ports of New York, Philadelphia, or Baltimore. Until 1783, the British navigation acts required an intermediate stop in an English port.

GEOGRAPHY. From its headwaters in Switzerland to its mouth in the Dutch North Sea, the Rhine is some 1,236 km (768 miles) long. The length of the Rhine is divided into three sections.

The Oberrhein (Upper Rhine) from Basel in Switzerland to Mainz in Germany is about 362 km (225 miles) long. In 1812, Johann Gottfried Tula (1770-1828), an engineer from Karlsruhe, put forth his plans to modernize the marshy and boggy portion of the Upper Rhine, which was periodically rampant with typhoid and dysentery. The plans were submitted to the administration of Baden; work was begun about 1828 and completed only in 1885. During the years 1817-74, the 354 km (220 miles) section between Basel and Worms was shortened artificially by about eighty-two km (fifty-one miles); moreover, the meandering channel, crossing a three to four km (two to two and a half miles) flood-plain of the Rhine, was narrowed to a channel of about 200 m (656 ft.).

The Mittel Rhein (Middle Rhine), being a short 124 km (seventy-seven miles), from Mainz to Bonn, is well known for its scenic aspect with vineyards lining the steep hills of the river banks. These hills are named the Schiefergebirge (shale or slate mountains).

This part of the Rhine contains some of the shallowest hazards (at the Binger Loch) and also some of the deepest portions. The deepest portions are 200-300 m (656-986 ft.) deep. In places, rapid currents persist. The narrowest part of the Rhine, at the famous rock outcrop the Lorelei, is only about 112 m (367 ft.) wide. By contrast, the Rhine at Mainz is almost 580 m (1,903 feet) wide. Most of the famous castles, castle ruins, and remains of toll stations are on the Middle Rhine.

The Lower Rhine from Bonn in Germany to Hoek van Holland in the Netherlands is thus about 750 km (468 miles) long. Here the bed of the river widens in the low lying and flat landscape. Here also the currents become much slower. Just below Lobith, the Rhine splits into two main channels. The larger channel to the south is termed the Waal and is used by modern ocean-going vessels as far inland as Düsseldorf.

Figure 4

THE MIDDLE
AND
UPPER RHINE

Legend

⌒⌒⌒⌒ THE RHINE RIVER

The other main channel, to the north, is called the Neder Rijn (Lower Rhine) or Lek. The two channels converge above Rotterdam and extend westward past Hoek van Holland. Another channel, still further to the north, originally termed the Oude Rijn (the Old Rhine, shown on figure 3 as "Rhine") runs by Leiden and out into the North Sea at Katwijk. This channel, being connected by canals to Rotterdam, Amsterdam, and Utrecht, was used mainly by smaller boats.

Average current speeds for the various portions are summarized in Table 6.6 on the next page. As mentioned earlier, the distance from Strasbourg (Strassburg) in the French province of Bas-Rhin to the Dutch city of Rotterdam is about 740 km (460 miles). Modern day current records show that free-floating barges or boats drifting over this distance downstream, travel at an average speed of three and one half km/hr, or somewhat more than two miles an hour. Until the middle of the 19th century, it would have taken travellers about nine days to go from Alsace in France to Rotterdam, that is, if they were not hindered by the numerous toll stations.

TABLE 6.6
THE RHINE CURRENTS

Cities	Distance in km	Current in km/hr	Floating Time in hrs	Ave. Time in hrs	Remarks
Basel to Canal du Rhone	20	8 to 4	5.0 to 2.5	3.3	Basel is at the German/Swiss border
Canal du Rhone to Breisach	41	4 to 2	0.5 to 10.0	13.7	
Breisach to Strassburg	69	6 to 3	0.0 to 11.0	15.3	
Strassburg to Iffezheim	39	5 to 3	3.0 to 7.0	9.8	
Iffezheim to Mannheim	94	7 to 5	8.8 to 13.0	15.7	
Mannheim to Mainz	69	5 to 4	7.3 to 13.0	15.3	Worms is ca. 23 km north of Mannheim
Mainz to Bingen	30	5 to 3	0.0 to 6.0	7.5	
Bingen to St. Goar	29	7 to 5	5.8 to 4.1	4.8	
St. Goar to Koblenz	35	6 to 5	7.0 to 5.8	6.4	
Koblenz to Köln	95	5 to 4	3.8 to 19.0	21.1	
Köln to Lobith	178	5 to 4	4.5 to 35.0	39.6	Krefeld is ca. 71 km north of Köln
Lobith to Dordrecht	105	5 to 3	5.0 to 21.0	26.3	Lobith is at the German/Dutch border
Dordrecht to Rotterdam	20	5 to 3	6.7 to 4.0	5.0	
Rotterdam to Hoek van Holland	28	5 to 3	9.3 to 5.6	7.0	Hoek van Holland is at the North Sea
	852			190.7	

Remarks:
Distance Basel to Lobith is 699 km (434 miles)
Distance Worms to Krefeld is 306 km (190 miles)

Today, there is constant traffic on the Rhine except during severe winters when it is frozen. And in fact, traffic kilometer markers are visible along the navigable part of the Rhine. The zero kilometer marker begins upstream at the bridge of the City of Konstanz in Germany. Downstream, at the German/Dutch border, near the village of Lobith, the markers read km 862 (535 miles). At Hoek van Holland the markers read km 1035 (643 miles).

INFAMOUS TOLL STATIONS ON THE RHINE. The navigable part of the Rhine thus extends from Konstanz, on the Bodensee, north and westward to its mouth near Hoek van Holland. The Romans were very active along the entire length of the Rhine and had major boat building centers on its left bank at Mainz in the Middle Rhine, and at Vetera (Xanten) and at Köln (Cologne) on the Lower Rhine. During the Middle Ages, sea-going vessels sailed up the Rhine to Köln. Smaller vessels could sail further up the Rhine, perhaps as far as the rapids at the Binger Loch (near Bingen). Eventually, in the years 1830-32, these shallows were blasted with dynamite and dredged to permit access even further upstream.

Table 6.7 on the next page shows the names of some seventy-five toll stations existing in the Middle Ages along the Rhine. In the short stretch between Mainz and Köln, a distance of 179 km (111 miles), there were thirty toll stations, or one toll station every six km (three and seven-tenths miles). These toll stations include many famous names, especially along the stretch of the river between Mainz and Koblenz.

One of the oldest toll stations was Sooneck Castle, near Bingen, which dates from 1015. Erected by Archbishop Willigis of Mainz, this castle was to become, eventually, one of the strongholds of the robber barons ("Raubritter" in German). Today, ruins of hilltop castles indicate where their former toll stations were located on the river below. Four of the Electors of the Holy Roman Empire controlled and derived an important source of revenue from various toll stations as listed below:

Kurmainz (Archbishop of Mainz)
Bingen	Ehrenfels
Rheinstein	Ober-Lahnstein
Trechtlinghausen	Mainz
Fürstenberg	

Kurköln (Archbishop of Köln)
Andernach	Linz
Bonn	Köln

Kurtrier (Archbishop of Trier)
Oberwesel	Koblenz
Boppard	Engers (Hammerstein)
Kapellen	Leutesdorf

Kurpfalz (Elector Palatine)
Bacharach	Kaub

At various times, there were as many as sixty-two toll stations in operation at any one time, as named in Table 6.7 on the next page. These toll stations were most active in the Middle Ages. The high fees and the piratical activities of the tolls generated the term "robber knights." These robber knights were especially active until the formation of the first Rheinische Städtebund (League of Rhenish Cities) which lasted, however, only from 1254 to 1257. The first Städtebund was composed of seventy cities but had only modest success. Finally, in 1282, Emperor Rudolf I (reigned 1273-1291) organized more effective resistance and succeeded in controlling the robber knights. The second League of Rhenish Cities, which was formed in 1381 and which lasted until 1388, resulted in a more or less permanent peace treaty.

TABLE 6.7

ANCIENT TOLL STATIONS ON THE RHINE

(after Aubin & Niessen, 1926; Niessen, 1946)

By Year 1200 (north to south)

r-Wyk b. Dursted*	r-Kaiserwerth*	l-St. Goar*
l-Thiel*	l-Neuss	l-Bingen*
r-Arnheim*	l-Koeln	r-Geisenheim
l-Nimwegen	l-Remagen	l-Mainz*
l-Schmithausen	r-Hammerstein	l-Oppenheim
r-Lobith	r-Leutesdorf*	l-Worms
r-Rees	l-Andernach*	l-Strassburg
r-Duisburg	l-Koblenz*	
r-Angermund	l-Boppard*	

By Year 1300 (north to south)

l-Huissen	r-Braubach	r-Ehrenfels
l-Buederich	r-Sterrenberg	l-Kastel
l-Rheinberg	(Camp)	r-Mannheim
l-Uerdingen	l-Oberwesel	r-Ketsch
r-Monheim	r-Kaub	l-Speyer
l-Worringen	l-Bacharach*	l-Rheinhausen
l-Bonn*	l-Fuerstenberg	l-Germersheim*
l-Sinzig	l-Trechinghausen	l-Hoerdt
r-Lahnstein*	l-Rheinstein	l-Merfeld

By Year 1400 (north to south)

l-Griethausen	r-Muehlheim	r-Udenheim*
r-Emmerich*	r-Honnef	r-Weisweil
l-Xanten	r-Linz*	r-Breisach
l-Orsoy*	l-Rheineck	l-Kems
r-Ruhrort	l-Kapellen	l-Basel
r-Duesseldorf*	r-Nierstein	l-Laufenburg
l-Zons*	r-Gernsheim	

By Year 1500 (North to south)

r-Engers	l-Neuenburg	l-Saeckingen
l-Selz	l-Rheinfelden	

Remarks: r = right bank; l = left bank

* = still active in 18th century

CASTLES ON THE RHINE. The main centers of the robber knights were the castles of Rheinstein, Reichenstein, Sooneck near Bingen, and Rheineck near Niederbreisig, on the Middle Rhine, all of which were destroyed about 1282. The fortress at Rheinfels proved more resistant.

During the religious strife at Köln between 1582 and 1586, the castles of Drachenfels and Godesburg were destroyed.

During the Thirty Years' War (1618-48), many of the castles between Koblenz and Mainz were attacked and partially destroyed. Some of these castles eventually were rebuilt.

The third major period of destruction for the castles came during the Wars of Louis XIV, especially during 1688-89. At least fourteen castles fell into French hands and suffered heavy damage.

The fourth major period of destruction came in 1792 during the French Revolution when many of the remaining castles fell into French hands and were dynamited to the ground.

LATER HISTORY. In 1520-21, the famous German engraver Albrecht Dürer (1471-1528) used river boats on the Rhine for his journey to The Netherlands. This trip was for the purpose of renewing his pension with Emperor Karl V (1519-1556).

At the Treaty of Westphalia in 1648, and also at the Treaty of Rijswick in 1697, provisions were made for eliminating many of the toll stations then still existing. As late as 1750, there were thirty-six toll stations between Heilbronn (on the Upper Rhine, near Stuttgart) and Rotterdam. Migrants complained that traversing this distance meant delays of four to six weeks. Table 6.6 on page 242 shows that floating travel time over this distance should have been in the order of six days.

The 1648 treaty provisions were further clarified and expanded in 1803 and again in 1815, at which time there were still sixteen to eighteen toll stations in the German sector. Even up to 1848, there were about eighteen toll stations; these were not completely eliminated until 1868.

Before the early part of the 19th century, the smaller ocean-going vessels required towing by horses. A smallish ship of, say 150 tons, would require ten to twelve horses in order to be drawn upstream as far upstream as Koblenz. The first steamship to travel the Rhine was the British ship the *Prince of Orange*. In 1816, this ship went under its own power from Rotterdam to Köln and was then towed upstream by horses to Koblenz. In 1824, a Dutch steamship, the *Rijn*, travelled upstream to Kaub, and in 1825, to Strasbourg.

With the advent of tourism along the Lower and Middle Rhine, the Köln-Düsseldorf Rhine Steamship Company (popularly known as the "KD"), was founded in 1826. Regular passenger boat service between Köln and Mainz began in 1827. This mass transport made travel along the Rhine much cheaper and quicker. Thanks to the various travel guides discussed earlier, an influx of English tourists invaded the Rhine during the summer months by the 1830's.

In 1832, the ship *Stadt Frankfurt* steamed to Basel in Switzerland. The 1840's saw the beginning of strong competition for trade and tourism by the railroads running along the banks of the Rhine. Even today, a series of luxury liners, such as the *M.S. Britannia*, ply the Rhine between Basel and Rotterdam. The modern steamers traverse the 800 odd km (about 497 miles) between the two cities with an average travel speed of fourteen knots (twenty-six km per hour, or sixteen miles per hour) downstream and eight and six-tenths knots (sixteen km per hour, or ten miles per hour) upstream. The cruises last a leisurely four days and include stopovers.

THE RHEINGOLD EXPRESS. Railway service along the Rhine was relatively late. In fact, the first stretch, between Köln and Bonn, was constructed only in 1844. Thereafter, tracks were built rapidly along both sides of the Rhine.

Beginning with the general use of railroads in Germany from about 1850, the main emigrant departure centers were shifted to the north German harbors of Bremen and Hamburg. Rotterdam became a relatively minor departure point for German travellers. The Lower and Middle Rhine channels retained and increased their importance as a commercial shipping lane, however. Whatever shipping records existed in Rotterdam were destroyed by bombing in World War II; there is however, a recent Shipping Museum in Rotterdam which is dedicated to recovering general historical information.

The rail system along the Rhine henceforth developed a reputation as a tourist route. Basking in the vast luxury of *The Rheingold Express*, today's rail traveller can cover the distance of 484 km (301 miles) from Amsterdam to Frankfurt in little more than five hours including a border crossing and short stops in eight major cities. The *Express* travels much of its route along the immediate left bank of the Rhine. Leaving Frankfurt, it covers the route of 423 km (263 miles) to München in scarcely more than four hours.

Today, one of the more spectacular sights along the Rhine is the island fortress called the Pfalzgrafenstein, or simply "der Pfalz." It is located on an island near Kaub am Rhein. It was built in 1326-27 by Emperor Ludwig IV, der Bayern, and has never been destroyed. The small castle, which has a pentagonal shape, was renovated in 1971 in bold red and white colors.

REFERENCES

Aubin, Hermann & Josef Niessen, 1926, *Geschichtlicher Handatlas der Rheinprovinz.* Verlag J. P. Bachem GmbH, Köln, 18 p., 56 illus.
Note especially map 30: *Zollstätten am Rhein,* i.e., Toll Stations on the Rhine.

Avenarius, Wilhelm, 1980, *Pfalzgrafenstein: in Alte Burgen, Schöne Schlösser.* Verlag Das Beste, Stuttgart, 238 p., illus.
_____, 1986, *Rheinland-Pfalz Burgen & Schlösser.* Graphoprint, Koblenz, 34 p., numerous illus.
The two publications contain a spectacular series of color photos of the better known castles on and near the Rhine.

Baedeker, Karl, 1886, *Die Rheinlande.* Verlag von Karl Baedeker, Leipzig, 32nd ed., 438 p., 31 maps.
A relatively late edition of the famous travel guide series which began in 1828, see earlier essay "The Rhine Travel Guides" in Part 5.

Dursthoff, Lutz, et al (ed.), 1988, *Die deutschen Burgen und Schlösser.* S. Fischer Verlag, Frankfurt/Main, 933 p.
A very comprehensive listing of German castles; published under the auspices of the German Federation of Castle owners.

Feger, Robert, 1974, *Burgen und Schlösser in Sudbaden.* Weidlich Verlag, Würzburg, 312 p.,
_____, 1978, *Ritter, Fursten und Melusinen.* Rombach Verlag, Freiburg, 175 p.
Deals mainly with castles in the German State of Baden.

Göck, Roland, 1979, *Der Rhein.* Präsentverlag, Gutersloh, 164 p., illus.
Basically a pictorial essay.

Hollenweger, Paula, 1980, *Sagen von Oberrhein.* Frenzel Verlag, Neuenburg am Rhein, 151 p.
The title translates as "Tales from the Upper Rhine."

Johnson, Paul, 1989, *Castles of England, Scotland and Wales.* Harper & Row, N.Y., 215 p., maps, illus.
Numerous illustrations of English castles, first printed in 1978; listed here for purposes of comparison.

Kalkwick, K. A., & A. I. J. M. Schellart, 1980, *Atlas van de Nederlandse Kastelen.* Sijthoff, Amsterdam, 246 p., maps, illus.
Comprehensive listing of Dutch castles.

Müller, Kristiane (ed.), 1991, *The Rhine*. APA Publications (HK) Ltd., Singapore, 330 p., illus., maps.
A rather uneven and historically incomplete series, by ten writers, of documentaries on the Rhine.

Müller-Ahlfeld, Theodor (ed.), 1969, *Der Rhein*. Rudolf Krämer-Badoni Verlag, Berlin, 144 p., illus.
_____, Willy Eggers, & Harald Busch (eds.), 1956, *Der Rhein von den Alpen bis zum Meer*. Umschau Verlag, Frankfurt/Main, 29 p., map, illus.
The two books are pictorial essays of the Rhine.

Niessen, Josef, 1946 (1950), *Geschichtlicher Handatlas der Deutschen Länder am Rhein: Mittel- und Niederrhein*. J. P. Bachem Verlag, Köln, 64 p., numerous maps.
Note especially map 20, *Rheingebiet um das Jahr 1610*, and map 34, *Zollstätten am Rhein*, that is, the Rhine about the year, 1610, and toll stations on the Rhine.

Pearson, A. J., 1919, *The Rhine and its Legends*. Coblence, 34 p., illus.
This work was reprinted by Mennonite Family History, Elverson, Pa., in 1992; it illustrates and relates legends about nineteen of the scenic wonders of the Rhine.

Römer, Gerhard (ed.), 1981, *Die Oberrheinlande in Alten Landkarten (1618-1828)*. Badischen Landesbibliothek, Karlsruhe, 131 p., illus.
The Upper Rhine in antique maps; contains good color photo reproductions, unfortunately in a small scale.

Schneider, H. J., 1983, *Der Rhein*. Insel Verlag, Frankfurt/Main, 443 p., illus.

Schneiders, Toni, 1982, *Der Rhein*. Herder Verlag, Freiburg, 212 p., illus.

Simrock, Karl, 1840, *Das malerische und romantische Rheinland*. Olms Presse, Hildesheim (reprint 1975), 488 p., 60 copperplate illus.
The reprints of old copper plate scenes are especially interesting and informative. For instance, some show sailing on the Rhine, apparently in an upstream direction.

Spence, Lewis, 1915, *Hero Tales and Legends of the Rhine*. Frederick A. Stokes Co., N.Y., 379 p.

Tillmann, Curt, 1961, *Lexikon der Deutschen Burgen und Schlösser*. Anton Hiersemann, Stuttgart, Bd. I, Aach bis Marzoll, p. 1-640; Bd. II, Maschau bis Zyrown, p. 641-1282; Bd. III, Nachträge, Literatur, Register, p. 1283-1781; Bd. IV, Atlas (numerous maps). Lexicon of German castles country-wide, with indexed maps.

von Lüttichan-Bärenstein, Hannibal (ed.), 1980, *Alte Burgen, Schöne Schlösser*. Verlag Das Beste, Stuttgart, 278 p., illus., map Map and color illustrations show the most important castles in Germany.

Winkler, Wilhelm, 1935, *Pfälzischer Geschichtsatlas*. Verlag der Pfälzischen Gesell. z. Förderung d. Wissenschaften, Neustadt / Haardt, 18 p., 40 illus. Note especially map 5, *Villages with the suffix heim, etc.*, also map 16, *German migration to SE Pa.* The suffix -heim is typical of the area known as the Palatinate.

N THE MODERN WORLD, WHEN CROSSING the Atlantic is a matter of hours, we look back on the travails of those who came to America in the 17th and 18th centuries. Even until about 1860, crossing the Atlantic was a matter of weeks on a slow, bouncy, sailing ship. Almost always this meant crowded and unclean quarters which smelled awful. The stench rapidly went from merely nauseating to mind numbing. Nor were the food and water appealing. A bland diet of heavily salted and dried fish or meat, dried beans, perhaps some bread and some rancid cheese or butter did little to quell the uneasy stomach of the weary traveller.

The 17th century immigrants came in big ships and small ships, the main English ports of embarkation being London, Bristol, and Liverpool. Boston was one of the earliest points of entry in America. Later, Philadelphia, New York and Baltimore were the main entry points. Philadelphia received the bulk of the immigrants during the 18th century while New York was the dominant port of entry by far during the 19th century and on into the 20th century.

According to the 17th century records of William Penn, some trips were "a mere twenty-eight days while a few were longer than six weeks" (as quoted in Balderston, 1963, p. 27). Penn's salesmanship was apparent as the twenty-eight days was an exception and a record set by the ship *Jeffrey*. Most sailing times westward across the Atlantic averaged around eight to ten weeks, with some as long as fifteen or even twenty weeks, especially for ships taking the "southern route" in the winter.

ACROSS THE ATLANTIC. Recognizing the fact that Jamestown (Virginia), St. Augustine (Florida), and Santa Fe (New Mexico) were among the earliest permanent settlements in America, colonization began in earnest only about 1620. The English colony and the two Spanish settlements mentioned here were established about 1607 and 1609, respectively.

Jamestown, located in a marshy area on the Jamestown River, had a precarious existence from the start. By 1609, there were some 500 inhabitants, but during the winter of 1609/10, nearly all died from disease and starvation so that only about sixty-five were left. Recent tabulation of the Jamestown colonists indicate that 7,549 colonists arrived between the years 1607 and 1624 of which 6,454 died not long after arriving. The main causes of death apparently were malnutrition, typhoid, and typhus. Three Germans, namely F. Unger, H. Keffler and F. Volday, participated in the settlement of Jamestown which was initially under the leadership of Captain John Smith (c.1579-1631).

The experiences of the settlers in Jamestown with the local Indian tribes is representative of many of the early colonies. The Jamestown massacre of 1622, which was carried out by a confederation of thirty Algonquian-speaking tribes, slowed the development of the small colony when some 350 white colonists were killed. The outgrowth of this hostile action was the Powhatan War which was a series of skirmishes lasting from 1622-44. During the final Indian raid on Jamestown in 1644, more than 500 white settlers were killed. A concerted action by the remaining whites and friendly Indian tribes led to retribution and a peace settlement.

The English Pilgrims, numbering 104 individuals, including thirty-five Puritans, departed Plymouth, England, after having lived for several years in Rotterdam. They departed aboard the *Mayflower* on September 16, 1620. They arrived at Cape Cod (Massachusetts) on November 19 after a trip of sixty-five days. The early arrivals were soon decimated by disease with one half of the passengers dying within three months of arrival.

The Dutch West Indies Company (founded in 1621) was responsible for the first Dutch settlements in America. Between 1624-26, the lower end of Manhattan Island in New York was populated, and by 1630, there were some 300 individuals there. The colony was taken over by the English in 1664 who changed its name from New Amsterdam to New York. Both the Dutch and English authorities favored Protestant emigrants over those of the Catholic faith.

Boston's first white inhabitant arrived in 1625. A colony of English Puritans was not formed until 1630, however. By 1675, Boston had a population estimated at 4,000.

During the period of 1631-34, there was heavy migration of Dutch, Swedes, and Finns, notably to the west and east banks of the Delaware River. By 1634, over 10,000 Europeans, mainly northern Europeans, had migrated to America. They spread along the coast from Massachusetts south to Delaware and Virginia, with scattered settlements as far south as South Carolina. Most of these settlements clung to the Atlantic coastline, or to river areas near the coast, such as the Delaware River, which now separates the states of Pennsylvania and Delaware.

In 1663, a colony of forty-one Dutch emigrants settled at the junction of the Horekill and lower Delaware Rivers in territory later known as Delaware. The colony was organized under communal terms. It had but a brief one year existence and was terminated in the Anglo-Dutch War of 1664. One of the leaders of the colony, Pieter Cornelisz Plockhoy (ca. 1620-1720), became a ward of the Mennonite colony at Germantown in the years 1694-1700.

By some estimates, the Dutch merchant fleet in the mid-17th century was comprised of some 16,000 vessels, or roughly one half of the European total. By 1700, this vast fleet was gradually being outnumbered by the English fleet. The Navigation Acts of England, between 1651 and 1673, decreed that imports to America first had to be carried to England by ships from the country of origin or by English ships. Henceforth, nearly all goods and passengers to America were carried on ships of English origin. The Navigation Acts were in effect until 1783.

EARLY PENNSYLVANIA SHIP ARRIVAL RECORDS. Some of the key records of the early arrivals in Pennsylvania were pieced together by Marion Balderston in her 1963 publication titled *William Penn's Twenty-three Ships* and in her 1967 publication titled *James Claypoole's Letter Book.* She refers mainly to the year 1682 and to ships landing in Philadelphia. These records were summarized and expanded in Walter Lee Sheppard's 1970 short paper titled *Digest of Ship and Passenger Arrivals in the Delaware.* Sheppard lists twenty-four ships arriving in 1683. The ship lists by Balderston and by Sheppard have been reformatted here as Tables 6.8 and 6.9. These important records provide a clue as to the annual volume of shipping and passenger traffic to America during this early formative period. Almost certainly, a continued search of English shipping records would aid immensely in filling in the gap of missing passengers going to America before 1728.

TABLE 6.8
PARTIAL LIST OF PASSENGER SHIPS TO PHILADELPHIA
for the Period 1681-1682

Order	Ship Name	Arrival Date	Size-Tons
1	The Bristol Factor	Dec., 1681	100
1	The John & Sarah	Mar., 1682	100
2	unknown	May, 1682	x
3	The Amity	Aug.. 1682	240
4	The Freeman	Aug., 1682	x
5	The Hester & Hannah	Aug., 1682	x
6	The Lyon	Aug., 1682	90
7	The Friendship	Aug., 1682	60
8	The Mary	Aug., 1682	46
9	The Society	Aug., 1682	100
10	The Golden Hinde	Sept., 1682	x
11	The Samuel	Sept., 1682	70
12	The Providence	Sept., 1682	50
13	The Friends Adventure	Sept., 1682	x
14	The Elizabeth, Ann & Catherine	Sept., 1682	250
15	The Hopewell	Oct., 1682	x
16	The Lamb	Oct., 1682	130
17	The Bristol Factor	Oct., 1682	100
18	The Welcome	Oct., 1682	284
19	The Jeffrey	Oct., 1682	500
20	The Submission	Nov., 1682	x
21	The Antelope	Dec., 1682	x
22	The Unicorn	Dec., 1682	300

Table 6.9
PARTIAL LIST OF PASSENGER SHIPS TO PHILADELPHIA
for the Period 1683

Order	Ship Name	Arrival Date	Size-Tons
1	The Bristol Merchant	Feb., 1683	300
2	The Thomas & Anne	Apr., 1683	x
3	The John & Elizabeth	May, 1683	70
4	The Grayhound	May, 1683	x
5	unknown	June, 1683	x
6	unknown	July, 1683	x
7	The Liverpool	July, 1683	130
8	The America	Aug., 1683	200
9	The Vine	Sept., 1683	x
10	The Eliza & Mary	Sept., 1683	x
11	The Endeavor	Sept., 1683	100
12	The Bristol Comfort	Oct., 1683	200
13	The Bristol Factor	Oct., 1683	100
14	The Concord	Oct., 1683	500
15	The Lyon	Oct., 1683	90
16	The Providence	Oct., 1683	50
17	The Unicorn	Oct., 1683	300
18	The Mary	Nov., 1683	x
19	The Jeffrey	Nov., 1683	500
20	The Morning Star	Nov., 1683	x
21	The Friendship	Nov., 1683	60
22	The Society	Nov., 1683	100
23	The Samuel & Mary	Nov., 1683	250
24	The Daniel & Elizabeth	Dec., 1683	x

The year 1683 was a peak year for immigrants arriving in Philadelphia with "more than a thousand" individuals arriving late in the year. Prominent among the arrivals was the Englishman James Claypoole who came on the ship *Concord* along with his wife, seven children, and five servants.

Most of the 17th century ships carried mainly cargo with a limited number of passengers. The *Samuel*, for instance, carried about 180 passengers which was an enormous number for those days.

The year 1683 also stands out as the year in which the first settlers of Germantown arrived. The two key ships were the *America* with Francis Daniel Pastorius and others, and the *Concord* with the much publicized group of thirteen heads of Quaker families from Crevelt (today Krefeld). The *Concord* was commemorated on April 29, 1983, by postage stamps issued jointly in Germany and in the United States.

Pastorius recorded his voyage: He departed from Frankfurt on April 2, 1683 on a barge trip down the Rhine. After stopovers in Köln (Cologne), Krefeld, and Rotterdam, he sailed to London on a small schooner on May 8. Pastorius departed Gravesend (near London) by sailing ship on June 8 and arrived in Philadelphia on August 20, a lengthy trip of seventy-four days across the Atlantic.

The *Concord*, with the thirteen heads of Quaker families, left Gravesend on July 24, 1683, and arrived in Philadelphia on October 6, 1683 after a trip of seventy-five days.

The ship which carried William Penn on his first trip to America in 1682, the *Welcome*, made the voyage in eight and one half weeks. It was also one of the larger ships, being 284 tons. The *Welcome* was however outclassed considerably by the *Jeffrey* and the *Concord*, both rated at 500 tons. The smaller ships, such as the *Providence*, weighed in at a mere 50 tons or less.

Two or three of the ships to Philadelphia in 1682 were plagued by smallpox. Penn himself was lucky to escape the disease as his ship, the *Welcome*, lost some thirty passengers out of "100 or so Quakers" to smallpox. Table 6.10 gives relevant data for William Penn's two trips to Philadelphia and for his return trips to England.

TABLE 6.10
PENN'S TRIPS TO AMERICA, 1682-1701

Penn's 1st trip (1682)
    Aug. 30 - sails for America
    Oct. 28 - lands at New Castle, Delaware, 60 days

Penn's return trip (1684)
    Aug. 18 - sails from Lewes, Delaware
    Oct. 3 - lands at Worthing, Sussex 47, days

Penn's 2nd trip (1699)
    Sept. 3 - departs from Isle of Wight
    Dec. 3 - arrives at Philadelphia, 92 days

Penn's return trip (1701)
    "Penn left America in early November, 1701 and reached England about a month later"

Steele's (1986) compilation of sailing records for ships from London to various ports in the Americas confirm sailing times mentioned above. His Table 4.13 summarizes the accounts of seventeen ships sailing during the years 1705-1739. In that Table, the time span from London to Philadelphia ranged from five weeks, five days to fifteen weeks, with an average of nine weeks, six days.

As one would expect, the trip westward across the Atlantic, against the prevailing winds and currents, was generally considerably longer than the return trip eastward. Modern day oceanographers recognize the warm, eastward flowing current as the Gulf Stream. The trip westward detoured considerably to the south in an attempt to avoid the main part of the Gulf Stream.

American statesman and scientist Benjamin Franklin (1706-1790), based on information from his cousin Timothy Folger, had printed in London about 1769-70 the first known map of the Gulf Stream. The publishing of this work was precipitated by complaints in London that westward bound mail packets often took two weeks longer than east bound mail packets. Not until much later was there improvement on the speed of trans-Atlantic travel. In his much publicized account of pioneering life in Missouri, the Rhinelander Gottfried Duden stated that his sailing ship left Rotterdam on May 30, 1824, and reached land in Chesapeake Bay on August 14, 1824, after a trip of seventy-six days. Some three years later, Duden's return trip to Holland, sailing with the current, was much shorter, being only twenty-nine days.

16TH CENTURY POPULATION ESTIMATES. The scattered records provide rough estimates of the population of the English colonies in America. The following estimates for the year 1700 are interesting for their extrapolation of migration patterns:

Massachusetts Bay	80,000
Virginia	55,000
Maryland	32,000
New York	30,000
Connecticut	30,000
Pennsylvania/Delaware	20,000
South Carolina	12,000
New Hampshire	10,000
Rhode Island	10,000
North Carolina	5,000

Total	284,000

By 1713, the European population in America is estimated at about 360,000; the figure for 1755 shows a large increase to some 1,500,000.

At the time of the Revolution, Philadelphia's population was estimated at some 34,000. It was in fact, second only to London in size in the British Empire.

STEAMBOATS ON THE ATLANTIC. Although the first American steam engine apparently was operational in mining activities in New Jersey as early as 1754, it was not until 1785 that the first experiments with steamboats operating on rivers took place in America.

Between 1785 and 1807, there were some sixteen steamboats trials in American inland waters. The first of these trials was by the American inventor John Fitch (1743-1798) with a boat he built in 1785. The trial had limited success. Fitch's second boat in 1787 was a bit more successful, operating under its own power on the Delaware River, near Philadelphia. Fitch made another limited attempt in 1790.

Another early steamboat trial was made by Oliver Evans in 1804, also near Philadelphia. All of these preliminary trials had an elementary steam engine and very primitive paddle-type equipment.

The early trials by the American engineer Robert Fulton (1765-1815) which involved putting a cumbersome engine in the Clermont and steaming on the Hudson River near Albany, N.Y., gained much attention. In 1807, Fulton was able to make the run from Albany to New York on the Hudson River, a distance of 160 miles and return; his boat averaged some five miles per hour and thus met the monopoly agreement required by New York State law.

Fulton was followed by American inventor John Stevens (1749-1838) about 1809 with steamboat runs on the Delaware River.

The massive nature of the early steam engines and the need of enormous quantities of wood for fuel by steamboats plying the rivers and inland water ways of America precluded their being adapted to ocean travel. It was decades before steam was a significant motive power on the trip across the Atlantic.

In fact, slow moving sailing ships were the primary mode of transportation across the Atlantic until the mid-1800's. Significantly, the early ocean-going steamships were not much faster. For instance, in 1819, the *Savannah*, using a combination of sail and auxiliary steam power, sailed from Savannah, Georgia, to Liverpool in twenty-seven days. The bulky steam engine on the *Savannah* had been used, however, only for about eighty hours.

A Canadian steamship, the *Royal William*, was another early ship with an auxiliary steam engine to cross the Atlantic; its maiden voyage in 1833 took twenty-five days. In 1838, there were eleven steamer sailings from New York to Europe. As steam engines became more and more efficient, they gradually took over the burden of driving ships to their destination, especially in a westerly direction.

Between 1848-1860, the number of steamships crossing the Atlantic grew tremendously, but these early ships were not cost effective when compared to sailing ships except for first-class passengers, mail, and the best paying freight. Sailing packets continued to carry immigrants and bulky freight. Even in the mid-19th century the health hazards were great. The *Leibnitz*, sailing from Hamburg to New York on November 2, 1867, arrived sixty-one days later. Of its 544 passengers, 108 had died; a mortality rate of almost 20%. Another, not unusual voyage was made by the ship *Lord Broughan* sailing in 1869 from Hamburg to New York; of its 383 passengers, seventy-five died, again a mortality rate of 20%.

The transition from the use of sailing ships to steamships lasted the better part of the 19th century; in fact, the first steamship without auxiliary sails crossed the Atlantic only in 1899. Although Tepper (1988) cites the following statistics for passenger arrivals in America, there was no clear transition between sailing ships and steamships:

Year	Passengers via Sailing Ships	Passengers via Steamships	Total Passengers
1856	136,459	5,111	141,571
1865	83,452	116,579	200,031
1873	8,715	259,573	268,288

The primary European firms carrying the increasingly heavy immigrant traffic to America in the mid 19th century were Hapag (1847) in Hamburg, Lloyd (1857) in Bremen, Cunard (1840) and White Star (1869) of Great Britain, the CGT (1869) in France, the Red Star Line (1872) in Belgium, and the Holland-America Line (1873) in the Netherlands.

The two German firms became especially prominent through their adaptation of steam ships and through promotional activities in northern and eastern Europe. American firms which held 82 percent of the market in 1840 held only 12 percent by 1890. In the 1870's, cross-Atlantic travel times averaged about seventeen days, which declined to about nine days in the 1890's. By this time, the Industrial Revolution was in full force.

BASIC MIGRATION PATTERNS IN AMERICA. In the late 17th century, and well into the 18th century, Philadelphia was one of the primary ports of entry into America. The notable William Penn was instrumental in expediting the migration of thousands of Quakers to America. The Society of Friends, however, was to remain a dominantly English phenomena and would never incorporate large numbers of continental Europeans. Many of the arrivals at Philadelphia were not members of the Society of Friends.

Plate 82-E published in 1932 by Paullin and Wright shows the distribution of Friends churches in America in 1775-76. Paullin's map and accompanying text record the number of Friends churches as being about 310, or almost ten percent of the total of 3,195 churches. The Friends churches were concentrated in and around Philadelphia and scattered in the foothills along the front of the Appalachian Mountain system. The distribution of the Friends churches, in ever diminishing numbers, goes as far north as Maine and as far south as Georgia. By this account, Penn's immigrant campaign was a huge success.

By contrast, the Mennonite and German Reformed Churches were largely composed of German and Swiss emigrants. In 1775-76, the Mennonite churches in America numbered a mere sixteen while the German Reformed churches numbered 159. Paullin's maps show the churches of the two groups concentrated in eastern Pennsylvania. The Mennonite churches, of course, were mainly in Montgomery and Lancaster counties.

After the Revolutionary War, and into the early 19th century, the tide of Protestant German and Swiss and immigrants of many other nationalities and religions rapidly spread westward across Pennsylvania, into Ohio and Indiana, and continued westward. Dunbar (1915) cites five key events which marked significant advances in migration patterns of Americans across the United States. These were:

1. 1787-1789: the governmental organization of the Ohio country and the Northwest Territory, and the beginning of a general migration into those regions.
2. 1807-1809: general public recognition of the value of steam as a means of propulsion. This included initially steamboat transportation.
3. 1828-1829: the beginning of the railway building period.
4. 1848-1849: the discovery of gold in California (which was in fact preceded a few years by a general migration to Oregon Territory).
5. 1869: the completion of the first transcontinental railway after two decades of intensive lobbying by interested beneficiaries.

EARLY COASTAL ROUTE 95. Plate 138-H in Paullin and Wright, 1932, is titled *Public Post Roads and Main Stage Routes, 1774.* These routes are confined to the eastern seaboard, stretching from Portland, Maine southward to St. Augustine, Florida. Thus until the late 18th century, there was no regular public access to lands within and beyond the north-south trending Appalachian Mountains.

Even upon reaching America, transportation inland could be, and usually was, a taxing experience until the mid-19th century. The 18th century was marked by poor roads often being only enlarged Indian trails. Of course, no steamships existed on the rivers or canals. Nor were there any railroads. Until after the Revolutionary War, the primary mode of transportation in America was by foot or on horseback. By this mode, the average rate of travel was some four miles an hour.

Typical of early roads in America was the so-called Boston Post Road. This was a horseback post road initiated in January, 1673 and ran from near Portsmouth (New Hampshire) 264 miles south through New York to Philadelphia and another 290 miles on to Williamsburg, Virginia. Initial post travel time from Boston to Williamsburg over the road was about four weeks. By 1720, there was regular mail service over the ninety-seven mile portion between New York and Philadelphia; this section became known as the "King's Highway." The King's Highway was soon expanded to include the meandering route of over 1,000 miles extending between the seaports of Boston (Massachusetts) and Charleston (South Carolina).

The coastal route was improved in 1737 and expanded 448 miles southward in 1753 to extend to Charleston in South Carolina. The first regular stage coach service over the King's Highway began to operate in 1750 with regular city-to-city service by 1756. Wagon travel was in general limited to the summer months. By 1793, one could travel the 209 miles from Boston to New York, by stage-coach, in four days, or some 52 miles per day.

Of course, the name "King's Highway" was dropped from general use with the advent of the Revolutionary War (1775-1783). The route was to prove a vital link for General George Washington's troops with their wagons and cannons.

In 1802, a trip by stagecoach from Boston, Mass. to Savannah, Georgia, covered the distance of some 1,046 miles in twenty-two and one half days for an average daily rate of about forty-six miles per day.

Today, the much travelled Highway 95 covers nearly the same route although on a straighter line and extends from Canada south to the tip of Florida.

BRIDGING THE ALLEGHENIES. The 500 mile Allegheny Mountain portion of the Appalachian Mountain system, that is, the mountainous terrain in Virginia, West Virginia, Maryland, and Pennsylvania, formed a formidable barrier to early land travel.

In 1773, at the instigation of Judge Richard Henderson, an important trail through the Alleghenies was opened. The American pioneer Daniel Boone (1734-1820), his brother Squire, seven families, and about forty men started on one of the earliest group migrations westward. Beginning from their settlement along the Yadkin River, deep in the interior of North Carolina, Boone initiated what later was to be called "Boone's Wilderness Road," across the southern end of the Alleghenies and through the Cumberland Gap.

By 1775, the Boone party reached the settlement subsequently named Boones Borough in northern Kentucky, some ninety miles southeast of Louisville, a town settled about 1778, on the Ohio River. Today, the trail across the Tennessee-Kentucky border, through the Cumberland Gap, is the relatively obscure Interstate Highway 25E.

Boone was followed almost immediately by other groups. A prominent pioneer was George Rogers Clark (1752-1818) who went to Kentucky in 1775. Clark actively participated in frontier warfare in various parts of the Ohio Valley against the Indians and, later, during the Revolutionary War, against the British. Several thousand people traversed the Wilderness Road during the Revolutionary period of 1776-1783.

By 1784, some 30,000 people had gone into the Kentucky region and were spreading southward into Tennessee. Another 12,000 followed in the summer of 1784. All these early Kentucky immigrants travelled either on foot with backpack, on horseback, or on foot with horsepack; travel time was in the order of one to two months. In 1792, Kentucky became the first state west of the Appalachians. In 1796, the trail was finally widened to accommodate wagons. Virtually all of the early immigrants, mainly of English background, were from either Virginia or North Carolina.

By about 1800, the Iroquois, or Mohawk Trail, from Albany, N.Y., westward some 360 miles to Buffalo, was one of the main trails into the interior. Records indicate that in 1824, travel by stage coach between Albany and western New York, during the "muddy season", took seven nights and six days. By 1830, there were five stage coach companies operating between Albany and Buffalo, even though the boat traffic on the parallel Erie Canal, starting in 1826, provided strong competition, but only in the summer. The canal was normally frozen about five months a year. The Mohawk Trail provided an important connection with shipping on the Great Lakes. Today, New York State Throughway 90 covers much of the same route.

Another Indian trail, called the Allegheny Path by the Indians, and later named the Pennsylvania Road (duplicating in part Forbes' Military Road, dating from 1758), ran from Philadelphia westward some 300 miles to the location of present-day Pittsburgh, i.e. twenty or more days by pack train to the junction of the Allegheny and Monongahela Rivers.

By 1727, Lancaster County became the settlement center for waves of Swiss and German Mennonites. Most of these Mennonites were farmers who developed the important grain growing area of Lancaster Co. The pious pioneers of the Lancaster area suffered through a period of great uncertainty during the French and Indian War of 1754-1763, especially before the military success of Forbes in 1758.

In Lancaster County, Pa., about 1750, the Conestoga freight wagon was devised and manufactured by the tens of thousands. This wagon, which became very popular, used hickory for wheels and frames because of its lightness and strength. The frames were normally of massive oak, sixteen feet long, while the wheels stood five feet high. The heavy construction required six strong horses in order to traverse the Alleghenies. The ox-bow shape of the Conestoga wagon prevented slippage of goods while going up and down the mountains. Needless to say, the cumbersome Conestoga was quickly discarded in the marshy terrain of western Ohio, Indiana, and Illinois.

By 1751, the Pennsylvania Road was one of the most important trails westward and remained so in the period prior to the Revolutionary War. The trail was named the Pennsylvania & Lancaster Turnpike upon its completion in 1795. At this date, broken stone and gravel formed the road surface from Philadelphia to Lancaster and thus was a primary improvement over most roads of the time.

One trip recorded for the year 1802 covered the 300 mile distance from Philadelphia to Pittsburgh by a combination of stagecoach, horseback, and walking which lasted some nine days, or an average of about thirty-five miles per day.

By 1820, the entire length of the Turnpike through Harrisburg, on to Pittsburgh, was surfaced with broken stone. In 1828, the mail run between Philadelphia and Pittsburgh was recorded as varying between fifty-two and seventy-two hours. Today, Pennsylvania Highway 76, although by-passing Lancaster to the north, covers the route from Philadelphia to Pittsburgh.

By 1791, stage coach lines began operation in all directions in America over the approximately 1,905 miles of post roads then in existence. One of the first guides of national scope to print a comprehensive list of United States roads was D. Hewitt's 1825 book titled *The American Traveller, etc.* which was printed in Washington by Davis & Force.

Probably the most important early federal road building project was the Cumberland Road (also later known as the National Road) which ran from Cumberland, Maryland, to Wheeling, Virginia. Congressional approval was granted in 1802 with actual work begun in Maryland in 1808. Between 1806 and 1838, there were more than thirty acts of Congress dealing with various legal issues, rights of way, and financing. The right of way was set at eighty feet with a road bed of broken stone from three inches up to a foot deep.

In Pennsylvania, part of the National Road duplicated Braddock's Military Road, a trail dating from 1755. Edward Braddock (1695-1755) ordered a trail constructed for use by his English army; he intended to drive the French out of the vicinity of a fort that was later to be the site of modern Pittsburgh. The well-known story of Edward Braddock's dismal failure has been repeated many times.

By 1817, the first 130 miles of the National Road connected the Frederick Pike, coming from the Atlantic coast at Baltimore, Maryland, across the Appalachian Mountains, with inland areas along the Ohio River. Almost immediately great stagecoach and freight lines were established on this route. Surveying of the route across Ohio, Indiana, and Illinois did not begin until 1820 and primary funds for construction of this section were not granted until 1825.

By 1833, the National Road reached Columbus, Ohio, and in 1852, it stretched westward to Vandalia, Illinois, and subsequently became the main artery for traffic westward. Today, the route is part of the much travelled and over-lapping coast-to-coast U.S. Highways 40 and 70.

In addition to the roads, two important trans-Appalachian canals were completed: the 363 mile Erie Canal in 1825, linking Albany to Buffalo, N.Y., and the 394 mile Pennsylvania Canal in 1834, linking Philadelphia to Pittsburgh. Both canals provided important routes for carriers of bulky freight westward across their respective states of New York and Pennsylvania. Travel was either by horse-drawn packet boat, for passenger use, at three or four miles per hour, or by line boat, which carried both freight and passengers, at about two miles per hour.

The Erie Canal, although built along relatively level terrain, contained some 200 locks which were utilized in going up and down slight changes in elevation. Each lock required time to maneuver so that in 1835, trips were taking up to seven days. The more difficult mountainous terrain in which the Pennsylvania canal had been built slowed progress even more so.

With the completion of the New York Central and New and Erie railroads in 1852, the Erie Canal was subjected to strong competition for freight and passenger traffic. Likewise, in 1853 the Pennsylvania and Baltimore and Ohio railroads provided strong competition for the Pennsylvania Canal.

STEAMBOATS ON THE OHIO AND MISSISSIPPI. After the Revolutionary War, the spearhead of westward expansion was through the Ohio Valley from Pittsburgh, Pennsylvania, and Wheeling, Virginia, westward, along the Ohio River to its junction with the Mississippi River, up and down the Mississippi River to St. Louis, Missouri, and New Orleans, Louisiana, and westward from St. Louis along the Missouri River toward St. Joseph.

During the first half of the 19th century, this great westward population expansion was due in large part to the introduction of free-floating boats on inland waterways. River transportation on the Ohio and the Mississippi Rivers was at first by rafts, by barges, by pole boats, by keelboats, and by flatboats. The distance of 1,950 miles from Pittsburgh, downstream, to New Orleans lasted from a month to six weeks. Rate of travel for loaded commercial boats, downstream, was five miles an hour.

It was one matter to float downstream and quite another matter to attempt to take a boat upstream. For instance, a seventy-five foot long keelboat making the upstream trip from New Orleans to Louisville, Kentucky, a distance of about 1,350 miles, took between three and four months. The round trip from Louisville to Pittsburgh, Pa, some 1,200 miles, lasted about two months.

Relatively few of the lighter and smaller keelboats made the trip upriver from New Orleans to Pittsburgh. Primitive techniques were used to literally drag a boat upstream. These included towing by men with ropes on a river bank, on rare occasions towing by horses, the common use of poles and periodically oars, the cordelle (a rope attached to a tree or post on the bank, using a pulley effect), and bushwhacking by grabbing overhanging branches. In contrast to the Rhine where the prevailing winds were often in the upstream direction, sails had limited effect on the Mississippi and the Ohio Rivers.

Needless to say, few passengers travelled upstream before the introduction of the steamboat. The first verified steamboat to cover the downstream distance from Pittsburgh to New Orleans was the 371 ton *New Orleans* in 1811-1812. She was built in Pittsburgh under the direct supervision of Nicholas Roosevelt who adhered to the design of Robert Fulton, primary owner, and American statesman Robert Livingston (1746-1813), another backer. Construction of the *New Orleans* lasted from

November, 1810 until October, 1911. She had her maiden voyage downstream from late October 1911 until mid-January, 1912.

Later in 1812, the *New Orleans* went upstream from New Orleans to Natchez, against the current for a distance of 313 miles, in seven days, or about three miles an hour. The *New Orleans* concentrated on the run between New Orleans and Natchez until it was sunk by a snag in 1814. Nevertheless, the *New Orleans* inaugurated a new era in the western migration of emigrants across the American continent.

By 1815, the *Enterprise* went up the Mississippi and Ohio Rivers from New Orleans to Pittsburgh.

In 1817, the *Washington* set a record for the upstream distance of 1,350 miles, from New Orleans to Louisville, Kentucky, of twenty-five days. The more usual port-to-port time was about thirty to thirty-five days. In 1820, the 355 ton *Paragon* travelled from New Orleans to Louisville, with full cargo, in seventeen days, seven hours. In 1833, the 286 ton *Tuscarora* made this upstream trip in seven days, six hours.

By the 1850's regular business trips for the 1,350 miles from New Orleans upstream to Louisville were made in five to six days. The 135 mile upstream trip from Louisville to Cincinnati was made in eleven to twelve hours, and the 470 miles trip from Cincinnati to Pittsburgh in about forty-five hours. The average time for downstream steamboat trips from Louisville to New Orleans decreased in 1815 from about ten days to some five days in 1860.

GERMAN TOURISTS AMONG MIDWEST TRAVELLERS. Gottfried Duden, a German physician by training, made an oft cited trip to America. The 1824 overland trip, from his landing at Chesapeake Bay, to a destination at St. Louis, Mo., probably used the Cumberland trail for the most part. His trip took about seventy-three days to cover the distance of more than 700 miles. Duden's propagandistic essay on his trip was originally published in German in 1829 and widely distributed among the Germans in the Rhineland; the Duden publication was translated and reprinted by the University of Missouri Press in 1980.

A well-known publication, also originally in German, was that of Alexander Philip Maximilian (1782-1867), Prince of Wied-Neuwied. Landing at Boston in May, 1832, the Prince travelled across the northern part of the United States, and up the Missouri River aboard the steamboats *Yellowstone* and *Assiniboine*, into the upper reaches of the Missouri River, travelling over a good portion of the 1804-06 trail-blazing route taken by explorers Meriwether Lewis (1774-1809) & William Clark (1770-1838). The extensive tour taken by the Prince lasted until July, 1834, when he returned to Europe via New York. The original German edition of his travels was published in three volumes in Koblenz during the years 1839-41 and reprinted in 1970. English translations were printed in 1843 and 1906. No doubt this massive work also did much to gain the interest of the 19th century migrants originating from the Rhineland.

Other German royalty included Karl Bernhard (1792-1862), Duke of Saxe-Weimar-Eisenach. The Duke travelled the American interior via steamboat, up the Mississippi River, in 1825-26. The report of these travels were printed in Germany in 1828 and also widely distributed. The Duke of Württemberg, Friedrich Paul Wilhelm, likewise was aboard a Mississippi River steamer, visting among other places, Louisville and St. Louis in 1822-1824. The travels were recorded in German in 1835.

SHADES OF MARK TWAIN. Samuel Langhorne Clemens (1835-1910) attained literary eminence during the years 1874-1884 under the pseudonym Mark Twain. Clemens had a varied occupational career during which he worked on steamboats on the Mississippi River in the years 1857-1861 and in fact became a licenced river boat pilot in 1859. He was well qualified to popularize the phenomena which marked transportation on the inland rivers of the United States. Twain's 1882 book *Life on the Mississippi* gives a vivid description, especially pages 103-104, of steamboat transportation hazards.

In the peak steamboat years from 1820 to 1880, nearly 6,000 steamboats were built along the Mississippi-Ohio River system. The three leading centers of steamboat construction were Pittsburgh, Cincinnati, and Louisville; these three rapidly growing cities accounted for nearly 4,500 of the total. Cincinnati went from a population of 2,540 in 1810 to 115,485 in 1850; Pittsburgh increased from 4,768 in 1810 to 46,601 in 1850, and Louisville went from 1,357 in 1810 to 77,860 in 1850.

Flimsy construction and high accident rates contributed to the nearly continual replacement of steamboats. Significantly, the longevity of any given steamboat, on western rivers, was a matter of a few years.

Steamboat operations on the Missouri River, westward from St. Louis, began in 1819 when the ninety-eight ton *Independence* went upstream a distance of some 250 miles. About the same time, Major Stephen H. Long, a U.S. Army officer, led a mapping expedition up the Missouri River; Long used the *Western Engineer* as far as Council Bluffs in Iowa.

The population of St. Louis had jumped to 77,860 by 1850. In the 1850's the 298 mile trip from St. Louis upstream to St. Joseph, Mo. was made port-to-port in sixty to seventy hours. By this time, St. Louis had become a center of steamboat operations on the Mississippi, while St. Joseph headquartered operations on the lower Missouri River.

The slow moving steamboats continued to be plagued by a high accident rate, by low water in the summer, and by iced-over rivers in the winter. Unfortunately for steamboat transportation, by 1860, Chicago, Pittsburgh, Cincinnati, Louisville, St. Louis, Memphis, Vicksburg, and New Orleans were all in communication by rail. The railroad lines subsequently bridged the Mississippi River at several places and barely slowed their westward expansion during the Civil War. By 1870, the more reliable and more frequent time schedules of the railroads superseded steamboat operations in all but the transportation of the most bulky freight. Railroads had an additional advantage of travelling nearly straight line distances, which in many cases were nearly one half of those travelled by steamboats travelling as they did over highly meandering rivers.

BEYOND THE MISSISSIPPI. Daniel Boone, having tired of the rush of migrants into Kentucky, went westward. By 1815, Boone and two sons initiated the trail later known as "Boone's Lick Road" which ran some 150 miles nearly due west from St. Charles, Mo. to Franklin, Mo. By 1830, the trail had been extended to Independence, Mo., just short of Kansas Territory.

One of the first overland trails to be used west of the Mississippi River on a regular basis was the Santa Fe Trail which ran from Independence, Mo. southwestward some 770 miles to Santa Fe, New Mexico. The trail was initiated about 1822 and was in constant use by about 1830. Between 1863 and 1871, the trail became the route of the well-known Santa Fe Railroad.

The Santa Fe trail was a precursor to the Oregon and California trails, but only by a few years. The latter were in full use in the 1840's. In fact, the first large body of migrants to reach the Pacific Coast went to Oregon territory in 1843. In 1844, about 1,400 individuals travelled the route of some 2,000 miles to Oregon, and in 1845, the various migrant bodies numbered almost 3,000.

The Oregon and California trails ran from staging areas in northwestern Missouri, western Iowa, and eastern Nebraska to the northern California and Oregon. The joint trail normally traversed Nebraska territory along the south side of the Platte river and therefore was sometimes called the Great Platte River road. The Platte River valley gained a poor reputation as "500 miles of dusty, sandy, flat prairie."

THE MORMON TREK. In a few years, the great Mormon migrations were to head west, generally keeping on the north side of the Platte River. In fact, the best documented accounts of migration along the Platte River are those meticulously kept by the Mormons.

In 1846/47, trailblazer Brigham Young (1801-1877) led the first band of 148 Mormons some 1,300 miles westward from Nauvoo, Illinois. In the first year, three permanent camps, with some 15,000 Mormons and 30,000 head of cattle, were established, extending across Iowa. After arriving at Council Bluffs, it was a major struggle for the migrants to build rafts in order to cross the Missouri River. This experience was to prove invaluable to the Mormons in later years. After crossing to the west side of the Missouri River, the leaders of the Mormon contingent established a winter camp in an area adjacent to the city later known as Omaha, Nebraska.

The 1846/47 Winter Camp, with some 3,400 inhabitants proved trying with its constricted temporary quarters and limited food supplies. Notable were the various outbreaks of scurvy, caused by diets deficient in vitamin C, especially the lack of citrus fruits, and also of potatoes, tomatoes, green peppers and cabbage. In 1847, the original group of 148 Mormons traversed about 1,073 miles along the north side of the North Platte River through Nebraska Territory. There were seventy-three wagons, ninety-three horses, fifty-two mules, sixty-six oxen, nineteen cows, seventeen dogs, and a few chickens. Progress was slow; there was the matter of building campsites, occasionally clearing trails, and the major effort of crossing the Platte River at Fort Laramie, Wyoming, and again at Mormon Ferry. On good days, the group might make fifteen to twenty miles. Normally, travel was delayed or lost entirely on Sunday. The leader of the advance party, Brigham Young, became wagon bound in the latter weeks of the trip; reference to stagnant water sources along the trip indicates that he probably had a moderate case of either dysentery, cholera, or typhoid.

Eventually Brigham Young and the 147 other Mormons arrived at the west side of the Wasatch Range in Utah Territory. Here the group founded Salt Lake City, near the southern end of the inland sea by the same name. The trip to the Salt Lake had lasted 111 days and thus averaged about ten miles per day.

The initial band of 148 migrants was soon followed: the number of inhabitants of Salt Lake City multiplied to 1,700 within four month's time and to almost 5,000 by the end of 1848. It was a phenomenal mass movement overland by a united group of religiously oriented people. Way stations established by the group had important consequences for later migrants and for the route of the first transcontinental railroad which eventually paralleled much of the Mormon route.

The final location of Brigham Young's group was not by chance. In fact, two important publications and their maps, both dating 1845, were closely studied for advice; these publications were John C. Fremont's report of his 1843-45 expeditions across the Great Basin, and Landsford Hasting's *Emigrant Guide to Oregon and California*.

Even in subsequent years, the westward journey remained challenging. The famous Mormon Handcart Company of 1856, consisting of 576 men, women, and children with handcarts, was caught in Wyoming territory by a winter storm. Before rescue teams of horses and wagons arrived, some 100 died.

By 1875, more than 350 other Mormon settlements were subsequently established along the west side of the mountains to the north and south of Salt Lake City. By 1870, Salt Lake City itself had grown to a population of 12,800 and possibly 70,000 Mormons were scattered north and south of Salt Lake City. By some estimates, however, the earliest migrants were subjected to eight to nine percent annual mortality rates by various factors such as diseases and lack of food.

By 1900, an estimated 100,000 Mormon migrants, many directly from Europe, especially from England, formed the backbone of the settlement of Utah and Idaho.

COMMERCIAL STAGE LINES IN THE WESTERN TERRITORIES. The first stage-coach service between Independence, Mo. and Salt Lake City began in the summer of 1850 and was supported by a mail contract. The service covered the 1,200 mile route in two to three weeks.

Butterfield's Overland Mail route, beginning about 1857, ran horse-drawn stage coaches from the Mississippi River to San Francisco. Butterfield's route, starting from St. Louis, Missouri, and Memphis, Tennessee, south through Ft. Smith, Arkansas, and across northern Texas to El Paso, and then on to Los Angeles, covered an oxbow route of some 2,729 miles. The fastest mail service was about twenty-four days.

In April, 1859, the Pony Express was organized. This route ran from St. Joseph, Missouri, via Salt Lake City, Utah, to Sacramento, California, over a distance of 1,966 miles. An enormous organization of 190 stations, 420 horses, and 400 station men was needed to keep the route operating. About eighty riders were continually in the saddle. The westbound route was covered in nine days, twenty-three hours and the eastbound route in eleven days, twelve hours. On the average, the pony riders covered 250 miles in a twenty-four hour day as compared with 100 to 125 miles by stage coaches. Needless to say, demand did not support this romantic organization and it lasted only about nineteen months.

Moreover, the Pony Express trail, in part, along the Platte River in Nebraska, became the route of the first transcontinental railway. Construction of the railway was begun in 1867 and it was completed on May 10, 1869; the much publicized railroad connection was achieved at Promontory, Utah. On January 10, 1870, the Utah Central Railroad connected Salt Lake City northward to Ogden. This connection allowed further population expansion of Salt Lake City and promoted development of the area, notably that of mining and smelting.

Western trails and railways are further discussed in the following section. The railroad building explosion in the United States in the 2nd half of the 19th century is exemplified by those built in the State of Kansas for which a vast amount of documentation is available.

REFERENCES

Adams, J. T., & R. V. Coleman, 1943, *Atlas of American History*. Charles Schribner's Sons, N.Y., 360 p., 147 maps.
Contains a good series of graphic maps.

Alexander, T. G., & J. B. Allen, 1984, *Mormons & Gentiles, A History of Salt Lake City*. Pruett Publ. Co., Boulder, Co, 360 p., illus.

Anonymous, 1884, "A Partial List of the Families Who Arrived at Philadelphia between 1682 and 1687." *Pennsylvania Mag. Hist. Biogr.*, vol. 8, p. 328-340 (editorial comments by F. D. Stone).

Anuta, M. J., 1983, *Ships of our Ancestors*. Ships of Our Ancestors, Inc., Menominee, Mich., 380 p.
Illustrations show 365 ships, mainly steam, dating from about 1857 and thus from the peak German immigration period.

Balderston, Marion, 1962, "The Real Welcome Passengers." *The Huntington Library Quarterly*, San Marino, Calif., vol. 26, p. 31-56
_____, 1963, "William Penn's Twenty-Three Ships." *Pennsylvania Gen. Mag.*, vol. 23, no. 2, p. 27-67
_____, 1965, "Pennsylvania's 1683 Ships and some of their Passengers." *Ibid*, vol. 24, p. 69-114
_____, 1967, *James Claypoole's Letter Book, London and Philadelphia, 1681-1684*. The Huntington Library, San Marino, Calif., 256 p.

Brown, J. E., & Dan Guravich, 1980, *The Mormon Trek West*. Doubleday & Co. Inc., Garden City, N.Y., 184 p., illus., maps.

Buck, A. J., 1914, *Travel and Description, 1765-1865*. Illinois State Historical Library, Springfield, 514 p.
Very professional compilation and annotation of 660 publications relating to travel and migration to Illinois for the period 1765-1865; also listed are 458 county histories and atlases of Illinois.

Bretting, Agnes, 1992, "The Journey, from the Old World to the New." In *Fame, Fortune, and Sweet Liberty*. Edition Temmen, p. 74-122, illus.
A good introduction to passenger ships, especially those emanating from Bremen and Hamburg in the 19th century.

Cramer, Zadok, 1814, *The Navigator*. Cramer, Spear & Eichbaum, Pittsburgh, 360 p., maps, 8th edition.
The various editions from 1801 to 1824, 12th edition, bridge the transition from free-floating craft to the use of steamboats along the Ohio, the Monongahela, the Alleghany, and the Mississippi Rivers.

As discussed in the essay *Early American Maps* in Part 3, *The Navigator* likely is an outgrowth of government hydrographic surveys dating from 1766.

Dohan, M. H., 1981, *Mr. Roosevelt's Steamboat, the First Steamboat to Travel the Mississippi*. Dodd, Mead & Co., N.Y., 194 p., illus., 3 maps.
An imaginative and well written tale involving hostile Indians and the New Madrid earthquake. Nicholas Roosevelt belonged to the dynamic lineage, of Dutch descent, which later provided two United States presidents.

Duden, Gottfried, 1980, *Report on a Journey to the Western States of North America (1824-1827)*. Univ. Missouri Press, 372 p., map.
Translation of the much publicized 1829 German book which influenced thousands of Rhinelanders to consider migration to America.

de Groot, Irene, & Robert Vorstman, 1980, *Maritime Prints by the Dutch Masters*. Gordon Fraser Gallery Ltd., London, 284 p., numerous illus.
One of the few books in print showing illustrations of early sailing ships.

Dunbar, Seymour, 1968 (reprint), *A History of Travel in America*. Green Press, N.Y. (copyright Bobbs - Merrill Co., 1915), Vol. I, 339 p., Vol., II, p. 341-740, Vol. III, p. 741-1124, Vol. IV, p. 1125-1529, 2 maps, numerous illus.
Reprinted also in 1937 in one volume by Tudor Publ., Co., N.Y. Dunbar's massive work would be a basic reference if the essential facts contained in the book were limited to about 500 pages.

Filby, R. W., 1988, *Passenger and Immigration Lists Bibliography 1538-1900*. Gale Research Co. Detroit (2nd ed.)
_____, & M. K. Meyer, 1981, *Passenger and Immigration Lists Index*. Gale Research Co., Detroit, Vol. I, A-G, 787 p., Vol. II, H-N, p. 788-1570, Vol. III, O-Z, p. 1571-2339
This is a standard and on-going work. The early volumes list 500,000 passengers to the U.S. and Canada in the 17th to 19th centuries - data is taken directly from the literature with little or no editing.

Gaustad, E. S., 1976, *Historical Atlas of Religion in America*. Harper & Row, N.Y., 189 p., 2 maps, numerous illus., revised edition.
An important source of tables and graphs related to American church history.

Greeley, Horace, 1964 (facsimile of 1860 edition), *An Overland Journey from New York to San Francisco in the Summer of 1859*. Alfred A. Knopf, N.Y., 326 p.
The well-known author travelled by rail to Missouri, then by stagecoach, via Denver, Ft. Laramie, Salt Lake City, Humboldt River, etc., to San Francisco.

Haites, E. F., James Mak, & G. M. Walton, 1975, *Western River Transportation, The Era of Early Internal Development 1810-1860*. John Hopkins Univ. Press, Baltimore, 209 p.

Haws, Duncan, & A. A. Hurst, 1986, *The Maritime History of the World*. Teredo Books, Ltd., Brighton, England, 2 vols., 960 p., 31 maps, 200 illus.

Hoffman, H. W., 1980, *Sagas of Old Western Travel and Transport*. Howell North Books, San Diego, 284 p.
Contains a good bibliography relating to transportation in the Far West.

Hulbert, A. B., 1904, *The Cumberland Road*. in Historic Highways of America, vol. 10, Arthur H. Clark Co., Cleveland, 208 p., 2 maps, illus.
The two index maps show the route of the first "national" road.

_____, 1920, *The Paths of Inland Commerce, a Chronicle of Trail, Road, and Waterways*. Yale Univ. Press, New Haven, Conn., 211 p., illus.

Hunter, L. C., 1949, *Steamboats on Western Rivers*. Harvard Univ. Press, Cambridge, Mass., 684 p., illus.
The author is recognized as a leading authority on the subject.

_____, 1985, *A History of Industrial Power in the United States 1780-1930. Volume Two: Steam Power*. Univ. Press of Virginia, Charlottesville, 732 p., illus.

Jackson, K. T. & J. T. Adams (eds.), 1978, *Atlas of American History*. Charles Schribner's Sons, N.Y., 294 p., 242 maps.
Revised from the 1943 edition by J. T. Adams and R. V. Coleman.

Jobe, Joseph (ed.), 1967, *The Great Age of Sail*. Edita Lausanne, S.A. Lausanne, 213 p., illus.

Kemp, Peter (ed.), 1976, *The Oxford Companion to Ships and the Sea*. Oxford Univ. Press, London, 972 p., illus.

Kemp, Peter & Richard Ormond, 1986, *The Great Age of Sail*. Phaidon Press, 192 p., 200 illus.

Lancour, Harold, 1963, *A Bibliography of Ship Passenger Lists, 1538-1825*. New York Public Library, 137 p., (3rd ed., revised by R. J. Wolfe and F. E. Bridgers).

Lewis, M. W., 1933, *The Development of Early Emigrant Trails in the United States East of the Mississippi River*. National Genealogical Soc., Special Publ. No. 3, 12 p., map (reprinted 1962, and later years).

Löschburg, Winfried, 1982, *A History of Travel*. Hippocrene Books, Inc. (English ed.), 190 p., numerous illus.

Maximilian, Alexander Philip, 1839-41, *Reise in das Innere Nord-America in den Jahren 1832 bis 1834*. Koblenz, 3 vols. (reprinted in 1906 in English by Arthur H. Clark Co., Cleveland as *Travels in the Interior of North America*, vol. 1, 393 p., vol. 2, 395 p., vol. 3, 346 p.

Paullin, C. O., & J. K. Wright, 1975, *Atlas of the Historical Geography of the U.S.*. Greenwood Press, 162 p., 166 pls.
The book was originally printed in 1932 and is important enough to have been reprinted. The numerous illustrations show data not available in other publications.

Ringwalt, J. L., 1888, *Development of Transportation Systems in the United States*. Privately printed, Philadelphia, Pa. 398 p., illus.
Reprinted by Johnson Reprint Corp., N.Y., 1966.

Rose, A. C., 1952, *Public Roads of the Past - 3500 B.C. to 1800 A.D.*. American Assoc. State Highway Officials, Washington, D.C., 101 p., illus.
_____, 1953, *Public Roads of the Past - Historic American Highways*. ibid, 183 p., illus., maps.
_____, 1976, *Historic American Roads*. Crown Publishers Inc., N.Y., 118 p., illus.
This is an unusual series of publications with data not normally available in other publications. Most major libraries contain all or part of the series.

Rupp, I. D., 1931, *A Collection of Upwards of Thirty Thousand Names of German, Swiss, Dutch, French, Portuguese, and other Immigrants to Pennsylvania Chronologically Arranged from 1727 to 1776*. Degner & Co., Leipzig, 478 + 89 p.
The original edition begun in 1856 is a partial listing and is now superseded by Strassburger & Hinke, 1934, cited below.

Sheppard, W. L., Jr. (ed.), 1985, *Passengers and Ships Prior to 1684*. Welcome Soc. of Pennsylvania, Phila., 245 p. Reprinted 1992 by Heritage Books, Inc., Bowie, Maryland.
Contains reprints of and corrections to articles by Balderston, Roach, Sheppard, Dallett, Bunting, & Dickson.

Steele, I. K., 1986, *The English Atlantic, 1675-1740*. Oxford Univ. Press, London, 400 p., illus.

Stover, J. F., 1978, *Iron Road to the West*. Columbia Univ. Press, N.Y., 266 p., maps, illus.
A very good documentary of American railroads for the critical formative period of 1830-1860.

Strassburger, R. B., 1934, *Pennsylvania German Pioneers. A Publication of the Original Lists of Arrivals in the Port of Philadelphia from 1727 to 1808*. Pennsylvania German Soc., Norristown, Pa., 3 vols. Edited by W. J. Hinke. Reprinted by Genealogical Publ. Co., Baltimore, 1966, in 2 vols., 776 p. +709 p.

Swetnam, George, 1964, *Pennsylvania Transportation*. Pennsylvania Historical Assoc., Gettysburg, 81 p., illus.

Taylor, G. R., 1951, *The Transportation Revolution 1815-1860*. Volume IV, The Economic History of the United States. Rinehart & Co., Inc., N.Y., 490 p., illus.

Tepper, Michael (ed.), 1980, *New World Immigrants (A Consolidation of Ship Passenger Lists ...)*. Genealogical Publ. Co., Baltimore, Vol. 1, 568 p., Vol. 2, 602 p.
_____, 1988, *American Passenger Arrival Records*. Genealogical Publ. Co., Inc., Baltimore, 134 p.
The two above publications contain reprints of many often utilized earlier publications.

Tolzmann, D. H. (ed.), 1991, *Germany and America, 1450-1700*. Heritage Books, Inc., Bowie, Md., 263 p., illus.
This interesting publication is a new imprint of J. F. Sachse's 1897 *History of the German role in the Discovery, Exploration and Settlement of the New World*.

_____, 1992, *The First Germans in America*. Heritage Books, Inc., Bowie, Md., circa 117 p.
Essentially a series of three reprints containing about 121 irregularly numbered pages. The work lists nearly 600 names of individuals residing in North America, mainly in Manhattan and New York, for

the period 1609 to 1683. The majority of names are of Dutch or Low German spelling.

Tunis, Edwin, 1952, *Oars, Sails and Steam*. World Publ. Co., Cleveland, 77 p.
Contains numerous illustrations of ancient, early and modern sailing ships.

Waitley, Douglas, 1970, *Roads of Destiny*. Robert E. Luce, Inc., Washington, 319 p., maps.
This is a lively discussion of early American roads and their utilization.

Wokeck, M. S., 1986, "Promoters and Passengers: The German Immigrant Trade, 1683-1775." In *The World of William Penn*. Univ. Pennsylvania Press, Phila., p. 259-278.

THE TRAILS OF KANSAS. THE HISTORY OF the three great trails across the unsettled Kansas territory (from the indigenous Kanza, or Kansa, Indian tribe), namely the Santa Fe, the California, and the Oregon trails, begins about 1822. In that year, a Missourian, William Becknell, went southwestward across Kansas territory with a pack train loaded with trading goods, hoping to do business with various Indian tribes. Becknell eventually wound up deep in Mexican territory where he was welcomed by local authorities, thereby establishing a regular trading route some 770 miles west to the city of Santa Fe. Fortunately for Becknell, the Mexican Revolution, which had begun in 1811 and was resolved internally in 1821, had broken down the non-intercourse rule which had earlier prevailed in Mexican territories.

In 1826 another entrepreneur, William Ashley, took a pack train from St. Louis, across Missouri and Kansas territory, some 2,000 miles to Oregon territory. Missouri had become a state in 1822; the town of Independence was established in 1827 in western Missouri and quickly became one of the primary outfitting posts for the trails westward. The highly fertile plains to the west took the French name "prairie"; Independence became the "prairie port" because of the thousands of "prairie schooners" (light-framed covered wagons) which eventually departed from its ports.

In 1830, Ashley was followed by William Sublette and a regular trading route subsequently was opened to Oregon. The important army post of Fort Leavenworth had been built in 1827 in Kansas territory on the west bank of the Missouri River and was situated twenty miles north of the Kansas River.

In 1839, Johann August Suter (1803-1880; also spelled Sutter, Suttor, and Sutor, being probably derived from the Latin word sutor, meaning shoemaker), an erstwhile refugee from Swiss bankruptcy laws, erected a trading post in northern California and eventually managed to finagle a large land grant from the Mexican government.

The real migration of the emigrants across the Oregon trail began in 1842 and increased to a flood in 1843. With the rumors about the discovery of gold at Suter's mill in California in 1848, another wave of migrants rushed westward following the Oregon trail in part and then diverging southward to California. Suter was dismayed to have hordes of would-be miners and riff-raff overrun his property.

The Mexican War of 1846-48 saw increased movement of army troops in both east and west directions along the Santa Fe Trail. Although these troops saw little combat from either the Mexicans or the indigenous Indian tribes, a typical regiment suffered casualties of about fifteen percent, this being from various diseases. Additionally, many individuals were incapacitated from long lasting effects of disease after their term of duty was completed. During the period of about 1821 to 1867, the scourge of malaria was especially important along the Santa Fe Trail, particularly on the eastern section between Franklin, Mo., and the Arkansas River in south central Kansas. During the pioneer days of 1840 to 1860, it has been estimated that nearly 1,000 trappers and traders used the Santa Fe trail. In the same period, some 250,000 to 500,000 migrants travelled over the Oregon and California trails. The migrants travelled in trains of not less than twenty-five wagons; some trains contained as many as 125 or even 250 wagons. Travel by wagons drawn by oxen over the open prairie was at the speed of twelve to fifteen miles a day; a good pair of Missouri mules could cover fifteen to twenty miles in a day. On the other hand, oxen could be sustained by the prairie grasses, while mules and horses required supplementary feeds of grain.

The trains usually left Missouri in late spring after the grass en route became green and high enough to support livestock; every effort was made to reach the destination before fall snows began in the Rocky and the Sierra Madre Mountains.

The migrants from the Old World and the New World took with them many infectious diseases which regularly took their toll. In some order of importance, these included malaria, bacillary or amoebic dysentery, cholera, typhoid, typhus, and small pox. In many cases, treatment was primitive or non-existent; woe to the sick individual who suffered a long trip on a box wagon.

Fortunately, smallpox vaccine had been discovered in 1796 and introduced to America by 1800 although many individuals, notoriously entire native Indian tribes, did not have the benefit of the vaccine. In the case of malaria, the effective treatment was quinine which was isolated from the bark of certain trees grown in Peru and was in fairly common use in America by 1840; surprisingly, it was not until 1880 that the discovery of the malaria parasite was made and only in 1895 was this parasite related to the anopheles mosquito. The cholera micro-organism, which left thousands dead in St. Louis in 1846, was discovered only in 1883. Typhoid fever, which was often water borne, was common prior to 1910. Typhus fever, usually louse or flea borne, was prevalent in winter climates when bathing and changes of clothes declined; it was not until 1909 that the common body louse was proved to be the primary carrier.

Other travel hazards were scurvy, measles, venereal diseases, starvation, and lack of water. The lives of many were saved unknowingly from the effects of dysentery by the common practice of boiling water for tea and coffee; the treeless plains offered only buffalo chips for fuel which fortunately burned like charcoal. Alkali dust blinded some on the trip across the great salt flats of Utah territory. Many perished along the way; a few grew tired of the rough journey and settled before reaching the promised land. Oddly enough, before the Civil War and before the introduction of repeating rifles, which were used to slaughter great masses of buffalo, the numerous native Indian tribes did not especially hinder the crossing of large groups of migrants.

EARLY TRAINS IN AMERICA. The economic viability of the early trains in America begins with the Pennsylvania Railroad which was organized in 1846. Eventually, this railroad connected New York City with Philadelphia, and then Pittsburgh, Chicago, and St. Louis. Somewhat later, the New York Central railroad connected New York City with Albany, Buffalo, Chicago, and St. Louis.

By 1854, there was a rail line from Chicago west to the Mississippi River at Rock Island, Ill., and the great movement westward was on.

During the Civil War years of 1861-65, transportation of large armies was facilitated by a railroad network covering much of the area east of the Mississippi River.

Table 6.11 gives a summary of key events in the history of American railroads.

TABLE 6.11
BRIEF HISTORY OF AMERICAN RAILROADS

1825	First locomotive to run on rails in America, at Hoboken, N.J.
1829	First steam engine to run on commercial railroad tracks in the U.S., at Honesdale, Pa.
1830	First regular passenger service by steam power, along 23 miles of track, at Charleston, S.C.
1837	First locomotive west of the Alleghenies, Sandusky to Springfield, Ohio
1838	New York City and Washington, D.C. linked by rail.
1848	First direct rail route between Boston and New York City; total U.S. track about 6,000 miles.
1848	Chicago acquired its first locomotive.
1850	President Millard Fillmore signed the first federal railroad land grant act.
1852	First locomotive west of the Mississippi River, ran west from St. Louis five miles; total U.S. track about 12,900 miles. Railroad from Baltimore completed west of Ohio River at Wheeling, W.Va.
1853	First all rail route between Chicago and eastern cities.
1854	Railroad from Chicago west to Mississippi River at Rock Island, Ill.
1856	First railroad bridge to span the Mississippi River, at Davenport, Iowa; rebuilt in the same year after burning.
1859	Railroads reached Missouri River at St. Joseph, Mo.; total U.S. track about 28,800 miles.
1860	First railroad in Kansas, Marysville & Elwood, 5.2 miles, Elwood to Wathena, Doniphan Co. Total U.S. track 30,626

miles; Chicago with 11 railroads became America's leading railway center.

1862 President Lincoln signed act authorizing construction of a railroad line from the Missouri River to the Pacific Ocean.

1869 Golden Spike ceremony at Promontory, Utah. Total U.S. track about 46,800 miles; gauge used by Union Pacific-Central Pacific set at standard 4' 8".

1869 First railroad bridge to span the Missouri River, at Kansas City, Mo.

1870 First coast to coast run, Boston to San Francisco.

1870 First railroad bridge across Ohio River, at Cincinnati.

1871-72 Peak mileage years for new track in U.S., 6,660 and 7,439 miles, respectively.

1881 Total track exceeded 100,000 miles.

1890 Total track in U.S. and Canada about 175,000 miles.

WEST OF THE MISSISSIPPI. By Act of May 26, 1830, Kansas was declared an informal part of Indian territory. Kansas was formally organized as a territory in 1854 and admitted to the Union in 1861. With the organization of the territory, a number of Emigrant Aid Companies were established in coastal cities in order to expedite the movement of immigrants westward. Notable among these companies were the Massachusetts Emigrant Aid Company and the Emigrant Aid Companies of New York and Connecticut. Their somewhat exaggerated promotions suggested that it was possible to travel from Boston to Kansas by train in five days. At any rate, capital investments by the aid companies did permit the acquisition of steam and water powered saw-mills and grist-mills, as well as printing presses and other technology generated by the budding Industrial Revolution.

In Kansas territory of 1854, there were no town or villages of any consequence settled by whites, only the three Army forts, namely Fort Leavenworth, Fort Riley, and Fort Atkinson.

In 1862, the Homestead Act provided that pioneers could obtain 160 acres of public land at no cost if the pioneer resided on and cultivated his land claim for five years; war veterans were given credit towards their residence requirement according to years of service. Alternatively, settlers had an option to purchase the land for $1.25 per acre. With the close of the Civil War in 1865 a great ex-soldier immigration poured into Kansas. Within ten years, twenty-six million acres in Kansas were acquired by would-be settlers. Peak immigration years were 1870-71.

So successful was the settlement policy that by 1878 Kansas bounded into first place among wheat producing states with a production of more than 33,000,000 bushels. Wheat and other grains literally flowed from the Midwest eastward and across the Atlantic in order to support a healthy balance of payments. The return import was, in many cases, high quality English steel rails for further expansion of the West.

Planning for a railroad from the Midwest to the Pacific began in 1853 with railroad surveys carried out by the U.S. Army Topographic engineers. However, construction began only in 1865 with the Union Pacific starting from Omaha, Nebraska. The line went westward across Nebraska along the Platte River valley, somewhat north of Kansas.

In May, 1869, the first transcontinental railroad connected the Union Pacific coming from Omaha with the Central Pacific coming from Sacramento. The well-publicized meeting point was Promontory, Utah.

In many cases, the railroads preceded instead of followed settlement, and in other cases, settlement was contemporaneous with the building of the railroads. The Federal Government contributed to the development and settlement of Kansas by authorizing grants of land to the railroads. Alternate sections of land, usually within twenty miles of the railroad right of way were granted. The railroads then sold much of this land to immigrants in order to finance the laying of tracks. During the late 1800's, almost one sixth of the area of Kansas was covered by grants of land to railroads.

A prime tactic of the railroads was to dispose of large tracts to "colonies" of settlers. Thus, in 1871, the Kansas Pacific Railroad sold 22,000 acres to a Swedish colony in Saline Co., 47,000 acres to a Scotch colony in Dickinson Co., 32,000 acres to an English colony in Clay Co., and 19,000 acres to a Welsh colony in Riley Co., Kansas.

In Kansas, the Atchison, Topeka & Santa Fe Railroad, better known as the "Santa Fe" was founded in 1859 by Cyrus Holliday. The railroad received a land grant of almost three million acres from the Federal Government via the State of Kansas in exchange for reduced rates on government traffic. Even though the land grant was not formally received until February, 1864, the Santa Fe started construction in Topeka in 1863 and went eastward to Atchison on the Missouri River, north of Kansas City. It went west to Newton by 1871, then to Great Bend, and by 1872 to the famous frontier town of Dodge City, all in Kansas. By 1881, the Santa Fe went westward to Deming, New Mexico.

The Kansas Pacific, which merged into the Union Pacific, opened a road between Kansas City and Lawrence, Kansas, in December, 1864, and westward to Salina on April 29, 1867, and Phil Sheridan (or, Sheridan, in westernmost Kansas) on April, 1869. By September, 1870, the line, then renamed the Kansas Pacific, reached Denver. The Kansas Pacific had initially received a direct land grant from the Federal Government for almost four million acres.

In the late 1800's, the four key railroads in Kansas were as follows:

1. Union Pacific: from Kansas City westward 420 miles.
2. Atchison, Topeka & Santa Fe: northeast to southwest, Atchison to Dodge City; westward across Kansas 446 miles.
3. Leavenworth, Lawrence & Galveston: north to south, from Lawrence southward to Texas.

4. Missouri River, Ft. Scott & Gulf: north to south, from Kansas City southward.

The tremendous expansion of the railroads in the United States during the latter part of the 19th century is exemplified by the rate of railroad building in Kansas. For instance, the 1877 map of Kansas by O.W. Gray in his *National Atlas of the U.S.* shows about 2,030 miles of track; evidently, some of the railroad track shown on the Gray map was only then in the planning stage. By comparison, George F. Cram's 1890 map titled *Railroad and County Map of Kansas* shows approximately 7,960 miles of railroad track. On the Cram map, all but four of Kansas' 105 counties were traversed by track; the four counties lacking track were in the extreme southwest corner. The Gray map is at a scale of one inch equals roughly nineteen miles, while the Cram map is at a scale of about one inch equals twenty miles. In Kansas, a multitude of small railroads were organized in the last half of the 19th century. Most had Denver or Pacific as part of their name. Few reached the high flying goals of either Denver or the Pacific. By 1890, most were merged into one of the main lines.

COWBOYS AND INDIANS. There was intense competition among the railroads for the transportation of people and goods, in both east and westward directions.

With the laying of the rails across Kansas, the years 1869-75 were times of the big buffalo hunts. Numerous hides were shipped by rail to eastern markets. But killing off the buffalo created friction with the indigenous Indian tribes and by 1880, the enormous herds of buffalo were reduced to a very minor number.

One major source of income to the railroads was the transportation of cattle for eastern markets. The period of the long cattle drives lasted from about 1865 to 1885.

The most famous of the several cattle trails was the Chisholm Trail. The original Chisholm trail, begun in 1865, just after the Civil War, started in the area between San Antonio and Austin, Texas, and went almost due north some 800 miles. Initially, the trail went to the Union Pacific depot at Abilene in central Kansas. In 1867 about 35,000 head of cattle, mainly longhorn steers from Texas, were shipped by train from Abilene. In 1871, the number was about 600,000. By that time, Abilene had become known as the first "Cowboy Capital of the West."

However, the Santa Fe, not to be outdone, enticed cattle owners to use their loading stations which cut off a significant portion of the trail drive. Thus, Dodge City, in south central Kansas became a major loading point, and by 1872, took the title of "Cowboy Capital of the World."

Even then, the southern Kansas prairie land was not free from Indian attacks. In August, 1874, six general land surveyors were attacked and killed by Cheyenne Indians in Meade Co. while laying out township lines. This infamous attack, designed to instill fear in the hearts of the early pioneers, became widely known as the Lone Tree Massacre. In 1874, a total of twenty-seven persons were killed by Indians in the State. The last year of Indian problems in Kansas was 1878 when some forty white persons were killed, many in Decatur Co., during the unauthorized migration of the Cheyennes northward through Kansas.

The Germans took a keen interest in tales of the wild West. Part of these tales were spread by the writing of Baron Ernst von Hesse-Wartegg (1854-1918). The Baron was born in Vienna to Austro-German nobility and spent most of his career travelling and writing about his travel experiences. Of his some forty books, at least eight dealt with travel in America. A trip across Kansas in 1877 describes in detail impressions of key cities which included, among others, the frontier town of Topeka and the sprawling and raw cowboy town of Dodge City. There are a number of interesting observations from the Baron's trip over 300 miles of the Santa Fe rail line. Almost surely, the writings of the Baron were known to and used by the prolific fiction writer Karl May (1842-1912) who was born in Saxony and never went to the American west. However, May's novels of the wild west, starting in 1882, created excitement in the minds nearly every 20th century German schoolchild and had a considerable effect in stimulating 1.5 million German-speaking people to migrate to the United States in the period after 1914.

SOUTH CENTRAL KANSAS. The Santa Fe had reached Newton, Kans., in 1871, a small community in south central Kansas which was incorporated in 1872. At this time, large efforts were made to attract Mennonites from Russia, Poland, and Prussia to settle on Santa Fe lands in Kansas. In early 1875, Carl B. Schmidt, Commissioner of Immigration for several railroads, most notably for the Atchison, Topeka and Santa Fe, travelled among the affluent Mennonites of West Prussia and organized the distribution of propaganda describing the great opportunities in Kansas.

There was a strong competition between the Santa Fe, the Kansas Pacific, and the Burlington & Quincy Railroads for these migrants. Frederick Hedde, state agent from Nebraska, represented the Burlington system. In 1871, he sent his subagent George Harris to Europe with 10,000 circulars printed in German. Kent K. Keman, was the Wisconsin state immigration agent active in Europe at the time.

The Northern Pacific probably used the most intensive recruiting methods in Europe. Initially, they advertised through the newspapers of two German cities, one in Gotha and the other in Frankfurt. The railroad was centered in Bismarck, N.Dak. By 1882, the Company had 124 general agents active in Europe. It is estimated that they distributed 623,590 brochures, and in addition, eventually ran ads in sixty-eight German newspapers.

Schmidt and the others were so successful that between 1873 and 1884, some 18,000 migrants from Prussia and Russia, most of them

German-speaking, came to the United States of which an estimated 5,000 settled in south central Kansas, especially along the Arkansas valley. The year 1874 was the peak migration year with about 1,275 Mennonite families, or about 3,000 individuals, going to the western States, of which perhaps 600 families went to the south central Kansas counties of Harvey, Marion, and Reno. For the year 1885, the estimate was some 1,400 persons going to western communities. Lesser numbers of Mennonites came also from southern Germany and from Switzerland. The names of many of the Mennonites settling in Kansas during the period of 1872-1904 are documented in a recent publication by Haury (1986).

Not all of the "Russian" immigration were Mennonites; the group of 1875-77, settling in Ellis Co., Ks., was predominantly Catholic.

In 1879, the hardy migrants from the Ukraine brought an important economic contribution, namely, the hard red Turkey winter wheat.

LAND OF THE POST ROCK. In north central Kansas and south central Nebraska, the physical and spiritual survival of the Mennonite and other communities was fundamentally dependent upon the Union Pacific and the smaller rail lines.

By 1867, the Union Pacific had reached Abilene and Salina, Kans., in central Kansas, and subsequently smaller railroads sprang up northward. One small railroad in north central Kansas was known by the quaint name of the Atchison, Solomon Valley & Denver R.R. (today, part of the Missouri Pacific Railroad). On this line, the first passenger train, coming from Salina a distance of sixty-four miles, reached Beloit, in Mitchell Co., on September 1, 1878. In the spring of 1879, the line reached Glen Elder, a small community incorporated in the same year. Continuing west, the line reached Cawker City on May 17, 1879, and Downs, another very small community in Osborne Co., on June 21, 1879. The distance from Beloit to Downs was twenty-four miles.

The Atchinson, Solomon Valley & Denver was a typical small railroad which was undercapitalized, went bankrupt, and was taken over by Jay Gould (1836-1892), the well-known American financier and railroad speculator. In 1872, Gould had gotten control of the Union Pacific by devious means. Gould became known as the archetypical "robber baron" as he fleeced friend and foe alike. Subsequently, Gould got control of the Missouri Pacific and eventually changed the names of the small north central Kansas railroads to Missouri Pacific.

During the period of 1863-1879, life on the plains of Kansas tried the optimism of even the hardiest souls. It was a time when coal replaced buffalo droppings for fuel, kerosene replaced candles for light, and frame wood houses replaced "soddies" (dirt block) for homes, all of which were made possible by the coming of the railroads. Individuals without earlier trying experiences, such as those encountered in the Civil War of 1861-65, became discouraged with the rigors of frontier life. Under the primitive conditions, many of the original homesteaders gave up their land rights with many going "back east." By some estimates, the grasshopper plague year of 1874 convinced some 25% of the settlers of north central Kansas to move on.

By about 1880, north central Kansas was reasonably well settled. The immigrants included individuals who were knowledgeable about quarrying techniques. Subsequently, the development of the peculiar phenomena of quarrying the famous Fencepost Limestone in order to support thousands of miles of fences stemmed from the combination of the meager local supply of trees and from the ready source of an uniquely adapted layer of limestone. Another advantage was that the rock would not burn on the occasion of the relatively frequent prairie fires. The Fencepost Limestone bed of the Greenhorn Limestone Formation occurred in a layer some eight to ten inches thick, near the ground surface, and spread out over much of fifteen counties. A rock post five or six feet long might weigh 350 to 400 pounds; most quarrying and setting of these blocks was by hand. From about 1884 to 1920 there were millions of posts carved out of the bedrock; apparently it was cost effective to quarry these backbreaking monsters even with the competition of substitutes provided by the railroads.

REFERENCES

Anonymous, 1877, *The National Atlas of the United States, etc.*. O. W. Gray & Son, Phila., 218 p., maps
The map of Kansas, p. 112-113, scale 1:1,140,000, shows Mitchell Co. villages of Naomi, Glen Elder, Cawker, Beloit, etc., but does not show Atchison, Solomon Valley & Denver R.R., only older railroads.

Anonymous, 1975, *Railroad Maps of the United States*. U.S. Govt. Printing Office, Washington, D.C., 118 p., illus.
_____, 1984, *Railroad Maps of North America - The First Hundred Years*. ibid, 206 p., illus.

Anonymous, 1983, *On the Kansas Pacific Railway*. Kansas History Quarterly., vol. 6, p. 164-172.

Anonymous, 1985, *Rand McNally Handy Railroad Atlas of the United States*. Rand McNally & Co., Chicago, Ill., 64 p., maps.

Anonymous, 1989, *Chronology of America's Railroads*. Assoc. American Railroads, Washington, D.C., factual brochure, 7 p.

Baughman, R. W., 1961, *Kansas in Maps*. Kansas State Historical Society, Topeka, Kans., 104 p., illus., maps.
_____, 1961, *Kansas Post Offices*. ibid, 256 p., illus.

Bryant, K. L., Jr., 1974, *History of the Atchison, Topeka & Santa Fe Railway*. Macmillan Publ. Co., N.Y.,

Bullard, W. C., 1990, *Bound for the Promised Land*. City of Independence (Mo.), National Frontier Trails Center, 48 p., illus.

Clark, I. G., 1958, *Then Came the Railroads*. Univ. Oklahoma Press, Norman, 336 p., illus.
Interesting narrative of important railroad events west of the Mississippi.

Evans, C. S., 1990, *A Guide to finding Kansas Maps*. Kansas Geol. Surv., Educational Series 8, 80 p.

Evans, H. C., (ed.), 1939, *Kansas, A Guide to the Sunflower State*. Hastings House, N.Y., 538 p. Reprinted in 1976 by Scholarly Press, Inc., St.Clair Shores, Mi.

Farley, A. W., 1959, "Samuel Hallett and the Union Pacific Railway Company in Kansas." *Kansas Historical Quarterly*, Topeka, 16 p.

Goetzmann, Wm. H., 1982, "Explorer, Mountain Man, and Scientist." In *Exploring the American West, 1803-1879*. U.S. Dept. Interior, Washington, D.C., National Park Handbook 116, p. 21-99, illus., maps
Shows indexed map of the four 1853-55 surveys for the transcontinental railroad route, which was completed in 1869.

Grant, H. R., 1987, "Building the Kansas Pacific Railway." *Kansas History Quarterly*, vol. 10, no. 2, p. 76-88

Grisafe, D. A., 1976, *Kansas Building Limestones*. Kansas Geol. Surv., Mineral Res., Ser. no. 4, 42 p., maps, illus.
Contains good color photographs of locally economically important rocks.

Hall, T. B., 1971, *Medicine on the Santa Fe Trail*. Morningside Bookshop, Dayton Oh, 161 p., maps, illus.
An excellent discussion of the primary diseases encountered in frontier America during the 19th century.

Haury, D. A. (ed.), 1986, *Index to Mennonite Immigrants on United States Passenger Lists, 1872-1904*. Mennonite Library & Archives, North Newton, Kans., 224 p.
Lists about 15,000 individuals, many eventually residing in Kansas, travelling on 209 ships.

McPherson, J. A., & Miller Williams (eds.), 1976, *Railroad Trains and Train People in American Culture*. Random House, N.Y., 186 p., illus.

Miller, Darrell (ed.), 1961, "Pioneer Plows and Steel Rails." *Downs News & Times*, Downs, Kans., 108 p. (misnumbered), 21 pls.

Muilenburg, Grace & Ada Swineford, 1975, *Land of the Post Rock*. Univ. Press of Kansas, Lawrence, 207 p., illus.
An in-depth and entertaining study of a quaint subject.

Rydjord, John, 1968, *Indian Place-Names*. Univ. Oklahoma Press, Norman, Okla.
_____, 1972, *Kansas Place-Names*. ibid, 613 p.

Socolofsky, H. E., & Huber Self, 1972, *Historical Atlas of Kansas*. Univ. Oklahoma Press, Norman, Okla., 70 maps, references-8 p., index-15 p.

Taylor, G. R., & I. D. Neu, 1956, *The American Railroad Network, 1861-1890*. Harvard Univ. Press, Cambridge, 113 p., 2 maps.
Maps show railways as of April 1, 1861.

Trautmann, Frederic, 1983, "Across Kansas by Train in 1877: The Travels of Ernst von Hesse-Wartegg." *Kansas History Quarterly*, vol. 6, p. 142-163, figs.

Wenger, Vernon, 1983, *A History of Railroad Construction and Abandonment within the State of Kansas*. Kansas Corporation Commission, Topeka, 96 page manuscript plus 11 page supplement, the supplement being dated Oct 1, 1990. Gives detailed information on virtually every railway in Kansas from about 1860 to the present; notes that Kansas railroad mileage expanded rapidly from about 4,200 miles in 1885 to about 8,800 miles in 1890.

Part 7

acob
Marzolf
of
Alsace

THE FOLLOWING NARRATIVE IS A TYPICAL Alsatian family history illustrated by the migration of the Marzolf family from the vicinity of the Upper Rhine in northeastern France to the central part of the United States. It is a tale of German-speaking people from the Alsace, a people who were exhausted by the Wars of the French Revolution (1792-1800) and the continuing Napoleonic Wars (1800-1815).

In 1795, the pacifistic Mennonites of Alsace had sent a petition to the "Division of Welfare" in Paris and received assurance that they were entirely free of military duty.

But by 1804, Napoleon Bonaparte I (1769-1821) had become Emperor of France and remained so until 1814. By the spring of 1807, Napoleon had some 600,000 troops in East Prussia. Largely, these troops lived off the land. In June, 1812, with some 300,000 troops in the main army, Napoleon undertook the well-known and ill-advised invasion of Russia. Obviously, with these massive armies in the field, Napoleon was in no mood to grant any exemption from service to religious dissidents.

In 1808, the Mennonites of Alsace sent a delegation to Paris with a petition for, among other requests, a continued exemption from military service. This petition was denied in January, 1809. Two more delegations to Paris in 1811 also received a negative response. Thus, the Mennonites began looking for alternative solutions to their problems.

By 1811, the economic crisis provoked by taxation for financing the wars, as well as overpopulation in many rural areas, convinced large parts of the population of Alsace to migrate, regardless of religious convictions.

THE MENNONITES OF ALSACE. The first documented, but obscure account of Mennonites at the small village of Steinseltz, a small farming community in northernmost Alsace, dates from 1699 when eleven Mennonite families were recorded as living there. The well-known Mennonite conferences held at Steinseltz, in France, in 1752, and at Essingen, near Landau in Germany, in 1759 and 1779, provide records linking the French/German border Mennonite groups.

The patriarch of the Marzolf clan in northern Alsace was one Wendel Marzolf who married a Susanna Müller (see Table 7.2 on page 302). They had at least three children, namely Georg (1775-1815), Jacob (1780-1870), and Barbara (1791-1880). No other data is currently available regarding the parents.

Georg Marzolf married Anna Maria Hausauer on 15 May 1796; the marriage was recorded in Steinseltz, which had been mentioned above.

About 1800, Georg's brother Jacob Marzolf married Elizabeth Hausauer, who evidently was a sister to Anna Maria. Thus, the two brothers married two sisters.

The six children of Georg and Anna Maria included four sons, namely Bernhard, b. 1799; Georg, b. 1801; Jakob, b. 1802; and Johannes, b. 1806 in Ingolsheim, near Steinseltz.

Apparently, (see for instance, Stumpf, 1973) initial migration involved for many a landward movement northward along the Rhine into the Palatinate of the German States, as it did for the Marzolf brothers; Georg Marzolf and his family went to Ingenheim, Jacob probably went to the Deutschhof.

Migration records indicate that the next move of the Georg Marzolf family occurred sometime before 1812 when they went from Ingenheim in the Palatinate, to Neuendorf in the Ukraine. The two younger daughters, Margarata and Elizabetha, evidently were born in Neuendorf in 1812 and 1814, respectively. No further records are currently known of this family.

JACOB MARZOLF (1780-1870). Jacob Marzolf, the younger son of Wendel and Susanna, was born either on 6 April 1780 or 17 April 1780, as various records indicate. Tradition states that he was born in Alsace, France, probably in the area very close to the German-French border, just south of the French town of Wissembourg.

About 1800, Jacob Marzolf married Elizabeth Hausauer. Her maiden name is variously spelled Hansoun, Hansauer, and Haussauer, the variations reflecting French, German, and English influences. She was born either on 20 February 1780, or more likely, on 18 January 1783 and claimed a French, i.e., Alsatian background.

The Jacob Marzolf family eventually numbered six children, namely George, b. about 1803, Jacob, b. 1805, Elizabeth, also b. 1805, Martin, b. 1807, Catherine, b. 1810, and Michael b, 1812. All of these children appear to have been born at Steinseltz or nearby Ingolsheim, in the Alsace. Possibly the family migrated (about 1810-1815) some five or ten miles northward across the border to the vicinity of another well-known Mennonite community, namely the Deutschhof, prior to their trip to America.

Between 1828 and 1837, the French government counted 26,019 emigrants from the Bas-Rhin area (northern Alsace) alone. Many were Mennonites seeking religious toleration. Doubtless, the French government encouraged the Germans in Alsace to resettle elsewhere.

The migration phenomena was not confined to the Alsace. Outside France, the year 1827-28 were peak years also of migration to America for Irish and German peoples.

WESTERN NEW YORK SETTLEMENT RECORDS. In late 1792, Theophile Cazenove, agent for various Dutch investment firms bought 1,500,000 acres in western New York. Subsequently, another 1,000,000 acres was purchased by the same group. Still later, they acquired more land in Pennsylvania. The Holland Land Co. was formed in late 1795 with a total acreage of about 2,733,000 acres combined from the various investment firms. After the War of 1812 (1812-1815), during which the City of Buffalo suffered heavy damage, both the U.S. Government and the Dutch investment firms were anxious to settle and populate western New York.

Survey and subdivision of the land controlled by The Holland Land Co. into lots was finished only in 1819. Cazenove had been succeeded in 1796 as General Agent in Philadelphia by P. Busti who in turn was succeeded in 1824 by J. J. van der Kemp. During the next forty-five years, there were a number of ordinary agents and subagents who promoted the development, improvement, and sale of these properties. Particularly active purchasers of the semi-virgin land were farmers of German background.

THE MARZOLF FAMILY'S JOURNEY TO AMERICA. An intensive search has been made of ship arrival records in the National Archives in Washington, D.C. No records have been found of the Marzolf family, nor of any related family names.

The Jacob Marzolf family came to the United States about 1828, landing probably either in New York City, or in Philadelphia. In addition to the eight family members mentioned above, the migrating group included Jacob's sister, Barbara, at least one daughter-in-law, a grand-daughter plus various Hausauers.

The exact route of the Marzolf family to America is as yet not documented; however one may speculate on their mode of travel. In those communities near the Rhine, the obvious mode of transportation is by barge down the Rhine to Rotterdam, and then across the Atlantic to the ports of New York, Philadelphia, or Baltimore.

The distance from Strasbourg (Strassburg) in Bas-Rhin to Rotterdam is about 740 km (460 miles). Modern day current records show that free-floating barges travel over this distance at an average speed of three and one half km/hr (some two miles/hr). Thus, it would have taken early 19th century travellers about nine days to go from the Alsace to Rotterdam by barge. The approximately 4,800 mile trip across the Atlantic by sailing ship must have taken four to six weeks, at least.

The idea of making a long trip to a strange land under primitive travel conditions was not readily accepted by all. It was a matter of push (poor economic conditions in France and southern Germany) and pull. In this case, the pull impetus was provided in part by The Holland Land Co. who were well along in their promotion scheme to settle western New York, as documented in the preceding paragraphs.

If the Marzolfs landed in New York City, they most likely would have gone by boat up the Hudson River to western New York. The Erie Canal, extending eastward from Tonawanda, N.Y., near Buffalo, to the Hudson River at Waterford, N.Y., near Troy, is about 363 miles long. It was completed on Oct. 26, 1825. The horse-drawn boat *Seneca Chief* left

Buffalo on that day and arrived in New York City on Nov. 4, or some nine days later. The return trip, partly upstream, took somewhat longer.

If the Marzolf family landed in Philadelphia, they probably would have gone first overland through the Reformed Mennonite community near Strasburg, Lancaster Co., Pa., via the Pennsylvania & Lancaster Turnpike Rd., which was completed in 1795, and then on to western New York.

By whatever route, the migrants, travelling from northeastern France to western New York, were faced with a strenuous trip of well over two months. With this background in mind, let's look now at the early American history of the Marzolf family.

THE JACOB MARZOLF FAMILY IN AMERICA. The various land records of Jacob and his son eldest son George for property in Erie Co., N.Y., are summarized below, courtesy of Robert A. Cramer, current resident of Buffalo:

August 5, 1829: Jacob Martzolf, George Martzolf, and Michael Osvalett (Oswalt) of Erie County bought for the sum of $320.00 part of lot 62 in the Township of Amherst, 76 acres from the Holland Land Co.
(This land was the south 1/3 of lot 62 on Eleven Mile Creek which is now called Ellicott Creek. Lot 62 is just north of the intersection of North Forest Rd. and Heim Rd. This is near the intersection of Routes 270 and 263).

In **1838**, Jacob Marzolf bought for $988.00 from Edward A. Hickox, part of Lot 18 (38 acres). Lot 18 is in Eggertsville (Amherst Township), bounded by Main St. and Eggert Rd.

October 1, 1845: John Reist of the Town of Amherst and Ann, his wife, sold for $1700.00 to George Martzolf, of the same place, land in Cheektowaga Township #12 in the 7th Range. By subdivision of said Township in lots, it is distinguished as the south part of lot no. 8 in said township bounded north by land conveyed by deed to Syloamus Colburn, etc. etc. (68 acres).
(Lot 8 in Cheektowaga is now part of greater Buffalo Airport, on Genesee St., which was formerly named Batavia Rd.).

In the 1850 U.S. Census for Amherst, the elders Jacob and Elizabeth Marzolf are shown in the household of their daughter Elizabeth and son-in-law Peter Goss. In the 1855 Census for the Town of Clarence, Jacob and Elizabeth are enumerated in the household of their grand-daughter Sarah and her husband Jacob Fisher.

Elizabeth Hausauer Marzolf died on/about 25 July 1866. Jacob died about 6 April 1870 and was buried in a cemetery near the City of Clarence, N.Y.

Barbara Marzolf (1791-1880), sister of Jacob, never married; she was buried in the Strickler Family Cemetery on Strickler Road, near Clarence, N.Y.

GEORGE MARZOLF (1803-1848). George Marzolf was born 20 February 1803 in the Alsace. He was the oldest of the six children of Jacob and Elizabeth (Hausauer) Marzolf. The family came to the United States about 1828, or when George was about twenty-five.

About 1826, George had already married Elizabeth Anna Sonya; her maiden name is variously spelled Sunya, Songe, and Sonyer, who was born, apparently in France, on 23 April 1803. The origin of this difficult family name currently eludes analysis as to etymological origin or even to proper spelling. It appears to be non-Germanic.

The George Marzolf family had eight children, who were: Elizabeth, b. 1826, Catherine, b. 1829, Jacob, b. 1831, Sarah, b. 1834, Martin, b. 1837, George, b. 1838, John, b. 1841, and Henry, b. 1844.

On 6 December 1831, George filed an U.S. Naturalization petition in Lancaster Township, Erie Co., N.Y. This petition indicated former allegiance to the "King of the French." On this petition, which was granted on 15 October 1844, the name was spelled Matzolf.

George's will was filed in Cheektowaga on 15 June 1848; he died the next day. On the will, the name was spelled Mortzolf. The will was witnessed by Mennonite Henry Herr and by John Longden. George was buried in the Williamsville, Erie Co., N.Y., Cemetery, Sect. A, Row 24, Grave 20. The weathered horizontal marker is still in place. A younger son, John, born in 1841, apparently died also in 1848. Likely, George and his son John were victims of one of the contagious diseases prevalent during this period, perhaps cholera.

The family group enumerated on the 1850 U.S. Census for Cheektowaga showed the following individuals: widow Elizabeth, 47; Elizabeth, 23; Jacob, 18; George, 14; Martin, 11; and Henry, 6. Comparison with later Census records and also Civil War records for the brothers Jacob, George, and Martin indicates that there are some minor discrepancies in the birth dates recorded on the 1850 census, possibly the census data was transmitted erroneously by a neighbor or one of the younger children.

The widow Elizabeth Anna (Sonya) Marzolf apparently followed her oldest son, Jacob, first to La Porte Co., Ind., later to Wathena, Doniphan Co., Ks., and finally in 1873, to Glen Elder, Mitchell Co., Ks. She was one of the first Reformed Mennonites to settle in Mitchell Co., Kans. She died 21 January 1897 and was buried in the Naomi Mennonite cemetery, south of Glen Elder, Kans.

FOUR BROTHERS, THREE WOUNDED OR DISABLED. Few families in the United States escaped direct involvement in the terrible tragedies of the Civil War. Religious convictions not withstanding, the four surviving sons of George Marzolf (1803-1848) contributed their fair share of the fight for freedom from slavery. The brothers Jacob, Martin, and George each served long terms of three years or more in upholding the Union cause; all three brothers suffered either from severe wounds or from diseases. The fourth and youngest brother, Henry, being born in 1844, was too young for the war and remained at home on the family farm to assist his mother and two older sisters.

Jacob initially had severe reservations about joining the armed forces. His wife, in fact, threatened to disown him if he went against the basic religious convictions of the family. However, after his two younger brothers had entered the conflict on the Union side in 1861, the next year Jacob felt a moral and family obligation to join the fray.

The oldest child of Jacob and Anna Elizabeth Marzolf, Emma, born in La Porte, Ind. in 1861, was scarcely more than a year old when on 11 August 1862, her father Jacob enlisted in the Union Army, Company I, 87th Regiment Infantry. This Regiment was organized and mustered in at South Bend, Ind. on 31 August 1862. At that time, a private's pay was reckoned at about $13.00 per month plus $3.00 clothing allowance.

The 87th Regiment fought various Civil War battles in Kentucky, Tennessee, Georgia, South Carolina, and North Carolina. In one infamous battle, at Chickamauga, Ga., on September 19/20, 1863, Jacob was wounded along with many others of his Company; in bloody hand-to-hand fighting for two days more than half of Jacob's Company were killed or wounded: of 366 active men, forty were killed, 142 wounded, and eight missing.

The two day battle of Chickamauga, Ga. was conducted over a stretch of about four miles, in dense woods and thick underbrush. The Union Army of Cumberland, numbering about 57,000, under General William S. Rosecrans (1819-1898) faced a formidable opponent of about 67,000 of the Confederate Army of Tennessee under the inept General Braxton Bragg (1817-1876). The Union army sustained 16,179 killed, wounded, or captured, or about 28.4%. The Confederate army counted 18,454 killed, wounded, or captured, or about 27.5%. The name Chickamauga is a Cherokee Indian name meaning "river of blood." During this, the bloodiest two day period of the Civil War, the west branch of Chickamauga Creek was literally a river of blood.

In the end, during the dusk hours of Sept. 20, the Federal forces made a slow retreat to Chattanooga, Tenn., some seven miles northward. The last area at Chickamauga to be evacuated was Snodgrass Hill. The remaining Union forces of some 27,000 on Snodgrass Hill were commanded by General George H. Thomas, who was subsequently nicknamed the "Rock of Chickamauga." The Confederate forces were slow to pursue.

The monument on Snodgrass Hill reads as follows:

Indiana's Tribute
To Her
Eighty Seventh Regiment Infantry

Colonel Newell Gleason, Commanding
Third Brigade (Van Derveer)
Third Division (Brannan)
Fourteenth Corps (Thomas)

September 19th, 1863, engaged near Hood's Bridge and tower south of the cross-roads. Supported the 9th Ohio when it charged the enemy and recaptured Burnham's Regular Battery; with the brigade withstood the last attack on the Union left.

September 20, 1863, from 11 A.M. to 1 P.M. was engaged in Kelly Field east of the LaFayette Road. About 11 A.M. the regiment was attacked with great fury; repulsing the enemy and drove him beyond the field.

About 1.30 P.M. retired to Snodgrass Hill, where this monument stands, and was engaged there until 7.30 P.M. Went into battle with effective force of 366; killed 7 officers, 33 enlisted men, wounded 4 officers, 138 enlisted men, missing 8, total casualties 190, percentage of loss 51.5.

All able forces were mobilized for the final battle which began in late October, 1863. The Union forces were encamped in and around the important railroad junction of Chattanooga. The Confederate forces occupied the rugged hills overlooking and surrounding the city, especially atop Missionary Ridge some two and one half miles to the east. After a series of further skirmishes in late November, 1863, the Union forces, with reinforcements, finally prevailed. With the Federal victory on Nov. 25, the Confederate forces began a retreat into Georgia; they had lost several hundred killed, more than 2,000 wounded and more than 4,000 captured. More importantly, the Confederate forces lost over sixty cannon and countless small arms, all of which was virtually irreplaceable at this stage of the War. The tide had turned; it was the beginning of the end for the Rebel cause.

During the War, the 87th Regiment had lost ten officers and eighty-one enlisted men killed or mortally wounded. Additionally, two officers and 190 enlisted men perished through fatigue and disease.

The Civil War records for Jacob can be summarized as follows:

1. enrolled August 11, 1862, Company I, 87th Regiment Infantry, in South Bend, Ind.
2. discharged June 9, 1865, as Corporal, near Washington, D.C.

3. length of service: 2 years, 9 months, 29 days.
4. wounded September 29, 1863, at Chickmauga, Ga.
5. physical description: 5'9", fair complexion, light hair, blue eyes.

When Jacob returned home to La Porte, Ind., in June, 1865, with a full beard, his daughter Emma, only four at that time, did not recognize the stranger at the gate. It had been a long and difficult war for mother "Eliza", who evidently spoke only meager English, and she had been compelled to take in washing in order to support herself and her daughter. The washing consisted of two batches a day during the week and three batches on Saturday. Other family support came from vegetable gardening.

Existing Civil War records for Jacob Marzolf show that the Marzolf name suffered through a variety of phonetic spellings, among them: Martsolf, Marcolf, Marsolf, Matsul, and Matsuff. There is little doubt, however, that the name is of Germanic origin. In spoken German, the 'z' becomes 'tz'. In German-American, the 'z' becomes a 'c' or a 's'. Census record spellings are given in the accompanying Table 7.1.

TABLE 7.1
FEDERAL AND STATE CENSUS RECORDS
OF JACOB MARZOLF (1831-1919)

Year	State	County	Township/City	Spelling
1840	x	x	x	x
1850	New York	Erie	Cheektowaga	Martzolf
1860	Indiana	La Porte	La Porte (City)	Marksull
1870	Kansas	Doniphan	Burr Oak	Marcolf
1875	Kansas	Mitchell	Walnut Creek	Marsolf
1880	Kansas	Mitchell	Walnut Creek	Martolph
1890	x	x	x	x
1900	Kansas	Mitchell	Walnut Creek	Marzolf
1910	Kansas	Mitchell	Walnut Creek	Marzolf

The Civil War records for brother Martin Marzolf, a blacksmith by trade, can be summarized as follows:

1. enrolled Sept. 23, 1861, Co. C., 10th Regiment Cavalry Vol., at Buffalo, N.Y.
2. discharged Dec. 30, 1863, as Corporal, at Warrenton, Va.
3. reenlisted Dec. 31, 1863, Amherst, N.Y.
4. discharged at Clouds Mills, Va., 26 June 1865, as Sergeant
5. length of service: 3 years, 9 months, 27 days.
6. wounded 9 June, 1863 at Brandy Station, Va. The wounds were later described as follows: four saber wounds, as follows, one across the left temple fracturing the skull, one on the right hip from thrust of saber to the hip bone, and two on the left shoulder.

7. physical description: 5'1/2", dark complexion, brown hair, grey eyes

In the Civil War records for Martin Marzolf, the name is spelled in six variations, being Marzolf, Martsolf, Martzolf, Martsolf, Marsolf, and Martsoff.

The Civil War records for brother George Marzolf, a farmer by trade, can be summarized as follows:

1. enrolled Aug. 20, 1861, Co. B, 6th Michigan Volunteer Infantry, at Kalamazoo, Mich.
2. discharged Aug. 23, 1864, at Kalamazoo, Mich.
3. length of service: 3 years, 3 days.
4. disabled with rheumatism, chronic diarrhea, and piles.
5. physical description: 5'4", dark complexion, black hair, brown eyes

George's duty at Vicksburg and at New Orleans indicates that he most likely contracted either malaria, yellow fever, or one of the dysenteries, or possibly all three. The Civil War records for George Marzolf show at least seven different spellings of the family name including Martsalf, Martsolf, Metsalf, Martsle, Martseld, Martzalf, and Mertzell.

After the Civil War, the four Marzolf brothers, Jacob, Martin, George, and Henry, all pulled their respective stakes in Indiana, New York, Michigan, and New York and became part of the great migration westward. The 1880 Census shows the four brothers living in Mitchell Co., Kansas, all within a one mile radius of the Naomi Post Office.

WESTWARD MIGRATION. Post Civil War days in Kansas were not without hazards. In western Kansas, attacks by the Cheyenne and Arapaho Indian tribes on the pioneers, who were encroaching on active buffalo hunting grounds, seemed to increase. Notable attacks are recorded for the years 1865, 1867, and 1868. The Limestone Creek massacre in Mitchell Co., Kans. in 1870 was followed by a similar attack in Meade Co. on 1874. The last large scale battle in western Kansas occurred in 1878, during the unauthorized migration of the Cheyennes northward. The relatively peaceful Pawnee tribe, indigenous to north central Kansas, and the Kansa and Wichita tribes of central Kansas, created a few minor disturbances. Similarly, the Comanche, Kiowa, Apache tribes of southwest Kansas and the Osage tribe of southeast Kansas provided relatively calm areas for settlement.

JACOB MARZOLF (1831-1919). Born 25 November 1831 at Williamsville (near Buffalo), Erie Co., N.Y., Jacob Marzolf was the third child and oldest son of George Marzolf and Elizabeth Anna Sonya Marzolf. Jacob was shown on the 1850 U.S. Census for Cheektowaga, Erie Co., N.Y. For some reason, he went to La Porte Co., Ind. in 1857. There he met Anna

Elizabeth Shafer (or Shaffer), who was born in Friedensdorf, near Marburg, province of Kassel, Germany.

"Eliza" came to the United States at age nineteen, this being in 1856, as a servant indentured to a Doctor, also of German origin. Her experience as a doctor's assistant was to serve Eliza well on the Kansas semifrontier. She was later to serve as a general practitioner in her isolated farm community. Indeed, her home remedies and common sense probably were superior to the general primitive knowledge then prevalent in the medical profession.

Jacob and Eliza were married either on 7 December 1858, or 7 November 1859, as various records state. They were married in La Porte, Ind., the Rev. J. S. McCloud officiating. To them were borne seven children as recorded in Table 7.2 on page 302, and as listed below.

Daughter Emma had been born in 1861, a year before Jacob enlisted for service in the Civil War. He returned home three years later.

In 1866, two significant events happened to the Jacob Marzolf family: son John H. was born and shortly thereafter, the family left La Porte Co., Ind. for Kansas. Jacob Marzolf was joined by his brother Martin. Initially, the two families settled along the Missouri River, at Wathena in Doniphan Co., in northeast Kansas. Here, Jacob's son George and his daughter Mary were born.

Most likely, the Marzolf families made the journey from Indiana to easternmost Kansas by railroad. By 1859, railroads did indeed exist over this distance of some 563 miles. It is a fairly simple matter to plot the trek from La Porte, Indiana, to Chicago, Illinois, via the Michigan Southern & Northern Indiana Railway, a distance of about fifty-nine miles. After changing to the St. Louis, Alton and Chicago Railway (later a part of the Illinois Central system), the group probably went south to Springfield, Illinois, and then west to Quincy, also in Illinois, a distance of about 298 miles.

It was then necessary to cross the Mississippi River by ferry to West Quincy, Missouri. The final rail journey of 206 miles was by the Hannibal & St. Joseph railroad to St. Joseph, Mo. where it would have been necessary to cross the Missouri River, again by ferry. A good maximum rail speed would have been twenty-five miles per hour and thus the actual rail travel time would have been possibly as little as twenty-two and one half hours. No doubt the average train speed was not that fast and, combined with train changes, stops at towns, and ferry crossings, one imagines that the trip took the better part of a week. Compared to other train fares of the time, adult fares would have been somewhat less that $10.00 for the entire trip.

In 1868, the brothers were joined by their mother Elizabeth Anna (Sonya) Marzolf and their older sister, Elizabeth (Marzolf) Farbaugh, a widow with three teen age children: Jacob, John, and Susan. Jacob Farbaugh, Sr. had died in 1857 in Erie Co., Ontario, Canada, and his widow Elizabeth had gone back to Erie Co., N.Y. in 1866. In the next few years, younger brothers George Marzolf and Henry Marzolf joined the family group in Doniphan Co., Kansas.

After a disastrous flood of the Missouri River in 1871, however, the families of Jacob and Martin Marzolf moved again, this time in covered wagons some 200 miles west (spring, 1872) to Walnut Creek Township in Mitchell Co., north central Kansas. The two Marzolf brothers were accompanied by Henry Kohler and his family. For the most part, they followed the "Pike's Peak Express Road". The dirt trail almost due westward, across the three unbridged rivers, namely, the Delaware, Little Blue, and Republican Rivers, lasted nearly a month. Progress was slow for one of the two horses died en route and was replaced in the hitches by the lone cow; the poor cow also provided some milk which was converted to butter by the jolting of the wagon. In Mitchell Co., Jacob's initial homestead was 160 acres.

The Marzolfs were part of the 1871-72 flood of migrants moving into the Solomon valley area. During the first decade, a series of small towns and villages, better known as Beloit, Glen Elder, Cawker City, and Downs, sprang up along the Solomon River. In 1868, the river was described as being about fifty feet wide, two to three feet deep in the dry season, and composed of clear water. The river was a key element in providing power for grain mills and, in the winter, ice for ice houses. The growth of trees in Mitchell Co was confined to the immediate banks of the Solomon River.

Life on the open prairie, some eight miles south of the Solomon River, was in a sod dug-out at first. Eventually, Jacob, who was a carpenter and a farmer, built a frame house with a partial basement of native limestone. Initially, fuel was provided mainly by buffalo and cow chips. The early settlers soon learned to judge by the color and age of the chips which would produced the best fire. Other fuels included long twisted grass, corn stalks, and sunflower stalks.

Butter, cream, and eggs constituted the main currency. These were traded for such merchandise as was available at the small local stores. A portion of the wheat and corn crops were bartered for milling at the nearest mill which was in Glen Elder, a day's trip away. Hogs, cattle, and wheat helped to pay taxes and to make improvements. The grain and livestock was hauled to the nearest rail line some 100 miles, or several days, away; the return trip always brought lumber, warm winter clothes, and other necessities.

Under the Timber Culture Act of 1873 established by the U.S. Congress, forty acres of a 160 acre claim had to be planted in trees and kept in healthy condition for ten years. Jacob added to his earlier holding by acquiring one of these claims.

The grasshopper plague in late July 1874 followed some six weeks of hot, dry weather which had shriveled the corn and other late crops; most foliage disappeared during the week or so of the grasshopper invasion. In the early spring of 1875, masses of white larva were noted in freshly plowed soil; fortunately, a cold, drizzling rain of four or five days apparently killed off most of the grasshopper larvae as there were few grasshoppers the following year.

THE NAOMI COMMUNITY. The community in which the Marzolfs lived was distinguished by the name Naomi. The Naomi Post Office was in existence from 4 Dec. 1873 to 23 Nov. 1885, according to a 1961 book by R. W. Baughman titled *Kansas Post Offices*. The Post Office was named after the wife of J. W. McGhee, an early settler, evidently Irish, along Walnut Creek. The name Naomi is a Biblical name, found in the Book of Ruth. The Naomi community is shown on the map of Kansas in the 1877 National Atlas of the U.S. published by O. W. Gray & Sons (Phila.). The Naomi Cemetery is clearly shown on the U.S. Geological Survey topographic map of 1953, titled Glen Elder South, Kansas, which is at a scale of 1:24,000.

In 1877, Jacob became a member of the Reformed Mennonite Church at Naomi, apparently for the first time; his wife joined in 1879. The small Naomi Church group in Mitchell Co. had originated about 1873 with the arrival of Jacob's mother, Elizabeth Anna (Sonya) Marzolf, and sister, Elizabeth (Marzolf) Farbaugh, mentioned above. Early services were held in the sod homes of various families. After Jacob built his frame house, the old sod home doubled both as a church and as a school. Early teachers at the school included Jacob's sister Elizabeth Farbaugh and George Mancha, who was also related to Jacob Marzolf.

In 1877, son Frank was born, and in 1883, daughter Sarah was born.

In the spring of 1879, the Atchinson, Solomon Valley & Denver R.R. reached Glen Elder in Mitchell Co., Kans. Subsequently, there was a determined effort by the U.S. government to register immigrants as citizens. Elizabeth (Marzolf) Farbaugh applied for citizenship and on the application was shown as a native of Germany. This application, dated 1 November 1879 renounced allegiance to William I, Emperor of Germany (this was actually Wilhelm I, ruled 1861-1888). The applications filed by her children shows them as natives of Canada and as former subjects of Queen Victoria of Great Britain (she reigned 1837-1901).

The winter wheat crops for three consecutive years 1879, 1880, and 1881, were a disaster. The later growing corn and vegetable crops were somewhat better in 1879 and 1880, but they also did very poorly in 1881. Still, the hardy pioneers survived and hung on. Additionally, there was a bitter two week January blizzard in 1880.

In 1884, Jacob gave one acre of ground for the Naomi Cemetery, and in 1887, he helped build the Naomi Church which became a Mennonite Landmark. The Naomi Church was located about nine miles south-southwest of Glen Elder, Kans., in SE 1/4 NE 1/4 Sec. 30, R9W, T7S, Walnut Creek Township. A number of Naomi Cemetery records predate 1884, the earliest being August, 1880; thus, the burial plot was probably in existence by the mid-1870's.

The first minister of the Naomi Church was George W. Mancha (1843-1918). Long time minister of the Naomi Church was Edwin F. Stouffer (1875-1963); in 1908, he was placed on probation as minister, later he became a full-fledged minister, and remained so until 1935, when, in the middle of the horrendous dust bowl years of 1933-37, he received permission from the Church to go back east, to Sterling, Ill. With the demise of the congregation, the one room frame church building at Naomi was torn down about 1965.

The years 1885, 1886, and 1887, once again were failures for the early wheat crop; 1887 was a bad year in Mitchell Co. for corn as well. The blizzard of 1886 was another discouraging factor. Starting New Years' eve, temperatures fell to twenty-two degrees below zero Fahrenheit and reached twenty-eight degrees below zero on January 7. Fierce, cold, strong winds, and drifting snow prevailed for some weeks. Prairie fires were another hazard, most notably during the spring of 1882 and again in 1887.

PENSION RECORDS. In 1890, Jacob applied for and received an Original Disability Pension for Civil War Veterans under Act of Congress approved 27 June 1890. Physical description of the claimant was:

Age - 58 years. Height - 5'8". Complexion - fair. Hair - light. Eyes - blue. Disabilities were: extreme nervousness as a result of sunstroke, loss of memory, rheumatism, constipation, diarrhea, etc.

(Oddly enough, after three generations, the physical description of Jacob Marzolf fits the current writer. It can only be a matter of cryptic genetic inheritance. The Civil War records show that Jacob's tall stature and fair complexion was indicative of a northern European inheritance; by contrast, the shorter stature, hair color, and apparently darker complexion of brothers Martin and George suggest a southern European inheritance).

In the first application, Jacob was classified as being "almost totally disabled." The 1890, 1898, and 1907 applications were signed as Jacob Martsolf. With the granting of the 1907 application, Jacob, aged seventy-six, was eligible to receive the munificent sum of $20 per month.

Still, $20 per month was a considerable sum of money considering the recession years of 1885-93 and the financial panic years of 1893-96. Moreover, the drought effects of the years 1893, 1894, and 1895 did little to quiet the anxieties of the midwesterners.

Jacob Marzolf remained in the area of Glen Elder until he died on 3 July, 1919, having lived eighty-eight years. His wife, Anna Elizabeth Shafer Marzolf died 3 March 1925, after a long life of more than eighty-eight years. Both are buried in the Naomi Mennonite Cemetery.

Martin Marzolf died on 18 Feb. 1925 in Mapleton, Bourbon Co., Kans., at the home of his oldest son Albert H. Marzolf. Martin is buried in the Prairie View Cemetery near Cawker City, Mitchell Co., Kans., at the side of his second wife.

George Marzolf died on 9 April 1891 near Corning, Nemaha Co., Ks. The exact burial place is unknown.

THE MARZOLF FAMILY THROUGH FIVE GENERATIONS. Table 7.2 shows, in addition to Marzolf and Hausauer, a predominance of family names of obviously German origin, including: Eschelman, Farbaugh, Fisher, Goss, Hagelberger, Heiman, Heins, Hoffmann, Kalbfleisch, Kramer, Müller, Rickoff, Reigle, Rohlf, Shafer, Weckesser, and Zimmerman. The names Farbaugh and Fisher, among others, probably show some changes in spelling from the original. For instance, Fisher was originally most likely Fischer, or perhaps even related to the Dutch name Visscher.

TABLE 7.2
THE MARZOLF FAMILY THROUGH FIVE GENERATIONS

1. Wendel Marzolf
   m. Susanna Müller
   11. Georg Marzolf (1775-1815)
        m. Anna Maria Hausauer (1778- ?)
        Bernhard Marzolf (1799-1812)
        Georg Marzolf (1801-1814)
        Jakob Marzolf (1802- ?)
        Johannes Marzolf (1806- ?)
        Margarata Marzolf (1812- ?)
        Elizabetha Marzolf (1814- ?)
   12. Jacob Marzolf (1780-1870)
        m. Elizabeth Hausauer (?1783- 1866)
        111. George Marzolf (1803-1848)
              m. Elizabeth Anna Sonya (1803-1897)
              1111. Elizabeth Marzolf (1826-1887)
                     m. Jacob Farbaugh
              1112. Catherine Marzolf (1829- ?)
                     m. Augustus Rohlf (Rolfin)
              1113. Jacob Marzolf (1831-1919)
                     m. Anna Elizabeth Shafer
                     11131. Emma Marzolf (1861-1931)
                             m. Charles R. Hendricks
                     11132. John H. Marzolf (1866-1935)
                             m. Anna Fisher
                     11133. George Marzolf (1869-1942)
                             m. 1st Bethsheba E. Supp
                             m. 2nd Sylvia Hollingshead
                             m. 3rd Margaret Adams Fisher

11134. Mary Marzolf (1872-1970)
    m. Edwin F. Stouffer
11135. Frank Marzolf (1877-1954)
    m. Mary Hoffmann
11136. Lucy Marzolf (1879-1882)
11137. Sara E. Marzolf (1883-1976)
    m. James T. Shull
1114. Sarah Marzolf (1834-1911)
    m. Jacob Fisher
1115. Martin Marzolf (1837-1925)
    m. 1st Susan Kelsey
11151. Albert Marzolf (1866-1955)
    m. 2nd Margaret Waddle Goodman
11152. William F. Marzolf (1871-1929)
11153. Charles Marzolf
11154. Fanny Marzolf
    m. ? Oliver
1116. George Marzolf (1838-1891)
    m. Laura Rachel Jones
11161. Nella Deloris Marzolf (1866- ?)
11162. Wellington Uzell Marzolf (1868- ?)
11163. Elbert J. Marzolf (1870- ?)
11164. Charles L. Marzolf (1876- ?)
11165. Bessie M. Marzolf (1880- ?)
1117. John Marzolf (1841-1848)
1118. Henry Marzolf (1844- ?)
    m. Salena ?
11181. John C. Marzolf (1844- ?)
11182. Elisabeth S. Marzolf (1869- ?)
11183. Charles D. Marzolf (1987- ?)
112. Jacob Marzolf (1805-1846)
    m. Louisa Kalbfleisch
1121. Alexander Marzolf
1122. Henry Marzolf (1836-1900)
1123. Jacob Marzolf (1838- ?)
1124. Elizabeth Marzolf
113. Elizabeth Marzolf (1805-1885)
    m. Peter Goss (six children)
114. Martin Marzolf (1807-1882)
    m. Magdalena Zimmerman
1141. Elizabeth Marzolf (1836- ?)
    m. George Zimmerman
1142. Magdalena Marzolf (1839- ?)
    m. Charles Heins
1143. Catherina Marzolf (1841- ?)
    m. Edgar Phelps

1144. Barbara Marzolf (1843-1924)
 m. Benjamin Miller
1145. Martin Marzolf (1846- ?)
 m. Finette Reigle
1146. George Marzolf (1849- ?)
 m. Catherine Rickoff
 11461. George Marzolf (1874- ?)
 11462. Katie Marzolf (1876- ?)
 11463. Willie Marzolf (1878- ?)
 11464. Lottie Marzolf (1879- ?)
1147. Jacob Marzolf (1851-1937)
 m. Catherine Garehime (1854-1933)
 11471. Henry Marzolf (1883-1964)
  m. Olive Lapp
 11472. John F. Marzolf (1885-1978)
  m. ? Berry
 11473. Elizabeth Marzolf (1887-1965)
  m. Peter Heiman (1885-1964)
 11474. Magdalena Marzolf
  m. ? Bates
 11475. William Marzolf
 11476. Andrew Marzolf (1892-1951)
 11477. Mary Marzolf (1897-1973)
115. Catherine Marzolf (1810- 1891)
 m. ? Kramer (six children)
116. Michael Marzolf (1812-1888)
 m. Magdalena Hagelberger
 1161. Catherina Marzolf (1834-1891)
 1162. Elizabeth Marzolf (1836- ?)
  m. Christian Allian
 1163. Sarah Marzolf (1838- ?)
  m. ? Weckesser
 1164. Joel Marzolf (1840-1918)
  m. 1st ? Jones
  m. 2nd ? Eschelman
  11641. Lucretia Marzolf
  11642. Michael Marzolf
  11643. Mary Marzolf
 1165. Susanne Marzolf (1841-1931)
  m. Isiah Town
 1166. Hannah Marzolf (1843- ?)
  m. Josiah Town
 1167. Michael (1849-1931)
  m. Hannah Stockdale
  11671. William Marzolf
  11672. Albert Marzolf

11673.   Martin Marzolf
1168.   Jacob Marzolf (1853- ?)
m. ? Stover
1169.   John Marzolf (1859- ?)
13.   Barbara Marzolf (1791-1880)
never married

ACKNOWLEDGEMENTS

The author acknowledges the fine assistance of the following individuals:

Mrs. Norm Bitterman, of Halkirk, Alberta, Canada
Robert A. Cramer, of Buffalo, N.Y.
Albert R. Hausauer, of Bismarck, N.D.
Kent Marzolf Litton, of Tempe, Ariz.
Mrs. Evelyn (Nusbaum) Lobdell, of Salina, Kans.
Mrs. Mary E. Martsolf, of Butler, Penna.
Edwin L. Marzolf, of Placentia, Calif.
Lawrence Marzolf, of Salina, Kans.
L. G. Meldrum, of the Indiana State Library, Archives Div.,
Indianapolis
Charles K. Nusbaum, of Dixon, Ill.
Mrs. Lucille (Nusbaum) Sharp, of St. Augustine, Fla.
Frank and Pauline (Kohler) Stouffer, of Beloit, Kans.
Jacob and Carol (Day) Stouffer, of Sterling, Ill.
Mrs. Del Tenopir, of Topeka, Kan.

REFERENCES

Bahlow, Hans, 1980, *Deutsches Namenlexicon*. Keyersche Verlagsbuchlandlung GMBH, München, 576 p. (original ed. 1967)
Shows the name Marzolf as the preferred spelling, being derived from the Latin Marcellus or Marcus; other spellings include Marzluff, Merzluft.

Baker, Oneta M., 1971, *A History of the Town of Clarence*. Buffalo & Erie Co. Historical Soc., N.Y., 8 p., illus.
_____, 1983, *History of the Town of Clarence*. Heart of the Lakes Publishing, Interlaken, N.Y., 619 p., illus.

Baughman, R. W., 1977, *Kansas Post Offices*. Kansas State Historical Soc., Topeka, Kans., 256 p., 16 maps (2nd. ed.)

Brechenmacher, J. K., 1957-60, *Etymologisches Wörterbuch der Deutschen Familiennamen*. C. A. Starke Verlag, Limburg a.d. Lahn, vol II, 879 p.
Shows Marzolf as preferred spelling, being derived from the Latin Marzellus and Markus.

Glover, W. H., 1971, *A History of the Town of Amherst*. Buffalo & Erie Co., Historical Soc., N.Y., 8 p., illus.

Hale, E. E., 1854, *Kanzas and Nebraska*. Phillips, Sampson & Co., Boston 256 p., map.
Basically an early summary of the various military expeditions across the area for the benefit of "Emigrant Aid Companies."

Haller, C. R., 1987, "From the Upper Rhine to the Missouri River." *Mennonite Family History*, Elverson, Pa., vol. VI, no. 3, p. 106-109, illus.
An early version of the Kansas-Marzolf Family history, now much expanded.

Kennedy, F. H. (ed.), 1990, *The Civil War Battlefield Guide*. Houghton Mifflin Co., 317 p., illus, numerous maps.
Good overview by numerous authors; includes maps and text for every important battle field of the Civil War. They give updated figures on casualties.

Korn, Jerry, 1985, *The Fight for Chattanooga: Chickamauga to Missionary Ridge*. Time-Life Books, Alexandria, Va., 176 p., illus., maps.

Laybourn, Norman, 1986, *L'Emigration des Alsaciens et des Lorrains du XVIIIe au XXe Siecle*. Assoc. Publ. Universites de Strasbourg, Vol. II, 501 p.

Includes incomplete chapter on "Les Mennonites", p. 354-357, and a sketchy list of later Mennonites on p. 34.; does not mention a Marzolf.

Marzolf, Stanley S., 1985, *Revision of Descendants of George Eberly and Judith Kuter, 1825-1984*. Privately printed, Normal Ill., 12 p.
Cites immigrant ancestor John Marzolf, 1840-1929, (no apparent relation to Jacob), resident of Illinois, as being born in Schalkendorf, 9 miles west of Hagenau, Bas-Rhin, Alsace.

Mershimer, Peggy M., 1991, *Descendancy Chart of Debold (Sr.) Martsolf (1779-1855)*. Privately printed, Slippery Rock, PA, 17 p.
Includes Pennsylvania Martsolfs, who have yet not been connected to the Illinois or Kansas Marzolfs mentioned above.

Mikula, E. J., 1971, *A History of the Town of Lancaster*. Buffalo & Erie Co. Historical Soc., N.Y., 8 p., illus.

Pieterse, W. C., 1976, *Inventory of the Archives of the Holland Land Company, 1789-1869*. Municipal Printing Office of Amsterdam, 75 p., 11 maps.
The best summary of Holland Land Company activities in western N.Y. It includes reproductions of some valuable early maps, partly in manuscript form.

Prentis, N. L., 1899, *A History of Kansas*. E. P. Greer, Winfield, Ks., 379 p., illus.
This is a standard work on the history of Kansas.

Reinstein, J. B., 1971, *A History of the Town of Cheektowaga*. Buffalo & Erie Co. Historical Soc., N.Y., 8 p., illus.

Reling, Dorothy & Mildred Reling, 1981, "Naomi Cemetery." In *Mitchell County Cemeteries, Vol. II*. North Central Kansas Genealogical Soc., Cawker City, Kans., 92 p.
Lists, on p. 6-11, Jacob Marzolf, 1831-1919, and his wife, etc. Through the extensive efforts of local historians, nearly all cemeteries in Mitchell Co. were catalogued in the four volume series.

Rydjord, John, 1968, *Indian Place-Names*. Univ. Oklahoma Press, Norman, 380 p.
Good discussion on the origin of Indian names in Kansas and their variations in spelling in the older literature.

Seguy, Jean, 1977, *Les Assemblees Anabaptistes-Mennonites de France*. Mouton & Co., Paris, 904 p.

Discusses Mennonite community at Steinseltz, Alsace, on pages 260-269, et seq.

Seguy, Jean, 1981, "Les Anabaptistes." In *Saisons d'Alsace*, n.s., no. 76, Strasbourg, p. 7-24.

Smith, H. P., 1884, *History of the City of Buffalo and Erie County*. D. Mason & Co., Syracuse, N. Y., Vol. I, 776 p., vol. 2, 554 p. + 136 p. + index 108 p.
Mentions a Philip Martzloff and a Jacob Martzloff; neither of apparent close relation to the current subject.

Stephenson, J. C., (ed.), 1977, "Downs, the First One Hundred Years." *Osborne County Farmer*, Osborne, Ks., 128 p., illus.
Mainly a compilation of newspaper and book articles concerning local history.

_____, 1979, "Downs Did It (1879-1979)." Centennial Volume. *Osborne County Farmer*, Osborne, Kans., 126 p., illus.

Stouffer, Frank & Pauline Stouffer, 1987, "The Reformed Mennonites of Mitchell County, Kansas." *Mennonite Family History*, Elverson, PA, Vol. IV, no. 3, p. 110-112, illus.

Stumpp, Karl, 1973, *The Emigration from Germany to Russia in the year 1763 to 1862*. Am. Hist. Soc. Germans from Russia, 1018 p., maps
Names Martzalff family on p. 703 and Marzolf families on p. 710, the first from Ingenheim/Bergzabern-Pf, and the second also from the French-German border area; both settled in "Neudorf", Chortitza district, Ukraine; book unfortunately not indexed, (the two families probably are related).

Terrell, W. H. H., 1867-69, *Report of the Adjutant General of the State of Indiana*. Alexander H. Conner Co., Indianapolis, Ind., vol. VI, 699 p.
The current subject, Jacob Marzolf, is listed on p. 418 as Jacob Matsol.

Turner, O., 1850, *Pioneer History of the Holland Purchase of Western New York*. Geo. H. Derby & Co., Buffalo, 670 p. (name index by L. C. Cooley, 1946)
Does not mention the family name Marzolf.

Young, S. M., 1965, *A History of the Town of Amherst, New York*. The Town Board of Amherst, N.Y., 306 p., illus.
Mentions Michael Martzolf, who evidently was related to the current subject.

ANABAPTISTS. A group of 16th century Reformers; the term is most commonly associated with those from northern Switzerland. Anabaptists believed in adult baptism and rejected the use of force, the bearing of arms, or the holding of government office.

Anabaptism proper began at Zürich, Switzerland, in 1525 under the leadership of Huldrych or Huldreich (Ulrich) Zwingli (1484-1531) and Conrad Grebel, among others. The term, for the most part, was later largely synonymized with the term Mennonites. See also RADICAL ANABAPTISTS, MARTYRS.

BENRATHER LINE. An imaginary line in Germany extending from Essen in the west past Leipzig in the east. The line marks the approximate division between Low German in the north and High German in the south. Named after the town of Benrather in Nordrhein-Westfalen. Also informally called the -maken/-machen line, compare the family names Schoenmaker and Schuhmacher.

CALVINISTS. Followers of John Calvin (1509-1564), an early Protestant Reformer who was a native of France but conducted most of his religious activity and writing in Geneva, Switzerland.

Eventually, Calvinism had a strong influence in The Netherlands after Prince Maurice of Orange converted to the faith in 1617. Another staunch Dutch Calvinist was Prince Willem III of Orange (1650-1702) who also became King of England.

CATHARTIC. A purgative agent, especially a laxative. Comparable to "Emetics," which, however, cause vomiting. Both were commonly used to treat many medical ailments before the 20th century.

CEROGRAPHY. A type of printing developed in the 19th century using engraving on a wax medium adhering to a metal plate. Used in the U.S. after 1824.

CONCEPT OF KÖLN (COLOGNE). On May 1, 1591, High German and Low German and Dutch Mennonites met in Köln to adopt a common confession of faith and to form an agreement on church regulations and conduct.

Mennonites of various congregations of the Rhine region from the North Sea south to Alsace and Switzerland were present. The agreement was signed by 15 representatives.

COPPER PLATE ENGRAVING. Engraving on copper plates was developed in Italy before 1446. Copper plate engraving allowed for greater detail than the then common woodcuts.

It reached a high point in the Netherlands and later in France in the 17th century, especially in the cartographic (map-making) industry, and in Germany, also in the 17th century, for illustrations of town views. Compare ICONOGRAPHY; WOODCUT.

DORDRECHT CONFESSION. Dordrecht is a Dutch City about 18 km (12 miles) southeast of Rotterdam. Its people accepted the Reformed faith in 1572. A Confession of Faith was adopted on April 21, 1632, and signed by 51 Flemish and Frisian Mennonite preachers as a basis of union.

DUNKARDS. Members of the German Baptist Brethren, opposed to military service and the taking of oaths.

DUTCH PROVINCES. In the Treaty of Utrecht of 1579, seven of the northern provinces of the Spanish Netherlands formed the Dutch Republic; they gained independence from their Spanish ruler in 1581.

Today, the twelve Dutch provinces are Friesland, Groningen, Drenthe, Noord Holland, Flevoland, Gelderland, Zuid Holland, Utrecht, Overijssel, Zeeland, Brabant, and Limburg.

The financial and governmental centers are concentrated in Amsterdam (North Holland) and The Hague (South Holland), respectively.

ERIE CANAL. An important transportation lane completed in 1825 which extends 363 miles across New York from Albany to Buffalo. It connects Lake Erie with the Atlantic Coast via the Hudson River.

GERMAN STATES. The more than three hundred semi-independent principalities of the 16th century have evolved into the following states: Baden-Württemberg, Bayern, Brandenburg, Hessen, Niedersachsen, Mecklenburg-Vorpommern, Nordrhein-Westfalen, Rheinland-Pfalz, Saarland, Sachsen, Sachsen-Anhalt, Schleswig-Holstein, and Thüringen.

The major metropolitan areas of Berlin, Bremen, and Hamburg retain a semi-independent status. The basic modern structure dates from the period of 1871 to 1918, a period called the Second Reich.

GUTENBERG BIBLE. Generally recognized as the first printed book, the Gutenberg Bible dates from the period of 1452-55 and was printed in Mainz by Johannes Gutenberg and his assistants.

HAPSBURG REGIME. (Habsburg in German). Ruling dynasty in the Holy Roman Empire during the period of 1278-1918. The long series of German Emperors of the House of Hapsburg, extending from 1438-1740 and from 1745-1806, was instrumental in leading the Empire through the Reformation up to the time of Napoleon. See Table 6.4 on page 228.

HOLY ROMAN EMPIRE. An Empire, consisting mainly of German States (plus Sicily) in some form of union, extending from A.D. 843 to 1806 This period is generally referred to as the First Reich.

ICONOGRAPHY. Pictorial illustration, usually of a religious subject. Iconography reached a high point in the German States with wood block engravings in the 14th and 15th centuries.

INCUNABULA. Books printed from moveable type during the period of about 1455 to not later than 1500. There are approximately 40,000 incunabula extant worldwide today.

INDUSTRIAL REVOLUTION. In the United States, a period occupying most of the 19th century; especially important during the second half of that century when railroads and steamships made the transportation of millions of migrants to America, and many back to Europe, much easier and cheaper. Compare STEAM POWER.

KEITHIAN CONTROVERSY. A split which developed among the Quakers in Pennsylvania in 1692. George Keith (1639?-1716) was a Scottish Presbyterian who converted to Quakerism in 1662 and went to America in 1687. His ideas of atonement differed from those of the main body of Quakers in Pennsylvania.

LABADISTS. Refers to the followers of Jean de Labadie (1610-1674) who was originally from Bordeaux, France. He joined the French Reformed Church in 1650. By 1664, he had moved to Middleburg, in The Netherlands, and by 1668, to Amsterdam. Later, he moved with several hundred followers to Herford, Westphalia, in Germany, and finally to Altona in Schleswig-Holstein. The Labadite group was never large, however vocal, and died out about 1732.

LITHOGRAPHY. A process of printing that uses stone as an engraving medium. Lithography was developed in Europe in the 19th century, especially for maps and other illustrations. First used in the U.S. in 1822.

LUTHERANS. One of the main components of the Protestant Church and of the Reformation, taking their name from the German theologian Martin Luther (1483-1546).

MARTYRS. The well-known book *Martyrs Mirror* written by Thieleman J. van Braght, a Dutch Mennonite, was printed in 1659. It was translated into German in 1748-1749 and into English in 1886. This account listed about 800 martyrs, most Anabaptists, who were killed in often gruesome ways for their faith. Various later accounts add several thousand names to the list of 16th century martyrs; these martyrs were resident in the

Lowlands and in Germany and Switzerland, mainly along the Rhine. Executions of Anabaptists began in 1525 in Switzerland, and did not terminate in Europe until about 1618.

MENNONITES. An Evangelical Protestant sect taking their name from Menno Simons (1492-1551), native of Witmarsum in Friesland, The Netherlands. The group name "Menists" was adopted about 1545. The Mennonites in general were opposed to taking oaths, holding public office, or performing military service. During the 16th and 17th centuries, the Mennonites became active in small groups all along the Rhine, especially along the left bank, from Switzerland north through Germany and The Netherlands.

MOVEABLE TYPE. Printer's type which was adapted by Gutenberg in the mid-15th century to speed up the printing process. The individual letters have the advantage of being able to be shifted where needed on the printing plate and can be used over and over.

PALATINATE. Historically speaking, a large area in southwestern Germany along the left bank, i.e., west bank of the Rhine River. The Latin term "Palatinum" appears on the Trier-Koblenzer Fragments, which are part of a manuscript map dating from about 1437. During the era of the Holy Roman Empire, the area was ruled by the Elector Palatine, for the most part resident in Heidelberg. After about 1544, Heidelberg and its University became a center of the Protestant movement.

The Palatinate occupied the southeastern half of the German State known today as Rheinland-Pfalz, that is, the Pfalz portion. In the war-torn era after 1685, the area furnished numerous emigrants to America, especially to Pennsylvania. The loose term Palatines includes many 18th century emigrants from Baden-Württemberg, that is, from the right or east bank of the Rhine.

PENNSYLVANIA DUTCH. A peculiar and unique language which developed in Pennsylvania in the 18th century, especially in Lancaster County. It embraced various German Rhenish dialects with a very heavy English overprint.

The basic German dialects are Rheinfränkisch (that is, from the Palatinate) combined with Alemannisch (that is, from Switzerland and the Alsace).

QUAKERS. Members of the Society of Friends, a Christian sect which was founded in England about 1650 by George Fox (1624-1691) and others. The organization was given the popular and unofficial name of Quakers about 1650.

The first Quaker missionaries went to Holland in 1653 and to Germany in 1657. William Penn was an ardent Quaker and was instrumental in encouraging numerous Quaker adherents to help settle Pennsylvania during the last part of the 17th century, especially after 1681. The Society of Friends was to remain largely an English, and later, an American phenomena.

RADICAL ANABAPTISTS (MÜNSTERITES). In 1532-35, the western German city of Münster was the scene of bitter struggles between the fanatic, revolutionary and left-wing Anabaptists led by the Dutchman Jan Beukelsz van Leiden, among others, and the Catholic forces of Bishop Franz of Waldeck, who was Franz, Graf von Waldeck and Bishop of Münster, Minden, and Osnabrück from 1530-1547.

In late 1535, the Anabaptist forces in Münster were wiped out and the leaders executed in early 1536. The Münsterites believed in the then alien ideas of communal property and in polygamy.

REFORMATION. The Reformation dates from about 1517 when Martin Luther (1483-1546) published, at Wittenberg in eastern Germany, his critic against the excesses of the Catholic Church. A high point of popular opinion against the Catholic Church came during the so-called Peasants War led by Thomas Münstzer, 1524-1525.

REPLICA-CASTING. The process utilized by Gutenberg in the mid-15th century to make a copy of a set of moveable type.

RHINE DELTA. The delta consists of four main channels in The Netherlands, most being now interconnected either naturally or artificially.

From north to south: the Oude Rijn, a minor waterway used mainly by smaller boats and serving Utrecht and Leiden; the Lek, serving Arnhem and the major shipping port of Rotterdam; the Waal being the main navigational channel eastward into Germany with two-thirds of the water flow, serving Nijmegen and Dordrecht; and the Maas flowing by Maastricht and Venlo.

In 1421, an enormous flood cut off Dordrecht from the mainland; subsequently, Rotterdam has served as the main port for the industrial area to the north.

STEAM POWER. A principal component of the Industrial Revolution. In America, successful steamboats date from about 1807 while steam engines were successfully employed by American railroads beginning about 1829.

UERDINGEN LINE. An imaginary line extending westward from the German City of Uerdingen in the Lower Rhine and separating in broad terms, the various dialects of The Netherlands north of the Rhine from those south of the Rhine. The area to the north is characterized by -ik/-ook/-lijk suffixes and to the south by -ich / -auch / -lich; compare the family names Hendriks and Hendrichs. In Germany, the Benrather Line (above), extending eastward, is similar.

VELLUM. Fine calf skin used as a printing medium until well into the 15th century. For instance, one fifth of the existing copies of the Gutenberg Bible were printed on vellum with the rest being printed on paper.

WENDISH. A relatively small group of West Slavic peoples. In the 19th century, they formed small enclaves in diverse areas such as central Texas, but are now principally assimilated into German-American culture.

WOODCUT. A block of wood upon which a design for printing is engraved. Especially common in Europe in the late 14th century through the 16th century for printing icons and playing cards. The first dated European woodcut stems from 1418. By the 17th century, wood cuts were generally replaced by copper and, later, steel plate engravings, the latter two media being much better adapted for printing maps.

Because of limitations in the program used for this index, an umlaut on a vowel (ä, ë, ö, ü) has been replaced by an 'e' following the vowel. Thus, Elizabeth Pfalzgräffin bei Rhein is entered as ELIZABETH, Pfalzgraeffin bei Rhein, and Matthäus Merian as MERIAN, Matthaeus. Names in the Reference and Acknowledgements sections have not been indexed. The same goes for names mentioned in the text as a reference or on acknowledgement. An exception on the latter rule has been made for authors and cartographers active before 1900, whose lives or achievements are discussed in the text; their names have been indexed.

In the case of names with prefixes, such as 'von', the prefix is treated as part of the surname, thus Baron von Meusebach can be found under VONMEUSEBACH, Baron. Noble and royal personages are indexed under their given name(s) followed by as much of their titles as is given in the text; Elector Johann Georg of Saxony is thus listed as JOHANN GEORG, Elector of Saxony.

CPSIA information can be obtained at www.ICGtesting.com
Printed in the USA
LVOW05s0018031014

407089LV00014B/201/P